Swift Cookbook
Second Edition

Over 60 proven recipes for developing better iOS applications with Swift 5.3

Keith Moon
Chris Barker

BIRMINGHAM - MUMBAI

Swift Cookbook
Second Edition

Group Product Manager: Ashwin Nair
Publishing Product Manager: Rohit Rajkumar
Senior Editor: Keagan Carneiro
Content Development Editor: Divya Vijayan
Technical Editor: Deepesh Patel
Copy Editor: Safis Editing
Project Coordinator: Kinjal Bari
Proofreader: Safis Editing
Indexer: Manju Arasan
Production Designer: Alishon Mendonca

First published: September 2017
Second edition: February 2021

Production reference: 1260221

Published by Packt Publishing Ltd.
Livery Place
35 Livery Street
Birmingham
B3 2PB, UK.

ISBN 978-1-83921-119-5

www.packt.com

I would like to thank my amazing and supportive wife, Alissa. Without her support and patience,this book would not have been possible.

– Keith Moon

For my partner, Mandy, who is the strongest and bravest woman I have ever met, and to our beautiful daughter, Madeleine – thank you both for your love and support.

For Harry and Nathan.

– Chris Barker

Contributors

About the authors

Keith Moon is an award-winning iOS developer, author, and speaker based in London. He has worked with some of the biggest companies in the world to create engaging and personal mobile experiences. Keith has been developing in Swift since its release, working on projects that are both fully Swift and mixed Swift and Objective-C. Keith has been invited to speak about Swift development at conferences from Moscow to Minsk and London.

Chris Barker is an iOS developer and tech lead for fashion retailer N Brown (JD Williams, SimplyBe, Jacamo), where he heads up the iOS team. Chris started his career developing .NET applications for online retailer dabs.com (now BT Shop) before he made his move into mobile app development with digital agency Openshadow (now MyStudioFactory Paris). There, he worked on mobile apps for clients such as Louis Vuitton, L'Oréal Paris, and the Paris Metro. Chris often attends and speaks at local iOS developer meetups and conferences such as NSManchester, Malaga Mobile, and CodeMobile.

About the reviewers

Juan Catalan is a software developer with more than 10 years of experience, having started learning iOS almost since its beginnings. He has worked as a professional iOS developer in many industries, including industrial automation, transportation, document management, fleet tracking, real estate, and financial services. Juan has contributed to more than 30 published apps, some of which have millions of users. He has a passion for software architecture, always looking for ways to write better code and optimize mobile apps.

George MacKay-Shore is an experienced software engineer who has worked in almost every field of the computing industry. His expertise ranges from embedded systems to games; from the public sector to FinTech; and all that is in between. He has a wide range of experience with many programming languages including C/C++, Swift, Java, TypeScript, and Python to name a few, and always strives to learn the newest innovative technologies.

Table of Contents

Preface

Since Apple announced the Swift programming language at WWDC 2014, it has gone on to become one of the fastest-growing programming languages. Swift is modern, open-source, and easy to use, and therefore its usefulness can extend beyond Apple's ecosystem, giving it the potential to be used across all platforms and for any scenario.

Swift 5.3 is the latest version of this exciting new programming language, giving you the tools to build performant and responsive apps with safe and clean code.

This book will guide you through Swift's features, building up your knowledge and toolset layer by layer, so you can use Swift to build the next great app or service.

You will be given useful, easy-to-follow recipes for using Swift to accomplish real-world tasks. Each recipe only uses concepts previously covered in the book so you will never feel lost.

Learn what makes Swift one of the fastest-growing and most exciting programming languages available today.

Who this book is for

If you are looking for a book to help you learn about the diverse features offered by Swift 5, along with tips and tricks to efficiently code and build applications, then this book is for you. Knowledge of Swift or general programming concepts will be beneficial.

What this book covers

Chapter 1, *Swift Building Blocks*, introduces you to the basic building blocks of Swift 5, its syntax, and the functionalities of basic Swift constructs. Also, this chapter will introduce you to Apple's Xcode IDE and Swift Playgrounds, which provides an ideal way to create, execute, debug, and understand the recipes contained in this book, thus setting you up to initiate the development process. In this chapter, you will learn how to write your first Swift program and understand the various basic elements of the Swift language.

Chapter 2, *Mastering the Building Blocks*, teaches you how to create more complex structures on the basis of the building blocks that you studied in the first chapter and the functionalities provided by the Swift standard library. You will get an understanding of how to bundle variables into tuples, order data with the help of an array, and store key-value pairs with dictionaries. You will also learn how to use the property observers and control the access to and visibility of your code. Then, you will learn how to extend the functionalities of your code using the extensions.

Chapter 3, *Data Wrangling with Swift Control Flow*, will teach you that programming is all about making decisions, therefore in this chapter, we will explore how to make decisions on the basis of the information gained and how to alter the control flow of the code. You will learn how to conditionally execute your code with if/else **statements**. You will also learn how to control the flow of execution of your code with switch statements, and then loop this code by understanding how to use for and while loops. You will then understand how to handle Swift errors with try, throw, do, and catch statements. Also, we will cover how a defer statement can be useful to change state once a function's execution is complete or to clean up values that are no longer needed.

Chapter 4, *Generics, Operators, and Nested Types*, provides you with an understanding of two advanced features of Swift, which are generics and operators. Using these features, you will learn how to build functionalities that are flexible and well defined. Also, you will understand how nested types allow logical grouping, access, and namespacing for your constructs.

Chapter 5, *Beyond the Standard Library*, takes you on a journey to explore the functionalities beyond the standard library provided by frameworks such as Foundation and UIKit. Learning how to use these functionalities will help you make full use of the Swift language.

Chapter 6, *Building iOS Apps with Swift*, is where we'll start the journey into building our very own iOS app. Taking everything we've learned and more from the previous chapters' recipes, this chapter will teach you how to get off the ground using Swift to build an iOS app.

Chapter 7, *Swift Playgrounds*, is where you will gain a total understanding of using Swift Playgrounds and explore advanced features other than those explored in previous chapters, to create fully interactive experiences.

Chapter 8, *Server-Side Swift*, introduces you to a totally different aspect of Swift programming: server-side programming with Swift. Also, you will gain an understanding of how to run Swift on Linux by installing the Swift toolchain. You will learn how to use a web server framework to build a REST API and how to host your API via a hosting service. You will also learn how to accomplish your tasks easily by understanding how to use Vapor, one of the most popular frameworks of Swift 5.

Chapter 9, *Performance and Responsiveness in Swift*, explores the more advanced concepts of Swift programming to provide an understanding of how certain Swift types are implemented and their performance characteristics. Also, you will learn how to perform asynchronous tasks using the Grand Central Dispatch API. Then, we'll explore the multi-threaded environment available on all Apple platforms and how to enhance the performance profile of your Swift constructs to build a fast and responsive app.

Chapter 10, *SwiftUI and Combine Framework*, dives straight into Apple's new UI framework, SwiftUI. With SwiftUI, we'll learn how to create iOS apps by exploring the declarative syntax used to achieve this. We'll also explore how easy it is for SwiftUI and UIKit to work together. In addition to SwiftUI, we'll also explore the basics of the new Combine framework and how this works alongside SwiftUI.

Chapter 11, *Using CoreML and Vision in Swift*, will dive into the frameworks offered by Apple and how we can use Swift code to harness machine learning techniques, as machine learning is becoming an increasingly hot topic. In this chapter, we'll cover CoreML and the Vision frameworks, using pre-trained models to identify objects in real time.

To get the most out of this book

To follow along with the examples in this book, you will need a computer running macOS Catalina (specifically version 10.15.4) or greater. You also need an Apple ID to download and install Xcode 12 from the Mac App Store. The chapter on server-side Swift (Chapter 8, *Server-Side Swift*) also requires a system running Ubuntu 20.04 LTS.

The code in this book has been tested against Swift 5.3, but should work with any newer versions of Swift.

Software/hardware covered in the book	OS requirements
macOS	10.15.4+ (Catalina)
Xcode	12+
Ubuntu (for Chapter 8, *Server-Side Swift*)	20.04 LTS

If you are using the digital version of this book, we advise you to type the code yourself or access the code via the GitHub repository (link available in the next section). Doing so will help you avoid any potential errors related to the copying and pasting of code.

Download the example code files

You can download the example code files for this book from GitHub at `https://github.com/PacktPublishing/Swift-Cookbook-Second-Edition`. In case there's an update to the code, it will be updated on the existing GitHub repository.

We also have other code bundles from our rich catalog of books and videos available at `https://github.com/PacktPublishing/`. Check them out!

Code in Action

Code in Action videos for this book can be viewed at `http://bit.ly/3shdTeQ`.

Download the color images

We also provide a PDF file that has color images of the screenshots/diagrams used in this book. You can download it here: `https://static.packt-cdn.com/downloads/9781839211195_ColorImages.pdf`.

Conventions used

There are a number of text conventions used throughout this book.

`CodeInText`: Indicates code words in text, database table names, folder names, filenames, file extensions, pathnames, dummy URLs, user input, and Twitter handles. Here is an example: "We can substitute `Grumble` wherever we would use `[Pug]` or `Array<Pug>`."

A block of code is set as follows:

```
let fraction = rating / total
let ratingOutOf5 = fraction * 5
let roundedRating = round(ratingOutOf5) // Rounds to the nearest
   // integer.
```

When we wish to draw your attention to a particular part of a code block, the relevant lines or items are set in bold:

```
class ProgrammeFetcher {
    typealias FetchResultHandler = (String?, Error?) -> Void
    func fetchCurrentProgrammeName(forChannel channel: Channel,
                                   resultHandler: FetchResultHandler) {
        // Get next programme
        let programmeName = "Sherlock"
        resultHandler(programmeName, nil)
    }
}
```

Any command-line input or output is written as follows:

```
$ mkdir css
$ cd css
```

Bold: Indicates a new term, an important word, or words that you see onscreen. For example, words in menus or dialog boxes appear in the text like this. Here is an example: "Select **System info** from the **Administration** panel."

Warnings or important notes appear like this.

Tips and tricks appear like this.

Sections

In this book, you will find several headings that appear frequently (*Getting ready*, *How to do it...*, *How it works...*, *There's more...*, and *See also*).

To give clear instructions on how to complete a recipe, use these sections as follows:

Getting ready

This section tells you what to expect in the recipe and describes how to set up any software or any preliminary settings required for the recipe.

How to do it...

This section contains the steps required to follow the recipe.

How it works...

This section usually consists of a detailed explanation of what happened in the previous section.

There's more...

This section consists of additional information about the recipe in order to make you more knowledgeable about the recipe.

See also

This section provides helpful links to other useful information for the recipe.

Get in touch

Feedback from our readers is always welcome.

General feedback: If you have questions about any aspect of this book, mention the book title in the subject of your message and email us at customercare@packtpub.com.

Errata: Although we have taken every care to ensure the accuracy of our content, mistakes do happen. If you have found a mistake in this book, we would be grateful if you would report this to us. Please visit www.packtpub.com/support/errata, selecting your book, clicking on the Errata Submission Form link, and entering the details.

Piracy: If you come across any illegal copies of our works in any form on the Internet, we would be grateful if you would provide us with the location address or website name. Please contact us at copyright@packt.com with a link to the material.

If you are interested in becoming an author: If there is a topic that you have expertise in and you are interested in either writing or contributing to a book, please visit authors.packtpub.com.

Reviews

Please leave a review. Once you have read and used this book, why not leave a review on the site that you purchased it from? Potential readers can then see and use your unbiased opinion to make purchase decisions, we at Packt can understand what you think about our products, and our authors can see your feedback on their book. Thank you!

For more information about Packt, please visit `packt.com`.

Swift Building Blocks 1

Since Apple announced the Swift programming language at WWDC 2014, it has gone on to become one of the fastest-growing programming languages. TIOBE is a company that measures software quality and publishes a ranking index of programming language usage. At the time of writing, Swift ranks as the 11th most popular language on this index. This is two places higher than when the first edition of this book was written (visit `http://www.tiobe.com/tiobe_index`).

Swift is a modern, general-purpose programming language that focuses on type safety and expressive and concise syntax. Positioned as a modern replacement for Objective-C, it has taken over from that older language as the future of development on Apple's platforms.

Occupying this niche alone would ensure Swift's place as a useful and important programming language. However, Apple's decision to open-source Swift has allowed its influence to extend beyond Apple's ecosystem, giving it the potential to be used across all platforms and for any scenario.

Since open-sourcing Swift, Apple has provided support for running your Swift code on Linux. In the later chapters, we will investigate using a Swift server to execute your code. In addition, the Swift Playgrounds iPad app turns your tablet into a lightweight **Integrated Development Environment (IDE)**. Despite these alternative ways to use and write Swift code, the simplest is still on a Mac and with Apple's Xcode IDE. At the beginning of this book, we will walk through setting that up and will then assume that the reader uses this development environment unless otherwise stated. Xcode also provides a perfect way to explore the structure and syntax of the Swift standard library, foundation, and any other framework available for iOS or Mac development in the form of its Playgrounds feature.

A **Swift Playground** is a simplified environment for executing Swift code. For our purposes, playgrounds provide an ideal way to create, run, and understand the recipes contained in this book. As such, it will also be assumed that the reader is using an Xcode Playground to implement the recipes contained in this book, unless otherwise stated.

Swift 5.3 is an important release, adding many language features that are crucial for Apple's SwiftUI framework, which we will cover in Chapter 10, *SwiftUI and Combine Framework*. Swift 5.3 will also be more compatible with future versions of Swift, which means that code written now with Swift 5.3 can run alongside code written with Swift 6 and beyond. This book will assume that the reader is using Swift 5.3; all code will work with this version.

In this chapter, we will look at the building blocks of the Swift language, examining the syntax and functionality of the basic Swift components that everything else is based on.

In this chapter, we will cover the following recipes:

- Creating your first Swift program
- Using Strings, Ints, Floats, and Bools
- Unwrapping optionals, and force unwrapping
- Reusing code in functions
- Encapsulating functionality in object classes
- Bundling values into structs
- Enumerating values with enums
- Passing around functionality with closures
- Using protocols to define interfaces

Technical requirements

All the code for this chapter can be found in the book's GitHub repository at https://github.com/PacktPublishing/Swift-Cookbook-Second-Edition/tree/master/Chapter01

Check out the following video to see the Code in Action: https://bit.ly/3rp0DnJ

Creating your first Swift program

In the first recipe, we will set up our development environment and use Swift Playgrounds to create our first piece of Swift code.

Getting ready

First, we must download and install Apple's IDE, Xcode, from the Mac App Store:

1. Open up the Mac App Store, either from the Dock or via Spotlight:

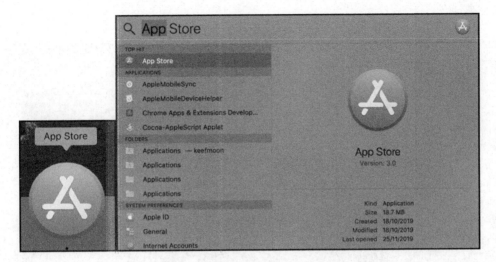

Figure 1.1 – App Store

2. Search for xcode:

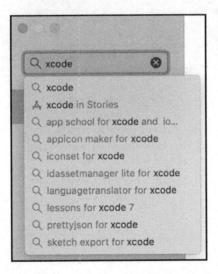

Figure 1.2 – Searching for xcode

3. Click on **GET**, followed by **Install**:

Figure 1.3 – Xcode in the App Store

 Xcode is a large download (nearly 8 GB), so this may take a while, depending on your internet connection.

4. Once downloaded, open Xcode from the App Store or the Dock:

Figure 1.4 – Opening Xcode

How to do it...

With Xcode downloaded, let's create our first Swift playground:

1. Launch Xcode from the icon in your Dock.
2. Choose **Get started with a playground** from the welcome screen:

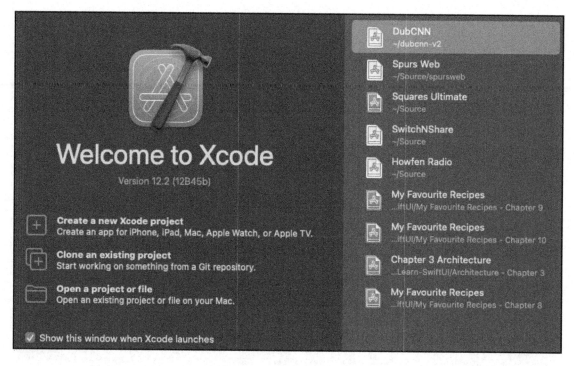

Figure 1.5 – Xcode, new project

3. Select **Blank** from the **iOS** tab of the template and then press **Next**:

Figure 1.6 – Xcode, selecting the project type

4. Choose a name and location for your playground and then press **Create**:

Figure 1.7 – Xcode, saving the project

Xcode playgrounds can be based on one of the three different Apple platforms: **iOS**, **tvOS**, and **macOS**. Playgrounds provide full access to the frameworks available to either iOS, tvOS, or macOS, depending on which you choose. An iOS playground will be assumed for the entirety of this book, chiefly because this is the platform of choice of the author. Where code does have UI components, the iOS platform will be used, unless stated otherwise.

You are now presented with a view that looks like this:

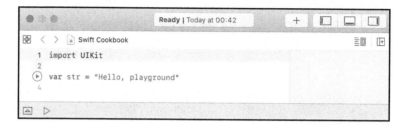

Figure 1.8 – Playground – code template

5. Let's replace the word `playground` with `Swift!`. Click on the play icon in the bottom left-hand corner of the window to execute the code in the playground:

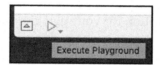

Figure 1.9 – Playground run/code execution

Congratulations! You have just run your first piece of Swift code.

On the right-hand side of the window, you will see the output of each line of code in the playground. We can see that our line of code has the output `Hello Swift!`

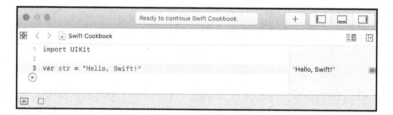

Figure 1.10 – The "Hello, Swift!" playground

There's more...

If you put your cursor over the output on the right-hand side, you will see two buttons, one that looks like an eye and another that is a rounded square:

Figure 1.11 – Playground, output

Click on the eye button to get a **Quick Look** box of the output. This isn't particularly useful for a text string, but can be useful for more visual output, such as colors and views:

Figure 1.12 – Playground output quick look

Click on the square button, and a box will be added inline, under your code, showing the output of the code. This can be really useful if you want to see how the output changes as you change the code:

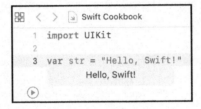

Figure 1.13 – Playground, inline output

See also

We will learn more about playgrounds and how we can take them further in Chapter 7, *Swift Playgrounds*.

Using Strings, Ints, Floats, and Bools

Many of the core operations in any programming language involve manipulating text, numbers, and determining true and false statements. Let's learn how to accomplish these operations in Swift by taking a look at its basic types and learning how to assign constants and variables. In doing so, we will touch on Swift's static typing and mutability system.

Getting ready

Open a new Swift Playground in Xcode. The previous recipe explains how to do this.

How to do it...

Let's run some Swift code that explores the basic types, and then we can walk through it step by step:

1. Type the following into the new playground file:

```swift
let phrase: String = "The quick brown fox jumps over the lazy dog"
let numberOfFoxes: Int = 1
let numberOfAnimals: Int = 2

let averageCharactersPerWord: Float = (3+5+5+3+5+4+3+4+3) / 9
print(averageCharactersPerWord) // 3.8888888

/*
phrase = "The quick brown ? jumps over the lazy ?" // Doesn't
compile
*/

var anotherPhrase = phrase
anotherPhrase = "The quick brown 🦊 jumps over the lazy 🐶"
print(phrase) // "The quick brown fox jumps over the lazy dog"
print(anotherPhrase) // "The quick brown 🦊 jumps over the lazy 🐶
"

var phraseInfo = "The phrase" + " has: "
print(phraseInfo) // "The phrase has: "

phraseInfo = phraseInfo + "\(numberOfFoxes) fox and \
  (numberOfAnimals) animals"
print(phraseInfo) // "The phrase has: 1 fox and 2 animals"

print("Number of characters in phrase: \(phrase.count)")

let multilineExplanation = """
Why is the following phrase often used?
"The quick brown fox jumps over the lazy dog"
This phrase contains every letter in the alphabet.
"""

let phrasesAreEqual = phrase == anotherPhrase
```

```
print(phrasesAreEqual) // false

let phraseHas43Characters = phrase.count == 40 + 3
print(phraseHas43Characters) // true
```

2. Press the play button at the bottom of the window to run the playground and verify that Xcode doesn't show any errors. Your playground should look like the following screenshot, with an output for each line in the timeline on the right-hand side and printed values in the console at the bottom:

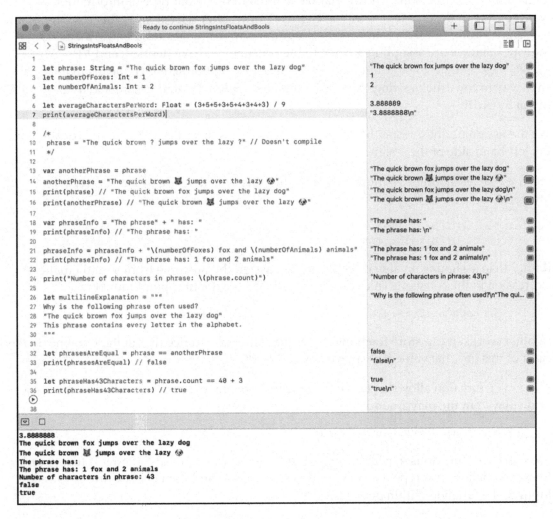

Figure 1.14 – Playground console output

How it works...

Let's step through the preceding code line by line to understand it.

In this line of code, we are assigning some text to a constant value:

```
let phrase: String = "The quick brown fox jumps over the lazy dog"
```

We define a new constant value by using the `let` keyword, and we give that constant a name, `phrase`. The colon : shows that we want to define what type of information we want to store in the constant, and that type is defined after the colon. In this case, we want to assign a string (`String` is how most programming languages refer to text). The = sign indicates that we are assigning a value to the constant we have defined, and "The quick brown fox jumps over the lazy dog" is a `String` literal, which means that it's an easy way to construct a string. Any text contained within " " marks is treated as a `String` literal by Swift.

We are assigning the `String` literal on the right-hand side of the = sign to the constant on the left-hand side of the = sign.

Next, we are assigning two more constants, but this time they are of the `Int` type, or integers:

```
let numberOfFoxes: Int = 1
let numberOfAnimals: Int = 2
```

Rather than assigning a value directly, we can assign the outcome from a mathematical expression to the constant. This constant is a `Float`, or floating-point number:

```
let averageCharactersPerWord: Float = (3+5+5+3+5+4+3+4+3) / 9
```

In other words, it can store fractions rather than integers. Notice that in the timeline on the right of this line, the value is displayed as 3.88889.

The `print` function allows us to see the output from any expression printed to the console or displayed in the playground:

```
print(averageCharactersPerWord)
```

We will cover functions in a later recipe, but for now, all you need to know is that in order to use a function, you type its name (in this case `print`) and then enclose any required input to the function within brackets, `()`.

When our code calls this function, the timeline to the right of the code displays the output of the statement as 3.88888, which differs from the line above it. The actual value of the mathematical expression we performed is 3.88888888... with an infinite number of 8s. However, the `print` function has rounded this up to just five decimal places and rounded it in a different way than the timeline for the line above. This potential difference between the true value of a floating-point number and how it's represented by the Swift language is important to remember when dealing with floats.

Next, you'll see some lines colored gray:

```
/*
phrase = "The quick brown ? jumps over the lazy ?" // Doesn't compile
*/
```

The playground doesn't produce an output for these lines because they are comments. The `/*` syntax before the line of code and the `*/` syntax after the line of code denote that this is a comment block, and therefore Swift should ignore anything typed in this block.

Remove `/*` and `*/` and you'll see that `// Doesn't compile` is still colored gray. This is because `//` also denotes a comment. Anything after this, on the same line, is also ignored.

If you now try and run this code, Xcode will tell you that there is a problem with this line, so let's look at the line to determine the issue.

On the left-hand side of the = sign, we have `phrase`, which we declared earlier, and now we are trying to assign a new value to it. We can't do this because we defined `phrase` as a constant using the `let` keyword. We should only use `let` for things we know will not change. This ability to define something as unchanging, or **immutable**, is an important concept in Swift, and we will revisit it in later chapters.

If we want to define something that can change, we declare it as a variable using the `var` keyword:

```
var anotherPhrase = phrase
```

Since `anotherPhrase` is a variable, we can assign a new value to it:

```
anotherPhrase = "The quick brown 🐱 jumps over the lazy 🐶"
```

Strings in Swift are fully *Unicode-compliant*, so we can have some fun and use emojis instead of words. Now, let's print out the values of our strings to see what values they hold:

```
print(phrase) // "The quick brown fox jumps over the lazy dog"
print(anotherPhrase) // "The quick brown 🐱 jumps over the lazy 🐶"
```

In the preceding lines, we have done the following:

- Defined a string called `phrase`
- Defined a string called `anotherPhrase` as having the same value as `phrase`
- Changed the value of `anotherPhrase`
- Printed the value of `phrase` and `anotherPhrase`

When we do this, we see that only `anotherPhrase` prints the new value that was assigned, even though the values of `phrase` and `anotherPhrase` were initially the same. Although `phrase` and `anotherPhrase` had the same value, they do not have an intrinsic connection; so, when `anotherPhrase` is assigned a new value, this does not affect `phrase`.

Strings can be easily combined using the + operator:

```
var phraseInfo = "The phrase" + " has: "
print(phraseInfo) // "The phrase has: "
```

This gives the result you would expect; the strings are concatenated.

You will often want to create strings by including values derived from other expressions. We can do this with `String` interpolation:

```
phraseInfo = phraseInfo + "\(numberOfFoxes) fox and \(numberOfAnimals)
    animals"
print(phraseInfo) // "The phrase has: 1 fox and 2 animals"
```

The values inserted after \ (and before) can be anything that can be represented as a string, including other strings, ints, floats, or expressions.

We can also use expressions with string interpolation, such as displaying the number of characters in a string:

```
print("Number of characters in phrase: \(phrase.count)")
```

Strings in Swift are collections, which are containers of elements; in this case, a string is a collection of characters. We will cover collections in more depth in the next chapter, but for now, it's enough to know that your collections can tell you how many elements they contain through their count property. We use this to output the number of characters in the phrase.

Multiline string literals can be defined using """ at the beginning and end of the string:

```
let multilineExplanation = """
Why is the following phrase often used?
"The quick brown fox jumps over the lazy dog"
```

```
This phrase contains every letter in the alphabet.
"""
```

The contents of the Multiline string must be on a separate line from the start and end signifiers. Within a Multiline string literal, you can use single quote characters " without needing to use an additional escape character, as you would with a single-line string literal.

Boolean, or `Bool`, values represent either true or false. In the next line, we evaluate the value of a Boolean expression and assign the result to the `phrasesAreEqual` constant:

```
let phrasesAreEqual: Bool = phrase == anotherPhrase
print(phrasesAreEqual) // false
```

Here, the equality operator, `==`, compares the values on its left and right and evaluates to `true` if the two values are equal, and `false` otherwise.

As we discussed earlier, although we assigned `anotherPhrase` the value of `phrase` initially, we then assigned a new, different value to `anotherPhrase`; therefore, `phrase` and `anotherPhrase` are not equal and the expression assigns the value of `false`.

Each side of the `==` operator can be any expression that evaluates to match the type of the other side, as we do with the following code:

```
let phraseHas43Characters: Bool = phrase.characters.count == 40 + 3
print(phraseHas43Characters) // true
```

In this case, the character count of `phrase` equals 43. Since `40 + 3` also equals 43, the constant is assigned the value of `true`.

There's more...

During this recipe, we defined a number of constants and variables, and when we did this, we also explicitly defined their type. For example, consider the following line of Swift code:

```
let clearlyAString: String = "This is a string literal"
```

Swift is a statically typed language. This means any constant or variable that we define has to have a specific type, and once defined it cannot be changed to a different type. However, in the preceding line of code, the `clearlyAString` constant is clearly a string! The right-hand side of the expression is a string literal, and therefore we know that the left-hand side will be a string. More importantly, the Swift compiler also knows this (a compiler is the program that turns Swift code into machine code).

Swift is all about being concise, so since the type can be inferred by the compiler, we do not need to explicitly state it. Instead of the preceding code, we can use the following code and it will still run, even though we didn't specify the type:

```
let clearlyAString = "This is a string literal"
```

In fact, all the type declarations that we have made so far can be removed! So, go back through the code we have already written and remove all type declarations (:String, :Int, :Float, and :Bool), as they can all be inferred. Run the playground to confirm that this is still valid Swift code.

See also

Further information regarding these base types in Swift can be found in Apple's documentation of the Swift language:

- **Ints, Floats, and Bools**: http://swiftbook.link/docs/the-basics

- **Strings and Characters**: http://swiftbook.link/docs/strings

Unwrapping optionals, and force unwrapping

In the real world, we don't always know the answer to a question, and problems can occur if we assume that we will always know the answer. The same is true in programming languages, especially when dealing with external systems that we may not control. In many languages, there is no way to call out that we might not know a value at any given time. This can lead to either fragile code or lots of checks to ensure a value exists before it can be used.

The term nil or null is used by programming languages to denote the absence of a value. Note that this is not the same as the number 0 or the empty (zero length) string "". Swift uses nil to indicate the absence of a value. Therefore, assigning nil to a value will remove any value that is currently assigned.

With a focus on Swift being type-safe and making it easier to write safe code, this ambiguity had to be addressed, and the Swift language does this with something called optionals. In this recipe, we will look at what optionals are in Swift, and how to handle and use them safely.

Getting started

Enter the following into a new playground:

```
var dayOfTheWeek: String = "Monday"
dayOfTheWeek = "Tuesday"
dayOfTheWeek = "Wednesday"
dayOfTheWeek = nil
```

When you try to run the code, you will see that the compiler has raised an error and will not let you assign `nil` to the `dayOfTheWeek` variable. Quite right too! The day of the week might change, but there will never not be a current day of the week.

As we declared the type to be `String`, that is what the compiler expects, and `nil` is not a string, so it can't be assigned to this variable.

The same is true even if you remove the type declaration and have the compiler infer it, as we did in the preceding recipe. This is because the type is inferred at the point the variable is declared, and since it is being assigned a string value, the type of `String` is inferred. All other uses of this variable are checked against this inferred type of `String`.

Delete the last line, as the compiler issue will prevent us from running further code in the playground.

How to do it...

We will look at a different scenario where it is appropriate to have an optional variable. Nick and Finn are playing a game. In each round, Finn will hold his hand behind his back and choose a number of fingers to hold up, Nick will guess how many fingers it is, and Finn will then show him how many fingers he had chosen to hold up.

To help keep track of the game, Nick stores how many fingers Finn has held up in a variable. When Finn shows his hand, Nick can enter a value for the number of fingers, but when Finn's hands are behind his back, Nick doesn't know how many fingers Finn is holding up, and so can't store a value.

Let's enter the following code:

```
// Start of the game
var numberOfFingersHeldUpByFinn: Int?
// Finn's hand behind his back
numberOfFingersHeldUpByFinn = nil
// Finn shows his hand
numberOfFingersHeldUpByFinn = 3
// Finn puts hand back behind his back
numberOfFingersHeldUpByFinn = nil
// Finn shows his hand
numberOfFingersHeldUpByFinn = 1
print(numberOfFingersHeldUpByFinn)
// End of the game
let lastNumberOfFingersHeldUpByFinn: Int = numberOfFingersHeldUpByFinn!
```

Unlike the days of the week example, this code compiles without issues, despite the fact that we assign nil to the variable. Let's look into why we were able to do that.

How it works...

We know that there will be times during the game when we don't know how many fingers are being held up, so the variable is optional; it may be an Int, or it may be nil. You will remember from earlier that nil does not mean 0. It is entirely possible that Finn may be holding up zero fingers (that is, a clenched fist) and this is a valid answer. In this scenario, nil represents a lack of knowledge regarding the number of fingers. To declare this variable as optional, we define the expected type, but with an additional ?:

```
var numberOfFingersHeldUpByFinn: Int?
```

In Swift, this is referred to as an optionally wrapped Int. We have wrapped the Int type in the concept of being optional. I am emphasizing this term **wrapping** because we will need to **unwrap** this optional type later on. At the start of the game, we don't know how many fingers are being held up, so we assign nil to this variable, which is allowable for optional variables:

```
numberOfFingersHeldUpByFinn = nil
```

Once Finn's hand is shown and we know how many fingers he has held up, we can assign that Int value to the variable:

```
numberOfFingersHeldUpByFinn = 3
```

Since the variable type is an optional `Int`, the valid values are either `Int` or `nil`; if we try something of another type, we will get a compiler error:

```
numberOfFingersHeldUpByFinn = "three" // Doesn't compile because "three"
isn't an Int or nil
```

As we discussed earlier, Swift has a static type system, so the type of variable can't be changed once it is declared. Therefore, although we have assigned a value of the `Int` type to the variable, this hasn't changed the variable type to the non-optional `Int`; its type remains `Int?`. Since the type is still optional, we can assign it a `nil` value when Finn puts his hands behind his back again:

```
numberOfFingersHeldUpByFinn = nil
```

When we print an optional variable, the output tells us that it is optional, for example, `Optional(1)`:

```
numberOfFingersHeldUpByFinn = 1
print(numberOfFingersHeldUpByFinn)
```

You will notice that the compiler highlights an issue that says **Expression implicitly coerced from 'Int?' to 'Any'** on the print line. We see this because we are passing an option value to the print comment, which is expecting a non-optional value. To solve this issue, we can provide a value to use if our optional value happens to be `nil`, and there is a really concise way to do this. The `??` operator can be applied after an optional value, and the value to the right of the operator will be used if the optional value is `nil`. This is called the **nil coalescing operator**:

```
print(numberOfFingersHeldUpByFinn ?? "Unknown")
```

At the end of the game, we want to store the number of fingers that Finn held up during the last round of the game. Since we know that we will play at least one round of the game, we know that there must be a value for the last number of fingers that were held up. Therefore, we declare the `lastNumberOfFingersHeldUpByFinn` variable as a non-optional `Int`:

```
let lastNumberOfFingersHeldUpByFinn: Int = numberOfFingersHeldUpByFinn!
```

However, our `numberOfFingersHeldUpByFinn` variable is an optional `Int`, and assigning a optional value to a non-optional variable causes a problem for the compiler since it can't be sure that it will be assigning a non-nil value. To get around this issue, we need to declare that this variable is now non-optional, even though we declared it as optional. We do this by adding `!` to the value.

If you remove ! from the preceding statement, the compiler will complain:

```
let lastNumberOfFingersHeldUpByFinn: Int = numberOfFingersHeldUpByFinn
    // Does not compile
```

In Swift terminology, by adding !, we are unwrapping the optional variable. Once it is unwrapped, and therefore non-optional, we can assign it to the lastNumberOfFingersHeldUpByFinn variable, which is also non-optional.

 Beware! Use of this forced unwrapping can be risky. When you forcibly unwrap an optional, you are declaring that you are sure that there will be a value in that variable at that point in the execution of the code. However, if the variable is nil, you will get an error while your code is running and the execution will terminate. If this code is running in an app, then the app will crash. We will see safer ways to unwrap an optional value in the later chapters.

Let's see what happens when we forcibly unwrap a variable that is set to nil. Imagine that we ended the game before playing the first round:

```
// Start of the game
var numberOfFingersHeldUpByFinn: Int?
// Hand behind his back
numberOfFingersHeldUpByFinn = nil
print(numberOfFingersHeldUpByFinn) // nil
// End of the game
let lastNumberOfFingersHeldUpByFinn: Int = numberOfFingersHeldUpByFinn!
```

This code will compile and run, but will crash at runtime because at the point that numberOfFingersHeldUpByFinn is assigned to lastNumberOfFingersHeldUpByFinn, the value of numberOfFingersHeldUpByFinn is nil.

There's more...

So far, we have seen non-optional variables, where a value of the correct type must be provided, and optional variables, where the value can either be the underlying type or nil. In a perfect world, this would be all we need. However, we may need to declare a variable that should be treated as non-optional, even if we don't know the value at the time it is declared. For these situations, we can declare a variable as an **implicitly unwrapped optional (IUO)** in Swift.

Run the following code in the playground:

```
var legalName: String!
// At birth
legalName = nil
// At birth registration
legalName = "Alissa Jones"
// At enrolling in school
print(legalName)
// At enrolling in college
print(legalName)
// Registering Marriage
legalName = "Alissa Moon"
// When meeting new people
print(legalName)
```

In the preceding example, we have declared a person's legal name, which is used at many points during their life, such as when registering for educational institutions. It can be changed, either by legal request or through marriage, and yet you would never expect someone's legal name to not exist. However, that is exactly what happens when someone is born! When a person is born, they don't have a legal name until their birth is registered. So, if we were trying to model this in code, a person's legal name could be represented as an **IUO**.

In code, we declare a variable to be an IUO by placing a ! sign after the type:

```
let legalName: String!
```

 IUOs present the same risk as forced unwrapping. You are promising that the variable has a value, even though it is possible that it could be `nil`. Although it's possible for the variable to be `nil`, when something tries to access it, a value will be there. If the variable is accessed, but doesn't contain a value, the execution will terminate and your app will crash.

There is some subtlety to how IUOs behave when they are assigned to other variables and the type is inferred. It's easiest to illustrate this with code, so enter the following into a playground:

```
var input: Int! = 5 // Int!
print(input) // 5
var output1 = input // Int?
print(output1 as Any) // Optional(5)
var output2 = input + 1 // Int
print(output2) // 5
```

When an IUO is assigned to a new variable, the compiler can't be sure that there is a non-nil value assigned. So, if an IUO is assigned to a new variable, as is the case with `output1` here, the compiler plays it safe and infers that the type of this new variable is an optional. If, however, the value of the IUO has been unwrapped, then the compiler knows that it has a non-nil value, and will infer a non-optional type. When assigning `output2`, the value of the input is unwrapped in order to add 1 to it. Therefore, the type of `output2` is inferred to be the non-optional `Int`.

See also

Further information regarding optionals can be found at `http://swiftbook.link/docs/the-basics`.

Reusing code in functions

Functions are a building block of almost all programming languages, allowing functionality to be defined and reused. Swift's syntax provides an expressive way to define your functions, creating concise and readable code. In this recipe, we will run through the different types of functions we can create, and understand how to define and use them.

How to do it...

Let's look at how functions are defined in Swift:

```
func nameOfFunction(parameterLabel1 parameter1: ParameterType1,
parameterLabel2 parameter2: ParameterType2,...) -> OutputType {
    // Function's implementation
    // If the function has an output type,
    // the function must return a valid value
    return output
}
```

Let's look at this in more detail to see how a function is defined:

- `func`: This indicates that you are declaring a function.
- `nameOfFunction`: This will be the name of your function and, by convention, is written in camel case (this means that each word, apart from the first, is capitalized and all spaces are removed). This should describe what the function does, and should provide some context to the value returned by the function, if one is returned. This will be how you will invoke the method from elsewhere in your code, so bear that in mind when naming it.
- `parameterLabel1 parameter1: ParameterType1`: This is the first input, or parameter, into the function. You can specify as many parameters as you like, separated by commas. Each parameter has a parameter name (`parameter1`) and type (`ParameterType1`). The parameter name is how the value of the parameter will be made available to your function's implementation. You can optionally provide a parameter label in front of the parameter name (`parameterLabel1`) that will be used to label the parameter when your function is used (at the call site).
- `-> OutputType`: This indicates that the function returns a value and indicates the type of that value. If no value is returned, this can be omitted.
- `{ }`: The curly brackets indicate the start and end of the function's implementation; anything within them will be executed when the function is called.
- `return output`: If the function returns a value, you type `return` and then the value to return. This ends the execution of the function; any code written after the return statement is not executed.

Now, let's put this into action.

Imagine that we are building a contacts app to hold the details of your family and friends, and we want to create a string of a contact's full name. Let's explore some of the ways in which functions can be used:

```
// Input parameters and output
func fullName(givenName: String,
              middleName: String,
              familyName: String) -> String {

    return "\(givenName) \(middleName) \(familyName)"
}
```

The preceding function takes three string parameters and outputs a string that puts all these together with spaces in between. The only thing this function does is take inputs and produce an output without causing any side effects; this type of function is often called a **pure function**. To call this function, we enter the name of the function followed by the input parameters within () brackets, where each parameter value is preceded by its label:

```
let myFullName = fullName(givenName: "Keith",
                          middleName: "David",
                          familyName: "Moon")

print(myFullName) // Keith David Moon
```

Functions with multiple parameters can get quite long, so to help with readability, the parameters can be placed on separate lines, as in the preceding example. This is true for both the definition of a function and when it is called. The convention is to align the start of the parameter name with the first parameter.

Since the function returns a value, we can assign the output of this function to a constant or a variable, just like any other expression.

The next function takes the same input parameters, but its purpose is not to return a value. Instead, it prints out the parameters as one string separated by spaces:

```
// Input parameters, with a side effect and no output
func printFullName(givenName: String,
                   middleName: String,
                   familyName: String) {

    print("\(givenName) \(middleName) \(familyName)")
}
```

We can call this function in the same way as the preceding function, although it can't be assigned to anything since it doesn't have a return value:

```
printFullName(givenName: "Keith", middleName: "David", familyName:
    "Moon")
```

The following function takes no parameters as everything it needs to perform its task is contained within it, although it does output a string. This function calls the fullName function we defined earlier, taking advantage of its ability to produce a full name when given the component names. Reusing functionality is the most useful feature that functions provide:

```
// No inputs, with an output
func authorsFullName() -> String {
```

```
        return fullName(givenName: "Keith",
                      middleName: "David",
                      familyName: "Moon")
    }
```

Since `authorsFullName` takes no parameters, we can execute it by entering the function name followed by empty brackets, `()`, and since it returns a value, we can assign the outcome of `authorsFullName` to a variable:

```
    let authorOfThisBook = authorsFullName()
```

Our final example takes no parameters and returns no value:

```
    // No inputs, no output
    func printAuthorsFullName() {

        let author = authorsFullName()
        print(author)
    }
```

You can call this function in the same way as the previous functions with no parameters, and there is no return value to assign:

```
    printAuthorsFullName()
```

As you can see from the preceding example, having input parameters and providing an output value are not required when defining a function.

There's more...

Now, let's look at a couple of ways of making your use of functions more expressive and concise.

Default parameter values

One convenience in Swift is the ability to specify default values for parameters. These allow you to omit the parameter when calling, as the default value will be provided instead. Let's use the same example as earlier in this recipe, where we are creating a contact app to hold information about our family and friends. Many of your family members are likely to have the same family name as you, so we can set the family name as the default value for that parameter. Therefore, the family name only needs to be provided if it is different from the default.

Enter the following code into a playground:

```
func fullName(givenName: String,
              middleName: String,
              familyName: String = "Moon") -> String {

    return "\(givenName) \(middleName) \(familyName)"
}
```

Defining a default value looks similar to assigning a value to the `familyName: String = "Moon"` parameter. When calling the function, the parameter with the default value does not have to be given:

```
let keith = fullName(givenName: "Keith", middleName: "David")
let alissa = fullName(givenName: "Alissa", middleName: "May")
let laura = fullName(givenName: "Laura",
                     middleName: "May",
                     familyName: "Jones")
print(keith) // Keith David Moon
print(alissa) // Alissa May Moon
print(laura)  // Laura May Jones
```

Parameter overloading

Swift supports parameter overloading, which allows for functions to have the same name and only be differentiated by the parameters that they take.

Let's learn more about parameter overloading by entering the following code into a playground:

```
func combine(_ givenName: String, _ familyName: String) -> String {
    return "\(givenName) \(familyName)"
}

func combine(_ integer1: Int, _ integer2: Int) -> Int {
    return integer1+integer2
}

let combinedString = combine("Finnley", "Moon")
let combinedInt = combine(5, 10)
print(combinedString) // Finnley Moon
print(combinedInt) // 15
```

Both the preceding functions have the name `combine`, but one takes two strings as parameters, and the other takes two Ints. Therefore, when we call the function, Swift knows which implementation we intended by the values we pass as parameters.

We've introduced something new in the preceding function declarations, anonymous parameter labels: `_ givenName: String`.

When we declare the parameters, we use an underscore, _, for the parameter label. This indicates that we don't want a parameter name shown when calling the function. This should only be used if the purpose of the parameters is clear without the labels.

See also

Further information about functions can be found at `http://swiftbook.link/docs/functions`.

Encapsulating functionality in object classes

Object-oriented programming is a common and powerful programming paradigm. At its core is the *object class*. Objects allow us to encapsulate data and functionality, which can then be stored and passed around.

In this recipe, we will build some class objects, break down their components, and understand how they are defined and used.

How to do it...

Let's write some code to create and use class objects, and then we will walk through what the code is doing:

1. First, create a `Person` class object:

```
class Person {
}
```

2. Within the curly brackets, { and }, add three constants representing the person's name, and one variable representing their country of residence:

```
let givenName: String
let middleName: String
let familyName: String
var countryOfResidence: String = "UK"
```

3. Below the properties, but still within the curly brackets, add an initialization method for our `Person` object:

```
init(givenName: String, middleName: String, familyName: String) {
    self.givenName = givenName
    self.middleName = middleName
    self.familyName = familyName
}
```

4. Next, add a variable as a property of the class, with a computed value:

```
var displayString: String {
    return "\(self.fullName()) - Location: \
      (self.countryOfResidence)"
}
```

5. Add a function within the `Person` object that returns the person's full name:

```
func fullName() -> String {
    return "\(givenName) \(middleName) \(familyName)"
}
```

6. Next, create a `Friend` object that extends the functionality of the `Person` object:

```
final class Friend: Person {
}
```

7. Within the `Friend` class object, add a variable property to hold details of where the user met the friend, and override the display string property to customize its behavior for `Friend` objects:

```
var whereWeMet: String?
override var displayString: String {
    let meetingPlace = whereWeMet ?? "Don't know where we met"
    return "\(super.displayString) - \(meetingPlace)"
}
```

8. In addition to the `Friend` object, create a `Family` object that extends the functionality of the `Person` object:

```
final class Family: Person {
}
```

9. Add a relationship property to our `Family` object and create an initializer method to populate it in addition to the other properties from `Person`:

```
final class Family: Person {

    let relationship: String
    init(givenName: String,
        middleName: String,
        familyName: String = "Moon",
        relationship: String) {

        self.relationship = relationship
        super.init(givenName: givenName,
                   middleName: middleName,
                   familyName: familyName)
    }
}
```

10. Give the `Family` object a custom `displayString` method that includes the value of the `relationship` property by adding this code within the `Family` object definition (within the curly brackets):

```
override var displayString: String {

    return "\(super.displayString) - \(relationship)"
}
```

11. Lastly, create instances of our new objects and print the display string to see how its value differs:

```
let steve = Person(givenName: "Steven",
                   middleName: "Paul",
                   familyName: "Jobs")

let richard = Friend(givenName: "Richard",
                     middleName: "Adrian",
                     familyName: "Das")
richard.whereWeMet = "Worked together at Travel Supermarket"

let finnley = Family(givenName: "Finnley",
                     middleName: "David",
                     relationship: "Son")

let dave = Family(givenName: "Dave",
                  middleName: "deRidder",
                  familyName: "Jones",
                  relationship: "Father-In-Law")
```

```
dave.countryOfResidence = "US"

print(steve.displayString)
// Steven Paul Jobs

print(richard.displayString)
// Richard Adrian Das - Worked together at Travel Supermarket

print(finnley.displayString)
// Finnley David Moon - Son

print(dave.displayString)
// Dave deRidder Jones - Father-In-Law
```

How it works...

Classes are defined with the `class` keyword. Class names start with a capital letter by convention, and the implementation of the class is contained, or "scoped", within curly brackets:

```
class Person {
    //...
}
```

An object can have property values, which are contained within the object. These properties can have initial values, as `countryOfResidence` does in the following code, although bear in mind that constants (defined with `let`) cannot be changed once the initial value has been set:

```
class Person {
    let givenName: String
    let middleName: String
    let familyName: String
    var countryOfResidence: String = "UK"
    //...
}
```

If your class were to just have the preceding property definitions, the compiler would raise a warning, as `givenName`, `middleName`, and `familyName` are defined as non-optional strings, but we have not provided any way to populate those values.

The compiler needs to know how the object will be initialized so that we can be sure that all the non-optional properties will indeed have values:

```
class Person {
    let givenName: String
    let middleName: String
    let familyName: String
    var countryOfResidence: String = "UK"
    init(givenName: String, middleName: String, familyName: String) {
        self.givenName = givenName
        self.middleName = middleName
        self.familyName = familyName
    }
    //...
}
```

`init` is a special method (functions defined within objects are called methods) that's called when the object is initialized. In the `Person` object of the preceding code, `givenName`, `middleName`, and `familyName` must be passed in when the object is initialized, and we assign those provided values to the object's properties. The `self.` prefix is used to differentiate between the property and the value passed in, as they have the same name.

We do not need to pass in a value for `countryOfResidence` as this has an initial value. This isn't ideal, though, as when we create a `Person` object, it will always have the `countryOfResidence` variable set to `"UK"`, and we will then have to change that value, if different, after initialization. Another way to do this would be to use a default parameter value, as seen in the previous recipe. Amend the `Person` object initialization to the following:

```
class Person {
    let givenName: String
    let middleName: String
    let familyName: String
    var countryOfResidence: String
    init(givenName: String,
        middleName: String,
        familyName: String,
        countryOfResidence: String = "UK") {

        self.givenName = givenName
        self.middleName = middleName
        self.familyName = familyName
        self.countryOfResidence = countryOfResidence
    }
    //...
}
```

Now, you can provide a country of residence in the initialization or omit it to use the default value.

Next, let's look at the `displayString` property of our `Person` class:

```
class Person {
    //...
    var displayString: String {
        return "\(self.fullName()) - Location: \
        (self.countryOfResidence)"
    }
    //...
}
```

This property declaration is different from the others. Rather than having a value assigned to it, it is followed by an expression contained within curly braces. This is a computed property; its value is not static but is determined by the given expression every time the property is accessed. Any valid expressions can be used to compute the property, but must return a value that matches the declared type of the property. The compiler will enforce this, and you can't omit the variable type for computed properties.

In constructing the return value above, we use `self.fullName()` and `self.countryOfResidence`. As we did in the preceding `init` method, we use `self.` to show that we are accessing the method and property of the current instance of the `Person` object. However, since `displayString` is already a property on the current instance, the Swift compiler is aware of this context and so those self references can be removed:

```
var displayString: String {
    return "\(fullName()) - Location: \(countryOfResidence)"
}
```

Objects can do work based on the information they contain, and this work can be defined in methods. Methods are just functions that are contained within classes and have access to all the object's properties. The `Person` object's `fullName` method is an example of this:

```
class Person {
    //...
    func fullName() -> String {
        return "\(givenName) \(middleName) \(familyName))"
    }
    //...
}
```

All the abilities of a function are available, which we explored in the last recipe, including optional inputs and outputs, default parameter values, and parameter overloading.

Having defined a `Person` object, we want to extend the concept of `Person` to define a friend. A friend is also a person, so it stands to reason that anything a `Person` object can do, a `Friend` object can also do. We model this inherited behavior by defining `Friend` as a subclass of `Person`. We define the class that our `Friend` class inherits from (called the "superclass"), after the class name, separated by `::`

```
final class Friend: Person {
    var whereWeMet: String?
    //...
}
```

By inheriting from `Person`, our `Friend` object inherits all the properties and methods from its superclass. We can then add any extra functionality we require. In this case, we add a property for details of where we met this friend.

The `final` prefix tells the compiler that we don't intend for this class to be subclassed; it is the final class in the inheritance hierarchy. This allows the compiler to make some optimizations as it knows it won't be extended.

In addition to implementing new functionalities, we can override functionalities from the superclass using the `override` keyword:

```
final class Friend: Person {
    //...
    override var displayString: String {

        let meetingPlace = whereWeMet ?? "Don't know where we met"
        return "\(super.displayString) - \(meetingPlace)"
    }
}
```

In the preceding code, we override the `displayString` computed property from `Person` as we want to add the "where we met" information. Within the computed property, we can access the superclass's implementation by calling `super.`, and then referencing the property or method.

Next, let's look at how we can customize how our subclasses are initialized:

```
final class Family: Person {

    let relationship: String

    init(givenName: String,
         middleName: String,
         familyName: String = "Moon",
         relationship: String) {
```

```
        self.relationship = relationship
        super.init(givenName: givenName,
                    middleName: middleName,
                    familyName: familyName)
    }
    //...
}
```

Our `Family` class also inherits from `Person`, but we want to add a `relationship` property, which should form part of the initialization, so we can declare a new `init` that also takes a relationship string value. That passed-in value is then assigned to the `relationship` property because the superclass's initializer is called.

 Subclasses must have all their non-optional properties assigned a value before the superclass's `init` method is called. If we had forgotten to assign a value to `relationship`, or we had assigned it after calling `super.init`, then our code would not compile.

With all our class objects defined, we can create instances of these objects and call methods and access properties of these objects:

```
let steve = Person(givenName: "Steven",
                    middleName: "Paul",
                    familyName: "Jobs")

let richard = Friend(givenName: "Richard",
                    middleName: "Adrian",
                    familyName: "Das")
richard.whereWeMet = "Worked together at Travel Supermarket"

let finnley = Family(givenName: "Finnley",
                    middleName: "David",
                    relationship: "Son")

let dave = Family(givenName: "Dave",
                middleName: "deRidder",
                familyName: "Jones",
                relationship: "Father-In-Law")
dave.countryOfResidence = "US"

print(steve.displayString)
// Steven Paul Jobs

print(richard.displayString)
// Richard Adrian Das - Worked together at Travel Supermarket

print(finnley.displayString)
```

```
// Finnley David Moon - Son

print(dave.displayString)
// Dave deRidder Jones - Father-In-Law
```

To create an instance of an object, we use the name of the object like a function, passing in any required parameters. This returns an object instance that we can then assign to a constant or variable.

When creating an instance, we are actually calling the object's `init` method, and you can do this explicitly, as follows:

```
let steve = Person.init(givenName: "Steven",
                        middleName: "Paul",
                        familyName: "Jobs")
```

However, to be concise, this is usually omitted.

There's more...

Class objects are **reference types**, which is a term that refers to the way they are stored and referenced internally. To see how these reference type semantics work, let's look at how an object behaves when it is modified:

```
class MovieReview {
    let movieTitle: String
    var starRating: Int // Rating out of 5
    init(movieTitle: String, starRating: Int) {
        self.movieTitle = movieTitle
        self.starRating = starRating
    }
}

// Write a review
let shawshankReviewOnYourWebsite = MovieReview(movieTitle: "Shawshank
  Redemption", starRating: 3)

// Post it to social media
let referenceToReviewOnTwitter = shawshankReviewOnYourWebsite
let referenceToReviewOnFacebook = shawshankReviewOnYourWebsite

print(referenceToReviewOnTwitter.starRating) // 3
print(referenceToReviewOnFacebook.starRating) // 3

// Reconsider the review
shawshankReviewOnYourWebsite.starRating = 5
```

```
// The change is visible from anywhere with a reference to the object
print(referenceToReviewOnTwitter.starRating) // 5
print(referenceToReviewOnFacebook.starRating) // 5
```

We defined a `MovieReview` class object, created an instance of that `MovieReview` object, and then assigned that review to two separate constants. As a class object is a reference type, it is a reference to the object that is stored in the constant, rather than a new copy of the object. Therefore, when we reconsider our review to give *The Shawshank Redemption* five stars (and rightly so!), we are changing the underlying object. All references that access that underlying object will receive the updated value when the `starRating` property is accessed.

See also

- Further information about classes can be found at `http://swiftbook.link/docs/classes-and-structures`.
- In `Chapter 9`, *Performance and Responsiveness in Swift*, we will examine reference semantics in more detail, and see how this affects performance.

Bundling values into structs

Class objects are great for encapsulating data and functionality within a unifying concept, such as a person, as they allow individual instances to be referenced. However, not everything is an object. We may need to represent data that is logically grouped together, but there isn't much more than that. It's **not** more than the sum of its parts; it is the sum of its parts.

For this, there are **structs**. Short for structures, structs can be found in many programming languages. Structs are **value types**, as opposed to classes, which are reference types, and, as such, behave differently when passed around. In this recipe, we will learn how structs work in Swift, and when and how to use them.

Getting ready

This recipe will build on top of the previous recipe, so open the playground you have used for the previous recipe. Don't worry if you didn't work through the previous recipe, as this one will contain all the code you need.

How to do it...

We have already defined a `Person` object as having three separate string properties relating to the person's name. However, these three separate strings don't exist in isolation from each other, as together they define a person's name. Currently, if you wanted to retrieve a person's name, you have to access three separate properties and combine them. Let's tidy this up by defining a person's name as its own struct:

1. Create a struct called `PersonName`:

   ```
   struct PersonName {
   }
   ```

2. Add three properties to `PersonName`, for `givenName`, `middleName` and `familyName`. Make the first two constants, and the last one a variable, as a family name can change:

   ```
   struct PersonName {
       let givenName: String
       let middleName: String
       var familyName: String
   }
   ```

3. Add a method to combine the three properties into a `fullName` string:

   ```
   func fullName() -> String {
       return "\(givenName) \(middleName) \(familyName)"
   }
   ```

4. Provide a method to change the family name property and prefix this method with the `mutating` keyword:

   ```
   mutating func change(familyName: String) {
       self.familyName = familyName
   }
   ```

5. Create a person name, passing in the property values:

   ```
   var alissasName = PersonName(givenName: "Alissa",
                                middleName: "May",
                                familyName: "Jones")
   ```

How it works...

Defining a struct is very similar to defining an object class, and that is intentional. Much of the functionality available to a class is also available to a struct. Therefore, you will notice that aside from using the `struct` keyword instead of `class`, the definition of a class and a struct are almost identical.

Within the `PersonName` struct, we have properties for the three components of the name and the `fullName` method we saw earlier to combine the three name components into a full name string.

The method we created to change the family name property has a new keyword that we haven't seen before, `mutating`:

```
mutating func change(familyName: String) {
    self.familyName = familyName
}
```

This keyword must be added to any method in a struct that changes a property of the struct. This keyword is to inform anyone using the method that it will change, or "mutate", the struct. Unlike class objects, when you mutate a struct, you create a copy of the struct with the changed properties. This behavior is known as **value-type semantics**.

To see this in action, let's first create a struct and then check that it behaves as we expect when we assign it to different values:

```
let alissasBirthName = PersonName(givenName: "Alissa",
                                  middleName: "May",
                                  familyName: "Jones")
print(alissasBirthName.fullName()) // Alissa May Jones
var alissasCurrentName = alissasBirthName
print(alissasCurrentName.fullName()) // Alissa May Jones
```

So far, so good. We have created a `PersonName` struct, assigned it to a constant called `alissasBirthName`, and then assigned that constant to a variable called `alissasCurrentName`.

Now let's see what happens when we mutate `alissasCurrentName`:

```
alissasCurrentName.change(familyName: "Moon")
print(alissasBirthName.fullName()) // Alissa May Jones
print(alissasCurrentName.fullName()) // Alissa May Moon
```

When we call the mutating method on the `alissasCurrentName` variable, only that variable is changed. This change is not reflected in `alissasBirthName`, even though these structs were once the same. This behavior would be different if `PersonName` was an object class, and we explored that behavior in the previous recipe.

There's more...

We can use how this value-type behavior interacts with constants and variables to restrict unintended changes.

To see this in action, first, let's amend our `Person` class to our new `PersonName` struct:

```
class Person {
    let birthName: PersonName
    var currentName: PersonName
    var countryOfResidence: String
    init(name: PersonName, countryOfResidence: String = "UK") {
        birthName = name
        currentName = name
        self.countryOfResidence = countryOfResidence
    }
    var displayString: String {
        return "\(currentName.fullName()) - Location: \
          (countryOfResidence)"
    }
}
```

We've added the `birthName` and `currentName` properties of our new `PersonName` struct type, and we initiate them with the same value when the `Person` object is created. Since a person's birth name won't change, we define it as a constant, but their current name can change, so it's defined as a variable.

Now, let's create a new `Person` object:

```
var name = PersonName(givenName: "Alissa", middleName: "May", familyName:
"Jones")
let alissa = Person(name: name)
print(alissa.currentName.fullName()) // Alissa May Jones
```

Since our `PersonName` struct has value semantics, we can use this to enforce the behavior that we expect our model to have. We would expect to not be able to change a person's birth name, and if you try, you will find that the compiler won't let you.

As we discussed earlier, changing the family name mutates the struct, and so a new copy is made. However, we defined `birthName` as a constant, which can't be changed, so the only way we would be able to change the family name would be to change our definition of `birthName` from `let` to `var`:

```
alissa.birthName.change(familyName: "Moon") // Does not compile.
  // Compiler tells you to change let to var
```

When we change `currentName` to have a new family name, which we can do since we defined it as a `var`, it changes the `currentName` property, but not the `birthName` property, even though these were assigned with the same value:

```
print(alissa.birthName.fullName()) // Alissa May Jones
print(alissa.currentName.fullName()) // Alissa May Jones
alissa.currentName.change(familyName: "Moon")
print(alissa.birthName.fullName()) // Alissa May Jones
print(alissa.currentName.fullName()) // Alissa May Moon
```

We have used a combination of objects and structs to create a model that enforces our expected behavior. This technique can help to reduce potential bugs in our code.

See also

- Further information about structs can be found at `http://swiftbook.link/docs/classes-and-structures`.

- In Chapter 9, *Performance and Responsiveness in Swift*, we will examine value semantics in more detail, and see how it affects performance.

Enumerating values with enums

Enumerations are a programming construct that lets you define a value type with a finite set of options. Most programming languages have enumerations (usually abbreviated to **enums**), although the Swift language takes the concept further than most.

An example of an enum from the iOS/macOS SDK is `ComparisonResult`, which you would use when sorting items. When comparing for the purposes of sorting, there are only three possible results from a comparison:

- `ascending`: The items are ordered in ascending order.
- `descending`: The items are ordered in descending order.
- `same`: The items are the same.

There are a finite number of possible options for a comparison result; therefore, it's a perfect candidate for being represented by an enum:

```
enum ComparisonResult : Int {
    case orderedAscending
    case orderedSame
    case orderedDescending
}
```

Swift takes the enum concept and elevates it to a first-class type. As we will see, this makes enums a very powerful tool for modeling your information.

This recipe will examine how and when to use enums in Swift.

Getting ready

This recipe will build on top of the earlier recipes, so open the playground you have used for the previous recipes. Don't worry if you haven't tried out the previous recipes, as this one will contain all the code you need.

How to do it...

In the *Encapsulating functionality in object classes* recipe, we created a `Person` object to represent people in our model and, in the *Bundling values into structs* recipe, we made a `PersonName` struct to hold information about a person's name. Now, let's turn our attention to a person's title (for example, Mr, Mrs), which precedes someone's full name. There are a small and finite number of common titles that a person may have; therefore an enum is a great way to model this information.

1. Create an enum to represent a person's title:

```
enum Title {
    case mr
    case mrs
```

```
        case mister
        case miss
        case dr
        case prof
        case other
    }
```

We define our enumeration with the `enum` keyword and provide a name for the enum. As with classes and structs, the convention is that this starts with a capital letter, and the implementation is defined within curly brackets. We define each enum option with the `case` keyword, and, by convention, these start with a lowercase character.

2. Assign the `mr` case of our `Title` enum to a value:

    ```
    let title1 = Title.mr
    ```

    Enums can be assigned by specifying the enum type, then a dot, and then the case. However, if the compiler can infer the enum type, we can omit the type and just provide the case, preceded by a dot.

3. Define a constant value, of the `Title` type, and then assign a case to it with the type inferred:

    ```
    let title2: Title
    title2 = .mr
    ```

How it works...

In many programming languages, including C and Objective-C, enums are defined as a type definition on top of an integer, with each case being given a defined integer value. In Swift, enums do not need to represent integers under the hood. In fact, they do not need to be backed by any type and can exist as their own abstract concepts. Consider the following example:

```
enum CompassPoint {
    case North, South, East, West
}
```

It doesn't make sense to map the compass points as integers, and in Swift we don't have to.

Note that we can define multiple cases on the same line by separating them with commas.

For `Title` also, an integer-based enum doesn't seem appropriate; however, a string-based one may be. So, let's declare our enum to be string-based:

```
enum Title: String {
    case mr = "Mr"
    case mrs = "Mrs"
    case mister = "Master"
    case miss = "Miss"
    case dr = "Dr"
    case prof = "Prof"
    case other // Inferred as "other"
}
```

The enum's raw underlying type is declared after its name and a : separator. The raw types that can be used to back the enum are limited to types that can be represented as a literal. This includes the following Swift base types:

- `String`
- `Int`
- `Float`
- `Bool`

These types can be used to back an enum because they conform to a protocol, called `RawRepresentable`. We will cover protocols later in the chapter.

Cases can be assigned a value of the raw type; however, certain types can be inferred, and so do not need to be explicitly declared. For int-backed enums, the inferred values are sequentially assigned starting at 0:

```
enum Rating: Int {
    case worst   // Infered as 0
    case bad     // Infered as 1
    case average // Infered as 2
    case good    // Infered as 3
    case best    // Infered as 4
}
```

For string-based enums, the inferred value is the name of the case, so the `other` case in our `Title` enum is inferred to be `other`.

We can get the underlying value of the enum in its raw type by accessing its `rawValue` property:

```
let title1 = Title.mr
print(title1.rawValue) // "Mr"
```

There's more...

As mentioned in the introduction to this recipe, Swift treats enums as a first-class type, and therefore they can have functionality that is not available to enums in most programming languages. This includes having computed variables and methods.

Methods and computed variables

Let's imagine that it is important for us to know whether a person's title relates to a professional qualification that the person holds. Let's add a method to our enum to provide that information:

```
enum Title: String {
    case mr = "Mr"
    case mrs = "Mrs"
    case mister = "Master"
    case miss = "Miss"
    case dr = "Dr"
    case prof = "Prof"
    case other // Inferred as "other"

    func isProfessional() -> Bool {
        return self == Title.dr || self == Title.prof
    }
}
```

For the list of titles that we have defined, `Dr` and `Prof` relate to professional qualifications, so we have our method return `true` if `self` (the instance of the enum type this method is called on) is equal to the `dr` case, or equal to the `prof` case.

In defining this method, we used | |, which is the OR logical operator. Using this operator returns a `true` Bool value if the expression on the left-hand side evaluates to `true` OR the expression on the right-hand side evaluates to `true`. Another useful common operator to know is the AND operator, `&&`, but this is not appropriate for this method.

This functionality feels more appropriate as a computed property since whether it `isProfessional` or not is intrinsic to the enum itself, and we don't need to do much work to determine the answer. So, let's change this into a property:

```
enum Title: String {
    case mr = "Mr"
    case mrs = "Mrs"
    case mister = "Master"
    case miss = "Miss"
    case dr = "Dr"
    case prof = "Prof"
    case other // Inferred as "other"
    var isProfessional: Bool {
        return self == Title.dr || self == Title.prof
    }
}
```

Now, we can determine whether a title is a professional title by accessing the computed property on it:

```
let loganTitle = Title.mr
let xavierTitle = Title.prof
print(loganTitle.isProfessional) // false
print(xavierTitle.isProfessional) // true
```

We can't store any additional information on an enum, over and above the enum value itself, but being able to define methods and computed properties that provide extra information about the enum is a really powerful option.

Associated values

Our string-based enum seems perfect for our title information, except that we have a case called `other`. If the person has a title that we hadn't considered when defining the enum, we can choose `other`, but that doesn't capture what the other title is. In our model, we would need to define another property to hold the value given for `other`, but that splits our definition of title over two separate properties, which could cause an unintended combination of values.

Swift enums have a solution for this situation, **associated values**. We can choose to associate a value with each enum case, allowing us to bind a non-optional string to our other case.

Let's rewrite our Title enum to use an associated value:

```
enum Title {
    case mr
    case mrs
    case mister
    case miss
    case dr
    case prof
    case other(String)
}
```

We have defined the other case to have an associated value by putting the value's type in brackets after the case declaration. We do not need to add associated values for every case. Each case declaration can have associated values of different types or none at all.

 Enums containing associated values cannot have a raw type as they are now too complex to be represented by one of these base types, so our Title enum is no longer string-based.

Now let's look at how we assign an enum case with an associated type:

```
let mister: Title = .mr
let dame: Title = .other("Dame")
```

The associated value is declared in brackets after the case, and the compiler enforces that the type matches the type declared in our enum definition. As we declared the other case to have a non-optional string, we are ensuring that a title of other cannot be chosen without providing details of what the other title is, and we don't need another property to fully represent Title in our model.

See also

Further information about enums can be found at http://swiftbook.link/docs/enums.

Passing around functionality with closures

Closures are also referred to as **anonymous functions**, and this is the best way to explain them. Closures are functions without a name and, like other functions, they can take a set of input parameters and can return an output. Closures behave like other primary types. They can be assigned, stored, passed around, and used as input and output to functions and other closures.

In this recipe, we will explore how and when to use closures in our code.

Getting ready

We will continue to build on our contacts app example from earlier in this chapter, so you should use the same playground as in the previous recipes.

If, however, you are implementing this in a new playground, first add the relevant code from the previous recipes:

```swift
struct PersonName {
    let givenName: String
    let middleName: String
    var familyName: String
    func fullName() -> String {
        return "\(givenName) \(middleName) \(familyName)"
    }
    mutating func change(familyName: String) {
        self.familyName = familyName
    }
}

class Person {
    let birthName: PersonName
    var currentName: PersonName
    var countryOfResidence: String
    init(name: PersonName, countryOfResidence: String = "UK") {
        birthName = name
        currentName = name
        self.countryOfResidence = countryOfResidence
    }
    var displayString: String {
        return "\(currentName.fullName()) - Location: \
        (countryOfResidence)"
    }
}
```

For explanations of how this code works, please refer to the previous recipes in this chapter.

How to do it...

Now, let's define a number of types of closures, which we will then work through step by step:

1. Define a closure to print this author's details that takes no input and returns no output:

```
// No input, no output
let printAuthorsDetails: () -> Void = {
    let name = PersonName(givenName: "Keith",
                          middleName: "David",
                          familyName: "Moon")
    let author = Person(name: name)
    print(author.displayString)
}
printAuthorsDetails() // "Keith David Moon - Location: UK"
```

2. Define a closure that creates a `Person` object. The closure takes no input, but returns a `Person` object as the output:

```
// No input, Person output
let createAuthor: () -> Person = {
    let name = PersonName(givenName: "Keith",
                          middleName: "David",
                          familyName: "Moon")
    let author = Person(name: name)
    return author
}
let author = createAuthor()
print(author.displayString) // "Keith David Moon - Location: UK"
```

3. Define a closure that prints a person's details, taking the three components of their name as `String` inputs, but returning no output:

```
// String inputs, no output
let printPersonsDetails: (String, String, String) -> Void = {
given,
  middle, family in
    let name = PersonName(givenName: given,
                          middleName: middle,
                          familyName: family)
```

```
        let author = Person(name: name)
        print(author.displayString)
    }
    printPersonsDetails("Kathleen", "Mary", "Moon")
    // "Kathleen Mary Moon - Location: UK"
```

4. Lastly, define a closure to create a person, taking the three name components as string inputs and returning a `Person` object as the output:

```
    // String inputs, Person output
    let createPerson: (String, String, String) -> Person = { given,
      middle, family in
        let name = PersonName(givenName: given,
                              middleName: middle,
                              familyName: family)
        let person = Person(name: name)
        return person
    }
    let felix = createPerson("Felix", "Robert", "Moon")
    print(felix.displayString) // "Felix Robert Moon - Location: UK"
```

How it works...

Let's take a look at the different types of closures we just implemented:

```
    // No input, no output
    let printAuthorsDetails: () -> Void = {
        let name = PersonName(givenName: "Keith", middleName: "David",
          familyName: "Moon")
        let author = Person(name: name)
        print(author.displayString)
    }
```

As a first-class type in Swift, closures can be assigned to constants or variables, and constants and variables need a type. To define a closure's type, we need to specify the input parameter types and the output type, and for the closure in the preceding code, the type is `() -> Void`. The `Void` type is another way of saying "nothing", so this closure takes no inputs and returns nothing, and the closure's functionality is defined within the curly brackets, as with other functions.

Now that we have this closure defined and assigned to the `printAuthorsDetails` constant, we can execute it like other functions, but with the variable name, instead of the function's name. With this closure, that will cause this author's details to be printed:

```
printAuthorsDetails() // "Keith David Moon - Location: UK"
```

The next closure type takes no input parameters, but returns a `Person` object, as you can see with the `() -> Person` type definition:

```
// No input, Person output
let createAuthor: () -> Person = {
    let name = PersonName(givenName: "Keith", middleName: "David",
      familyName: "Moon")
    let author = Person(name: name)
    return author
}
let author: Person = createAuthor()
print(author.displayString) // "Keith David Moon - Location: UK"
```

Since it has an output, the execution of the closure returns a value that can be assigned to a variable or constant. In the preceding code, we execute the `createAuthor` closure and assign the output to the `author` constant. Since we defined the closure type as `() -> Person`, the compiler knows that the output type is a `Person`, and so the type of constant can be inferred. Since we don't need to declare it explicitly, let's remove the type declaration:

```
let author = createAuthor()
print(author.displayString) // "Keith David Moon - Location: UK"
```

Next, let's take a look at a closure that takes input parameters:

```
// String inputs, no output
let printPersonsDetails: (String, String, String) -> Void = { given,
  middle, family in
    let name = PersonName(givenName: given, middleName: middle,
      familyName: family)
    let author = Person(name: name)
    print(author.displayString)
}
printPersonsDetails("Kathleen", "Mary", "Moon") // "Kathleen Mary Moon
  - Location: UK"
```

You will remember, from the recipe on functions, that we can define parameter labels, which determine how the parameters are referenced when the function is used, and parameter names, which define how the parameter is referenced from within the function. In closures, these are defined a bit differently:

- Parameter labels cannot be defined for closures, so, when calling a closure, the order and parameter type have to be used to determine what values should be provided as parameters:

```
(String, String, String) -> Void
```

- Parameter names are defined inside the curly brackets, followed by the in keyword:

```
given, middle, family in
```

Putting it all together, we can define and execute a closure with inputs and an output, as follows:

```
// String inputs, Person output
let createPerson: (String, String, String) -> Person = { given, middle,
  family in
    let name = PersonName(givenName: given,
                          middleName: middle,
                          familyName: family)
    let person = Person(name: name)
    return person
}
let felix = createPerson("Felix", "Robert", "Moon")
print(felix.displayString) // "Felix Robert Moon – Location: UK"
```

There's more...

We've seen how we can store closures, but we can also use them as method parameters. This pattern can be really useful when we want to be notified when a long-running task is completed.

Let's imagine that we want to save the details of our Person object to a remote database, maybe for backup or use on other devices. We may want to be notified when this process has completed, so we execute some additional code, perhaps printing a completion message, or update some UI. While the actual saving implementation is outside the scope of this recipe, we can amend our Person class to allow this save functionality to be called, passing a closure to execute on completion.

Add a method to save to a remote database, taking in a completion "handler", and store it for subsequent execution:

```
class Person {
    //....
    var saveHandler: ((Bool) -> Void)?
    func saveToRemoteDatabase(handler: @escaping (Bool) -> Void) {
        saveHandler = handler
        // Send person information to remove database
        // Once remote save is complete, it calls saveComplete(Bool)
        // We'll fake it for the moment, and assume the save is
          // complete.
        saveComplete(success: true)
    }
    func saveComplete(success: Bool) {
        saveHandler?(success)
    }
}
```

We define an optional variable to hold on to the save handler during the long-running save operation. Our closure will take a `Bool` to indicate whether the save was a success:

```
var saveHandler: ((Bool) -> Void)?
```

Let's now define a method to save our `Person` object, which takes a closure as a parameter:

```
func saveToRemoteDatabase(handler: @escaping (Bool) -> Void) {
    saveHandler = handler
    // Send person information to remove database
    // Once remote save is complete, it calls saveComplete(Bool)
    // We'll fake it for the moment, and assume the save is complete.
    saveComplete(success: true)
}
```

Our function stores the given closure in the variable and then starts the process to save to the remote database (the actual implementation of this is outside the scope of this recipe). This save process will call the `saveComplete` method when completed.

We added a modifier, `@escaping`, just before the closure type definition. This tells the compiler that, rather than using the closure within this method, we intend to store the closure and use it later. The closure will be *escaping* the scope of this method. This modifier is needed to prevent the compiler from doing certain optimizations that would be possible if the closure was *nonescaping*. It also helps users of this method understand whether the closure they provide will be executed immediately, or at a later time.

With the save operation complete, we can execute the `saveHandler` variable, passing in the `success` Boolean:

```
func saveComplete(success: Bool) {
    saveHandler?(success)
}
```

Since we stored the closure as an optional, we need to unwrap it by adding a `?` after the variable name. If `saveHandler` has a value, the closure will be executed; if it is `nil`, the expression is ignored.

Now that we have a function that takes a closure, let's see how we call it:

```
let fox = createPerson("Fox", "Richard", "Moon")
fox.saveToRemoteDatabase(handler: { success in
    print("Saved finished. Successful: \(success)")
})
```

Swift provides a more concise way to provide closures to functions. When a closure is the last (or only) parameter, Swift allows it to be provided as a **trailing closure**. This means the parameter name can be dropped and the closure can be specified after the parameter brackets. So, we can rewrite the preceding with the following, neater, syntax:

```
let fox = createPerson("Fox", "Richard", "Moon")
fox.saveToRemoteDatabase() { success in
    print("Saved finished. Successful: \(success)")
}
```

See also

Further information about closures can be found at `http://swiftbook.link/docs/closures`.

Using protocols to define interfaces

Protocols are a way to describe the interface that a type provides. They can be thought of as a contract, defining how you can interact with instances of that type. Protocols are a great way to abstract the "what" something does from "how" it does it. As we will see in subsequent chapters, Swift adds functionalities to protocols, that make them even more useful and powerful than in many other programming languages.

Getting ready

We will continue to build on examples from the previous recipes, but don't worry if you haven't followed these recipes yet as all the code you need is listed in the upcoming sections.

How to do it...

In the last recipe, we added a method to our `Person` class that (given the full implementation) would save it to a remote database. This is a very useful functionality, and as we add more features to our app, there will likely be more types that we also want to save to a remote database:

1. Create a protocol to define how we will interface with anything that can be saved in this way:

```
protocol Saveable {
    var saveNeeded: Bool { get set }
    func saveToRemoteDatabase(handler: @escaping (Bool) -> Void)
}
```

2. Update our `Person` class so that it conforms to the `Saveable` protocol:

```
class Person: Saveable {
    //....
    var saveHandler: ((Bool) -> Void)?
    var saveNeeded: Bool = true
    func saveToRemoteDatabase(handler: @escaping (Bool) -> Void) {
        saveHandler = handler
        // Send person information to remove database
        // Once remote save is complete, it calls
          // saveComplete(Bool)
        // We'll fake it for the moment, and assume the save is
          // complete.
        saveComplete(success: true)
    }
    func saveComplete(success: Bool) {
        saveHandler?(success)
    }
}
```

How it works...

Protocols are defined with the `protocol` keyword, and the implementation is contained within curly brackets. As we have seen with other type definitions, it is conventional to begin a protocol name with a capital letter. It is also convention to name a protocol as either something that the type **is** or something that it **does.** In this protocol, we are declaring that any type of implementation is **saveable.**

Types conforming to this protocol have two parts of the interface to implement. Let's look at the first:

```
var saveNeeded: Bool { get set }
```

The `Saveable` protocol declares that anything implementing it needs to have a variable called `saveNeeded`, which is a `Bool`. This property will indicate that the information held in the remote database is out of date and a save is needed. In addition to the usual property declaration, a protocol requires us to define whether the property can be accessed (`get`) and changed (`set`), which is added in curly brackets after the type declaration. Removing the set keywords makes it a read-only variable.

 Defining a protocol property as read-only doesn't prevent an implementing type from allowing the property to be set, just that the setting of that property isn't defined in the interface.

The second part of our protocol definition is to describe the method we can call to save the information to the remote database:

```
func saveToRemoteDatabase(handler: @escaping (Bool) -> Void)
```

This `func` declaration is exactly the same as other function declarations we have seen. However, the implementation of this function, which would have been contained in curly brackets, is omitted. Any type conforming to this protocol must provide this function and its implementation.

Now that we have defined our protocol, we need to implement the `Saveable` protocol on our `Person` class that we have been using throughout this chapter:

```
class Person: Saveable {
    //....
    var saveHandler: ((Bool) -> Void)?
    func saveToRemoteDatabase(handler: @escaping (Bool) -> Void) {
        saveHandler = handler
        // Send person information to remove database
        // Once remote save is complete, it calls saveComplete(Bool)
```

```
        // We'll fake it for the moment, and assume the save is
          // complete.
        saveComplete(success: true)
    }
    func saveComplete(success: Bool) {
        saveHandler?(success)
    }
}
```

Conforming to a protocol looks similar to how a class inherits from another class, as we saw earlier in this chapter. The protocol name is added after the type name, separated by :. By adding this conformance, the compiler will complain that our `Person` object doesn't implement part of the protocol, as we haven't declared a `saveNeeded` property. So let's add that:

```
class Person: Saveable {
    //....
    var saveHandler: ((Bool) -> Void)?
    var saveNeeded: Bool = true
    func saveToRemoteDatabase(handler: @escaping (Bool) -> Void) {
        saveHandler = handler
        // Send person information to remove database
        // Once remote save is complete, it calls saveComplete(Bool)
        // We'll fake it for the moment, and assume the save is
          // complete.
        saveComplete(success: true)
    }
    func saveComplete(success: Bool) {
        saveHandler?(success)
    }
}
```

We'll add a default value of `true` since when an instance of this object is created, it won't be in the remote database, and so it will need to be saved.

There's more...

Protocol conformance can be applied to classes, structs, enums, and even other protocols. The benefit of a protocol is that it allows an instance to be stored and passed without needing to know how it's implemented under the hood. This provides many benefits, including testing using mock objects and changing implementations without changing how and where the implementations are used.

Let's add a feature to our app that lets us set a reminder for a contact's birthday, which we will also want to save to our remote database.

We can use protocol conformance to give our reminder the same, consistent, save functionality interface, even though a reminder may have a very different implementation for saving.

Let's create our `Reminder` object and have it conform to the `Saveable` protocol:

```
class Reminder: Saveable {
    var dateOfReminder: String // There is a better way to store dates,
      // but this suffice currently.
    var reminderDetail: String // eg. Ali's birthday
    init(date: String, detail: String) {
        dateOfReminder = date
        reminderDetail = detail
    }
    var saveHandler: ((Bool) -> Void)?
    var saveNeeded: Bool = true
    func saveToRemoteDatabase(handler: @escaping (Bool) -> Void) {
        saveHandler = handler
        // Send reminder information to remove database
        // Once remote save is complete, it calls
          // saveComplete(success: Bool)
        // We'll fake it for the moment, and assume the save is
          // complete.
        saveComplete(success: true)
    }
    func saveComplete(success: Bool) {
        saveHandler?(success)
    }
}
```

Our `Reminder` object conforms to `Saveable` and implements all the requirements.

We now have two objects that represent very different things and have different functionalities, but they both implement `Saveable`, and therefore we can treat them in a common way.

To see this in action, let's create an object that will manage the saving of information in our app:

```
class SaveManager {
    func save(_ thingToSave: Saveable) {
        thingToSave.saveToRemoteDatabase { success in
            print("Saved! Success: \(success)")
        }
    }
}
let nick = createPerson("Nick", "Edward", "Moon") // This closure was
```

```
    // covered in the previous recipe
let birthdayReminder = Reminder(date: "12/06/2008", detail: "Nick's
    Birthday")
let saveManager = SaveManager()
saveManager.save(nick)
saveManager.save(birthdayReminder)
```

In the preceding example, `SaveManager` doesn't know the underlying type that it is being passed, but it doesn't need to. It receives instances that conform to the `Saveable` protocol and therefore can use that interface to save each instance.

See also

Further information about protocols can be found at `http://swiftbook.link/docs/ protocols`.

Mastering the Building Blocks

2

The previous chapter explained the basic types that form the building blocks of the Swift language. In this chapter, we will build on this knowledge to create more complex structures, such as arrays and dictionaries, before moving on and looking at some of the little gems Swift offers, such as tuples and typealias. Finally, we'll round off this chapter by looking at extensions and access control – both of which are key components that contribute to a sound yet efficient codebase.

In this chapter, we will cover the following recipes:

- Bundling variables into tuples
- Ordering your data with arrays
- Containing your data in sets
- Storing key-value pairs with dictionaries
- Subscripts for custom types
- Changing your name with typealias
- Getting property changing notifications using property observers
- Extending functionality with extensions
- Controlling access with access control

Let's get started!

Technical requirements

All the code for this chapter can be found in this book's GitHub repository at `https://github.com/PacktPublishing/Swift-Cookbook-Second-Edition/tree/master/Chapter02`

Check out the following video to see the Code in Action: `https://bit.ly/2YGayJh`

Bundling variables into tuples

A **tuple** is a combination of two or more values that can be treated as one. If you have ever wished you could return more than one value from a function or method, you should find tuples very interesting.

Getting ready

Create a new playground and add the following statement:

```
import Foundation
```

This example uses one function from `Foundation`. We will delve into Foundation in more detail in Chapter 5, *Beyond the Standard Library*, but for now, we just need to import it.

How to do it...

Let's imagine that we are building an app that pulls movie ratings from multiple sources and presents them together to help the user decide which movie to watch. These sources may use different rating systems, such as the following:

- Number of stars out of 5
- Points out of 10
- Percentage score

We want to normalize these ratings so that they can be compared directly and displayed side by side. We want all the ratings to be represented as a number of stars out of 5, so we will write a function that will return the number of whole stars out of 5. We will then use this to display the correct number of stars in our **user interface (UI)**.

Our UI also includes a label that will read **x Star Movie**, where **x** is the number of stars. It would be useful if our function returned both the number of stars and a string that we can put in the UI. We can use a tuple to do this. Let's get started:

1. Create a function to normalize the star ratings. The following function takes a rating and a total possible rating, and then returns a tuple of the normalized rating and a string to display in the UI:

```
func normalizedStarRating(forRating rating: Float,
    ofPossibleTotal total: Float) -> (Int, String) {

}
```

2. Inside the function, calculate the fraction of the total score. Then, multiply that by our normalized total score, 5, and round it to the nearest whole number:

```
let fraction = rating / total
let ratingOutOf5 = fraction * 5
let roundedRating = round(ratingOutOf5) // Rounds to the nearest
    // integer.
```

3. Still within the function, take the rounded fraction and convert it from a `Float` into an `Int`. Then, create the display string and return both `Int` and `String` as a tuple:

```
let numberOfStars = Int(roundedRating) // Turns a Float into an Int
let ratingString = "\(numberOfStars) Star Movie"
return (numberOfStars, ratingString)
```

4. Call our new function and store the result in a constant:

```
let ratingAndDisplayString = normalisedStarRating(forRating: 5,
                                ofPossibleTotal: 10)
```

5. Retrieve the number of stars rating from the tuple and print the result:

```
let ratingNumber = ratingAndDisplayString.0
print(ratingNumber) // 3 - Use to show the right number of stars
```

6. Retrieve the display string from the tuple and print the result:

```
let ratingString = ratingAndDisplayString.1
print(ratingString) // "3 Star Movie" - Use to put in the label
```

With that, we have created and used a tuple.

How it works...

A tuple is declared as a comma-separated list of the types it contains, within brackets. In the preceding code, you can see a tuple being declared as (Int, String). The function, normalizedStarRating, normalizes the rating and creates numberOfStars as the closest round number of stars and ratingString as a display string. These values are then combined into a tuple by putting them, separated by a comma, within brackets; that is, (numberOfStars, ratingString). This tuple value is then returned by the function.

Next, let's look at what we can do with that returned tuple value:

```
let ratingAndDisplayString = normalizedStarRating(forRating: 5,
                                ofPossibleTotal: 10)
```

Calling our function returns a tuple that we store in a constant called ratingAndDisplayString. We can access the tuple's components by accessing the numbered member of the tuple:

```
let ratingNumber = ratingAndDisplayString.0
print(ratingNumber) // 3 - Use to show the right number of stars

let ratingString = ratingAndDisplayString.1
print(ratingString) // "3 Star Movie" - Use to put in the label
```

 As is the case with most numbered systems in programming languages, the member numbering system starts with 0. The number that's used to identify a certain place within a numbered collection is called an index.

There is another way to retrieve the components of a tuple that can be easier to remember than the numbered index. By specifying a tuple of variable names, each value of the tuple will be assigned to the respective variable names. Due to this, we can simplify accessing the tuple values and printing the result:

```
let (nextNumber, nextString) = normalizedStarRating(forRating: 8,
                                ofPossibleTotal: 10)
print(nextNumber) // 4
print(nextString) // "4 Star Movie"
```

Since the numerical value is the first value in the returned tuple, this gets assigned to the nextNumber constant, while the second value, the string, gets assigned to nextString. These can then be used like any other constant and removes the need to remember which index refers to which value.

There's more...

As we mentioned previously, accessing a tuple's components via a number is not ideal as we have to remember their order in the tuple to ensure that we are accessing the correct one. To provide some context, we can add labels to the tuple components, which can be used to identify them when they are accessed. Tuple labels are defined in a similar way to parameter labels, preceding the type and separated by a :. Let's add labels to the function we created in this recipe and then use those labels to access the tuple values:

```
func normalizedStarRating(forRating rating: Float,
                    ofPossibleTotal total: Float)
                    -> (starRating: Int, displayString: String) {

    let fraction = rating / total
    let ratingOutOf5 = fraction * 5
    let roundedRating = round(ratingOutOf5) // Rounds to the nearest
        // integer.
    let numberOfStars = Int(roundedRating) // Turns a Float into an Int
    let ratingString = "\(numberOfStars) Star Movie"

    return (starRating: numberOfStars, displayString: ratingString)
}

let ratingAndDisplayString = normalizedStarRating(forRating: 5,
                            ofPossibleTotal: 10)

let ratingInt = ratingAndDisplayString.starRating
print(ratingInt) // 3 - Use to show the right number of stars

let ratingString = ratingAndDisplayString.displayString
print(ratingString) // "3 Stars" - Use to put in the label
```

As part of the function declaration, we can see the tuple being declared:

```
(starRating: Int, displayString: String)
```

When a tuple of that type is created, the provided values are preceded by the label:

```
return (starRating: numberOfStars, displayString: ratingString)
```

To access the components of the tuple, we can use these labels (although the number of indexes still work):

```
let ratingValue = ratingAndDisplayString.starRating
print(ratingValue) // 3 - Use to show the right number of stars

let ratingString = ratingAndDisplayString.displayString
print(ratingString) // "3 Stars" - Use to put in the label
```

Tuples are a convenient and lightweight way to bundle values together.

In this example, we created a tuple with two components. However, a tuple can contain any number of components.

See also

Further information about tuples can be found in Apple's documentation on the Swift language at `https://docs.swift.org/swift-book/ReferenceManual/Types.html`.

Ordering your data with arrays

So far in this book, we have learned about many different Swift constructs: **classes**, **structs**, **enums**, **closures**, **protocols**, and **tuples**. However, it is rare to deal with just one instance of these on their own. Often, we will have many of these constructs, and we need a way to collect multiple instances and place them in useful data structures. Over the next few recipes, we will examine three collection data structures provided by Swift; that is, **arrays**, **sets**, and **dictionaries** (dictionaries are often called **hash tables** in other programming languages):

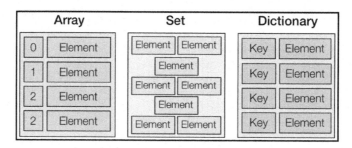

Figure 2.1 – Collection of data structures

While doing this, we will look at how to use them to store and access information, and then examine their relative characteristics.

Getting started

First, let's investigate **arrays**, which are ordered lists of elements. We won't be using any components from the previous recipes, so you can create a new playground for this recipe.

How to do it...

Let's use an array to organize a list of movies to watch:

1. Create an array called `moviesToWatch`. This will hold our strings:

   ```
   var moviesToWatch: Array<String> = Array()
   ```

2. Append three movies to the end of our movie list array:

   ```
   moviesToWatch.append("The Shawshank Redemption")
   moviesToWatch.append("Ghostbusters")
   moviesToWatch.append("Terminator 2")
   ```

3. Print the names of each movie in the list, in turn:

   ```
   print(moviesToWatch[0]) // "The Shawshank Redemption"
   print(moviesToWatch[1]) // "Ghostbusters"
   print(moviesToWatch[2]) // "Terminator 2"
   ```

4. Print a count of the number of movies in the list so far:

   ```
   print(moviesToWatch.count) // 3
   ```

5. Insert a new movie into the list so that it's the third one in it. Since arrays are zero-based, this is done at index 2:

   ```
   moviesToWatch.insert("The Matrix", at: 2)
   ```

6. Print the list count to check it has increased by one and print the newly updated list:

```
print(moviesToWatch.count) // 4
print(moviesToWatch)
// The Shawshank Redemption
// Ghostbusters
// The Matrix
// Terminator 2
```

7. Use the `first` and `last` array properties to access their respective values and print them:

```
let firstMovieToWatch = moviesToWatch.first
print(firstMovieToWatch as Any) // Optional("The Shawshank
  Redemption")
let lastMovieToWatch = moviesToWatch.last
print(lastMovieToWatch as Any) // Optional("Terminator 2")
```

8. Use an index subscript to access the second movie in the list and print it. Then, set a new value to that same subscript. Once you've done that, print the list count to check the number of movies that haven't changed and print the list to check that the second array element has changed:

```
let secondMovieToWatch = moviesToWatch[1]
print(secondMovieToWatch) // "Ghostbusters"
moviesToWatch[1] = "Ghostbusters (1984)"
print(moviesToWatch.count) // 4
print(moviesToWatch)
// The Shawshank Redemption
// Ghostbusters (1984)
// The Matrix
// Terminator 2
```

9. Create a new array of spy movies by initializing it with some movies using the array literal syntax:

```
let spyMovieSuggestions: [String] = ["The Bourne Identity",
                                     "Casino Royale",
                                     "Mission Impossible"]
```

10. Combine the two arrays we have created using the addition operator (+) and assign them back to the `moviesToWatch` variable. Then, print the array count so that it reflects the two lists combined and print the new list:

```
moviesToWatch = moviesToWatch + spyMovieSuggestions
print(moviesToWatch.count) // 7
print(moviesToWatch)
// The Shawshank Redemption
// Ghostbusters (1984)
// The Matrix
// Terminator 2
// The Bourne Identity
// Casino Royale
// Mission Impossible
```

11. Next, use an array convenience initializer to create an array that contains three entries that are the same. Then, update each array element so that the rest of their movie titles are shown:

```
var starWarsTrilogy = Array<String>(repeating: "Star Wars: ",
  count: 3)
starWarsTrilogy[0] = starWarsTrilogy[0] + "A New Hope"
starWarsTrilogy[1] = starWarsTrilogy[1] + "Empire Strikes Back"
starWarsTrilogy[2] = starWarsTrilogy[2] + "Return of the Jedi"
print(starWarsTrilogy)
// Star Wars: A New Hope
// Star Wars: Empire Strikes Back
// Star Wars: Return of the Jedi
```

12. Let's replace part of our existing movie list with our `starWarsTrilogy` list, and then print the count and list:

```
moviesToWatch.replaceSubrange(2...4, with: starWarsTrilogy)
print(moviesToWatch.count) // 7
print(moviesToWatch)
// The Shawshank Redemption
// Ghostbusters (1984)
// Star Wars: A New Hope
// Star Wars: Empire Strikes Back
// Star Wars: Return of the Jedi
// Casino Royale
// Mission Impossible
```

13. Lastly, remove the last movie in the list and check that the array count has reduced by one:

```
moviesToWatch.remove(at: 6)
print(moviesToWatch.count) // 6
print(moviesToWatch)
// The Shawshank Redemption
// Ghostbusters (1984)
// Star Wars: A New Hope
// Star Wars: Empire Strikes Back
// Star Wars: Return of the Jedi
// Casino Royale
```

With that, we've looked at many ways we can create and manipulate arrays.

How it works...

When creating an array, we need to specify the type of elements that will be stored in the array. The array element type is declared in angular brackets as part of the array's type declaration. In our case, we are storing strings:

```
var moviesToWatch: Array<String> = Array()
moviesToWatch.append("The Shawshank Redemption")
moviesToWatch.append("Ghostbusters")
moviesToWatch.append("Terminator 2")
```

The preceding code uses a Swift language feature called **generics**, which can be found in many programming languages, and will be covered in detail in Chapter 4, *Generics, Operators, and Nested Types*.

The append method of Array will add a new element to the end of the array. Now that we have put some elements in the array, we can retrieve and print those elements:

```
print(moviesToWatch[0]) // "The Shawshank Redemption"
print(moviesToWatch[1]) // "Ghostbusters"
print(moviesToWatch[2]) // "Terminator 2"
```

Elements in an array are numbered with a zero-based index, so the first element in the array is at index 0, the second is at index 1, the third is at index 2, and so on. We can access the elements in the array using a subscript, in which we provide the index of the element we want to access. A subscript is specified in square brackets, after the array instance's name.

When an element is accessed using the index subscript, no check is done to ensure you have provided a valid index. In fact, if an index is provided that the array doesn't contain, this will cause a crash. Instead, we can use some index helper methods on `Array` to ensure that we have an index that is valid for this array. Let's use one of these helper methods to check an index that we know is valid for our array, and then another that we know is not valid:

```
let index5 = moviesToWatch.index(moviesToWatch.startIndex,
                            offsetBy: 5,
                            limitedBy: moviesToWatch.endIndex)
print(index5 as Any) // Optional(5)

let index10 = moviesToWatch.index(moviesToWatch.startIndex,
                            offsetBy: 10,
                            limitedBy: moviesToWatch.endIndex)
print(index10 as Any) // nil
```

The `index` method lets us specify the index we want as an offset of the first index parameter, but as something that's limited by the last index parameter. This will return the valid index if it is within the bounds, or `nil` if it is not. By the end of the playground, the `moviesToWatch` array contains six elements, in which case retrieving index 5 is successful but index 10 returns `nil`.

In the next chapter, we will cover how to make decisions based on whether this index exists, but for now, it's just useful to know that this method is available.

Arrays have a `count` property that tells us how many elements they store. So, when we add an element, this value will change:

```
print(moviesToWatch.count) // 3
```

Elements can be inserted anywhere in the array using the same zero-based index that we used in the preceding code:

```
moviesToWatch.insert("The Matrix", at: 2)
```

So, by inserting `"The Matrix"` at index 2, it will be placed at the third position in our array, and all the elements at position 2 or greater will be moved down by 1.

This increases the array's count:

```
print(moviesToWatch.count) // 4
```

The array also provides some helpful computed properties for accessing elements at either end of the array:

```
let firstMovieToWatch = moviesToWatch.first
print(firstMovieToWatch as Any) // Optional("The Shawshank Redemption")
let lastMovieToWatch = moviesToWatch.last
print(firstMovieToWatch as Any) // Optional("Terminator 2")
let secondMovieToWatch = moviesToWatch[1]
print(secondMovieToWatch) // "Ghostbusters"
```

These properties are optional values as the array may be empty, and if it is, these will be nil. However, accessing an array element via an index subscript returns a non-optional value.

In addition to retrieving values via the subscript, we can also assign values to an array subscript:

```
moviesToWatch[1] = "Ghostbusters (1984)"
```

This will replace the element at the given index with the new value.

When we created our first array, we created an empty array and then appended values to it. Additionally, an array literal can be used to create an array that already contains values:

```
let spyMovieSuggestions: [String] = ["The Bourne Identity",
                                     "Casino Royale",
                                     "Mission Impossible"]
```

An array type can be specified with the element type enclosed by square brackets, and the array literal can be defined by comma-separated elements within square brackets. So, we can define an array of integers like this:

```
let fibonacci: [Int] = [1, 1, 2, 3, 5, 8, 13, 21, 34, 55]
```

As we learned in the previous chapter, the compiler can often infer the type from the value we assign, and when the type is inferred, we don't need to specify it. In both the preceding arrays, spyMovieSuggestions and fibonacci, all the elements in the array are of the same type; that is, String and Int, respectively. Since these types can be inferred, we don't need to define them:

```
let spyMovieSuggestions = ["The Bourne Identity", "Casino Royale",
  "Mission Impossible"]
let fibonacci = [1, 1, 2, 3, 5, 8, 13, 21, 34, 55]
```

Arrays can be combined using the + operator:

```
moviesToWatch = moviesToWatch + spyMovieSuggestions
```

This will create a new array by appending the elements in the second array to the first.

The array provides a convenience initializer that will fill an array with repeating elements. We can use this initializer to create an array with the name of a well-known movie trilogy:

```
var starWarsTrilogy = Array<String>(repeating: "Star Wars: ", count: 3)
```

We can then combine subscript access, string appending, and subscript assignment to add the full movie name to our trilogy array:

```
starWarsTrilogy[0] = starWarsTrilogy[0] + "A New Hope"
starWarsTrilogy[1] = starWarsTrilogy[1] + "Empire Strikes Back"
starWarsTrilogy[2] = starWarsTrilogy[2] + "Return of the Jedi"
```

The array also provides a helper for replacing a range of values with the values contained in another array:

```
moviesToWatch.replaceSubrange(2...4, with: starWarsTrilogy)
```

Here, we have specified a range using . . . to indicate a range between two integer values, inclusive of those values. So, this range contains the integers 2, 3, and 4.

We will specify ranges in this way in subsequent chapters. Alternatively, you can specify a range that goes up to, but not including, the top of the range. This is known as a half-open range:

```
moviesToWatch.replaceSubrange(2..<5, with: starWarsTrilogy)
```

For our arrays, we've added elements, accessed them, and replaced them, so we need to know how to remove elements from an array:

```
moviesToWatch.remove(at: 6)
```

Provide the index of the element to the remove method. By doing this, the element at that index will be removed from the array, and all the subsequent elements will move up one place to fill the empty space. This will reduce the array's count by 1:

```
print(moviesToWatch.count) // 6
```

There's more...

If you are familiar with Objective-C, you will have used `NSArray`, which provides similar functionalities to a Swift array. You may also remember that `NSArray` is immutable, which means its contents can't be changed once it's been created. If you need to change its contents, then an `NSMutableArray` should be used instead. Due to this, you may be wondering if Swift has similar concepts of mutable and immutable arrays. It does but rather than using separate mutable and immutable types, you create a mutable array by declaring it as a variable and an immutable array by declaring it as a constant:

```
let evenNumbersTo10 = [2, 4, 6, 8, 10]
evenNumbersTo10.append(12) // Doesn't compile

var evenNumbersTo12 = evenNumbersTo10
evenNumbersTo12.append(12) // Does compile
```

To understand why this is the case, it's important to know that an array is a value type, as are the other collection types in Swift.

As we saw in the previous chapter, a value type is immutable in nature and creates a changed copy whenever it is mutated. Therefore, by assigning the array to a constant using `let`, we prevent any new value from being assigned, making mutating the array impossible.

See also

Further information about arrays can be found in Apple's documentation on the Swift language at `https://developer.apple.com/documentation/swift/array`.

Arrays use generics to define the element type they contain. Generics will be discussed in detail in `Chapter 4`, *Generics, Operators, and Nested Types*.

Containing your data in sets

The next collection type we will look at is a **set**. Sets differ from arrays in two important ways. The elements in a set are stored *unordered*, and each unique element is only held once. In this recipe, we will learn how to create and manipulate sets.

How to do it...

First, let's explore some ways we can create sets and perform set algebra on them:

1. Create an array that contains the first nine Fibonacci numbers, and also a set containing the same:

```
let fibonacciArray: Array<Int> = [1, 1, 2, 3, 5, 8, 13, 21, 34]
let fibonacciSet: Set<Int> = [1, 1, 2, 3, 5, 8, 13, 21, 34]
print(fibonacciArray.count) // 9
print(fibonacciSet.count) // 8
```

2. Print out the number of elements in each collection using the `count` property. Despite being created with the same elements, the count value is different:

```
print(fibonacciArray.count) // 9
print(fibonacciSet.count) // 8
```

3. Insert an element into a set of animals, remove an element, and check whether a set contains a given element:

```
var animals: Set<String> = ["cat", "dog", "mouse", "elephant"]
animals.insert("rabbit")
print(animals.contains("dog")) // true
animals.remove("dog")
print(animals.contains("dog")) // false
```

4. Create some sets containing common mathematical number groups. We will use these to explore some methods for set algebra:

```
let evenNumbers = Set<Int>(arrayLiteral: 2, 4, 6, 8, 10)
let oddNumbers: Set<Int> = [1, 3, 5, 7, 9]
let squareNumbers: Set<Int> = [1, 4, 9]
let triangularNumbers: Set<Int> = [1, 3, 6, 10]
```

5. Obtain the union of two sets and print the result:

```
let evenOrTriangularNumbers = evenNumbers.union(triangularNumbers)
    // 2, 4, 6, 8, 10, 1, 3, unordered
print(evenOrTriangularNumbers.count) // 7
```

6. Obtain the intersection of two sets and print the result:

```
let oddAndSquareNumbers = oddNumbers.intersection(squareNumbers)
    // 1, 9, unordered
print(oddAndSquareNumbers.count) // 2
```

7. Obtain the symmetric difference of two sets and print the result:

```
let squareOrTriangularNotBoth =
    squareNumbers.symmetricDifference(triangularNumbers)
    // 4, 9, 3, 6, 10, unordered
print(squareOrTriangularNotBoth.count) // 5
```

8. Obtain the result of subtracting one set from another and print the result:

```
let squareNotOdd = squareNumbers.subtracting(oddNumbers) // 4
print(squareNotOdd.count) // 1
```

Next, we will examine the set membership comparison methods that are available:

1. Create some sets with overlapping membership:

```
let animalKingdom: Set<String> = ["dog", "cat", "pidgeon",
                                  "chimpanzee", "snake",
"kangaroo",
                                  "giraffe", "elephant", "tiger",
                                  "lion", "panther"]

let vertebrates: Set<String> = ["dog", "cat", "pidgeon",
                                "chimpanzee", "snake", "kangaroo",
                                "giraffe", "elephant", "tiger",
                                "lion", "panther"]

let reptile: Set<String> = ["snake"]

let mammals: Set<String> = ["dog", "cat", "chimpanzee",
                            "kangaroo", "giraffe", "elephant",
                            "tiger", "lion", "panther"]

let catFamily: Set<String> = ["cat", "tiger", "lion", "panther"]

let domesticAnimals: Set<String> = ["cat", "dog"]
```

2. Use the `isSubset` method to determine whether one set is a subset of another. Then, print the result:

```
print(mammals.isSubset(of: animalKingdom)) // true
```

3. Use the `isSuperset` method to determine whether one set is a superset of another. Then, print the result:

```
print(mammals.isSuperset(of: catFamily)) // true
```

4. Use the `isStrictSubset` method to determine whether one set is a strict subset of another. Then, print the result:

```
print(vertebrates.isStrictSubset(of: animalKingdom)) // false
print(mammals.isStrictSubset(of: animalKingdom)) // true
```

5. Use the `isStrictSuperset` method to determine whether one set is a strict superset of another. Then, print the result:

```
print(animalKingdom.isStrictSuperset(of: vertebrates)) // false
print(animalKingdom.isStrictSuperset(of: domesticAnimals))  // true
```

6. Use the `isDisjoint` method to determine whether one set is disjointed with another. Then, print the result:

```
print(catFamily.isDisjoint(with: reptile)) // true
```

How it works...

Sets are created in almost the same way as arrays, and like arrays, we have to specify the element type that we will be stored in them:

```
let fibonacciArray: Array<Int> = [1, 1, 2, 3, 5, 8, 13, 21, 34]
let fibonacciSet: Set<Int> = [1, 1, 2, 3, 5, 8, 13, 21, 34]
```

Arrays and sets store their elements differently. If you provide multiple elements of the same value to an array, it will store them multiple times. A set works differently; it will only store one version of each unique element. Therefore, in the preceding Fibonacci number sequence, the array stores two elements for the first two values, 1, 1, but the set will store this as just one 1 element. This leads to the collections having different counts, despite being created with the same values:

```
print(fibonacciArray.count) // 9
print(fibonacciSet.count) // 8
```

This ability to store elements uniquely is made possible due to a requirement that a set has regarding the type of elements it can hold. A set's elements must conform to the `Hashable` protocol. This protocol requires a `hashValue` property to be provided as an `Int`, and the set uses this `hashValue` to do its uniqueness comparison. Both the `Int` and `String` types conform to `Hashable`, but any custom types that will be stored in a set will also need to conform to `Hashable`.

A set's `insert`, `remove`, and `contains` methods work as you would expect, with the compiler enforcing that the correct types are provided. This compiler type checking is done thanks to the **generics** constraints that all the collection types have. We will cover generics in more detail in `Chapter 4`, *Generics, Operators, and Nested Types*.

Union

The `union` method returns a set containing all the unique elements from the set that the method is called on, as well as the set that was provided as a parameter:

```
let evenOrTriangularNumbers = evenNumbers.union(triangularNumbers)
    // 2,4,6,8,10,1,3,unordered
```

The following diagram depicts the **Union** of **Set A** and **Set B**:

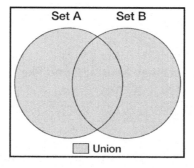

Figure 2.2 – Union of sets

Intersection

The `intersection` method returns a set of unique elements that were contained in both the set that the method was called on and the set that was provided as a parameter:

```
let oddAndSquareNumbers = oddNumbers.intersection(squareNumbers)
    // 1, 9, unordered
```

The following diagram depicts the **Intersection** of **Set A** and **Set B**:

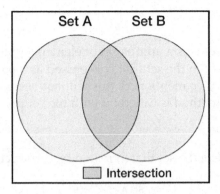

Figure 2.3 – Set intersection

Symmetric difference

The `symmetricDifference` method returns a set of unique elements that are in either the set the method is called on, or the set that's provided as a parameter, but not elements that are in both:

```
let squareOrTriangularNotBoth =
    squareNumbers.symmetricDifference(triangularNumbers)
// 4, 9, 3, 6, 10, unordered
```

 This `set` operation is sometimes referred to as method is so `exclusiveOr`, both other programming languages, including previous versions of Swift.

The following diagram depicts the **Symmetric Difference** of **Set A** and **Set B**:

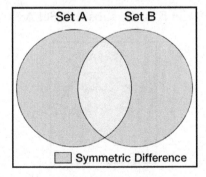

Figure 2.4 – Symmetric difference

Subtracting

The `subtracting` method returns a unique set of elements that can be found in the set the method was called on, but not in the set that was passed as a parameter. Unlike the other set manipulation methods we've mentioned, this will not necessarily return the same value if you swap the set that the method is called on with the set provided as a parameter:

```
let squareNotOdd = squareNumbers.subtracting(oddNumbers) // 4
```

The following diagram depicts the set that's created by **Subtracting Set B** from **Set A**:

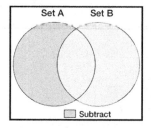

Figure 2.5– Subtracting a set

Membership comparison

In addition to set manipulation methods, there are a number of methods we can use to determine information about set membership.

The `isSubset` method will return true if all the elements in the set that the method is called on are contained within the set that's passed as a parameter:

```
print(mammals.isSubset(of: animalKingdom)) // true
```

The following diagram depicts **Set B** as the **subset** of **Set A**:

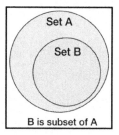

Figure 2.6 – Subset

This will also return true if the two sets are equal (they contain the same elements). If you only want a true value if the set that the method is called on is a subset and *not* equal, then you can use `isStrictSubset`:

```
print(vertebrates.isStrictSubset(of: animalKingdom)) // false
print(mammals.isStrictSubset(of: animalKingdom)) // true
```

The `isSuperset` method will return true if all the elements in the set that have been passed as a parameter are within the set that the method is called on:

```
print(mammals.isSuperset(of: catFamily)) // true
```

The following diagram depicts **Set A** as the **superset** of **Set B**:

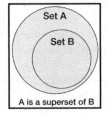

Figure 2.7 – Superset

This will also return true if the two sets are equal (they contain the same elements). If you only want a true value if the set that the method is called on is a superset and not equal, then you can use `isStrictSuperset`:

```
print(animalKingdom.isStrictSuperset(of: vertebrates))     // false
print(animalKingdom.isStrictSuperset(of: domesticAnimals)) // true
```

The `isDisjoint` method will return true if there are no common elements between the set that the method is called on and the set that was passed as a parameter:

```
print(catFamily.isDisjoint(with: reptile)) // true
```

The following diagram shows that **Set A** and **Set B** are **disjoint**:

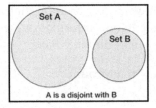

Figure 2.8 – Disjoint

As with arrays, a set can be declared immutable by assigning it to a `let` constant instead of a `var` variable:

```
let planets: Set<String> = ["Mercury", "Venus", "Earth",
                            "Mars", "Jupiter", "Saturn",
                            "Uranus", "Neptune", "Pluto"]
planets.remove("Pluto") // Doesn't compile
```

This is because a set, like the other collection types, is a value type. Removing an element would mutate the set, which creates a new copy, but a `let` constant can't have a new value assigned to it, so the compiler prevents any mutating operations.

See also

Further information about arrays can be found in Apple's documentation on the Swift language at `https://docs.swift.org/swift-book/LanguageGuide/CollectionTypes.html`.

Sets use generics to define the element types they contain. Generics will be discussed in detail in `Chapter 4`, *Generics, Operators, and Nested Types*.

Storing key-value pairs with dictionaries

The last collection type we will look at is the **dictionary**. This is a familiar construct in programming languages, where it is sometimes referred to as a **hash table**. A dictionary holds a collection of pairings between a key and a value. The **key** can be any element that conforms to the `Hashable` protocol (just like elements in a set), while the **value** can be any type. The contents of a dictionary is not stored in order, unlike an array; instead, the *key* is used both when storing a value and as a lookup when retrieving a value.

Getting ready

In this recipe, we will use a dictionary to store details of people at a place of work. We need to store and retrieve a person's information based on their role in the organization, such as a company directory. To hold this person's information, we will use a modified version of our `Person` class from `Chapter 1`, *Swift Building Blocks*.

Enter the following code into a new playground:

```
struct PersonName {
    let givenName: String
```

```
        let familyName: String
}

enum CommunicationMethod {
    case phone
    case email
    case textMessage
    case fax
    case telepathy
    case subSpaceRelay
    case tachyons
}

class Person {
    let name: PersonName
    let preferredCommunicationMethod: CommunicationMethod
    convenience init(givenName: String,
                     familyName: String,
                     commsMethod: CommunicationMethod) {
        let name = PersonName(givenName: givenName, familyName:
          familyName)
        self.init(name: name, commsMethod: commsMethod)
    }
    init(name: PersonName, commsMethod: CommunicationMethod) {
        self.name = name
        preferredCommunicationMethod = commsMethod
    }

    var displayName: String {
        return "\(name.givenName) \(name.familyName)"
    }
}
```

How to do it...

Let's use the `Person` object we defined previously to build up our workplace directory using a dictionary:

1. Create a `Dictionary` for the employee directory:

```
var crew = Dictionary<String, Person>()
```

2. Populate the dictionary with employee details:

```
crew["Captain"] = Person(givenName: "Jean-Luc",
                         familyName: "Picard",
```

```
                                      commsMethod: .phone)

    crew["First Officer"] = Person(givenName: "William",
                                   familyName: "Riker",
                                   commsMethod: .email)

    crew["Chief Engineer"] = Person(givenName: "Geordi",
                                    familyName: "LaForge",
                                    commsMethod: .textMessage)

    crew["Second Officer"] = Person(givenName: "Data",
                                    familyName: "Soong",
                                    commsMethod: .fax)

    crew["Councillor"] = Person(givenName: "Deanna",
                                familyName: "Troi",
                                commsMethod: .telepathy)

    crew["Security Officer"] = Person(givenName: "Tasha",
                                      familyName: "Yar",
                                      commsMethod: .subSpaceRelay)

    crew["Chief Medical Officer"] = Person(givenName: "Beverly",
                                           familyName: "Crusher",
                                           commsMethod: .tachyons)
```

3. Retrieve an array of all the keys in the dictionary. This will give us an array of all the roles in the organization:

```
let roles = Array(crew.keys)
print(roles)
```

4. Use a key to retrieve one of the employees and print the result:

```
let firstRole = roles.first! // Chief Medical Officer
let cmo = crew[firstRole]! // Person: Beverly Crusher
print("\(firstRole): \(cmo.displayName)")
// Chief Medical Officer: Beverly Crusher
```

5. Replace a value in the dictionary by assigning a new value against an existing key. The previous value for the key is discarded when a new value is set:

```
print(crew["Security Officer"]!.name.givenName) // Tasha

crew["Security Officer"] = Person(givenName: "Worf",
                                  familyName: "Son of Mogh",
                                  commsMethod: .subSpaceRelay)

print(crew["Security Officer"]!.name.givenName) // Worf
```

With that, we have learned how to create, populate, and look up values in a dictionary.

How it works...

As with the other collection types, when we create a dictionary, we need to provide the types that the dictionary will be holding. For dictionaries, there are two types that we need to define. The first is the type of the key (which must conform to `Hashable`), while the second is the type of the value being stored against the key. For our dictionary, we are using `String` for the key and `Person` for the values being stored:

```
var crew = Dictionary<String, Person>()
```

As with an array, we can specify a `dictionary` type using square brackets and create one using a dictionary literal, where `:` separates the key and the value:

```
let intByName: [String: Int] = ["one": 1, "two": 2, "three": 3]
```

Therefore, we can change our dictionary definition so that it looks like this:

```
var crew: [String: Person] = [:]
```

The `[:]` symbol denotes an empty dictionary as a dictionary literal.

Elements are added to a dictionary using a subscript. Unlike an array, which takes an `Int` index in the subscript, a dictionary takes the key and then pairs the given value with the given key. In the following example, we are assigning a `Person` object to the `"Captain"` key:

```
crew["Captain"] = Person(givenName: "Jean-Luc",
                         familyName: "Picard",
                         commsMethod: .phone)
```

If no value currently exists, the assigned value will be added. If a value already exists for the given key, the old value will be replaced with the new value and the old value will be discarded.

There are properties on the dictionary that provide all the keys and values. These properties are of a custom collection type that can be passed to an array initializer to create an array:

```
let roles = Array(crew.keys)
print(roles)
```

To display all the dictionary's keys, as provided by the `keys` property, we can either create an array or iterate over the collection directly. We will cover iterating over a collection's values in the next chapter, so for now, we will create an array.

Next, we will use one of the values from an array of keys, alongside the crew, to retrieve full details about the associated `Person`:

```
let firstRole = roles.first! // Chief Medical Officer
let cmo = crew[firstRole]! // Person: Beverly Crusher
print("\(firstRole): \(cmo.displayName)")
// Chief Medical Officer: Beverly Crusher
```

We get the first element using the `first` property, but since this is an optional type, we need to force unwrap it using `!`. We can pass `firstRole`, which is now a non-optional `String` to the dictionary subscript, to get the `Person` object associated with that key. The return type for retrieving the value via subscript is also optional, so it also needs to be force unwrapped before we print its values.

 Force unwrapping is usually an unsafe thing to do since if we force unwrap a value that turns out to be `nil`, our code will crash. We advise you to check that a value isn't `nil` before unwrapping the optional. We will cover how to do this in the next chapter.

There's more...

In this recipe, we used strings as the keys for our dictionary. However, we can also use a type that conforms to the `Hashable` protocol.

One downside of using `String` as a key for our employee directory is that it is very easy to mistype an employee's role or look for a role that you expect to exist but doesn't. So, we can improve our implementation by using something that conforms to `Hashable` and is better suited to being used as a key in our model.

We have a finite set of employee roles in our model, and an **enumeration** is perfect for representing a finite number of options, so let's define our roles as an enum:

```
enum Role: String {
    case captain = "Captain"
    case firstOfficer = "First Officer"
    case secondOfficer = "Second Officer"
    case chiefEngineer = "Chief Engineer"
    case councillor = "Councillor"
    case securityOfficer = "Security Officer"
    case chiefMedicalOfficer = "Chief Medical Officer"
}
```

Now, let's change our `Dictionary` definition so that it uses this new enum as a key, and then insert our employees using these enum values:

```
var crew = Dictionary<Role, Person>()

crew[.captain] = Person(givenName: "Jean-Luc",
                        familyName: "Picard",
                        commsMethod: .phone)

crew[.firstOfficer] = Person(givenName: "William",
                             familyName: "Riker",
                             commsMethod: .email)

crew[.chiefEngineer] = Person(givenName: "Geordi",
                              familyName: "LaForge",
                              commsMethod: .textMessage)

crew[.secondOfficer] = Person(givenName: "Data",
                              familyName: "Soong",
                              commsMethod: .fax)

crew[.councillor] = Person(givenName: "Deanna",
                           familyName: "Troi",
                           commsMethod: .telepathy)

crew[.securityOfficer] = Person(givenName: "Tasha",
                                familyName: "Yar",
                                commsMethod: .subSpaceRelay)

crew[.chiefMedicalOfficer] = Person(givenName: "Beverly",
                                    familyName: "Crusher",
                                    commsMethod: .tachyons)
```

You will also need to change all the other uses of `crew` so that they use the new enum-based key.

Let's take a look at how and why this works. We created `Role` as a `String`-based enum:

```
enum Role: String {
    //...
}
```

Defining it in this way has two benefits:

- We intend to display these roles to the user, so we will need a string representation of the `Role` enum, regardless of how we defined it.
- Enums have a little bit of protocol and generics magic in them, which means that if an enum is backed by a type that implements the `Hashable` protocol (as `String` does), the enum also automatically implements the `Hashable` protocol. Therefore, defining `Role` as being String-based satisfies the dictionary requirement of a key being `Hashable` without us having to do any extra work.

With our `crew` dictionary now defined as having a Role-based key, all subscript operations have to use a value in the role enum:

```
crew[.captain] = Person(givenName: "Jean-Luc",
                        familyName: "Picard",
                        commsMethod: .phone)
let cmo = crew[.chiefMedicalOfficer]
```

The compiler enforces this, so it's no longer possible to use an incorrect role when interacting with our employee directory. This pattern of using Swift's constructs and type system to enforce the correct use of your code is something we should strive to do, as it can reduce bugs and prevent our code from being used in unexpected ways.

See also

Further information about dictionaries can be found in Apple's documentation on the Swift language at `http://swiftbook.link/docs/collections`.

Subscripts for custom types

By using collection types, we have seen that their elements are accessed through subscripts. However, it's not just collection types that can have subscripts; your own custom types can provide subscript functionality too.

Getting ready

In this recipe, we will create a simple game of *tic-tac-toe*, also known as *Noughts and Crosses*. To do this, we need a three-by-three grid of positions, with each position being filled by either a nought from Player 1, a cross from Player 2, or nothing. We can store these positions in an array of arrays.

The initial game setup code uses the concepts we've already covered in this book, so we won't go into its implementation. Enter the following code into a new playground so that we can see how subscripts can improve its usage:

```swift
enum GridPosition: String {
    case player1 = "o"
    case player2 = "x"
    case empty = " "
}

struct TicTacToe {
    var gridStorage: [[GridPosition]] = []
    init() {
        gridStorage.append(Array(repeating: .empty, count: 3))
        gridStorage.append(Array(repeating: .empty, count: 3))
        gridStorage.append(Array(repeating: .empty, count: 3))
    }
    func gameStateString() -> String {
        var stateString = "--------------\n"
        stateString += printableString(forRow: gridStorage[0])
        stateString += "--------------\n"
        stateString += printableString(forRow: gridStorage[1])
        stateString += "--------------\n"
        stateString += printableString(forRow: gridStorage[2])
        stateString += "--------------\n"
        return stateString
    }
    func printableString(forRow row: [GridPosition]) -> String {
        var rowString = "| \(row[0].rawValue) "
        rowString += "| \(row[1].rawValue) "
        rowString += "| \(row[2].rawValue) |\n"
        return rowString
    }
}
```

How to do it...

Let's run through how we can use the tic-tac-toe game defined previously, as well as how we can improve how it is used, using a subscript. We will also examine how this works:

1. Let's create an instance of our `TicTacToe` grid:

```
var game = TicTacToe()
```

2. For a player to make a move, we need to change the `GridPosition` value that's been assigned to the relevant place in the array of arrays. This is used to store the grid positions. Player 1 will place a nought in the middle position of the grid, which would be row position 1, column position 1 (since it's a zero-based array):

```
// Move 1
game.gridStorage[1][1] = .player1
print(game.gameStateString())
/*
------------
|   |   |   |
------------
|   | o |   |
------------
|   |   |   |
------------
*/
```

3. Next, Player 2 places their cross in the top-right position, which is row position 0, column position 2:

```
// Move 2
game.gridStorage[0][2] = .player2
print(game.gameStateString())
/*
------------
|   |   | x |
------------
|   | o |   |
------------
|   |   |   |
------------
*/
```

We can make moves in our game. We can do this by adding information directly to the `gridStorage` array, which isn't ideal. The player shouldn't need to know how the moves are stored, and we should be able to change how we store the game information without having to change how the moves are made. To solve this, let's create a subscript of our game struct so that making a move in the game is just like assigning a value to an array.

4. Add the following subscript method to the `TicTacToe` struct:

```
struct TicTacToe {
    var gridStorage: [[GridPosition]] = []
    //...
    subscript(row: Int, column: Int) -> GridPosition {
        get {
            return gridStorage[row][column]
        }
        set(newValue) {
            gridStorage[row][column] = newValue
        }
    }
    //...
}
```

5. So, now, we can change how each player makes their move and finish the game:

```
// Move 1
game[1, 1] = .player1
print(game.gameStateString())
/*
    -------------
    |   |   |   |
    -------------
    |   | o |   |
    -------------
    |   |   |   |
    -------------
*/

// Move 2
game[0, 2] = .player2
print(game.gameStateString())
/*
    -------------
    |   |   | x |
    -------------
    |   | o |   |
    -------------
```

```
    |   |   |   |
    -------------
 */

// Move 3
game[0, 0] = .player1
print(game.gameStateString())
/*
    -------------
 | o |   | x |
    -------------
 |   | o |   |
    -------------
 |   |   |   |
    -------------
 */

// Move 4
game[1, 2] = .player2
print(game.gameStateString())
/*
    -------------
 | o |   | x |
    -------------
 |   | o | x |
    -------------
 |   |   |   |
    -------------
 */

// Move 5
game[2, 2] = .player1
print(game.gameStateString())
/*
    -------------
 | o |   | x |
    -------------
 |   | o | x |
    -------------
 |   |   | o |
    -------------
 */
```

6. Just like when using an array, we can use a subscript to access the value, as well as assign a value to it:

```
let topLeft = game[0, 0]
let middle = game[1, 1]
```

```
let bottomRight = game[2, 2]
let p1HasWon = (topLeft == .player1)
             && (middle == .player1)
             && (bottomRight == .player1)
```

How it works...

Subscript functionality can be defined within a class, struct, or enum, or declared within a protocol as a requirement. To do this, we can define `subscript` (which is a reserved keyword that activates the required functionality) with input parameters and an output type:

```
subscript(row: Int, column: Int) -> GridPosition
```

This subscript definition works like a computed property, where `get` can be defined to allow you to access values through `subscript` and `set` can be defined to assign values using `subscript`:

```
subscript(row: Int, column: Int) -> GridPosition {
    get {
        return gridStorage[row][column]
    }
    set(newValue) {
        gridStorage[row][column] = newValue
    }
}
```

Any number of input parameters can be defined, and these should be provided as comma-separated values in the subscript:

```
game[1, 2] = .player2 // Assigning a value
let topLeft = game[0, 0] // Accessing a value
```

There's more...

Just like parameters defined in a function, `subscript` parameters can have additional labels. If defined, these become required at the call site, so the `subscript` we added can alternatively be defined as follows:

```
subscript(atRow row: Int, atColumn column: Int) -> GridPosition
```

In this case, when using the `subscript`, we would also provide the labels in the `subscript`:

```
game[atRow: 1, atColumn: 2] = .player2 // Assigning a value
let topLeft = game[atRow: 0, atColumn: 0] // Accessing a value
```

See also

Further information about subscripts can be found in Apple's documentation on the Swift language at `http://swiftbook.link/docs/subscripts`.

Changing your name with typealias

The `typealias` declaration allows you to create an alias for a type (and is therefore pretty accurately named!). You can specify a name that can be used in place of any given type of definition. If this type is quite complex, a typeAlias can be a useful way to simplify its use.

How to do it...

We will use a typealias to replace an array definition:

1. First, let's create something we can store in an array. In this instance, let's create a `Pug` struct:

```
struct Pug {
    let name: String
}
```

2. Now, we can create an array that will contain instances of a `Pug` struct:

```
let pugs = [Pug]()
```

 As you may or may not know, the collective noun for a group of pugs is called a **grumble**.

3. We can set up a `typealias` to define an array of pugs as a `Grumble`:

```
typealias Grumble = [Pug]
```

4. With this defined, we can substitute `Grumble` wherever we would use `[Pug]` or `Array<Pug>`:

```
var grumble = Grumble()
```

5. However, this isn't some new type – it is just an array with all the same functionalities:

```
let marty = Pug(name: "Marty McPug")
let wolfie = Pug(name: "Wolfgang Pug")
let buddy = Pug(name: "Buddy")
grumble.append(marty)
grumble.append(wolfie)
grumble.append(buddy)
```

There's more...

The preceding example allows us to use types in a more natural and expressive way. In addition, we can use a `typealias` to simplify a more complex type that may be used in multiple places.

To see how this might be useful, we can partially build an object to fetch program information:

```
enum Channel {
    case BBC1
    case BBC2
    case BBCNews
    //...
}

class ProgrammeFetcher {
    func fetchCurrentProgrammeName(forChannel channel: Channel,
        resultHandler: (String?, Error?) -> Void) {
        // ...
        // Do the work to get the current programme
        // ...
        let exampleProgramName = "Sherlock"
        resultHandler(exampleProgramName, nil)
    }
    func fetchNextProgrammeName(forChannel channel: Channel,
        resultHandler: (String?, Error?) -> Void) {
        // ...
        // Do the work to get the next programme
        // ...
```

```
            let exampleProgramName = "Luther"
            resultHandler(exampleProgramName, nil)
      }
  }
```

In the `ProgrammeFetcher` object, we have two methods that take a channel and a result handler closure. The result handler closure has the following definition. We have to define this twice; once for each method:

```
(String?, Error?) -> Void
```

Instead, we can define this closure definition with a `typealias` called `FetchResultHandler` and replace each method definition with a reference to this `typealias`:

```
class ProgrammeFetcher {
    typealias FetchResultHandler = (String?, Error?) -> Void
    func fetchCurrentProgrammeName(forChannel channel: Channel,
                              resultHandler: FetchResultHandler) {
        // Get next programme
        let programmeName = "Sherlock"
        resultHandler(programmeName, nil)
    }
    func fetchNextProgrammeName(forChannel channel: Channel,
                           resultHandler: FetchResultHandler) {
        // Get next programme
        let programmeName = "Luther"
        resultHandler(programmeName, nil)
    }
}
```

Not only does this save us from defining the closure type twice, but it is also a better description of the function that the closure performs.

Using `typealias` doesn't affect how we provide closure to the method:

```
let fetcher = ProgrammeFetcher()
fetcher.fetchCurrentProgrammeName(forChannel: .BBC1,
    resultHandler: { programmeName, error in
    print(programmeName as Any)
})
```

See also

Further information about typealias can be found in Apple's documentation on the Swift language at http://swiftbook.link/docs/declarations.

Getting property changing notifications using property observers

It's common to want to know when a property's value changes. Perhaps you want to update the value of another property or update some user interface element. In Objective-C, this was often accomplished by writing your own getter and setter or using **Key-Value Observing (KVO)**, but in Swift, we have native support for property observers.

Getting ready

To examine property observers, we should create an object with a property that we want to observe. Let's create an object that manages users and a property that holds the current user's name:

```
class UserManager {
    var currentUserName: String = "Emmanuel Goldstein"
}
```

We want to present some friendly messages when the current user changes. We'll use property observers to do this.

How to do it...

Let's get started:

1. Amend the currentUserName property definition so that it looks as follows:

```
class UserManager {
    var currentUserName: String = "Emmanuel Goldstein" {
        willSet (newUserName) {
            print("Goodbye to \(currentUserName)")
            print("I hear \(newUserName) is on their way!")
        }
        didSet (oldUserName) {
            print("Welcome to \(currentUserName)")
```

```
                    print("I miss \(oldUserName) already!")
                }
            }
        }
```

2. Create an instance of `UserManager` and change the current username. This will generate friendly messages:

```
let manager = UserManager()

manager.currentUserName = "Dade Murphy"
// Goodbye to Emmanuel Goldstein
// I hear Dade Murphy is on their way!
// Welcome to Dade Murphy
// I miss Emmanuel Goldstein already!

manager.currentUserName = "Kate Libby"
// Goodbye to Dade Murphy
// I hear Kate Libby is on their way!
// Welcome to Kate Libby
// I miss Dade Murphy already!
```

How it works...

Property observers can be added within curly brackets after the property declaration, and there are two types: `willSet` and `didSet`.

The `willSet` observer will be called before the property is set and provides the value that will be set on the property. This new value can be given a name within brackets; for example, `newUserName`:

```
willSet (newUserName) {
    //...
}
```

The `didSet` observer will be called after the property is set and provides the value that the property had before being set. This old value can be given a name within brackets; for example, `oldUserName`:

```
didSet (oldUserName) {
    //...
}
```

There's more...

The new value and old value that are passed into the property observers have implicit names, so there is no need to explicitly name them. The `willSet` observer is passed a value with an implicit name of `newValue`, and the `didSet` observer is passed a value with an implicit name of `oldValue`.

Therefore, we can remove our explicit names and use the implicit value names:

```
class UserManager {
    var currentUserName: String = "Emmanuel Goldstein" {
        willSet {
            print("Goodbye to \(currentUserName)")
            print("I hear \(newValue) is on their way!")
        }
        didSet {
            print("Welcome to \(currentUserName)")
            print("I miss \(oldValue) already!")
        }
    }
}
```

See also

Further information about property observers can be found in Apple's documentation on the Swift language at `http://swiftbook.link/docs/properties`.

Extending functionality with extensions

Extensions let us add functionality to our existing classes, structs, enums, and protocols. This can be especially useful when the original type is provided by an external framework, which means you aren't able to add functionality directly.

Getting ready

Imagine that we often need to obtain the first word from a given string. Rather than repeatedly writing the code to split the string into words and then retrieving the first word, we can extend the functionality of `String` to provide its own first word.

How to do it...

Let's get started:

1. Create an extension of `String`:

```
extension String {

}
```

2. Within the extension's curly brackets, add a function that returns the first word from the string:

```
extension String {
    func firstWord() -> String {
        let spaceIndex = firstIndex(of: " ") ?? endIndex
        let word = prefix(upTo: spaceIndex)
        return String(word)
    }
}
```

3. Now, we can use this new method on `String` to get the first word from a phrase:

```
let llap = "Live long, and prosper"
let firstWord = llap.firstWord()
print(firstWord) // Live
```

How it works...

We can define an extension using the `extension` keyword and then specify the type we want to extend. The implementation of this extension is defined within curly brackets:

```
extension String {
    //...
}
```

Methods and computed properties can be defined in extensions in the same way that they can be defined within classes, structs, and enums. Here, we will add a firstWord function to the String struct:

```
extension String {
    func firstWord() -> String {
        let spaceIndex = firstIndex(of: " ") ?? endIndex
        let word = prefix(upTo: spaceIndex)
        return String(word)
    }
}
```

The implementation of the firstWord method is not important for this recipe, so we'll just touch on it briefly.

In Swift, String is a collection, so we can use the collection methods to find the first index of an empty space. However, this could be nil since the string may contain only one word or no characters at all, so if the index is nil, we must use the endIndex instead. The nil coalescing operator (??) is only used to assign endIndex if firstIndex(of: " ") is nil. More generally, it will evaluate the value on the left-hand side of the operator, unless it is nil, in which case it will assign the value on the right-hand side.

Then, we use the index of the first space to retrieve the substring up to the index, which has a SubString type. We then use that to create and return a String.

Extensions can implement anything that uses the existing functionality, but they can't store information in a new property. Therefore, computed properties can be added, but stored properties cannot. Let's change our firstWord method so that it's a computed property instead:

```
extension String {
    var firstWord: String {
        let spaceIndex = firstIndex(of: " ") ?? endIndex
        let word = prefix(upTo: spaceIndex)
        return String(word)
    }
}
```

There's more...

Extensions can also be used to add protocol conformance, so let's create a protocol that we want to add conformance to:

1. The protocol declares that something can be represented as an `Int`:

```
protocol IntRepresentable {
    var intValue: Int { get }
}
```

2. We can extend `Int` and have it conform to `IntRepresentable` by returning itself:

```
extension Int: IntRepresentable {
    var intValue: Int {
        return self
    }
}
```

3. Next, we'll extend `String`, and we'll use an `Int` constructor that takes a `String` and returns an `Int` if our `String` contains digits that represent an integer:

```
extension String: IntRepresentable {
    var intValue: Int {
        return Int(self) ?? 0
    }
}
```

4. We can also extend our own custom types and add conformance to the same protocol, so let's create an `enum` that can be `IntRepresentable`:

```
enum CrewComplement: Int {
    case enterpriseD = 1014
    case voyager = 150
    case deepSpaceNine = 2000
}
```

5. Since our enum is Int-based, we can conform to `IntRepresentable` by providing a `rawValue`:

```
extension CrewComplement: IntRepresentable {
    var intValue: Int {
        return rawValue
    }
}
```

6. We now have `String`, `Int`, and `CrewComplement` all conforming to `IntRepresentable`, and since we didn't define `String` or `Int`, we have only been able to add conformance through the use of extensions. This common conformance allows us to treat them as the same type:

```
var intableThings = [IntRepresentable]()
intableThings.append(55)
intableThings.append(1200)
intableThings.append("5")
intableThings.append("1009")
intableThings.append(CrewComplement.enterpriseD)
intableThings.append(CrewComplement.voyager)
intableThings.append(CrewComplement.deepSpaceNine)

let over1000 = intableThings.compactMap { $0.intValue > 1000 ?
  $0.intValue: nil }
print(over1000)
```

The preceding example includes the use of `compactMap` and the ternary operator, which haven't been covered in this book. Further information can be found in the *See also* section.

See also

Further information about extensions can be found in Apple's documentation on the Swift language at `http://swiftbook.link/docs/extensions`.

The documentation for `compactMap` can be found at `https://developer.apple.com/documentation/swift/sequence/2950916-compactmap`.

Further information about the ternary operator can be found at `https://docs.swift.org/swift-book/LanguageGuide/BasicOperators.html#ID71`.

Controlling access with access control

Swift provides fine-grained access control, allowing you to specify the visibility that your code has to other areas of code. This enables you to be deliberate about the interface you provide to other parts of the system, thus encapsulating implementation logic and helping separate the areas of concern.

Swift has five access levels:

- **Private**: Only accessible within the existing scope (defined by curly brackets) or extensions in the same file.
- **File private**: Accessible to anything in the same file, but nothing outside the file.
- **Internal**: Accessible to anything in the same module, but nothing outside the module.
- **Public**: Accessible both inside and outside the module, but cannot be subclassed or overwritten outside of the defining module.
- **Open**: Accessible everywhere, with no restrictions in terms of its use, and can therefore be subclassed and overwritten.

These can be applied to types, properties, and functions.

Getting ready

To explore each of these access levels, we need to step outside our playground comfort zone and create a module. To have something that will hold our module and a playground that can use it, we will need to create an Xcode workspace:

1. In Xcode, select **File** | **New** | **Workspace...** from the menu:

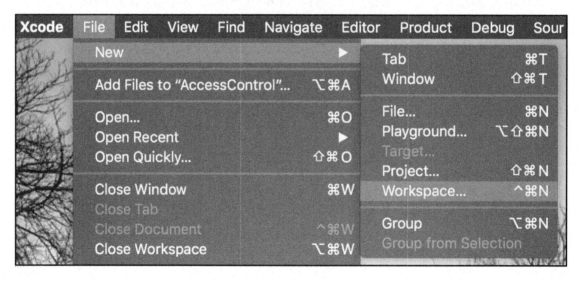

Figure 2.9 – Xcode – New project

2. Give your workspace a name, such as `AccessControl`, and choose a save location. You will now see an empty workspace:

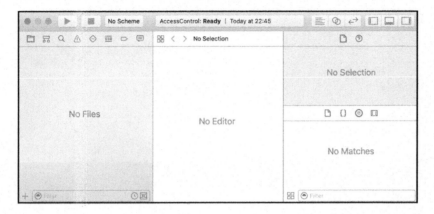

Figure 2.10 – Xcode – New project structure

In this workspace, we need to create a module. To illustrate the access controls that are available, let's have our module represent something that tightly controls which information it exposes, and which information it keeps hidden. One thing that fits this definition is Apple; that is, the company.

3. Create a new project from the Xcode menu by selecting **File** | **New** | **Project...**:

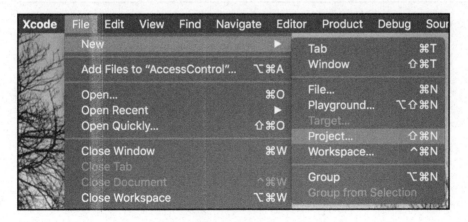

Figure 2.11 – New project

4. From the template selector, select **Framework**:

Figure 2.12 – New project framework

5. Name the project `AppleInc`:

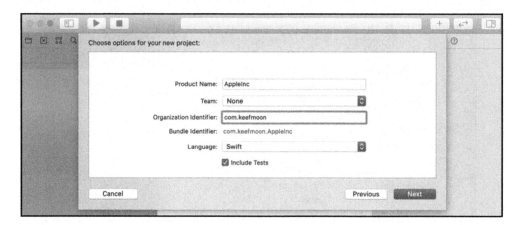

Figure 2.13 – Naming the project

6. Choose a location. Then, at the bottom of the window, ensure that **Add to:** has been set to the workspace we just created:

Figure 2.14 – New project workspace group

7. Now that we have a module, let's set up a playground to use it in. From the Xcode menu, select **File** | **New** | **Playground...**:

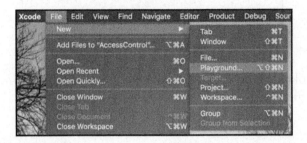

Figure 2.15 – New playground

8. Give the playground a name and save it to a location:

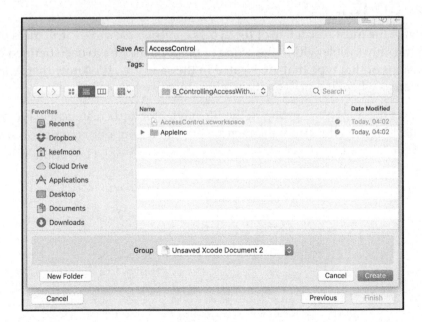

Figure 2.16 – New project

9. This playground will not be added to the workspace automatically; you will need to locate the playground you just created and drag it into the file explorer pane on the left-hand side of your workspace.

10. Press the run button on the Xcode toolbar to build the `AppleInc` module:

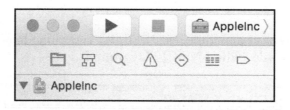

Figure 2.17 – Xcode toolbar

11. Select the playground from the file navigator and add an import statement to the top of the file:

```
import AppleInc
```

We are now ready to look into the different access controls that are available.

How to do it...

Let's investigate the most restrictive of the access controls: `private`. Structures marked as `private` are only visible within the scope of the type they have been defined in, as well as any extensions of that type that are located in the same file. We know that Apple has super-secret areas where it works on its new products, so let's create one:

1. Select the `AppleInc` group in the file navigator and create a new file by selecting **File | New | File...** from the menu. Let's call it `SecretProductDepartment`.

2. In this new file, create a `SecretProductDepartment` class using the `private` access control:

```
class SecretProductDepartment {

    private var secretCodeWord = "Titan"
    private var secretProducts = ["Apple Glasses",
                                  "Apple Car",
                                  "Apple Brain Implant"]

    func nextProduct(codeWord: String) -> String? {
        let codeCorrect = codeWord == secretCodeWord
        return codeCorrect ? secretProducts.first : nil
```

```
        }
    }
```

Next, let's look at the `fileprivate` access control. Structures marked as `fileprivate` are only visible within the file that they are defined in, so a collection of related structures defined in the same file will be visible to each other, but anything outside the file will not see these structures.

When you buy an iPhone from the Apple Store, it's not made in-store; it's made in a factory that the public doesn't have access to. So, let's model this using `fileprivate`.

3. Create a new file called `AppleStore`. Then, create structures for `AppleStore` and `Factory` using the `fileprivate` access control:

```
public enum DeviceModel {
    case iPhone12
    case iPhone12Mini
    case iPhone12Pro
    case iPhone12ProMax
}

public class AppleiPhone {

    public let model: DeviceModel

    fileprivate init(model: DeviceModel) {
        self.model = model
    }
}

fileprivate class Factory {
    func makeiPhone(ofModel model: DeviceModel) -> AppleiPhone {
        return AppleiPhone(model: model)
    }
}

public class AppleStore {

    private var factory = Factory()

    public func selliPhone(ofModel model: DeviceModel)
                            -> AppleiPhone {
        return factory.makeiPhone(ofModel: model)
    }
}
```

To investigate the `public` access control, we will be defining something that is visible outside the defining module but cannot be subclassed or overridden. Apple itself is the perfect candidate to model this behavior as certain parts of it are visible to the public. However, it closely guards its image and brand, so *subclassing* Apple to alter and customize it will not be allowed.

4. Create a new file called `Apple` and create a class for Apple that uses the `public` access control:

```
public class Person {

    public let name: String

    public init(name: String) {
        self.name = name
    }
}

public class Apple {

    public private(set) var ceo: Person
    private var employees = [Person]()
    public let store = AppleStore()
    private let secretDepartment = SecretProductDepartment()

    public init() {
        ceo = Person(name: "Tim Cook")
        employees.append(ceo)
    }

    public func newEmployee(person: Person) {
        employees.append(person)
    }

    func weeklyProductMeeting() {

        var superSecretProduct =
          secretDepartment.nextProduct(codeWord: "Not sure...
            Abracadabra?") // nil

        // Try again
        superSecretProduct =
          secretDepartment.nextProduct(givenCodeWord: "Titan")
        print(superSecretProduct as Any) // "Apple Glasses"
    }
}
```

Lastly, we have the `open` access control. Structures defined as `open` are available outside the module and can be subclassed and overridden without restriction. To explain this last control, we want to model something that exists within Apple's domain but is completely open and free from restrictions. So, for this, we can use the Swift language itself!

Swift has been open sourced by Apple, so while they maintain the project, the source code is fully available for others to take, modify, and improve.

5. Create a new file called `SwiftLanguage` and create a class for the Swift language that uses the `open` access control:

```
open class SwiftLanguage {

    open func versionNumber() -> Float {
        return 5.1
    }

    open func supportedPlatforms() -> [String] {
        return ["iOS", "macOS", "tvOS", "watchOS", "Linux"]
    }
}
```

We now have a module that uses Swift's access controls to provide interfaces that match our model and provide the appropriate visibility.

How it works...

Let's examine our `SecretProductDepartment` class to see how its visibility matches our model:

```
class SecretProductDepartment {
    private var secretCodeWord = "Titan"
    private var secretProducts = ["Apple Glasses",
                                  "Apple Car",
                                  "Apple Brain Implant"]
    func nextProduct(codeWord: String) -> String? {
        let codeCorrect = codeWord == secretCodeWord
        return codeCorrect ? secretProducts.first : nil
    }
}
```

The `SecretProductDepartment` class is declared without an access control keyword, and when no access control is specified, the default control of `internal` is applied. Since we want the secret product department to be visible within Apple, but not from outside Apple, this is the correct access control to use.

The two properties of the `secretCodeWord` and `secretProducts` classes are marked as private, thus hiding their values and existence from anything outside the `SecretProductDepartment` class. To see this restriction in action, add the following to the same file, but outside the class:

```
let insecureCodeWord = SecretProductDepartment().secretCodeWord
```

When you try to build the module, you are told that `secretCodeWord` can't be accessed due to the `private` protection level.

While these properties are not directly accessible, we can provide an interface that allows the information to be provided in a controlled way. This is what the `nextProduct` method provides:

```
func nextProduct(codeWord: String) -> String? {
    let codeCorrect = codeWord == secretCodeWord
    return codeCorrect ? secretProducts.first : nil
}
```

If the correct codeword is passed, it will provide the name of the next product from the secret department, but the details of all other products, and the codeword itself, will be hidden. Since this method doesn't have a specified access control, it is set to the default of `internal`.

It's not possible for contents within a structure to have a more permissive access control than the structure itself. For instance, we can't define the `nextProduct` method as being `public` because this is more permissive than the class it is defined in, which is only `internal`.
Thinking about it, this is the obvious outcome as you cannot create an instance of an internal class outside of the defining module, so how can you possibly call a method on a class instance that you can't even create?

Next, let's look at the `AppleStore.swift` file we created. The purpose here is to provide people outside of Apple with the ability to purchase an iPhone through the Apple Store, but to restrict the creation of iPhones to just the factories where they are built, and then restrict access to those factories to just the Apple Store:

```
public enum DeviceModel {
    case iPhone12
```

```
        case iPhone12Mini
        case iPhone12Pro
        case iPhone12ProMax
    }

    public class AppleiPhone {
        public let model: DeviceModel
        fileprivate init(model: DeviceModel) {
            self.model = model
        }
    }

    public class AppleStore {
        private var factory = Factory()
        public func selliPhone(ofModel model: DeviceModel)
                            -> AppleiPhone {
            return factory.makeiPhone(ofModel: model)
        }
    }
```

Since we want to be able to sell iPhones outside of the `AppleInc` module, the `DeviceModel` enum and the `AppleiPhone` and `AppleStore` classes are all declared as `public`. This has the benefit of making them available outside the module but preventing them from being subclassed or modified. Given how Apple protects the look and feel of their phones and stores, this seems correct for this model.

The Apple Store needs to get their iPhones from somewhere; that is, from the factory:

```
    fileprivate class Factory {
        func makeiPhone(ofModel model: DeviceModel) -> AppleiPhone {
            return AppleiPhone(model: model)
        }
    }
```

By making the `Factory` class `fileprivate`, it is only visible within this file, which is perfect because we only want the Apple Store to be able to use the factory to create iPhones.

We have also restricted the iPhone's initialization method so that it can only be accessed from structures in this file:

```
    fileprivate init(model: DeviceModel)
```

The resulting iPhone is public, but only structures within this file can create iPhone class objects in the first place. In this case, this is done by the factory.

Next, let's look at the `Apple.swift` file:

```swift
public class Person {
    public let name: String
    public init(name: String) {
        self.name = name
    }
}

public class Apple {
    public private(set) var ceo: Person
    private var employees = [Person]()
    public let store = AppleStore()
    private let secretDepartment = SecretProductDepartment()
    public init() {
        ceo = Person(name: "Tim Cook")
        employees.append(ceo)
    }
    public func newEmployee(person: Person) {
        employees.append(person)
    }
    func weeklyProductMeeting() {
        var superSecretProduct =
          secretDepartment.nextProduct(givenCodeWord: "Not sure...
            Abracadabra?") // nil
        // Try again
        superSecretProduct =
          secretDepartment.nextProduct(givenCodeWord: "Titan")
        print(superSecretProduct) // "Apple Glasses"
    }
}
```

The preceding code made both the `Person` and `Apple` classes public, along with the `newEmployee` method. This allows new employees to join the company. The CEO, however, is defined as both public and private:

```swift
public private(set) var ceo: Person
```

We can define a separate, more restrictive, access control for setting a property than the one that was set for getting it. This has the effect of making it a read-only property from outside the defining structure. This provides the access we require since we want the CEO to be visible outside of the `AppleInc` module, but we want to only be able to change the CEO from within Apple.

The final access control is `open`. We applied this to the `SwiftLanguage` class:

```
open class SwiftLanguage {
    open func versionNumber() -> Float {
        return 5.0
    }
    open func supportedPlatforms() -> [String] {
        return ["iOS", "macOSX", "tvOS", "watchOS", "Linux"]
    }
}
```

By declaring the class and methods as `open`, we are allowing them to be subclassed, overridden, and modified by anyone, including those outside the `AppleInc` module. With the Swift language being fully open source, this matches what we are trying to achieve.

There's more...

With our module fully defined, let's see how things look from outside the module. We need to build the module to make it available to the playground. Select the playground; it should contain a statement that imports the `AppleInc` module:

```
import AppleInc
```

First, let's look at the most accessible class that we created; that is, `SwiftLanguage`. Let's subclass the `SwiftLanguage` class and override its behavior:

```
class WinSwift: SwiftLanguage {
    override func versionNumber() -> Float {
        return 5.3
    }
    override func supportedPlatforms() -> [String] {
        var supported = super.supportedPlatforms()
        supported.append("Windows")
        return supported
    }
}
```

Since `SwiftLanguage` is `open`, we can subclass it to add more supported platforms and increase its version number.

Next, let's create an instance of the `Apple` class and see how we can interact with it:

```
let apple = Apple()

let keith = Person(name: "Keith Moon")
```

```
apple.newEmployee(person: keith)

print("Current CEO: \(apple.ceo.name)")
let craig = Person(name: "Craig Federighi")
apple.ceo = craig // Doesn't compile
```

We can create `Person` and provide it to Apple as a new employee since the `Person` class and the `newEmployee` method are declared as public. We can retrieve information about the CEO, but we aren't able to set a new CEO as we defined the property as `private` `(set)`.

Another one of the public interfaces `selliPhone` provided by the module allows us to buy an iPhone from the Apple Store:

```
// Buy new iPhone
let boughtiPhone = apple.store.selliPhone(ofModel: .iPhone12Pro)
// This works

// Try and create your own iPhone
let buildAniPhone = AppleiPhone(model: .iPhone12Pro)
// Doesn't compile
```

We can retrieve a new iPhone from the Apple Store because we declared the `selliPhone` method as `public`. However, we can't create a new iPhone directly since the iPhone's `init` method is declared as `fileprivate`.

See also

Further information about access control can be found in Apple's documentation on the Swift language at `http://swiftbook.link/docs/access-control`.

3
Data Wrangling with Swift Control Flow

Programming is all about making decisions. The purpose of most code involves taking information, inspecting it, making decisions, and producing an output. So far, we have seen a lot of ways to represent information, but in this chapter, we will explore how to make decisions based on that information using a number of Swift's control flow statements. We will find out how they differ and the situations where each is appropriate.

In this chapter, we will cover the following recipes:

- Making decisions with `if/else`
- Handling all the cases with `switch`
- Looping with `for` loops
- Looping with `while` loops
- Handling errors with `try`, `throw`, `do`, and `catch`
- Checking upfront with `guard`
- Doing it later with `defer`
- Bailing out with `fatalError` and `precondition`

Technical requirements

All the code for this chapter can be found in this book's GitHub repository at `https://github.com/PacktPublishing/Swift-Cookbook-Second-Edition/tree/master/Chapter03`

Check out the following video to see the Code in Action: `https://bit.ly/3aq66Us`

Making decisions with if/else

The if/else statement is a cornerstone of almost every programming language. It enables code to be executed conditionally, based on the outcome of a Boolean statement. In this recipe, we will see how if/else can be used, including some ways that are unique to Swift.

Getting ready

If you have ever played pool, you'll know that the aim of the game (when playing standard 8-ball pool) is to pot all the balls of one type and then to pot the black ball. When using American pool balls, they are numbered 1-15, and have a different pattern depending on their type. Balls 1-7 have a solid color, balls 9-15 are white with a colored stripe around them, and ball 8 is black:

Figure 3.1 – American pool balls

In this recipe, we will write a function that will take the number on a pool ball and return the type of ball it is.

How to do it...

Let's use an if/else control flow statement to write a function to return the right pool ball type:

1. Create an enum to describe the possible ball types:

```
enum PoolBallType {
    case solid
    case stripe
```

```
        case black
    }
```

2. Create the method that will take an `Int` and return `PoolBallType`:

```
func poolBallType(forNumber number: Int) -> PoolBallType {
    if number < 8 {
        return .solid
    } else if number > 8 {
        return .stripe
    } else {
        return .black
    }
}
```

3. Use this function and test that we get the expected results:

```
let two = poolBallType(forNumber: 2) // .solid
let eight = poolBallType(forNumber: 8) // .black
let twelve = poolBallType(forNumber: 12) // .stripe
```

How it works...

Within the function, we define three code paths: `if`, `else if`, and `else`:

```
if <#a boolean expression#> {
    <#executed if boolean expression above is true#>
} else if <#other boolean expression#> {
    <#executed if other boolean expression above is true#>
} else {
    <#executed if neither boolean expressions are true#>
}
```

First, we want to determine whether the ball is solid. Since we know that the balls numbered 1-7 are solid, we can test whether the ball number is less than 8, with `number < 8`. If this is `true`, we return the `.solid` case of our `enum`.

If it is `false`, the `else if` Boolean expression is evaluated. As balls 9-15 are striped, we can test whether the ball number is more than 8, with `number > 8`. If this is `true`, we return the `.stripe` case of our `enum`.

Lastly, if both the preceding Boolean expressions are `false`, we return the `.black` case of our `enum`, since that can only happen if the number is exactly 8.

The `else if` and `else` blocks are optional, and you can declare multiple `else if` to cover additional conditions. Let's expand our preceding example with an extra `else if` to better decide the pool ball type.

As we stated previously, pool balls are numbered between 1 and 15, but we don't take into account those upper and lower bounds in our implementation. So if we were to provide the function with ball number 0, it would return `.solid`, and if we were to provide ball number 16, it would return `.stripe`, which doesn't accurately reflect our intention:

```
let zero = poolBallType(forNumber: 0) // .solid
let sixteen = poolBallType(forNumber: 16) // .stripe
```

Let's modify our function to only return a pool ball type if the number is between 1 and 15, and return `nil` otherwise:

```
func poolBallType(forNumber number: Int) -> PoolBallType? {
    if number > 0 && number < 8 {
        return .solid
    } else if number > 8 && number < 16 {
        return .stripe
    } else if number == 8 {
        return .black
    } else {
        return nil
    }
}
```

Now we have four code branches in our `if` statement, and we can use the AND operator, `&&`, to combine Boolean statements (the OR operator, `||`, is also available).

We can now call our function for both numbers within the expected 1-15 range and outside it:

```
let two = poolBallType(forNumber: 2) // .solid
let eight = poolBallType(forNumber: 8) // .black
let twelve = poolBallType(forNumber: 12) // .stripe
let zero = poolBallType(forNumber: 0) // nil
let sixteen = poolBallType(forNumber: 16) // nil
```

Our improved function will produce `nil` for numbers outside of the expected range.

There's more...

There are some other ways we can use if/else statements.

Understanding conditional unwrapping

The function we created earlier returns an optional value, so if we want to do anything useful with the resulting value, we need to unwrap the optional. So far, the only way we have seen how to do this is by force unwrapping, which will cause a crash if the value is nil.

Instead, we can use an if statement to *conditionally unwrap* the optional, turning it into a more useful, non-optional value.

Let's create a function that will print information about a pool ball of a given number. If the provided number is valid for a pool ball, it will print the ball's number and type; otherwise, it will print a message explaining that it is not a valid number.

Since we will want to print the value of the PoolBallType enum, let's make it String backed, which will make printing its value easier:

```
enum PoolBallType: String {
    case solid
    case stripe
    case black
}
```

Now, let's write the function to print the pool ball details:

```
func printBallDetails(ofNumber number: Int) {
    let possibleBallType = poolBallType(forNumber: number)
    if let ballType = possibleBallType {
        print("\(number) - \(ballType.rawValue)")
    } else {
        print("\(number) is not a valid pool ball number")
    }
}
```

The first thing we do in our printBallDetails function is to get the ball type for the given number:

```
let possibleBallType = poolBallType(forNumber: number)
```

In our improved version of this function, this returns an optional version of the PoolBallType enum. We want to include the rawValue of the returned enum as part of printing the ball details. Since the returned value is optional, we need to unwrap it first:

```
if let ballType = possibleBallType {
    print("\(number) - \(ballType.rawValue))")
}
```

In this `if` statement, instead of defining a Boolean expression, we are assigning our optional value to a constant; the `if` statement uses this to *conditionally unwrap* the optional. The optional value is checked to see whether it is `nil`; if it is not `nil`, then the value is unwrapped and assigned to the constant as a non-optional value. That constant becomes available within the scope of the curly brackets following the `if` statement. We use that `ballType` non-optional value to obtain the raw value for the `print` statement.

Since the `if` branch of the `if-else` statement is followed when the optional value has a value, then the `else` branch is followed when the optional value is `nil`.

As this means that the given number is not valid for a pool ball, we print a relevant message:

```
else {
    print("\(number) is not a valid pool ball number")
}
```

We can now call our new function with the same values as before to print out the pool ball type:

```
printBallDetails(ofNumber: 2)   // 2 - solid
printBallDetails(ofNumber: 8)   // 8 - black
printBallDetails(ofNumber: 12)  // 12 - stripe
printBallDetails(ofNumber: 0)   // 0 is not a valid pool ball number
printBallDetails(ofNumber: 16)  // 16 is not a valid pool ball number
```

We've used conditional unwrapping to print the pool ball type, if valid, or explain it's not valid.

Chaining optional unwrapping

The ability of `if` statements to conditionally unwrap optionals can be chained together to produce some useful and concise code. The following example is a bit contrived, but it illustrates how we can use a single `if` statement to unwrap a chain of optional values.

When you play a game of pool, called a *frame*, the type of the first ball you pot becomes the type you need to pot for the rest of the frame, and your opponent has to pot the opposite type.

Let's define a frame of pool and say that we want to track what type of ball each player will be potting:

```
class PoolFrame {
    var player1BallType: PoolBallType?
```

```
        var player2BallType: PoolBallType?
}
```

We will also create a `PoolTable` object that has an optional `currentFrame` property, which will contain information about the current frame if one is in progress:

```
class PoolTable {
    var currentFrame: PoolFrame?
}
```

We now have a pool table that has an optional frame and a frame that has an optional ball type for each player.

Now, let's write a function that prints the ball type for player 1 in the current frame. It is possible that the current frame is `nil` because there is no frame currently being played, or that player 1's ball type is `nil` because a ball hasn't yet been potted. Therefore, we need to account for either of those being `nil`:

```
func printBallTypeOfPlayer1(forTable table: PoolTable) {
    if let frame = table.currentFrame, let ballType =
      frame.player1BallType {
        print(ballType.rawValue)
    } else {
        print("Player 1 has no ball type or there is no current frame")
    }
}
```

Our function is given a `PoolTable`, and to print player 1's ball type, we first need to check and unwrap the `currentFrame` property, and then we need to check and unwrap the current frame's `player1BallType` property.

We could do this by nesting our `if` statements:

```
func printBallTypeOfPlayer1(forTable table: PoolTable) {
    if let frame = table.currentFrame {
        if let ballType = frame.player1BallType {
            print(ballType.rawValue)
        } //... handle else
    } //... handle else
}
```

Instead, we can handle this chained unwrapping in one `if` statement by performing the unwrapping statement sequentially, separated by commas, and each statement can access the unwrapped values from the previous statements:

```
func printBallTypeOfPlayer1(forTable table: PoolTable) {
    if let frame = table.currentFrame, let ballType =
```

```
        frame.player1BallType {
          print("\(ballType)")
      } //... handle else
   }
```

The first statement unwraps the `currentFrame` property, and the second statement uses that unwrapped frame to unwrap player 1's ball type.

Let's use the function we've just created:

1. First, we'll create a table, and without a current frame print player 1's ball type, which won't be available:

   ```
   //
   // Table with no frame in play
   //
   let table = PoolTable()
   table.currentFrame = nil
   printBallTypeOfPlayer1(forTable: table)
   // Player 1 has no ball type or there is no current frame
   ```

2. Next, we can create a current frame, but as player 1's ball type is still `nil`, the function prints the same output:

   ```
   //
   // Table with frame in play, but no balls potted
   //
   let frame = PoolFrame()
   frame.player1BallType = nil
   frame.player2BallType = nil
   table.currentFrame = frame
   printBallTypeOfPlayer1(forTable: table)
   // Player 1 has no ball type or there is no current frame
   ```

3. If we set player 1's ball type, now our function prints the type:

   ```
   //
   // Table with frame in play, and a ball potted
   //
   frame.player1BallType = .solid
   frame.player2BallType = .stripe
   printBallTypeOfPlayer1(forTable: table)
   // solid
   ```

We've created a method that can chain conditional unwrappings, only printing a value when all the values in the chain are non-nil.

Using enums with associated values

As we saw in the *Enumerating values with enums* recipe from Chapter 1, *Swift Building Blocks*, enums can have associated values, and we can use an `if` statement to both check an enum's case and extract the associated value in one expression.

Let's create an enum to represent the result of the pool game, with each case having an associated message:

```
enum FrameResult {
    case win(congratulations: String)
    case lose(commiserations: String)
}
```

Next, we'll create a function that takes a `Result` and prints either the congratulatory message or the commiseration message:

```
func printMessage(forResult result: FrameResult) {
    if case Result.win(congratulations: let winMessage) = result {
        print("You won! \(winMessage)")
    } else if case Result.lose(commiserations: let loseMessage) =
        result {
        print("You lost :( \(loseMessage)")
    }
}
```

Calling this function will print the result, followed by the relevant message:

```
let result = Result.win(congratulations: "You're simply the best!")
printMessage(forResult: result) // You won! You're simply the best!
```

The `if case` block will be executed if the value on the right-hand side of the `=` matches the case on the left-hand side. In addition, you can specify a local constant for the associated value (`winMessage` in the following example), which is then available within the subsequent block:

```
if case Result.win(congratulationsMessage: let winMessage) = result {
    print("You won! \(winMessage)")
}
```

We've used the `if case` statement to both check the case of an enum value and access its associated value in one go.

See also

Further information about if/else can be found in Apple's documentation on the Swift language at `http://swiftbook.link/docs/statements`.

Handling all cases with switch

`switch` statements allow you to control the flow of execution by testing one specific value in multiple ways. In Objective-C and other languages, `switch` statements can only be used on values that can be represented by an integer, and are most commonly used to make decisions based on enumeration cases.

As we have seen, **enumerations** have become a lot more powerful in Swift, as they can be based on more than just integers, and so too can `switch` statements.

`switch` statements in Swift can be used on any type and have advanced pattern-matching functionality.

In this recipe, we will explore both simple and advanced usage of `switch` control flow statements to control logic.

Getting ready

If you are old enough to remember the early days of the home computer, you may also remember text-based adventures. These were simple games that usually described a scene and then let you move around by typing a command to move north, south, east, or west. You would find and pick up items, and could often combine them to solve puzzles.

We can use `switch` statements to control the logic of a simple text adventure.

How to do it...

Let's create parts of a text-based adventure, and use `switch` statements to make the decisions:

1. Define an `enum` to represent the directions we can travel in:

    ```
    enum CompassPoint {
        case north
        case south
    ```

```
        case east
        case west
    }
```

2. Create a function that describes what the player of the text adventure will see when they look in that direction:

```
func lookTowards(_ direction: CompassPoint) {

    switch direction {
    case .north:
        print("To the north lies a winding road")
    case .south:
        print("To the south is the Prancing Pony tavern")
    case .east:
        print("To the east is a blacksmith")
    case .west:
        print("The the west is the town square")
    }
}


lookTowards(.south) // To the south is the Prancing Pony tavern
```

In our text adventure, users can pick up items and attempt to combine them to produce new items and solve problems.

3. Define our available items as an enum:

```
enum Item {
    case key
    case lockedDoor
    case openDoor
    case bluntKnife
    case sharpeningStone
    case sharpKnife
}
```

4. Write a function that takes two items and tries to combine them into a new item. If the items cannot be combined, it will return nil:

```
func combine(_ firstItem: Item, with secondItem: Item) -> Item? {

    switch (firstItem, secondItem) {
    case (.key, .lockedDoor):
        print("You have unlocked the door!")
        return .openDoor
    case (.bluntKnife, .sharpeningStone):
        print("Your knife is now sharp")
```

```
                    return .sharpKnife
            default:
                print("\(firstItem) and \(secondItem) cannot be combined")
                return nil
            }
        }
        let door = combine(.key, with: .lockedDoor) // openDoor
        let oilAndWater = combine(.bluntKnife, with: .lockedDoor) // nil
```

5. In our text adventure, the player will meet different characters and can interact with them. Define the characters that the player can meet:

```
enum Character: String {
    case wizard
    case bartender
    case dragon
}
```

6. Write a function that allows the player to say something, and optionally provide a character to whom it will be said. The interaction that will occur will depend on what is said and the character it is said to:

```
func say(_ textToSay: String, to character: Character? = nil) {

    switch (textToSay, character) {
    case ("abracadabra", .wizard?):
        print("The wizard says, \"Hey, that's my line!\"")
    case ("Pour me a drink", .bartender?):
        print("The bartender pours you a drink")
    case ("Can I have some of your gold?", .dragon?):
        print("The dragon burns you to death with his fiery
breath")
    case (let textSaid, nil):
        print("You say \"\(textSaid)\", to no-one.")
    case (_, let anyCharacter?):
        print("The \(anyCharacter) looks at you, blankly")
    }
}
say("Is anybody there?")
  // You say "Is anybody there?", to no-one.
say("Pour me a drink", to: .bartender)
  // The bartender pours you a drink
say("Can I open a tab?", to: .bartender)
  // The bartender looks at you, blankly
```

How it works...

Within the `lookTowards` function, we want to print a different message for each possible `CompassPoint` case; to do this, we use a `switch` statement:

```swift
func lookTowards(_ direction: CompassPoint) {
    switch direction {
    case .north:
        print("To the north lies a winding road")
    case .south:
        print("To the south is the Prancing Pony tavern")
    case .east:
        print("To the east is a blacksmith")
    case .west:
        print("The the west is the town square")
    }
}
```

At the top of the `switch` statement, we define the value that we want to switch on; then we define what we want to be done when that value matches each of the defined cases using the `case` keyword and then the matching pattern:

```swift
switch <#value#> {
case <#pattern#>:
    <#code#>
case <#pattern#>:
    <#code#>
//...
}
```

Each `case` statement is evaluated in turn, and if the pattern matches the value, the subsequent code is executed.

 If you are familiar with `switch` statements from Objective-C, you may remember that you needed to add `break;` at the end of each `case` statement to stop the execution from falling through to the next `case` statement. This is not needed in Swift; the break in execution is implied by the beginning of the next `case` statement. The only time this isn't the case, it is because your `case` statement is intentionally empty; in these cases, you need to add `break` to tell the compiler that it is intentionally blank for this case. If you do want execution to fall through to the next `case` statement, you can add `fallthrough` at the end of the `case` statement.

In our `combine` function, we have two values that we want to switch based on their values. We can provide multiple values to the `switch` statement in the form of a tuple:

```swift
func combine(_ firstItem: Item, with secondItem: Item) -> Item? {
    switch (firstItem, secondItem) {
    //....
    }
}
```

For each `case` statement, we define the valid value for each part of the tuple:

```swift
case (.key, .lockedDoor):
    print("You have unlocked the door!")
    return .openDoor
```

A `switch` statement in Swift requires that every possible case is covered; however, you can cover all the remaining possibilities in one go using the `default` case:

```swift
switch (firstItem, secondItem) {
//...
default:
    print("\(firstItem) and \(secondItem) cannot be combined")
    return nil
}
```

For our preceding `combine` function, you will notice that the player will only be able to combine the items if they provide them in the right order:

```swift
let door1 = combine(.key, with: .lockedDoor) // openDoor
let door2 = combine(.lockedDoor, with: .key) // nil
```

This is not the desired behavior, as there is no way for the player to know the correct order. To solve this, we can add multiple patterns to each `case` statement. So, when the player provides the `key` and `lockedDoor` items, we can handle the order `key`, `lockedDoor`, and the order `lockedDoor`, `key` with the same `case` statement, using the following format:

```swift
switch <#value#> {
case <#pattern#>, <#pattern#>:
    <#code#>
default:
    <#code#>
}
```

So, we can add the opposite item order as another pattern to each case:

```
func combine(_ firstItem: Item, with secondItem: Item) -> Item? {
    switch (firstItem, secondItem) {
    case (.key, .lockedDoor), (.lockedDoor, .key):
        print("You have unlocked the door!")
        return .openDoor
    case (.bluntKnife, .sharpeningStone), (.sharpeningStone,
      .bluntKnife):
        print("Your knife is now sharp")
        return .sharpKnife
    default:
        print("\(firstItem) and \(secondItem) cannot be combined")
        return nil
    }
}
```

Now the items can be combined in any order:

```
let door1 = combine(.key, with: .lockedDoor) // openDoor
let door2 = combine(.lockedDoor, with: .key) // openDoor
```

For our `say` method, we again have two values that we want to switch on: the text that the player says, and the character to whom it is said. Since the `character` value is optional, we will need to unwrap the value to compare it with non-optional values:

```
func say(_ textToSay: String, to character: Character? = nil) {
    switch (textToSay, character) {
    case ("abracadabra", .wizard?):
        print("The wizard says, "Hey, that's my line!"")
        //...
    }
}
```

In a `switch` statement, when the value is optional, you can compare it to a non-optional value by adding a `?` to wrap it as an optional, making the comparison valid. In the preceding instance, we are comparing the optional `character` value to `.wizard?`.

Where we have two values for a certain set of options, we may only care about one of the values, and the other value could be anything and the case would still be valid. In our example, once all the specific `textToSay` and character pairings have been handled, and the case where there is no character is handled, we want to unwrap and retrieve the character, but we don't care about the `textToSay` value, so we can use `_` to indicate that any value is acceptable:

```
func say(_ textToSay: String, to character: Character? = nil) {
    switch (textToSay, character) {
```

```
//...
case (_, let anyCharacter?):
    print("The \(anyCharacter) looks at you, blankly)")
}
}
```

To retrieve the value of the character entered as part of this `case` statement rather than declaring a value to be matched, we define a constant that will receive the value, and since the value we are switching on is optional, we also add `?`, which will unwrap the value if not `nil`, and assign it to the constant.

See also

Further information about `switch` can be found in Apple's documentation on the Swift language at `http://swiftbook.link/docs/switch`.

Looping with for loops

`for` loops allow you to execute code for each element in a collection or range. In this recipe, we will explore how to use `for` loops to perform actions on every element in a collection.

How to do it...

Let's create some collections and then use `for` loops to act on each element in the collection:

1. Create an array of elements, so we can do something with every item in the array:

   ```
   let theBeatles = ["John", "Paul", "George", "Ringo"]
   ```

2. Create a loop to go through our `theBeatles` array and print each string element that the `for` loop provides:

   ```
   for musician in theBeatles {
       print(musician)
   }
   ```

3. Create a `for` loop that executes some code a set number of times, instead of looping through an array. We can do this by providing a range instead of a collection:

```
// 5 times table
for value in 1...12 {
    print("5 x \(value) = \(value*5)")
}
```

4. Create a `for` loop to print the keys and values of a dictionary. Dictionaries contain pairings between a key and a value, so when looping through a dictionary, we will be provided with both the key and the value in the form of a tuple:

```
let beatlesByInstrument = ["rhythm guitar": "John",
                           "bass guitar": "Paul",
                           "lead guitar": "George",
                           "drums": "Ringo"]
for (key, value) in beatlesByInstrument {
    print("\(value) plays \(key)")
}
```

How it works...

Let's look at how we looped through our `theBeatles` array:

```
for musician in theBeatles {
    print(musician)
}
```

We specify the `for` keyword and then we provide a name for the local variable that will be used for each element in the collection or range. Then, the `in` keyword is provided, followed by the collection or range that will be looped through:

```
for <#each element#> in <#collection or range#> {
    <#code to execute#>
}
```

For range-based loops, the value provided for each loop is the next integer in the range:

```
for value in 1...12 {
    print("5 x \(value) = \(value*5)")
}
```

A range can be a *closed range,* where the range includes the start value and the end value, like the one specified above. Or it can be a *half-open range,* which goes up to, but doesn't include, the last value, like the following code:

```
for value in 1..<13 {
    print("5 x \(value) = \(value*5)")
}
```

When looping through a dictionary, we need to be provided with both the key and value; to do this, we provide a tuple that will receive each key and value in the dictionary:

```
for (key, value) in beatlesByInstrument {
    print("\(value) plays \(key)")
}
```

We can define the tuple and name each of the values. This name can then be used in an execution block. Let's change the tuple labels to better describe the values:

```
for (instrument, musician) in beatlesByInstrument {
    print("\(musician) plays \(instrument)")
}
```

Giving the tuple meaningful names in the preceding example makes the code easier to read.

See also

Further information about `for-in` loops can be found in Apple's documentation on the Swift language at `http://swiftbook.link/docs/for-in`.

Looping with while loops

`for` loops are great when you know how many times you intend to loop, but if you want to loop until a certain condition is met, you need a `while` loop.

A `while` loop has the following syntax:

```
while <#boolean expression#> {
    <#code to execute#>
}
```

The code block will execute over and over until the Boolean expression returns `false`. Therefore, it's a common pattern to change some value in the code block that may cause the Boolean expression to change to `false`.

 If there is no chance of the Boolean expression becoming `true`, the code will loop forever, which can lock up your app.

In this recipe, we will look at situations where a `while` loop can be useful for repeating actions.

Getting ready

This recipe will involve simulating the random flip of a coin. To flip our coin, we will need to randomly pick either heads or tails, so we will need to use a random number generator from the Foundation framework. We will discuss Foundation further in Chapter 5, *Beyond the Standard Library*, but for now, we just need to import the Foundation framework at the top of our playground:

```
import Foundation
```

This will give us the ability to generate a random number, which we will use now.

How to do it...

Let's work out how many times in a row we can flip a coin and get heads:

1. Create an `enum` to represent a coin flip, and use the random number generator to randomly choose heads or tails:

```
enum CoinFlip: Int {
    case heads
    case tails

    static func flipCoin() -> CoinFlip {
        return CoinFlip(rawValue: Int(arc4random_uniform(2)))!
    }
}
```

2. Create a function that will return the number of heads in a row from coin flips. The function will flip the coin within a `while` loop and continue to loop while the coin flip results in heads:

```
func howManyHeadsInARow() -> Int {

    var numberOfHeadsInARow = 0
    var currentCoinFlip = CoinFlip.flipCoin()

    while currentCoinFlip == .heads {
        numberOfHeadsInARow = numberOfHeadsInARow + 1
        currentCoinFlip = CoinFlip.flipCoin()
    }
    return numberOfHeadsInARow
}

let noOfHeads = howManyHeadsInARow()
```

How it works...

In our function, we start by keeping track of how many coin flips in a row are heads and keep a reference to the current coin flip, which will form the condition for the `while` loop:

```
func howManyHeadsInARow() -> Int {
    var numberOfHeadsInARow = 0
    var currentCoinFlip = CoinFlip.flipCoin()
    //...
}
```

In our `while` loop, we will continue to loop and execute the code in the following block while the current coin flip is heads:

```
while currentCoinFlip == .heads {
    numberOfHeadsInARow = numberOfHeadsInARow + 1
    currentCoinFlip = CoinFlip.flipCoin()
}
```

Within the code block, we add one to our running total and we re-flip the coin. We are flipping the coin and assigning it to `currentCoinFlip`, which will get rechecked on the next loop and if it is still heads, the next loop will be executed. Since we are changing something that affects the `while` condition, such that it could eventually be `false`, we can be sure that we won't be stuck in the loop forever.

As soon as the coin flip is tails, the `while` loop condition will be `false`, and so the execution will move on and return the running total we have been keeping:

```
return numberOfHeadsInARow
```

Now, every time you call the function, the coin will be randomly flipped and the number of heads in a row will be returned, so each time it's called, you may get a different value returned. Try it out a few times:

```
let noOfHeads = howManyHeadsInARow()
```

There's more...

We can actually simplify our `while` loop by doing the coin flip as part of the loop continuation checking:

```
func howManyHeadsInARow() -> Int {
    var numberOfHeadsInARow = 0
    while CoinFlip.flipCoin() == .heads {
        numberOfHeadsInARow = numberOfHeadsInARow + 1
    }
    return numberOfHeadsInARow
}
```

Each time through the loop, the `while` condition is evaluated, which involves re-flipping the coin and checking the outcome.

This is more concise and removes the need to track `currentCoinFlip`.

See also

Further information about `while` loops can be found in Apple's documentation of the Swift language at `http://swiftbook.link/docs/while`.

Handling errors with try, throw, do, and catch

Errors happen during programming. These errors may be due to your own code behaving in unexpected ways, or due to unexpected information or behavior from external systems. When these errors happen, it's important to handle them appropriately. Good error handling can separate a good app from a great app.

Swift provides a deliberate and flexible pattern for handling errors, allowing specific errors to be cascaded through a complex system.

In this recipe, we will discover how to define errors, and throw them when necessary.

How to do it...

To examine error handling, we will model a process that can go wrong, and for me, that is cooking a meal:

1. First, let's define the steps involved in cooking a meal as states that the meal will transition through:

```
enum MealState {
    case initial
    case buyIngredients
    case prepareIngredients
    case cook
    case plateUp
    case serve
}
```

2. Create an object to represent the meal we will be cooking. This object will hold the state of the meal as it moves through the process:

```
class Meal {
    var state: MealState = .initial
}
```

We want to allow the meal to transition between states, but not all state transitions should be possible. For instance, you can't move from buying ingredients to serving the meal. The meal should move sequentially from one state to the next. We can provide these restrictions by only allowing the state to be set from within the object itself, using access controls that we explored in the previous chapter.

3. Define the `state` property as only being privately settable:

```
class Meal {
    private(set) var state: MealState = .initial
}
```

4. To allow the state to be changed from outside the object, create a function that will throw an error if the state transition isn't possible:

```
class Meal {

    private(set) var state: MealState = .initial

    func change(to newState: MealState) throws {

        switch (state, newState) {

        case (.initial, .buyIngredients),
            (.buyIngredients, .prepareIngredients),
            (.prepareIngredients, .cook),
            (.cook, .plateUp),
            (.plateUp, .serve):
            state = newState

        default:
            throw MealError.canOnlyMoveToAppropriateState
        }
    }
}
```

In keeping with Swift's protocol-orientated approach, errors in Swift are defined as a protocol, `Error`. This approach allows you to construct your own type to represent errors within your code, and just have it conform to the `Error` protocol.

A common approach is to define errors as enums, with the enum cases representing the different types of errors that can occur.

5. Define the error thrown in the preceding `Meal` class:

```
enum MealError: Error {
    case canOnlyMoveToAppropriateState
}
```

6. Try to execute our error throwing method within a do block and catch any errors that may occur:

```
let dinner = Meal()
do {
    try dinner.change(to: .buyIngredients)
    try dinner.change(to: .prepareIngredients)
    try dinner.change(to: .cook)
    try dinner.change(to: .plateUp)
    try dinner.change(to: .serve)
    print("Dinner is served!")
} catch let error {
    print(error)
}
```

How it works...

The metaphor used in Swift error handling (as well as other languages) is *throwing* and *catching*. A method can *throw* an error if a problem occurs during its execution, at which point nothing further in the method will be executed, and the error is passed back to where the method was called from.

In order to receive this error (perhaps to provide the details of the error to the user), you must *catch* the error at the place the method is called.

To throw an error, you have to declare that the method has the potential to throw an error. Declaring that a method throws allows the compiler to expect potential errors from the method and ensure that you don't forget to catch these errors.

Methods can be declared as potentially throwing an error using the throws keyword:

```
func change(to newState: MealState) throws {
    //...
}
```

Within our change state method, we only change the state if we are moving to the next sequential state. Anything else isn't allowed and should throw an error. We can do this using the throw keyword, followed by a value that conforms to the Error protocol:

```
func change(to newState: MealState) throws {
    //...
    default:
        throw MealError.canOnlyMoveToAppropriateState
    }
}
```

When we create the `Meal` object and move through the states of preparing the meal, each change of state can throw an error. When we call a method that is marked as possibly throwing an error, we have to do it a certain way. We define a `do` block, within which we may call methods that can throw, and we then define a `catch` block that will be executed if any of these methods do throw an error. Each call to a throwing method must be prefixed with the `try` keyword:

```
let dinner = Meal()
do {
    try dinner.change(to: .buyIngredients)
    try dinner.change(to: .prepareIngredients)
    try dinner.change(to: .cook)
    try dinner.change(to: .plateUp)
    try dinner.change(to: .serve)
    print("Dinner is served!")
} catch let error {
    print(error)
}
```

If any of these methods does throw an error, execution will immediately move to the `catch` block. Therefore, by placing code after the `try` methods are called, we are guaranteeing that it will only be executed if the methods do not throw an error. By printing `Dinner is served!` after all the state transitions are called, we know this will only print if we have successfully moved through all the states. Try changing the order of these state change calls, and you'll see that the error is printed, and `Dinner is served!` is not.

In our `catch` block, after the `catch` keyword, we can define the local constant that we want the caught error to be assigned to. However, if we don't specify a local constant here, Swift will implicitly create one for us called `error`, so we can actually omit the constant declaration in the `catch` block and still print the value of the error:

```
do {
    //...
} catch {
    print(error)
}
```

Swift has defined the error for us, so we can still print the value.

There's more...

We have seen how we can throw and catch errors, but we mentioned in the introduction that we can cascade errors through a system, so let's look at how we can do this.

In our meal preparation example, we allow the meal state to be changed externally through a `change` method that can throw an error. Instead, let's change it to a private method, so we can only call it from within the class:

```
class Meal {
    private(set) var state: MealState = .initial
    private func change(to newState: MealState) throws {
        switch (state, newState) {
        case (.initial, .buyIngredients),
            (.buyIngredients, .prepareIngredients),
            (.prepareIngredients, .cook),
            (.cook, .plateUp),
            (.plateUp, .serve):
            state = newState
        default:
            throw MealError.canOnlyMoveToAppropriateState
        }
    }
}
```

Next, let's create some specific methods for moving to each state:

```
class Meal {
    //...
    func buyIngredients() throws {
        try change(to: .buyIngredients)
    }
    func prepareIngredients() throws {
        try change(to: .prepareIngredients)
    }
    func cook() throws {
        try change(to: .cook)
    }
    func plateUp() throws {
        try change(to: .plateUp)
    }
    func serve() throws {
        try change(to: .serve)
    }
}
```

You'll notice that when we call the `change` method from within each of the new methods, we don't need to use a `do` and `catch` block to catch the error; this is because we have defined each of the new methods as potentially throwing an error, so if the call to the `change` method throws an error, this error will be passed to the caller of our new method as though it were throwing an error.

This mechanism allows errors that may occur many levels deep in your code to surface and be handled appropriately.

We now need to amend our meal preparation code to use these new methods:

```
let dinner = Meal()
do {
    try dinner.buyIngredients()
    try dinner.prepareIngredients()
    try dinner.cook()
    try dinner.plateUp()
    try dinner.serve()
    print("Dinner is served!")
} catch let error {
    print(error)
}
```

Let's add the ability to actually affect our meal. We'll add a method to add salt to the meal and a property to allow us to track how much salt is added. Add these to the end of the Meal class:

```
class Meal {
    //...
    private(set) var saltAdded = 0
    func addSalt() throws {
        if saltAdded >= 5 {
            throw MealError.tooMuchSalt
        } else if case .initial = state, case .buyIngredients = state {
            throw MealError.wrongStateToAddSalt
        } else {
            saltAdded = saltAdded + 1
        }
    }
}
```

There are two ways in which adding salt can throw an error, either because we are in the wrong state to add salt (we can't add salt until after we have bought the ingredients), or because we have added too much salt. Let's add these two new errors to our MealError enum:

```
enum MealError: Error {
    case canOnlyMoveToAppropriateState
    case tooMuchSalt
    case wrongStateToAddSalt
}
```

We now have three possible errors that can occur during the preparation of a meal, and we may want to handle those errors differently. We can use multiple `catch` blocks to filter just specific errors that we want to catch, allowing us to handle each error separately:

```
let dinner = Meal()
do {
    try dinner.buyIngredients()
    try dinner.prepareIngredients()
    try dinner.cook()
    try dinner.plateUp()
    try dinner.serve()
    print("Dinner is served!")
} catch MealError.canOnlyMoveToAppropriateState {
    print("It's not possible to move to this state")
} catch MealError.tooMuchSalt {
    print("Too much salt!")
} catch MealError.wrongStateToAddSalt {
    print("Can't add salt at this stage")
} catch {
    print("Some other error: \(error)")
}
```

 It is important to ensure that all possible errors are handled by the `catch` blocks, as an unhandled error will result in a crash. It is, therefore, safest to add an unfiltered `catch` block at the end to catch any errors not caught by the previous blocks.

Since functions can throw an error, and closures are a type of function that can be passed as a parameter, we can have a function that takes a throwing closure where it can also throw an error. It may be that the only errors our function will throw are errors produced by the throwing closure that was passed as a parameter.

When that is true, a function can be defined as re-throwing, using the `rethrows` keyword.

This situation is quite confusing, so let's look at an example:

```
func makeMeal(using preparation: (Meal) throws -> ()) rethrows -> Meal {
    let newMeal = Meal()
    try preparation(newMeal)
    return newMeal
}
```

This `makeMeal` function takes a closure as a parameter; that closure takes a `Meal` object as a parameter and doesn't return anything, but may throw an error.

The purpose of this function is to handle the creation of the `meal` object for you, just leaving you to do any meal preparation within the block; it then returns the meal that was created and prepared. Let's see it in use:

```
do {
    let dinner = try makeMeal { meal in
        try meal.buyIngredients()
        try meal.prepareIngredients()
        try meal.cook()
        try meal.addSalt()
        try meal.plateUp()
        try meal.serve()
    }
    if dinner.state == .serve {
        print("Dinner is served!")
    }
} catch MealError.canOnlyMoveToAppropriateState {
    print("It's not possible to move to this state")
} catch MealError.tooMuchSalt {
    print("Too much salt!")
} catch MealError.wrongStateToAddSalt {
    print("Can't add salt at this stage")
}
```

The `makeMeal` function only throws errors thrown by the closure parameter, so it can be declared as re-throwing. Declaring a function of this type with the `rethrows` keyword isn't required, it can be declared with `throws` instead. However, the compiler can make additional optimizations for a re-throwing function.

See also

Further information about error handling can be found in Apple's documentation on the Swift language at `http://swiftbook.link/docs/error-handling`.

Checking upfront with guard

We have seen in previous recipes how we can use `if` statements to check Boolean expressions and unwrap optional values. It's a common use case to want to do some checks and conditional unwrapping at the beginning of a block of code, and then only execute the subsequent code if everything is as expected. This usually results in wrapping the whole block of code in an `if` statement:

```
if <#boolean check and unwrapping#> {
    <#a block of code#>
    <#that could be quite long#>
}
```

Swift has a better solution expressly for this purpose; the `guard` statement.

In this recipe, we will learn how to use the `guard` statement to return early from a method.

Getting ready

Let's imagine that we have some data that came from an external source, and we want to turn it into model objects that our code can understand, with the intention of displaying it to the user. We can use `guard` statements to ensure the data is correctly formatted, bailing early if it isn't.

How to do it...

We will take some information about the planets of the solar system, which could have come from an external source, and turn it into a model we can understand:

1. Create the planet data in the form of an array of dictionaries:

```
// From https://en.wikipedia.org/wiki/Solar_System
let inputData: [[String: Any]] = [
    ["name": "Mercury",
     "positionFromSun": 1,
     "fractionOfEarthMass": 0.055,
     "distanceFromSunInAUs": 0.4,
     "hasRings": false],
    ["name": "Venus",
     "positionFromSun": 2,
     "fractionOfEarthMass": 0.815,
     "distanceFromSunInAUs": 0.7,
     "hasRings": false],
```

```
        ["name": "Earth",
         "positionFromSun": 3,
         "fractionOfEarthMass": 1.0,
         "distanceFromSunInAUs": 1.0,
         "hasRings": false],
        ["name": "Mars",
         "positionFromSun": 4,
         "fractionOfEarthMass": 0.107,
         "distanceFromSunInAUs": 1.5,
         "hasRings": false],
        ["name": "Jupiter",
         "positionFromSun": 5,
         "fractionOfEarthMass": 318.0,
         "distanceFromSunInAUs": 5.2,
         "hasRings": false],
        ["name": "Saturn",
         "positionFromSun": 6,
         "fractionOfEarthMass": 95.0,
         "distanceFromSunInAUs": 9.5,
         "hasRings": true],
        ["name": "Uranus",
         "positionFromSun": 7,
         "fractionOfEarthMass": 14.0,
         "distanceFromSunInAUs": 19.2,
         "hasRings": false],
        ["name": "Neptune",
         "positionFromSun": 8,
         "fractionOfEarthMass": 17.0,
         "distanceFromSunInAUs": 30.1,
         "hasRings": false]
    ]
```

2. Define a `Planet` struct that will be created from the data:

```
struct Planet {
    let name: String
    let positionFromSun: Int
    let fractionOfEarthMass: Double
    let distanceFromSunInAUs: Double
    let hasRings: Bool
}
```

3. Taking this one step at a time, create a function that will take one-planet dictionaries and make a `Planet` struct, if it can. We'll use a `guard` statement to ensure that the dictionary has all the values we expect:

```
func makePlanet(fromInput input: [String: Any]) -> Planet? {

    guard
        let name = input["name"] as? String,
        let positionFromSun = input["positionFromSun"] as? Int,
        let fractionOfEarthMass = input["fractionOfEarthMass"] as?
          Double,
        let distanceFromSunInAUs = input["distanceFromSunInAUs"]
          as?
          Double,
        let hasRings = input["hasRings"] as? Bool
        else {
            return nil
        }

    return Planet(name: name,
                positionFromSun: positionFromSun,
                fractionOfEarthMass: fractionOfEarthMass,
                distanceFromSunInAUs: distanceFromSunInAUs,
                hasRings: hasRings)
}
```

4. Now that we can handle individual planet data, create a function that will take an array of planet dictionaries and make an array of `Planet` structs, using a `guard` statement to ensure that we successfully create a `Planet` struct:

```
func makePlanets(fromInput input: [[String: Any]]) -> [Planet] {

    var planets = [Planet]()
    for inputItem in input {
        guard let planet = makePlanet(fromInput: inputItem) else {
            continue }
        planets.append(planet)
    }

    return planets
}
```

How it works...

The guard statement works in a very similar way to an if statement, as optional values can be unwrapped and chained together in the same way. Since our planet data contains strings, ints, floats, and Booleans, the dictionary is of the [String: Any] type. So, to create our Planet struct, we will need to check if the expected values exist for given keys and cast them to the correct type.

In our makePlanet function, we use the guard keyword and then access and conditionally cast all the values we require from the planet data dictionary. If any of these conditional casts fail, the else block, which is defined after the guard statement, is executed. We have defined our function to return an optional Planet, so if we don't have the information expected, the guard will fail, and return nil:

```
func makePlanet(fromInput input: [String: Any]) -> Planet? {
    guard
        let name = input["name"] as? String,
        let positionFromSun = input["positionFromSun"] as? Int,
        let fractionOfEarthMass = input["fractionOfEarthMass"] as?
          Double,
        let distanceFromSunInAUs = input["distanceFromSunInAUs"] as?
          Double,
        let hasRings = input["hasRings"] as? Bool
        else {
            return nil
    }
    return Planet(name: name,
                  positionFromSun: positionFromSun,
                  fractionOfEarthMass: fractionOfEarthMass,
                  distanceFromSunInAUs: distanceFromSunInAUs,
                  hasRings: hasRings)
}
```

Any value unwrapped by the guard statement is made available to any code below the guard statement in the same scope; this makes the guard statement perfect for ensuring that input values are as expected before continuing. This removes the need to nest our code within an if block. The unwrapped values are then used to initialize the Planet struct.

As we have seen, a guard statement is for breaking execution when the guard condition fails, and therefore, the compiler ensures that an execution breaking statement is placed in the else block; this could be, for example, return, break, or continue.

In the `makePlanets` function, we use a `for` loop to iterate through the dictionaries and try to create a `Planet` struct from each one. If our `makePlanet` call returns `nil`, we call `continue` to skip this iteration of the `for` loop and jump to the next iteration:

```
func makePlanets(fromInput input: [[String: Any]]) -> [Planet] {
    //...
    for inputItem in input {
        guard let planet = makePlanet(fromInput: inputItem) else {
            continue }
        planets.append(planet)
    }
    //...
}
```

There's more...

The `makePlanets` function accepts an array of planet data dictionaries and returns an array of `Planet` structs. If the array provided is empty, we may decide that this is not a valid input to our function and we want to throw an error; `guard` can help with this too.

We can check that any conditional statement is true with `guard` and if it isn't, we can throw an error:

```
enum CreationError: Error {
    case noData
}

func makePlanets(fromInput input: [[String: Any]]) throws -> [Planet] {
    guard input.count > 0 else { throw CreationError.noData }
    //...
}
```

See also

Further information about `guard` statements can be found in Apple's documentation on the Swift language at http://swiftbook.link/docs/guard.

Doing it later with defer

Typically, when we call a function, control passes from the call site to the function, then the statements within the function are executed sequentially until either the end of the function or until a `return` statement. Control then returns to the call site. In the following diagram, the `print` statements are executed in the order 1, 2, then 3:

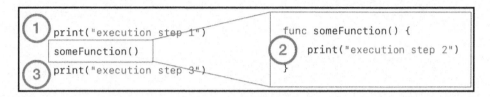

Figure 3.2 – print statement

Sometimes, it can be useful to execute some code after the function has returned, but before control has been returned to the call site. This is the purpose of Swift's `defer` statement. In the following example, step 3 is executed after step 2, even though it is defined above it:

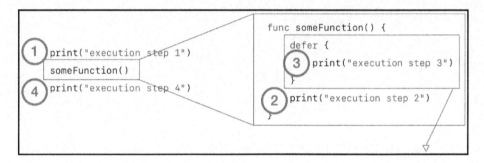

Figure 3.3 – defer statement

In this recipe, we will explore how to use `defer`, and when it can be helpful.

Getting ready

A `defer` statement can be useful to change the state once a function's execution is complete or to clean up values that are no longer needed. Let's look at an example of updating the state with a `defer` statement.

How to do it...

Imagine that we have movie reviews with star ratings, and we want to classify them based on their star rating:

1. Define the options that a movie review may be classified into:

```
enum MovieReviewClass {
    case bad
    case average
    case good
    case brilliant
}
```

2. Create an object to do the classification:

```
class MovieReviewClassifier {

    func classify(forStarsOutOf10 stars: Int) -> MovieReviewClass {
        if stars > 8 {
            return .brilliant // 9 or 10
        } else if stars > 6 {
            return .good // 7 or 8
        } else if stars > 3 {
            return .average // 4, 5 or 6
        } else {
            return .bad // 1, 2 or 3
        }
    }
}
```

3. Use the classifier to classify the review:

```
let classifier = MovieReviewClassifier()
let review1 = classifier.classify(forStarsOutOf10: 9)
print(review1) // brilliant
```

This works great, but for the purpose of this example, let's imagine that this classification was a long-running process, and we wanted to keep track of the state of the classifier, so we can externally check if the classifier was in the middle of classifying or was completed.

4. Define the possible classification states:

```
enum ClassificationState {
    case initial
    case classifying
```

```
        case complete
    }
```

5. Update our classifier class to hold and update the state, using a `defer` statement to move to the complete state:

```
class MovieReviewClassifier {

    var state: ClassificationState = .initial

    func classify(forStarsOutOf10 stars: Int) -> MovieReviewClass {

        state = .classifying

        defer {
            state = .complete
        }

        if stars > 8 {
            return .brilliant // 9 or 10
        } else if stars > 6 {
            return .good // 7 or 8
        } else if stars > 3 {
            return .average // 4, 5 or 6
        } else {
            return .bad // 1, 2 or 3
        }
    }
}
```

6. Use the classifier to classify the review and check the state:

```
let classifier = MovieReviewClassifier()
let review1 = classifier.classify(forStarsOutOf10: 9)
print(review1) // brilliant
print(classifier.state) // complete
```

How it works...

The `classify` method we defined above takes an input rating and then returns `MovieReviewClass` based on this rating:

```
func classify(forStarsOutOf10 stars: Int) -> MovieReviewClass {

    //...
```

```
        if stars > 8 {
            return .brilliant // 9 or 10
        } else if stars > 6 {
            return .good // 7 or 8
        } else if stars > 3 {
            return .average // 4, 5 or 6
        } else {
            return .bad // 1, 2 or 3
        }
    }
```

While doing that, it also updates a `state` value to indicate where the method is in the classification process:

```
state = .classifying

defer {
    state = .complete
}
```

The `defer` statement allows the state to be updated once the method has returned.

If we were to write this method without the `defer` statement, we would have to transition to the `complete` state within each branch of the `if` statement before returning a value, as nothing after this will be executed. The end of that method will look as follows:

```
if stars > 8 {
    state = .complete
    return .brilliant // 9 or 10
} else if stars > 6 {
    state = .complete
    return .good // 7 or 8
} else if stars > 3 {
    state = .complete
    return .average // 4, 5 or 6
} else {
    state = .complete
    return .bad // 1, 2 or 3
}
```

This repetition of updating the state can be avoided when we use the `defer` statement:

```
defer {
    state = .complete
}
```

To defer code, simply use the `defer` keyword, with the code to be deferred defined in curly brackets; this code will be run after the method has returned, but before the control flow is returned to the caller.

There's more...

You can define multiple `defer` statements within a method, and they are executed in the reverse order that they were defined, so the last `defer` statement defined is the first one executed after the method returns.

To demonstrate, add a new state that we'll switch to when completing classifications subsequent to the first:

```
enum ClassificationState {
    case initial
    case classifying
    case complete
    case completeAgain
}
```

Now, let's amend our classifier to keep track of the number of classifications it makes and changes to the `completeAgain` state if more than one classification has been completed:

```
class MovieReviewClassifier {
    var state: ClassificationState = .initial
    var numberOfClassifications = 0
    func classify(forStarsOutOf10 stars: Int) -> MovieReviewClass {
        state = .classifying
        defer {
            numberOfClassifications += 1
        }
        defer {
            if numberOfClassifications > 0 {
                state = .completeAgain
            } else {
                state = .complete
            }
        }
        if stars > 8 {
            return .brilliant // 9 or 10
        } else if stars > 6 {
            return .good // 7 or 8
        } else if stars > 3 {
            return .average // 4, 5 or 6
        } else {
```

```
            return .bad // 1, 2 or 3
        }
    }
}
```

Now change how we use the classifier; the second time we use it, it will complete with a different state:

```
let classifier = MovieReviewClassifier()
let review1 = classifier.classify(forStarsOutOf10: 9)
print(review1) // brilliant
print(classifier.state) // complete
print(classifier.numberOfClassifications) // 1

let review2 = classifier.classify(forStarsOutOf10: 2)
print(review2) // bad
print(classifier.state) // completeAgain
print(classifier.numberOfClassifications) // 2
```

Since we have now defined two `defer` statements, let's take another look to understand the order in which they are executed:

```
defer {
    numberOfClassifications += 1
}
defer {
    if numberOfClassifications > 0 {
        state = .completeAgain
    } else {
        state = .complete
    }
}
```

As discussed earlier, the last defined `defer` statement is executed first. So on the first classification, once the method returns, the last `defer` statement is executed and the state is changed to `complete`, because `numberOfClassifications` will be 0. Next, the first `defer` statement is executed, which adds 1 to the `numberOfClassifications` variable, which will now be 1.

On the second classification, once the method returns, the last `defer` statement will execute and change the state to `completeAgain` since `numberOfClassifications` is greater than 0. Finally, the first `defer` statement will execute, incrementing `numberOfClassifications` and making it 2.

If the `defer` statements had been the other way around, the state would always change to `completeAgain`, as `numberOfClassifications` would have incremented to 1 before the check was made.

See also

Further information about `defer` statements can be found in Apple's documentation on the Swift language at `http://swiftbook.link/docs/defer`.

Bailing out with fatalError and precondition

It's comforting to think that in the code you write, everything will always happen as expected, and your program can handle any eventuality. However, sometimes things can go wrong – really wrong. A situation could arise that you know is possible but don't expect to ever happen, and the program should terminate if it does. In this recipe, we will look at two issues like this: `fatalError` and `precondition`.

Getting ready

Let's reuse our example from the previous recipe; we have an object that can be used to classify movie reviews based on how many stars out of 10 the review gave the movie. However, let's simplify its use, and say that we only intend for a classifier object to classify one, and only one, movie review.

How to do it...

Let's set up our movie classifier to only be used once, and only accept ratings out of 10:

1. Define the classification state and the movie review class:

```
enum ClassificationState {
    case initial
    case classifying
    case complete
}

enum MovieReviewClass {
    case bad
    case average
```

```
            case good
            case brilliant
    }
```

2. Redefine our classifier object, using `precondition` and `fatalError` to indicate situations that are not expected to occur and would cause a problem:

```swift
class MovieReviewClassifier {
    var state: ClassificationState = .initial
    func classify(forStarsOutOf10 stars: Int) -> MovieReviewClass {
        precondition(state == .initial, "Classifier state must be
            initial")
        state = .classifying
        defer {
            state = .complete
        }
        if stars > 8 && stars <= 10 {
            return .brilliant // 9 or 10
        } else if stars > 6 {
            return .good // 7 or 8
        } else if stars > 3 {
            return .average // 4, 5 or 6
        } else if stars > 0 {
            return .bad // 1, 2 or 3
        } else {
            fatalError("Star rating must be between 1 and 10")
        }
    }
}

let classifier = MovieReviewClassifier()
let review1 = classifier.classify(forStarsOutOf10: 9)
print(review1) // brilliant
print(classifier.state) // complete
```

How it works...

We only want to use the classifier once; therefore, when we begin to classify a movie review, the current state should be `initial` as this object has never classified before and shouldn't be in the middle of classifying. If that is not the case, the classifier is being used incorrectly, and we should terminate the execution of the code:

```swift
func classify(forStarsOutOf10 stars: Int) -> MovieReviewClass {
    precondition(state == .initial, "Classifier state must be initial")
    //...
}
```

We state a precondition using the `precondition` keyword, provide a Boolean statement that we expect to be true, and an optional message. If this Boolean statement is not true, the execution of the code will terminate and the message will be displayed in the console.

In our example, we are making it a precondition that the state must be `initial` when calling this method.

When our classifier performs the classification, it expects a number of stars between 1 and 10. However, the method accepts an `Int` as a parameter; so, any integer value can be provided, positive or negative. If the value provided is not between 1 and 10 and the classifier cannot provide a valid `MovieReviewClass`, then the classifier is being used incorrectly, and we should terminate the execution of the code:

```
func classify(forStarsOutOf10 stars: Int) -> MovieReviewClass {
    //...
    if stars > 8 && stars <= 10 {
        return .brilliant // 9 or 10
    } else if stars > 6 {
        return .good // 7 or 8
    } else if stars > 3 {
        return .average // 4, 5 or 6
    } else if stars > 0 {
        return .bad // 1, 2 or 3
    } else {
        fatalError("Star rating must be between 1 and 10")
    }
}
```

The if-else statement covers all the valid `MovieReviewClass` options for the provided stars, so if none of these are triggered, we use a fatal error to indicate incorrect usage. This is done using the `fatalError` keyword, providing an optional message.

See also

Further information about `fatalError` can be found in Apple's documentation on the Swift language at `http://swiftbook.link/docs/fatalerror`.

Generics, Operators, and Nested Types

4

Swift provides a number of advanced features for building functionality that is flexible but well defined so that it feels like you are extending the language itself. In this chapter, we will examine two of these features: **generics** and **operators**. We will also see how nested types allow logical grouping, access control, and namespacing for your constructs.

In this chapter, we will cover the following recipes:

- Using generics with types
- Using generics with functions
- Using generics with protocols
- Using advanced operators
- Defining option sets
- Creating custom operators
- Nesting types and namespacing

Technical requirements

All the code for this chapter can be found in this book's GitHub repository at `https://github.com/PacktPublishing/Swift-Cookbook-Second-Edition/tree/master/Chapter04`

Check out the following video to see the Code in Action: `https://bit.ly/39I7wuy`

Using generics with types

When we build things in Swift that interact with other types, we often specify the type we are interacting with directly. This is helpful because it means we know the capabilities that the type has; we can put those capabilities to use and ensure that the outputs have the correct type. However, we now have a construct that can only interact with the specified type; it can't be reused with other types, even if the concepts are the same.

Generics give us the advantage of having a defined type while being generically applicable to other types. It is, perhaps, best illustrated with an example.

In this recipe, we will create a generic class that stores the last five things it was given and returns them all upon request.

Getting ready

We will create a custom collection object that will store the last five strings that the user copied so that they can paste not just the last string copied, but any of the last five. You can add strings to the list and ask for all the strings in the list, which will be returned newest to oldest:

```
class RecentList {
    var slot1: String?
    var slot2: String?
    var slot3: String?
    var slot4: String?
    var slot5: String?
    func add(recent: String) {
        // Move each slot down 1
        slot5 = slot4
        slot4 = slot3
        slot3 = slot2
        slot2 = slot1
        slot1 = recent
    }
    func getAll() -> [String] {
        var recent = [String]()
        if let slot1 = slot1 {
            recent.append(slot1)
        }
        if let slot2 = slot2 {
            recent.append(slot2)
        }
        if let slot3 = slot3 {
```

```
            recent.append(slot3)
        }
        if let slot4 = slot4 {
            recent.append(slot4)
        }
        if let slot5 = slot5 {
            recent.append(slot5)
        }
        return recent
    }
}
let recentlyCopiedList = RecentList()
recentlyCopiedList.add(recent: "First")
recentlyCopiedList.add(recent: "Next")
recentlyCopiedList.add(recent: "Last")
var recentlyCopied = recentlyCopiedList.getAll()
print(recentlyCopied) // Last, Next, First
```

This is great – it does just what we want. Now, let's say that we want to add a list of five recent contacts to a contacts app. The concept is exactly the same as the list of copied strings, as we want to do the following:

- Add something to a list.
- Get all the things on the list so that we can present them to the user.

However, because we specified that the `RecentList` object can only work with strings, it can't work with my custom `Person` object. We can use generics to make this more useful.

Let's see how to do this by making `RecentList` use generics.

How to do it...

We will update our `RecentList` code to use generics, so it can be used with other types:

1. Amend the `RecentList` object to define a generic type, `ListItemType`, which we use in place of `String`:

```
class RecentList<ListItemType> {

    var slot1: ListItemType?
    var slot2: ListItemType?
    var slot3: ListItemType?
    var slot4: ListItemType?
    var slot5: ListItemType?
```

```
func add(recent: ListItemType) {
    // Move each slot down 1
    slot5 = slot4
    slot4 = slot3
    slot3 = slot2
    slot2 = slot1
    slot1 = recent
}

func getAll() -> [ListItemType] {
    var recent = [ListItemType]()
    if let slot1 = slot1 {
        recent.append(slot1)
    }
    if let slot2 = slot2 {
        recent.append(slot2)
    }
    if let slot3 = slot3 {
        recent.append(slot3)
    }
    if let slot4 = slot4 {
        recent.append(slot4)
    }
    if let slot5 = slot5 {
        recent.append(slot5)
    }
    return recent
}
}
```

2. Provide a specified type, String, when creating RecentList, which will be used to replace the generic type for this instance of RecentList:

```
let recentlyUsedWordList = RecentList<String>()
recentlyUsedWordList.add(recent: "First")
recentlyUsedWordList.add(recent: "Next")
recentlyUsedWordList.add(recent: "Last")
var recentlyUsedWords = recentlyUsedWordList.getAll()
print(recentlyUsedWords) // Last, Next, First
```

Instead of using generics, we could have replaced all the String references in Recent1List with Any, which would allow it to accept any type. However, this would allow the list to be made up of different types of things, which is not what we want. It would also require us to cast values that are returned, to make them useful.

Let's examine how our newly genericized `RecentList` can be used for the other example we discussed earlier, the list of recent contacts.

3. Create a simple `Person` object:

```
class Person {

    let name: String
    init(name: String) {
        self.name = name
    }
}
```

4. Create some people to add to our recent contact list:

```
let rod = Person(name: "Rod")
let jane = Person(name: "Jane")
let freddy = Person(name: "Freddy")
```

5. Create a new `RecentList`, providing the specific `Person` type:

```
let lastCalledList = RecentList<Person>()
```

6. Add person objects to this list:

```
lastCalledList.add(recent: freddy)
lastCalledList.add(recent: jane)
lastCalledList.add(recent: rod)
```

7. Get all the people in the list, and since this is typed as an array of `Person` objects, print their `name` property:

```
let lastCalled = lastCalledList.getAll()
for person in lastCalled {
    print(person.name)
}
// Rod
// Jane
// Freddy
```

We now have a generic `RecentList` class that we have used with both strings and a custom `Person` class.

How it works...

To add generics to a `class` or `struct`, the generic type is defined in angle brackets after the class or struct name, and can be given any type name, although it should begin with a *capital letter* like other type names:

```
class RecentList<ListItemType> {
    //...
}
```

This generic type now becomes a stand-in for the specific type that will be specified when it is used, and we can use this wherever we would use the specific type.

It can be used as a property type:

```
var slot1: ListItemType?
```

As a parameter value:

```
func add(recent: ListItemType)
```

And as a return type:

```
func getAll() -> [ListItemType]
```

In many other programming languages that have a generics system, the generic type is often given a one-letter type name, usually `T`. Swift aims to be concise, but not at the expense of clarity, so I suggest using a more descriptive type name.

A descriptive type name becomes especially important if you have multiple generic types, which you can have as a comma-separated list within the angle brackets:

```
class RecentList<ListItemType, SomeOtherType> {
    //...
}
```

We have now created a generic `RecentList` object that can be used with any type.

There's more...

While being extremely generic has its advantages, you may wish to constrain which types can be used for the generic type, especially if you need to use some features of that constrained type.

Let's say that in addition to returning an array of items from `RecentList`, we want to be able to print out the list directly. To do this, we need to ensure that the type of item used in `RecentList` is something that can be converted into a *string* to be printed. There is already a `CustomStringConvertible` protocol that defines this behavior, so we want to ensure that any specific type used with `RecentList` conforms to `CustomStringConvertible`:

```
class RecentList<ListItemType: CustomStringConvertible> {
    //...
}
```

We add the constraint after the generic type name, separated by a colon, similar to how we specify protocol conformance and class inheritance. Indeed, while this example constrains the generic type to implement a protocol, we can instead specify a class that the specific type must be, or inherit from.

Now that we have this constraint, we can be sure that any specific type given will conform to `CustomStringConvertible`, and will therefore have a `description` string that we can print, so let's create a method to do that:

```
class RecentList<ListItemType: CustomStringConvertible> {
func printRecentList() {
    for item in getAll() {
        let printableItem = String(describing: item)
        print(printableItem)
    }
}
 //...
```

The only thing left to do is to make our `Person` class conform to `CustomStringConvertible` so that it can continue to be used as a specific type in `RecentList`:

```
extension Person: CustomStringConvertible {
    public var description: String {
        return name
    }
}
```

Now we can use this functionality with our `String` type's `RecentlyList` and our `Person` type's `RecentList`:

```
// Using String type
let recentlyUsedWordList = RecentList<String>()
recentlyUsedWordList.add(recent: "First")
recentlyUsedWordList.add(recent: "Next")
recentlyUsedWordList.add(recent: "Last")
```

```
recentlyUsedWordList.printRecentList()
// Last
// Next
// First

// Using Person type
let rod = Person(name: "Rod")
let jane = Person(name: "Jane")
let freddy = Person(name: "Freddy")
let lastCalledList = RecentList<Person>()
lastCalledList.add(recent: freddy)
lastCalledList.add(recent: jane)
lastCalledList.add(recent: rod)
lastCalledList.printRecentList()
// Rod
// Jane
// Freddy
```

By constraining the generic type, we could use features that we knew the type would have, to provide additional functionality.

See also

Further information about generic types can be found in Apple's documentation on the Swift language at `http://swiftbook.link/docs/generics`.

Using generics with functions

In addition to being able to specify generic types, you can use generics to build functions that are both widely applicable and strongly typed. In this recipe, we will use generics with functions.

How to do it...

We will use generics to create a function to help with placing values into a dictionary:

1. Create a generic function that inserts the same value into a dictionary for multiple keys:

   ```
   func makeDuplicates<ItemType>(of item: ItemType,
       withKeys keys: Set<String>) -> [String: ItemType] {
   ```

```
        var duplicates = [String: ItemType]()
        for key in keys {
            duplicates[key] = item
        }
        return duplicates
    }
```

2. Use this function, passing in a single value and multiple keys, and the value is stored against each of the given keys:

```
let awards: Set<String> = ["Best Director",
                           "Best Picture",
                           "Best Original Screenplay",
                           "Best International Feature"]
let oscars2020 = makeDuplicates(of: "Parasite", withKeys: awards)
print(oscars2020["Best Picture"] ?? "")
// Parasite
print(oscars2020["Best International Feature"] ?? "")
// Parasite
```

How it works...

Just like generics for types, the generic type for a function is specified within angle brackets:

```
func makeDuplicates<ItemType>(of item: ItemType,
    withKeys keys: Set<String>) -> [String: ItemType] {
    //...
}
```

The defined generic type name can then be used as a type definition within the rest of the function definition. In our example, we want to define the type of our input item to be duplicated, and we also want the values that are held in the dictionary to be returned to be of the same type.

Instead of using generics, we could have used the Any type in place of the generic type:

```
func makeDuplicates(of item: Any, withKeys keys: Set<String>) -> [String:
Any] {
    //...
}
```

However, this approach presents a few problems for anyone using this function:

- They will get back a dictionary containing values of the `Any` type, which will need to be cast to a more useful type.
- Without seeing the implementation, they can't be sure that the dictionary contains values of the same type. One key may have a `String` stored against it, and another may have an `Int`.
- Without seeing the implementation, they can't be sure that the values of the returned dictionary are of the same type as the item provided.

By using a generic type, we allow the functionality to be widely applicable while enforcing our type logic at compile time.

You'll notice that unlike instantiating a type with generics, we don't need to explicitly state the specific type to use when executing the function:

```
let oscars2020 = makeDuplicates(of: "Parasite", withKeys: awards)
```

This is because the compiler is able to infer it from the type of the first parameter provided. Since `Parasite` is a string, and the compiler knows that the parameter has the `ItemType` generic type, the compiler infers that for this use of the method, the `ItemType` generic type becomes the specific type of `String`.

There's more...

We can increase the usability of our function by providing a generic type for the set of keys we provide as the second parameter:

```
func makeDuplicates<ItemType, KeyType>(of item: ItemType, withKeys
   keys: Set<KeyType>) -> [KeyType: ItemType] {
      var duplicates = [KeyType: ItemType]()
      for key in keys {
         duplicates[key] = item
      }
      return duplicates
}
```

Multiple generic types are defined just as they were in the previous recipe, as a comma-separated list within the angle brackets.

All the collection types in Swift (array, dictionary, set, and so on) use generics, and in the preceding function, we are passing the generic type from our function into the set. Therefore, `KeyType` must conform to `Hashable`, since this is required for use in a `Set`.

If we wanted to make this constraint explicit or constrain the generic type for some other reason, this is defined after a colon:

```
func makeDuplicates<ItemType, KeyType: Hashable>(of item: ItemType,
    withKeys keys: Set<KeyType>) -> [KeyType: ItemType] {
    var duplicates = [KeyType: ItemType]()
    for key in keys {
        duplicates[key] = item
    }
    return duplicates
}
```

Just as with the previous example, if both specific types we are using can be inferred from the input or output, we don't need to specify it:

```
let awards: Set<String> = ["Best Director",
                           "Best Picture",
                           "Best Original Screenplay",
                           "Best International Feature"]
let oscars2020 = makeDuplicates(of: "Parasite", withKeys: awards)
print(oscars2020["Best Picture"]) // Parasite
print(oscars2020["Best International Feature"]) // Parasite
```

We have used two generic types to improve the flexibility of our function.

See also

Further information about generic functions can be found in Apple's documentation on the Swift language at http://swiftbook.link/docs/generic-functions.

Using generics with protocols

So far in this chapter, we have seen how to use generics within types and functions. In this recipe, we will round off our journey through generics in Swift by looking at how they can be used in protocols. This will allow us to produce abstract interfaces while maintaining strongly typed requirements that allow for a more descriptive model.

In this recipe, we will build a model for a transport app in the UK with the goal of providing the distance and duration of a journey for different methods of transport.

How to do it...

The ways that people travel can be very different, so let's start by defining transport methods in a generic way, and then specify what those travel methods are:

1. Define a protocol to define the features of a transport method:

```
protocol TransportMethod {
    associatedtype CollectionPoint
    var defaultCollectionPoint: CollectionPoint { get }
    var averageSpeedInKPH: Double { get }
}
```

2. Create a struct for traveling by train that implements the `TransportMethod` protocol:

```
struct Train: TransportMethod {
    typealias CollectionPoint = TrainStation
    // User's home or nearest station
    var defaultCollectionPoint: TrainStation {
        return TrainStation.BMS
    }
    var averageSpeedInKPH: Double {
        return 100
    }
}
```

3. We need to define the `TrainStation` type that we put as `CollectionPoint`. Let's do that as an enum:

```
enum TrainStation: String {
    case BMS = "Bromley South"
    case VIC = "London Victoria"
    case RAI = "Rainham (Kent)"
    case BTN = "Brighton (East Sussex)"
    // Full list of UK train stations codes at
    // http://www.nationalrail.co.uk/static/documents/content
        // /station_codes.csv
}
```

4. Since we plan to calculate the distance and duration of a journey, let's create a `Journey` object to represent that journey from a starting point to an endpoint:

```
class Journey<TransportType: TransportMethod> {
    let start: TransportType.CollectionPoint
    let end: TransportType.CollectionPoint
    init(start: TransportType.CollectionPoint,
```

```
        end: TransportType.CollectionPoint) {
        self.start = start
        self.end = end
    }
}
```

5. Add the transport method as a property of the journey as this will be used for the duration calculation:

```
class Journey<TransportType: TransportMethod> {
    let start: TransportType.CollectionPoint
    let end: TransportType.CollectionPoint
    let method: TransportType
    init(method: TransportType,
        start: TransportType.CollectionPoint,
        end: TransportType.CollectionPoint) {
        self.start = start
        self.end = end
        self.method = method
    }
}
```

6. To calculate the distance of our journey, we need the start and end to have definite locations. So, define a protocol that provides this location:

```
protocol TransportLocation {
    var location: CLLocation { get }
}
```

7. Import the `CoreLocation` framework at the top of the playground:

```
import CoreLocation
```

8. Constrain `CollectionPoint` associated type on `TransportMethod`, so that it must conform to the `TransportLocation` protocol we have just created:

```
protocol TransportMethod {
    associatedtype CollectionPoint: TransportLocation
    var defaultCollectionPoint: CollectionPoint { get }
    var averageSpeedInKPH: Double { get }
}
```

9. Use the location on the start and end of the `CollectionPoint` to calculate the distance and duration of the journey:

```
class Journey<TransportType: TransportMethod> {
    var start: TransportType.CollectionPoint
    var end: TransportType.CollectionPoint
```

```
let method: TransportType
var distanceInKMs: Double
var durationInHours: Double
init(method: TransportType,
     start: TransportType.CollectionPoint,
     end: TransportType.CollectionPoint) {
    self.start = start
    self.end = end
    self.method = method
    // CoreLocation provides the distance in meters,
    // so we divide by 1000 to get kilometers
    distanceInKMs = end.location.distance(from: start.location)
      / 1000
    durationInHours = distanceInKMs / method.averageSpeedInKPH
}
}
```

10. Ensure our `TrainStation` enum conforms to `TransportLocation`, which is now a requirement:

```
enum TrainStation: String, TransportLocation {
    case BMS = "Bromley South"
    case VIC = "London Victoria"
    case RAI = "Rainham (Kent)"
    case BTN = "Brighton (East Sussex)"
    // Full list of UK train stations codes can be found at
    // http://www.nationalrail.co.uk/static/documents/content
      // /station_codes.csv
    var location: CLLocation {
        switch self {
        case .BMS:
            return CLLocation(latitude: 51.4000504,
                              longitude: 0.0174237)
        case .VIC:
            return CLLocation(latitude: 51.4952103,
                              longitude: -0.1438979)
        case .RAI:
            return CLLocation(latitude: 51.3663,
                              longitude: 0.61137)
        case .BTN:
            return CLLocation(latitude: 50.829,
                              longitude: -0.14125)
        }
    }
}
```

11. Use our `Journey` object to calculate the distance and duration of a train journey:

```
let trainJourney = Journey(method: Train(),
                           start: TrainStation.BMS,
                           end: TrainStation.VIC)
let distanceByTrain = trainJourney.distanceInKMs
let durationByTrain = trainJourney.durationInHours
print("Journey distance: \(distanceByTrain) km")
print("Journey duration: \(durationByTrain) hours")
```

How it works...

At the outset, it may not be clear which is the best structure to use to define a transport method, and there might be different structures appropriate for different travel methods. Therefore, we can define a transport method as a protocol that appropriate types can conform to:

```
protocol TransportMethod {
    associatedtype CollectionPoint
    var defaultCollectionPoint: CollectionPoint { get }
    var averageSpeedInKPH: Double { get }
}
```

We define an associated generic type that we name `CollectionPoint`, which will represent the type of location that someone can be collected from when using this transport method. By using generics, we have ultimate flexibility in how a transport method chooses to define what can serve as a collection point.

Having defined an associated type, it can then be used as a placeholder in properties and methods for the specific type that will be defined when the protocol is used. We use it to define a default collection point that each transport method should provide.

Each transport method also provides an average speed, which will be used later in calculating the travel time.

Let's look at a concrete example of a transport method to help define the model further:

```
struct Train: TransportMethod {
    typealias CollectionPoint = TrainStation
    // User's home or nearest station
    var defaultCollectionPoint: TrainStationPoint {
        return TrainStation.BMS
    }
    var averageSpeedInKPH: Double {
        return 100
```

```
        }
    }
```

For `Train` to conform to the `TransportMethod` protocol, we must provide a specific version of the `CollectionPoint` generic type that is required by the protocol. In the case of traveling by train, the collection point will be a train station, so we now have to define the `TrainStation` type:

```
enum TrainStation: String {
    case BMS = "Bromley South"
    case VIC = "London Victoria"
    case RAI = "Rainham (Kent)"
    case BTN = "Brighton (East Sussex)"
    // Full list of UK train stations codes at
    // http://www.nationalrail.co.uk/static/documents/content
      // /station_codes.csv
}
```

Since there are a finite number of train stations that are discretely definable, an `enum` is a good way to represent them. I've only listed a small number above, for brevity.

Our goal is to model a journey and calculate the duration of the journey over specific transport methods, so let's create a `Journey` object:

```
class Journey<TransportType: TransportMethod> {
    let start: TransportType.CollectionPoint
    let end: TransportType.CollectionPoint
    init(start: TransportType.CollectionPoint,
         end: TransportType.CollectionPoint) {
        self.start = start
        self.end = end
    }
}
```

A journey takes place from one point to another, so we take the journey's start and end as input parameters. We need to have the flexibility to provide any type as the start and end, but we need them to be types connected to a transport method, with the same type for the start and end values. To accomplish this, we can have a generic type constrained to conform to the `TransportMethod` protocol; we can then define our start and end property types by referencing the `CollectionPoint` associated type of the generic type.

Our goal is to calculate the duration of a journey. To do this, we will need the speed of travel during the journey and the distance from start to end. Our `TransportMethod` protocol defines that it will provide an average speed, so let's also take the transport method as an input to our journey:

```
class Journey<TransportType: TransportMethod> {
    let start: TransportType.CollectionPoint
    let end: TransportType.CollectionPoint
    let method: TransportType
    init(method: TransportType,
        start: TransportType.CollectionPoint,
        end: TransportType.CollectionPoint) {
        self.start = start
        self.end = end
        self.method = method
    }
}
```

To get the distance of the journey, we need to calculate the distance between the start and end, but the type of both the start and end of the journey is the generic `CollectionPoint` type, which could be any type, and so does not have any location information that we can use to calculate distance.

To solve this, let's constrain `CollectionPoint` so that it must conform to a new protocol, `TransportLocation`:

```
protocol TransportLocation {
    var location: CLLocation { get }
}
```

Anything conforming to `TransportLocation` must provide a location in the form of a `CLLocation` object. The `CLLocation` object is part of the `CoreLocation` framework on iOS. Further investigation of the `CoreLocation` framework is outside the scope of this book, but it's enough to know that it provides ways to calculate the distance between two `CLLocation` objects, and we need to include the following at the top of this playground to use it:

```
import CoreLocation
```

With our `TransportLocation` protocol defined, we can constrain the `CollectionPoint` associated type on the `TransportMethod` protocol:

```
protocol TransportMethod {
    associatedtype CollectionPoint: TransportLocation
    var defaultCollectionPoint: CollectionPoint { get }
    var averageSpeedInKPH: Double { get }
}
```

Since our `CollectionPoint` will now conform to `TransportLocation`, and therefore must have a location property, we can go back to our `Journey` object and use this to calculate the distance of the journey and the duration:

```
class Journey<TransportType: TransportMethod> {
    var start: TransportType.CollectionPoint
    var end: TransportType.CollectionPoint
    let method: TransportType
    var distanceInKMs: Double
    var durationInHours: Double
    init(method: TransportType,
         start: TransportType.CollectionPoint,
         end: TransportType.CollectionPoint) {
        self.start = start
        self.end = end
        self.method = method
        // CoreLocation provides the distance in meters,
        // so we divide by 1000 to get kilometers
        distanceInKMs = end.location.distance(from: start.location) /
            1000
        durationInHours = distanceInKMs / method.averageSpeedInKPH
    }
}
```

The last thing we need to do is to ensure that our `TrainStation` enum conforms to `TransportLocation` as this is now a requirement. To do this, we just need to declare conformance and add a `location` property:

```
enum TrainStation: String, TransportLocation {
    case BMS = "Bromley South"
    case VIC = "London Victoria"
    case RAI = "Rainham (Kent)"
    case BTN = "Brighton (East Sussex)"
    // Full list of UK train stations codes can be found at
    // http://www.nationalrail.co.uk/static/documents/content
     // /station_codes.csv
    var location: CLLocation {
        switch self {
```

```
        case .BMS:
            return CLLocation(latitude: 51.4000504,
                                longitude: 0.0174237)
        case .VIC:
            return CLLocation(latitude: 51.4952103,
                                longitude: -0.1438979)
        case .RAI:
            return CLLocation(latitude: 51.3663,
                                longitude: 0.61137)
        case .BTN:
            return CLLocation(latitude: 50.829,
                                longitude: -0.14125)
        }
    }
}
```

Let's see how we would use our travel model to create a journey with specific types:

```
let trainJourney = Journey(method: Train(),
                            start: TrainStation.BMS,
                            end: TrainStation.VIC)
let distanceByTrain = trainJourney.distanceInKMs
let durationByTrain = trainJourney.durationInHours
print("Journey distance: \(distanceByTrain) km")
print("Journey duration: \(durationByTrain) hours")
```

We have used generics with protocols to create a generic system without prescribing the type of Swift construct we need to use.

There's more...

In this recipe, we made one type conform to `TransportMethod` – this was our `Train` struct. Let's look at another to see how tackling things in a protocol-oriented way allows flexibility in implementation.

In the next `TransportMethod`, we will implement `Road`, but there are a number of different vehicle types that we can use to travel by road, and they may have different average speeds. Since we have a finite list of options for travel by road, let's define it using an `enum`:

```
enum Road: TransportMethod {
    typealias CollectionPoint = CLLocation
    case car
    case motobike
    case van
```

```
        case hgv
        // The users home or current location
        var defaultCollectionPoint: CLLocation {
            return CLLocation(latitude: 51.1,
                                  longitude: 0.1)
        }
        var averageSpeedInKPH: Double {
            switch self {
            case .car: return 60
            case .motobike: return 70
            case .van: return 55
            case .hgv: return 50
            }
        }
    }
```

A journey by train has a finite list of collection points, which is the train stations but almost anywhere can be a collection point when traveling by road. Therefore, we can define the collection point for `Road` to be any `CLLocation`, but `CLLocation` doesn't conform to `TransportLocation`. We can solve this by extending `CLLocation` to add conformance:

```
    extension CLLocation: TransportLocation {
        var location: CLLocation {
            return self
        }
    }
```

Now, we can define a journey by road and calculate the duration:

```
    let start = CLLocation(latitude: 51.3994669,
                              longitude: 0.0116888)
    let end = CLLocation(latitude: 51.2968654,
                            longitude: 0.5053609)
    let roadJourney = Journey(method: Road.car,
                                start: start,
                                end: end)
    let distanceByRoad = roadJourney.distanceInKMs
    let durationByRoad = roadJourney.durationInHours
    print("Journey distance: \(distanceByRoad) km")
    print("Journey duration: \(durationByRoad) hours")
```

By taking a protocol-orientated approach to tackling the task of calculating a journey's duration, and by using protocol generics, we were able to use completely different, but appropriate, implementations for two transport methods while providing an interface so that they can be handled in a common way.

For a train journey, we used an `enum` to model the train stations and a `struct` to model the transport method, and for `road`, we implemented an `enum` for the transport method and used the `CLLocation` object for the transport location.

See also

Further information about associated types can be found in Apple's documentation on the Swift language at `http://swiftbook.link/docs/associated-types`.

Using advanced operators

Swift is a programming language that takes a relatively small number of well-defined principles and builds on them to create expressive and powerful language features. The concept of mathematical operators, such as +, -, *, and / for addition, subtraction, multiplication, and division, respectively, seems so fundamental as to not warrant a mention. However, in Swift, this common mathematical functionality is built on top of an underlying operator system that is extensible and powerful.

In this recipe, we will look at some of the more advanced operators provided by the Swift standard library, and in the next recipe, we will create our own custom operators.

How to do it...

The operators we will explore are known as bitwise operators and are used to manipulate numerical bit representations.

An integer value in Swift can be represented in its binary form by prefixing the integer literal with `0b`:

```
let zero: Int   = 0b000
let one: Int    = 0b001
let two: Int    = 0b010
let three: Int  = 0b011
let four: Int   = 0b100
let five: Int   = 0b101
let six: Int    = 0b110
let seven: Int  = 0b111
```

A bit is the smallest value in a computer system, consisting of either a 1 or 0. The integers mentioned here can be represented by three bits, which are clearly visible when represented in binary form, as illustrated in the preceding snippet. The integer `six` can be represented by the three bits 1, 1, and 0.

These binary representations are really useful when you need to represent multiple options in one value. For example, let's say that we want to indicate which devices are supported for a specific feature of an app. The available devices are as listed:

- Phone
- Tablet
- Watch
- Laptop
- Desktop
- TV
- Brain implant

Certain features may be appropriate for all the devices, or you may still be working on a feature, and so it isn't currently appropriate for any device, or it may be a combination of different devices. We can have Boolean values for each of the devices to indicate whether the feature is supported for that device, but this is not the best solution as there is nothing intrinsically tying the properties to each other, and you can forget to update some of the values as circumstances change.

Instead, we can represent all the supported devices with one integer value, and use each bit of the integer to represent a different device:

```
let phone: Int        = 0b0000001
let tablet: Int       = 0b0000010
let watch: Int        = 0b0000100
let laptop: Int       = 0b0001000
let desktop: Int      = 0b0010000
let tv: Int           = 0b0100000
let brainImplant: Int = 0b1000000

var supportedDevices: Int
```

To see how this enables us to store multiple devices in one value, let's add together a number of device values:

```
phone  = 0b0000001  +
tablet = 0b0000010  +
tv     = 0b0100000
-------------------
phone
tablet = 0b0100011
tv
```

As each device is represented by a different bit, the device values are combined by adding the values, and they don't overlap.

To test whether a particular device or combination of devices is supported, we can use a bitwise **AND** operation. A bitwise AND operation will compare the corresponding bits for two different binary values and will set that bit to 1 in a new binary value if both bit input values are 1. As an example, let's test whether phones are supported in the combined value we created earlier:

```
Supported Devices    = 0b 0 1 0 0 0 1 1
Phone                = 0b 0 0 0 0 0 0 1
AND Operation Result = 0b 0 0 0 0 0 0 1
```

The result only has a 1-bit value for the rightmost bit because this is the only bit that was set to 1 in both the `Supported Devices` value and the `Phone` value.

Once we have that result, we can directly compare it to the value for `Phone`, and if they are equal, then we know that the value of the supported devices included the `Phone` value:

```
AND Operation Result = 0b 0 0 0 0 0 0 1
Phone                = 0b 0 0 0 0 0 0 1
```

We now have a way to combine the possible options into one value, and a way to compare those values to see whether one is contained in another, using bitwise operations. The Swift standard library contains bitwise operators that allow us to perform these operations as easily as other mathematical operations, such as +, -, *, and /.

Typically, an operator will be in the following form:

```
<#left hand side value#> <#operator#> <#right hand side value#>
```

As it is when adding two numbers together:

```
2 + 3
```

In the preceding example, we have these:

- 2: This is the left-hand side value.
- +: This is the operator.
- 3: This is the right-hand side value.

The **bit shift operator** (<<) will take an integer value on the left-hand side and shift it by the number of bit positions to the right-hand side. Therefore, we can use this to express our intention better when declaring the device values:

```
let phone: Int       = 1 << 0 // 0b0000001
let tablet: Int      = 1 << 1 // 0b0000010
let watch: Int       = 1 << 2 // 0b0000100
let laptop: Int      = 1 << 3 // 0b0001000
let desktop: Int     = 1 << 4 // 0b0010000
let tv: Int          = 1 << 5 // 0b0100000
let brainImplant: Int = 1 << 6 // 0b1000000
```

The bitwise **AND** operator (&) will perform the same bit comparison that was previously described manually, and we can use this to create a function to determine whether a particular device exists within the value for the supported devices:

```
supportedDevices = phone + tablet + tv

func isSupported(device: Int) -> Bool {
    let bitWiseANDResult = supportedDevices & device
    let containsDevice = bitWiseANDResult == device
    return containsDevice
}

let phoneSupported = isSupported(device: phone)
print(phoneSupported) // true

let brainImplantSupported = isSupported(device: brainImplant)
print(brainImplantSupported) // false
```

The Swift standard library also provides operators for the following logical operations:

- **OR**: The OR operation, denoted by |, compares bits and sets the corresponding bit to 1 if either value has the bit set to 1. For our devices, this will mean creating a union between two device combinations:

```
let deviceThatSupportUIKit = phone + tablet + tv
let stationaryDevices = desktop + tv
let stationaryOrUIKitDevices = deviceThatSupportUIKit |
  stationaryDevices
let orIsUnion = stationaryOrUIKitDevices == (phone + tablet + tv +
  desktop)
print(orIsUnion) // true
```

- **XOR (exclusive or)**: The XOR operation, denoted by ^, will only set the bit to 1 if either value has the bit set to 1, but not if they both do:

```
let onlyStationaryOrUIKitDevices = deviceThatSupportUIKit ^
  stationaryDevices
let xorIsUnionMinusIntersection = onlyStationaryOrUIKitDevices == (phone +
  tablet + desktop)
print(xorIsUnionMinusIntersection) // true
```

We have seen some of the advanced operators available to us, provided by the Swift standard library.

See also

Further information about advanced operators can be found in Apple's documentation on the Swift language at `http://swiftbook.link/docs/advanced-operators`.

Defining option sets

The use of bitwise operations to hold multiple options in one value is a common pattern and is used throughout the **Cocoa Touch framework**, with one example being `UIDeviceOrientation`. In Swift, there is a protocol, `OptionSet`, that formalizes this pattern and provides additional convenience. In this recipe, we will explore how to define your own option sets.

How to do it...

Let's rewrite our example from the last recipe, which defined supported device values, to use an `OptionSet`:

```
struct Devices: OptionSet {
    let rawValue: Int
    static let phone      = Devices(rawValue: 1 << 0)
    static let tablet     = Devices(rawValue: 1 << 1)
    static let watch      = Devices(rawValue: 1 << 2)
    static let laptop     = Devices(rawValue: 1 << 3)
    static let desktop    = Devices(rawValue: 1 << 4)
    static let tv         = Devices(rawValue: 1 << 5)
    static let brainImplant = Devices(rawValue: 1 << 6)
    static let none: Devices = []
    static let all: Devices = [.phone,
                               .tablet,
                               .watch,
                               .laptop,
                               .desktop,
                               .tv,
                               .brainImplant]
    static let stationary: Devices = [.desktop, .tv]
    static let supportsUIKit: Devices = [.phone,
                                         .tablet,
                                         .tv]
}

let supportedDevices: Devices = [.phone,
                                 .tablet,
                                 .watch,
                                 .tv]
```

How it works...

The `OptionSet` protocol requires a `rawValue` property, and the convention is to define static constants for each of the options. Additionally, convenient combinations of options can also be defined as static constants, and `OptionSet` provides a convenience initializer, which allows an array of options to be provided, then the options are combined through bitwise addition and stored as one value.

The `OptionSet` protocol provides set-like manipulation and comparison methods that perform the same bitwise operations that we covered in the last recipe:

```
// Contains / AND and comparison
let phoneIsSupported = supportedDevices.contains(.phone)

// Union / OR
let stationaryOrUIKitDevices =
  Devices.supportsUIKit.union(Devices.stationary)

// Intersection / AND
let stationaryAndUIKitDevices =
  Devices.supportsUIKit.intersection(Devices.stationary)
```

Many of the set methods that we examined in `Chapter 2`, *Mastering the Building Blocks,* are also provided.

See also

Further information about the `OptionSet` protocol can be found in Apple's documentation on the Swift language at `http://swiftbook.link/docs/optionset`.

Creating custom operators

In an earlier recipe, we looked at some of the advanced operators that Swift offers on top of the common mathematical operators. In this recipe, we will look at how we can create our own operators, enabling very concisely expressive behaviors that feel like part of the language.

The custom operator we will create will be used to append the information in one value to the information in another value, producing a new value that contains the second value, followed by the first. The functionality we are looking to achieve is similar to the >> Unix command.

Getting ready

Let's understand how the Unix command, >>, works, and in this recipe, we will implement something similar in Swift using a custom operator.

Since macOS is Unix-based, we can provide Unix commands within **Terminal**. Open up the **Terminal** application on your Mac:

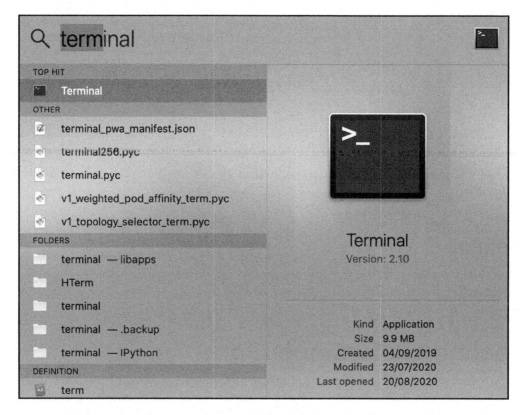

Figure 4.1 – Spotlight search

Type `cd ~/Desktop` and press *Enter to* move to the folder containing all the files and folders on your desktop. Type `touch Tasks.txt` and then press *Enter to* create a blank text file on your desktop, called `Tasks.txt`.

To add tasks to our tasks text file we can type the following command, followed by *Enter*:

```
echo "buy milk" >> Tasks.txt
```

If you open the text file on your desktop, you'll see that we have added **buy milk** on the first line.

Enter another task in the same way:

```
echo "mow the lawn" >> Tasks.txt
```

Reopen the `Tasks.txt` file, and you will see that **mow the lawn** has been added on the second line:

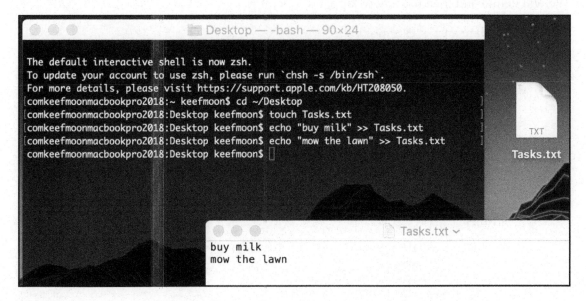

The default interactive shell is now zsh.
To update your account to use zsh, please run `chsh -s /bin/zsh`.
For more details, please visit https://support.apple.com/kb/HT208050.

Figure 4.2 – Task result

Add a few more tasks in the same way, and you'll see that each task is appended to the text file on the next line.

The command we issue in Terminal takes the following form:

```
<#What to append#> >> <#Where to append it#>
```

Let's create similar behavior in Swift; however, we can't use the same command string, >>, as this is already defined as bit shifting to the right, so let's make it >>>.

How to do it...

We will define and then use a new "append" operator >>>:

1. Declare an `infix operator`:

   ```
   infix operator >>>
   ```

2. Define the behavior for our operator when used with two strings:

   ```
   func >>> (lhs: String, rhs: String) -> String {
       var combined = rhs
       combined.append(lhs)
       return combined
   }
   ```

3. Define the behavior for our operator when appending a `String` to an array of strings:

   ```
   func >>> (lhs: String, rhs: [String]) -> [String] {
       var combined = rhs
       combined.append(lhs)
       return combined
   }
   ```

4. Define the behavior for our operator when appending an array of strings to another array of strings:

   ```
   func >>> (lhs: [String], rhs: [String]) -> [String] {
       var combined = rhs
       combined.append(contentsOf: lhs)
       return combined
   }
   ```

5. With these implementations in place, use our new operator to append things:

   ```
   let appendedString = "Two" >>> "One"
   print(appendedString) // OneTwo

   let appendedStringToArray = "three" >>> ["one", "two"]
   print(appendedStringToArray) // ["one", "two", "three"]

   let appendedArray = ["three", "four"] >>> ["one", "two"]
   print(appendedArray)  // ["one", "two", "three", "four"]
   ```

6. Refactor the preceding two operator implementations to use a generic element type for arrays:

```
func >>> <Element>(lhs: Element,
                     rhs: Array<Element>) -> Array<Element> {
    var combined = rhs
    combined.append(lhs)
    return combined
}

func >>> <Element>(lhs: Array<Element>,
                     rhs: Array<Element>) -> Array<Element> {
    var combined = rhs
    combined.append(contentsOf: lhs)
    return combined
}
```

7. Use the operator with arrays of any type:

```
let appendedIntToArray = 3 >>> [1, 2]
print(appendedIntToArray) // [1, 2, 3]

let appendedIntArray = [3, 4] >>> [1, 2]
print(appendedIntArray) // [1, 2, 3, 4]
```

We can implement our custom append operator for our own custom types too.

8. Create a `Task` and a `TaskList` to hold it:

```
struct Task {
    let name: String
}

class TaskList: CustomStringConvertible {
    private var tasks: [Task] = []
    func append(task: Task) {
        tasks.append(task)
    }
    var description: String {
        return tasks.map { $0.name }.joined(separator: "\n")
    }
}
```

9. Extend `TaskList` to add support for our new append operator:

```
extension TaskList {
    static func >>> (lhs: Task, rhs: TaskList) {
        rhs.append(task: lhs)
```

```
        }
    }
```

10. Append a `Task` to a `TaskList` using our custom operator:

```
let shoppingList = TaskList()
Task(name: "get milk") >>> shoppingList
print(shoppingList)
Task(name: "get teabags") >>> shoppingList
print(shoppingList)
```

How it works...

First, we declared an `infix operator`:

```
infix operator >>>
```

Operators can come in three types:

- `prefix` – Operates on one value and is placed before the value. An example is the NOT operator:

  ```
  let trueValue = !falseValue
  ```

- `postfix` – Operates on one value and is placed after the value. An example is the force unwrap operator:

  ```
  let unwrapped = optional!
  ```

- `infix` - Operates on two values and is placed between them. An example is the addition operator:

  ```
  let five = 2 + 3
  ```

Once we have defined the operator, we can write top-level functions that implement the behavior for each pair of types: one on the **left-hand side (LHS)** and one on the **right-hand side (RHS)**. Method parameter overloading allows us to specify the operator implementation for multiple-type pairings.

We can define how to append one string to another when our operator is used with strings:

```
func >>> (lhs: String, rhs: String) -> String {
    var combined = rhs
    combined.append(lhs)
    return combined
}
```

We can implement appending a `String` to an array of strings:

```
func >>> (lhs: String, rhs: [String]) -> [String] {
    var combined = rhs
    combined.append(lhs)
    return combined
}
```

We can also implement appending the elements in an array of strings to another array of strings:

```
func >>> (lhs: [String], rhs: [String]) -> [String] {
    var combined = rhs
    combined.append(contentsOf: lhs)
    return combined
}
```

This allows us to use the operator with strings and arrays of strings, as those are the implementations we defined:

```
let appendedString = "Two" >>> "One"
print(appendedString) // OneTwo

let appendedStringToArray = "three" >>> ["one", "two"]
print(appendedStringToArray) // ["one", "two", "three"]

let appendedArray = ["three", "four"] >>> ["one", "two"]
print(appendedArray)  // ["one", "two", "three", "four"]
```

We can implement our appending operator on every type of array that we think might be useful, but instead, we can implement it as a generic function and have it work for all arrays.

So, we can refactor the preceding two array implementations to use a generic element type:

```
func >>> <Element>(lhs: Element,
                   rhs: Array<Element>) -> Array<Element> {
    var combined = rhs
    combined.append(lhs)
    return combined
}

func >>> <Element>(lhs: Array<Element>,
                   rhs: Array<Element>) -> Array<Element> {
    var combined = rhs
    combined.append(contentsOf: lhs)
    return combined
}
```

This allows us to use arrays of ints without having to explicitly define them for int arrays:

```
let appendedIntToArray = 3 >>> [1, 2]
print(appendedIntToArray) // [1, 2, 3]

let appendedIntArray = [3, 4] >>> [1, 2]
print(appendedIntArray)  // [1, 2, 3, 4]
```

We can also implement it for our own custom types. Let's create `Task` and `TaskList`, which might benefit from using the operator:

```
struct Task {
    let name: String
}

class TaskList: CustomStringConvertible {
    private var tasks: [Task] = []
    func append(task: Task) {
        tasks.append(task)
    }
    var description: String {
        return tasks.map { $0.name }.joined(separator: "\n")
    }
}
```

We've added `CustomStringConvertible` conformance so that we can easily print out the result.

An alternative to implementing the use of an operator as a top-level function is to declare it within the relevant type as a static function. We'll declare it within an extension on our `TaskList` object, but we can just as easily declare it within the main `TaskList` class declaration:

```
extension TaskList {
  static func >>> (lhs: Task, rhs: TaskList) {
    rhs.append(task: lhs)
  }
}
```

Implementing this within a type has a few advantages: The implementation code is right next to the type itself, making it easier to find, and taking advantage of any values or types that might have a private, or otherwise restricted, access control, which will prevent them from being visible to a top-level function.

Now we can use our >>> operator to append a `Task` to a `TaskList`:

```
let shoppingList = TaskList()
Task(name: "get milk") >>> shoppingList
print(shoppingList)
Task(name: "get teabags") >>> shoppingList
print(shoppingList)
```

We have created a custom operator, to allow more concise and expressive code.

There's more...

Operators don't just work individually – they are often used within the same expression as other operators; the mathematical operators are a helpful example of this:

```
let result = 6 + 8 / 2 / 4
```

The order that each of these operations is performed in will affect the result. To understand the order in which the operations are performed, we can add brackets that will perform the same function:

```
let result = 6 + ((8 / 2) / 4)
```

In Swift, the decision about how to order the operations is made using two concepts – precedence and associativity:

- **Precedence**: This defines how important the operation type is. Therefore the operations with the highest precedence are performed first; for example, multiplication (*) has higher precedence than addition (+) and is therefore always performed first.
- **Associativity**: This defines which side, left or right, a value should associate itself with for evaluation when it has an operation with the same precedence on either side. This has the effect of defining the order that operations of the same precedence should be evaluated in: left to right or right to left.

Let's use this information to understand the operation ordering of the preceding mathematical operation. We have an expression comprising of one addition and two division operations. Division operations have higher precedence than addition operations; therefore, the division operations are evaluated first:

```
let result = 6 + (8 / 2 / 4)
```

We now have two division operations that need to be evaluated before the addition operation. Since both are division operators, they have the same precedence, so we have to look at associativity to know in which order to evaluate them. The division operation has an associativity of `left`, so they should be evaluated from left to right. Therefore, 8 / 2 is evaluated first and 4 / 4 is evaluated next. This gives us the following:

```
let result = 6 + ((8 / 2) / 4)
```

We need to define precedence and associativity for our custom operator, as the compiler does not currently know how it should be ordered within an expression containing multiple operations. Because of this, the following expression will not compile:

```
let multiOperationArray = [5,6] >>> [3,4] >>> [1,2] + [9,10] >>> [7,8]
print(multiOperationArray)
```

Precedence and associativity are defined within a precedence group, and an operator can either conform to an existing group or one that has been newly defined.

Let's define a new precedence group for our appending operator:

```
precedencegroup AppendingPrecedence {
    associativity: left
    higherThan: AdditionPrecedence
    lowerThan: MultiplicationPrecedence
}
```

Here, we give it the name `AppendingPrecedence` and define its values within curly brackets. We'll set its associativity to the left to match mathematical operations, and to establish precedence, we define that this precedence group is higher than another precedence group and lower than some other precedence groups. For the appending operator, we'll set the precedence to be higher than addition, so it will be evaluated before the addition operators but after the multiplication operators. Both the `AdditionPrecedence` and `MultiplicationPrecedence` groups are defined by the *standard library*.

Now that we have a precedence group defined, we can ensure that our custom operator conforms to it:

```
infix operator >>> : AppendingPrecedence
```

With precedence and associativity declared, the composite expression previously created will now compile:

```
let multiOperationArray = [5,6] >>> [3,4] >>> [1,2] + [9,10] >>> [7,8]
print(multiOperationArray) // [1,2,3,4,5,6,7,8,9,10]
```

We have defined how our custom operator works alongside other operators, allowing for complex combinations.

See also

Further information about custom operators can be found in Apple's documentation on the Swift language at `http://swiftbook.link/docs/custom-operators`.

Nesting types and namespacing

In Objective-C, all objects are at the **top level** and are given a global scope. They can be said to be in the same **namespace**. This is one reason for the convention among Objective-C developers, including Apple, of prefixing their class names with two- or three-letter identifiers.

These prefix characters allow similarly named classes from different frameworks to be differentiated, for example, *UIView* from *UIKit* and *SKView* from *SpriteKit*. Swift solves this problem by allowing types to be nested within other types, providing namespacing with nested types and modules.

Any type can be defined as being nested within another type. This allows us to tightly associate one type with another, in addition to providing namespacing, which helps differentiate types with the same name. In this recipe, we will create some nested types to see if it affects how they are referenced.

How to do it...

Let's build a system to monitor a physical device and the user interface that it displays. Both the device and the user interface have the concept of orientation, although each has a differing definition:

1. Define a class to represent the device:

```
class Device {
    enum Category {
        case watch
        case phone
        case tablet
    }
    enum Orientation {
        case portrait
        case portraitUpsideDown
        case landscapeLeft
        case landscapeRight
    }
    let category: Category
    var currentOrientation: Orientation = .portrait
    init(category: Category) {
        self.category = category
    }
}
```

Within this class, we have defined two enums, which only have value when used in relation to the Device class. Nesting the type also allows us to simplify the names of these types. It would be customary to name them DeviceCategory and DeviceOrientation to avoid confusion, but since they are nested, we can remove the Device prefix.

Any use of the nested types, within the type that contains them, can be used without any qualifiers; however, this is not the case for use outside of the containing type.

2. Access nested types from outside the containing type using dot syntax:

```
let phone = Device(category: .phone)
let desiredOrientation: Device.Orientation = .portrait
let phoneHasDesiredOrientation = phone.currentOrientation ==
    desiredOrientation
```

To reference a nested type, we must first specify the containing type, so the Orientation enum, within the Device class, becomes Device.Orientation.

3. Define a struct to represent a user interface:

```
struct UserInterface {
    struct Version {
        let major: Int
        let minor: Int
        let patch: Int
    }
    enum Orientation {
        case portrait
        case landscape
    }
    let version: Version
    var orientation: Orientation
}
```

Our `UserInterface` struct also includes a nested `Orientation` enum, but as these two enums lie in different namespaces, there is no naming conflict. As before, the nested types can be used without any qualifiers in the containing type.

Let's see how these two nested types can be used in conjunction with one another.

4. Create a function to convert from device orientation to user interface orientation:

```
func uiOrientation(for deviceOrientation: Device.Orientation) ->
  UserInterface.Orientation {
    switch deviceOrientation {
    case Device.Orientation.portrait,
      Device.Orientation.portraitUpsideDown:
        return UserInterface.Orientation.portrait
    case Device.Orientation.landscapeLeft,
      Device.Orientation.landscapeRight:
        return UserInterface.Orientation.landscape
    }
}
let phoneUIOrientation = uiOrientation(for:
  phone.currentOrientation)
print(phoneUIOrientation) // UserInterface.Orientation.portrait
```

How it works...

Our orientation conversion function specifies the full enum case for the `switch` statement and the `return` statements; for example:

```
Device.Orientation.portrait
UserInterface.Orientation.portrait
```

However, as we've seen previously when the compiler knows the type of the enum, only the case needs to be specified; the enum type can be removed. For our function, the input parameter type is `Device.Orientation` and the return type is `UserInterface.Orientation`, so the compiler does know enum types, and therefore we can remove the types:

```
func uiOrientation(for deviceOrientation: Device.Orientation) ->
UserInterface.Orientation {
    switch deviceOrientation {
    case .portrait, .portraitUpsideDown:
        return .portrait
    case .landscapeLeft, .landscapeRight:
        return .landscape
    }
}
```

Note that the `switch` case contains `.portrait` and returns `.portrait`, but these are cases from different enums, and the compiler knows the difference.

There's more...

We've seen how namespacing separates types nested within different containing types, but types within modules are also namespaced. This allows you to name your types without fear of collision with types in other modules.

Let's imagine that we are building an app for hospitals to keep track of their events and resources. As part of this, we create a class to represent surgical operations that we intend to track:

```
class Operation {
    let doctorsName: String
    let patientsName: String
    init(doctorsName: String, patientsName: String) {
        self.doctorsName = doctorsName
        self.patientsName = patientsName
    }
}
```

There is another class called `Operation`, provided by the **Foundation** framework, that can be used to execute and manage a long-running task. We can use both types of `Operation` side by side, because the `Foundation` framework is exposed as a module, and so the long-running `Operation` class can be used by referencing the `Foundation` module:

```
import Foundation

let medicalOperation = Operation(doctorsName: "Dr. Crusher",
                                 patientsName: "Commander Riker")
let longRunningOperation = Foundation.Operation()
```

We've seen how you can disambiguate two types with the same name, using the module they are within.

See also

Further information about nested types can be found in Apple's documentation on the Swift language at `http://swiftbook.link/docs/nested-types`.

5
Beyond the Standard Library

Apple's intention when open-sourcing Swift was to provide a cross-platform, general-purpose programming language that is ready to use. The Swift standard library provides core language features and common collection types. However, this does not provide everything needed to get up and running.

Therefore, Apple provides a framework called **Foundation** to help you perform common programming tasks that aren't covered by the core Swift language and the standard library.

The Foundation framework that you will use when developing for Apple platforms is *closed-sourced*, which means the underlying code is not accessible and only the API is visible. However, when Apple open-sourced Swift and made it available for Linux, it became necessary to provide the Foundation framework as well. To this end, Apple has released an open source, Swift-based version of Foundation as a core library, available here: `https://github.com/apple/swift-corelibs-foundation`.

In this chapter, we will cover the following recipes:

- Comparing dates with Foundation
- Fetching data with `URLSession`
- Working with JSON
- Working with XML

Technical requirements

All the code for this chapter can be found in this book's GitHub repository at `https://github.com/PacktPublishing/Swift-Cookbook-Second-Edition/tree/master/Chapter05`

Check out the following video to see the Code in Action: `https://bit.ly/3cIcNUK`

Comparing dates with Foundation

This recipe will focus on one area of Foundation that is very widely used, that is, date and time manipulation and formatting.

We will create a function that determines how long there is until Christmas and returns this information as a string that can be displayed to a user.

Getting ready

Create a new iOS playground and import the Foundation framework at the top of the playground:

```
import Foundation
```

How to do it...

Let's create a function that will return a string telling us how long there is until Christmas that we can then print:

1. Define the function:

```
func howLongUntilChristmas() -> String {

}
```

2. Within the function, get the current calendar and time zone:

```
let calendar = Calendar.current
let timeZone = TimeZone.current
```

3. Get the current date and time and use the calendar to get the current year:

```
let now = Date()
let yearOfNextChristmas = calendar.component(.year, from: now)
```

4. Define date components that correspond to midnight on Christmas Day:

```
var components = DateComponents(calendar: calendar,
                                timeZone: timeZone,
                                year: yearOfNextChristmas,
                                month: 12,
                                day: 25,
                                hour: 0,
```

```
                              minute: 0,
                              second: 0)
```

5. Get a `Date` object from those components:

   ```
   var christmas = components.date!
   ```

6. If we have already passed Christmas for this year, we need to adjust the component to refer to Christmas of the next year:

   ```
   // If we have already had Christmas this year,
   // then we need to use Christmas next year.
   if christmas < now {
     components.year = yearOfNextChristmas + 1
     christmas = components.date!
   }
   ```

7. Create `DateComponentsFormatter` to format how the time until Christmas is displayed:

   ```
   let componentFormatter = DateComponentsFormatter()
   componentFormatter.unitsStyle = .full
   componentFormatter.allowedUnits = [.month, .day, .hour, .minute,
       .second]
   ```

8. Use `DateComponentFormatter` to return a string for the time between now and next Christmas:

   ```
   return componentFormatter.string(from: now, to: christmas)!
   ```

9. Below the `howLongUntilChristmas` function, use this function to create a string, and print the outcome:

   ```
   let timeUntilChristmas = howLongUntilChristmas()
   print("Time until Christmas: \(timeUntilChristmas)")
   ```

How it works...

In *Step 1*, we create our `howLongUntilChristmas` function, then in *Step 2*, we get the currently set calendar and time zone as they will be needed for the date calculations to come:

```
let calendar = Calendar.current
let timeZone = TimeZone.current
```

While retrieving the current time zone is self-explanatory, it is not immediately obvious what the `Calendar` type represents and why we need to retrieve it.

How dates are represented is not as universally agreed as you might believe. Certain time components are mostly universal, such as the length of years and days, as they are connected to astronomical events, such as the time it takes for the Earth to perform one revolution of the Sun, and for the Earth to complete one rotation around its own axis, respectively. However, other time components, such as months and weeks and how the years are numbered, are rooted in the culture that created them.

 The calendar used throughout Europe and most of the world is known as the **Gregorian calendar**, introduced in 1582 by Pope Gregory XIII, replacing the Julian calendar. There are about 40 different calendars currently in use around the world, including Gregorian, Chinese, Hebrew, Islamic, Persian, Ethiopian, and Balinese Pawukon.

The way in which we present how long there is until Christmas will depend on the calendar that is relevant to the user. This is why we ask for the current calendar, which the user can change if they want a different representation.

Our next task is to get the current date and time:

```
let now = Date()
```

In *Step 3*, the default initializer for the `Date` value type uses the current date and time as its value. Note that this date value is set at the point of creation; it does not continually update with the current date and time.

In this step, we get a date and time for the next Christmas. We know the time, day, and month of Christmas, so to construct a date for Christmas, we just need to know the year. There is a method on `Calendar` called `component` that allows us to retrieve specific components from a `Date` value:

```
let yearOfNextChristmas = calendar.component(.year, from: now)
```

We now have the current year, within the user's current calendar; we can use it to create the Christmas date.

In *Step 4*, we create an instance of `DateComponents`, passing in the calendar, time zone, and the fact that we are defining December 25 at midnight, for the current year:

```
var components = DateComponents(calendar: calendar,
                                timeZone: timeZone,
                                year: yearOfNextChristmas,
                                month: 12,
```

```
            day: 25,
            hour: 0,
            minute: 0,
            second: 0)
```

In *Step 5*, we create a `Date` object from `DateComponents`. This is of an optional type as we may not have provided enough information to the components to generate a date; however, since we know that we have, we can force-unwrap this optional:

```
var christmas = components.date!
```

Next, we need to handle an edge case; what if we have already had Christmas this year? For example, let's imagine that the current date is December 27, 2020; we are trying to find the date of the next Christmas, but if we use the current year, we will get December 25, 2020, which is the Christmas just gone. So, in *Step 6*, we add 1 to the current year to get next Christmas, December 25, 2021:

```
if christmas < now {
    components.year = yearOfNextChristmas + 1
    christmas = components.date!
}
```

To account for this, we check whether the Christmas for this year is before `now`; if it is, we bump the year component to next year and recreate the Christmas date from `DateComponent`.

We now have the current `Date` and the next Christmas `Date`, and Foundation provides functionality to calculate the time difference between two dates and format it to display to a user, through the use of `DateComponentsFormatter`.

In *Step 7*, we create `DateComponentsFormatter`, and set `unitStyle` to `full`, which will provide a string using the full unit name, without abbreviation. We configure how we want the date and time divided for display, using `allowedUnits`:

```
let componentFormatter = DateComponentsFormatter()
componentFormatter.unitsStyle = .full
componentFormatter.allowedUnits = [.month, .day, .hour, .minute,
    .second]
```

In *Step 8*, we can retrieve a string from the formatter that describes the time between the two dates given, with the settings provided to the formatter. Since `DateComponentsFormatter` returns an optional string, we unwrap and return it:

```
return componentFormatter.string(from: now, to: christmas)!
```

Our `howLongUntilChristmas` method will provide a string describing how long until Christmas, which we can then print out.

See also

There is a lot more to discover in Foundation, so check out the documentation for further functionality:

- Swift 3 documentation for Foundation: `http://swiftbook.link/docs/foundation`
- Open source repository for Foundation: `https://github.com/apple/swift-corelibs-foundation`

Fetching data with URLSession

Every app worth building will need to send or receive information from the internet at some point and therefore, networking support is a critical part of any development platform. In Swift, this support for networking is provided by the Foundation framework.

When we need to retrieve information from the internet, we send out a request to a server on the internet, and that server sends a response that hopefully contains the information we requested.

In this recipe, we will learn how to send network requests and receive a response using the Foundation framework.

Getting ready

It is helpful to know of the different components that Foundation provides that deal with networking and what they do:

- `URL`: The address of a resource on a remote server. It contains information about the server and where the resource can be found on the server.
- `URLRequest`: Represents the request that will be made to the remote server. Defines the URL of the resource, how the request should be sent, metadata in the form of headers, and data that should be sent with it.

- `URLSession`: Manages the communication with remote servers, holds the configuration for that communication, and creates and optimizes the underlying connections.
- `URLSessionDataTask`: An object that manages the state of the request and delivers the response.
- `URLResponse`: Holds the metadata of the response from the remote server.

How to do it...

Let's use these networking tools to retrieve an image from a remote server:

1. Import `PlaygroundSupport` and set up indefinite execution for this playground:

```
import PlaygroundSupport

PlaygroundPage.current.needsIndefiniteExecution = true
```

2. Import Foundation and create an instance of `URLSession`:

```
import Foundation
let config = URLSessionConfiguration.default
let session = URLSession(configuration: config)
```

3. Next, we will construct a request for a remote image:

```
let urlString = "https://imgs.xkcd.com/comics/api.png"
let url = URL(string: urlString)!
let request = URLRequest(url: url)
```

4. Now that we have our `URLRequest`, we can create a data task to retrieve the image from the remote server:

```
let task = session.dataTask(with: request, completionHandler: {
    (data, response, error) in

})
```

5. We will take the image data and put it in a `UIImage` object to display it. So, we need to import the `UIKit` framework, which provides `UIImage`. So, let's import `UIKit` at the top of the playground:

```
import UIKit
```

6. Check for image data in the completion handler and create a `UIImage` object:

```
let task = session.dataTask(with: request) { (data, response,
error)
  in
    guard let imageData = data else {
        return // No Image, handle error
    }
    _ = UIImage(data: imageData)
}
```

7. Call `resume` on the task to start it:

```
task.resume()
```

How it works...

Let's walk through the previously mentioned steps to understand what we are doing:

```
import PlaygroundSupport

PlaygroundPage.current.needsIndefiniteExecution = true
```

Playgrounds execute the code they contain from top to bottom. When the end of the playground page is reached, the playground stops executing. In our example, the task is created and started, but then the playground reaches the end of the page before the image has been fully retrieved, because this happens asynchronously. If the playground were to stop execution here, the completion handler would never be executed, and we wouldn't see the image. This isn't a problem in a normal app that is continually running while it is in use; it is just specific to how Swift playgrounds work.

To solve this, we need to tell the playground that we don't want it to stop executing when it reaches the end of the page and instead, it should run indefinitely while we wait for the response to be received. This is done by importing the `PlaygroundSupport` framework in *Step 1* and setting `needsIndefiniteExecution` to be `true` on the current `PlaygroundPage`.

```
import Foundation
let config = URLSessionConfiguration.default
let session = URLSession(configuration: config)
```

In *Step 2*, when creating `URLSession`, we pass in a `URLSessionConfiguration` object, which allows configuring the time it takes for a request to time out and cache responses, among other things. For our purposes, we will just use the default configuration.

```
let urlString = "https://imgs.xkcd.com/comics/api.png"
let url = URL(string: urlString)!
let request = URLRequest(url: url)
```

In *Step 3*, we will be requesting the image from the excellent webcomic *XKCD* (http://xkcd.com). We can create the URL from a string, and then create a `URLRequest` request from the URL.

```
let task = session.dataTask(with: request, completionHandler: { (data,
   response, error) in


})
```

In *Step 4*, we do not create a data task directly; instead, we ask our `URLSession` instance to create the data task, and we pass in `URLRequest` and a completion handler. The completion handler will be fired once a response has been received from the remote server or some error has occurred.

The completion handler has three inputs, all optional:

- `data: Data`: The data returned in the body of the response; if our request was successful, this will contain our image data.
- `response: URLResponse`: The response metadata, including response headers. If the request was over HTTP/HTTPS, then this will be `HTTPURLResponse`, which will contain the HTTP status code.
- `error: Error`: If the request was unsuccessful, due to a network issue, for example, this value will have the error, and the data and response value will be `nil`. If the request was successful, this error value will be `nil`.

```
let task = session.dataTask(with: request) { (data, response, error) in
    guard let imageData = data else {
        return // No Image, handle error
    }
    _ = UIImage(data: imageData)
}
```

In *Step 6*, we check for response data and turn it into an image. To do this, we will need to construct a `UIImage` object from the data. `UIImage` is a class that represents an image on iOS and can be found in the `UIKit` framework. So, we also needed to import `UIKit` at the top of the playground, as we have done in *Step 5*.

Since we don't plan on doing anything with the image in this example, we are just going to view it in a playground preview; the compiler will complain if we assign it to a value that is never used. Therefore, we replace a normal value assignment with _, which allows the UIImage object to be generated without it being assigned to anything.

```
task.resume()
```

In *Step 7*, we have created the data task to retrieve the image, but we need to actually start the task to make the request. To do that, we call resume on the task.

When we run the playground, you will eventually see that the image value has been populated in the playground's right sidebar, and you can click on the preview icon to see the image that has been downloaded:

Figure 5.1 – Retrieved image displayed in the playground timeline

See also

- Further information about networking can be found in Apple's networking overview: http://swiftbook.link/docs/networking
- More information can also be found in Apple's URL Session programming guide: http://swiftbook.link/docs/urlsession-guide

Working with JSON

As discussed in the last recipe, almost every app will need to exchange information with the internet at some point, and in that recipe, we retrieved an image from a remote server. Very often, your app will need to retrieve more varied data, perhaps relating to the result of a search, or information about a shared state held on the server.

This information can be represented in any number of ways, but one of the most common ways is as **JavaScript Object Notation (JSON)**, which is a text-based structure for representing information. A JSON object contains key-value pairs, where the keys are strings and the values can be strings, numbers, Booleans, null, other objects, or arrays.

For example, information about a person could be expressed with this JSON object:

```
{
  "name": {
    "givenName": "Keith",
    "middleName": "David",
    "familyName": "Moon"
  },
  "age": 40,
  "heightInMetres": 1.778,
  "isBritish": true,
  "favouriteFootballTeam": null
}
```

The following is an example of an array of JSON objects:

```
[
  {
    "name": {
      "givenName": "Keith",
      "middleName": "David",
      "familyName": "Moon"
    },
    "age": 40,
    "heightInMetres": 1.778,
    "isBritish": true,
    "favouriteFootballTeam": null
  },
  {
    "name": {
      "givenName": "Alissa",
      "middleName": "May",
      "familyName": "Moon"
    },
    "age": 35,
```

```
      "heightInMetres": 1.765,
      "isBritish": false,
      "favouriteFootballTeam": null
   }
]
```

Foundation provides tools for reading information from and writing information as JSON data. In this recipe, we will interact with a JSON-based **Application Programming Interface (API)**, to both send and receive information.

Getting ready

Our goal is to interact with the GitHub API and create an issue for this book's repository. A full explanation of Git and GitHub is beyond the scope of this book; suffice to say that it's a service that stores versioned copies of your source code. Resources relevant to this book are stored in repositories on GitHub, and a GitHub user can create *issues* that serve as bug reports or feature requests.

If you don't already have one, then you will need to sign up for a GitHub account:

1. Go to `https://github.com`.
2. Fill in your details and press **Sign up for GitHub**.

Once you have created a GitHub account, you will need to create a personal access token, which we will use to authenticate some of the requests to the GitHub API. To create a personal access token, use the following steps:

1. Go to the settings page (`https://github.com/settings/tokens`) and click on **Generate new token**.
2. Give the token a name and check the box next to **repo**:

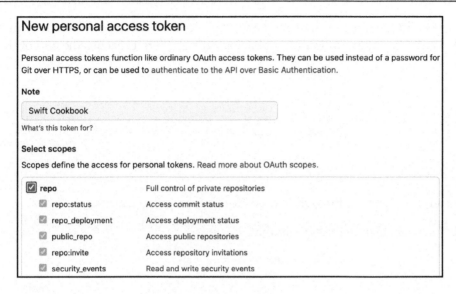

Figure 5.2 – Creating a personal access token

3. Click on **Generate token** at the bottom of the page. You will now see your newly generated personal access token.

4. Copy this token and paste it somewhere, as we will need it later:

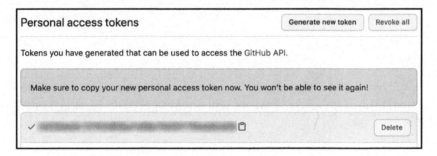

Figure 5.3 – The generated personal access token

How to do it...

To create our issue, we will first retrieve all of Packt Publishing's public repositories, and then find the relevant repository for this book. We will then create a new issue in this repository.

As in the preceding recipe, we will need a `URLSession` object to perform our requests, and we need to tell the playground not to finish executing when it reaches the end of the playground:

```
import Foundation
import PlaygroundSupport

PlaygroundPage.current.needsIndefiniteExecution = true

let config = URLSessionConfiguration.default
let session = URLSession(configuration: config)
```

Our first step is to fetch all the public repositories for a given user:

1. Let's create a function to do that:

```
func fetchRepos(forUsername username: String) {

    let urlString = "https://api.github.com/users/\(username)/repos"
    let url = URL(string: urlString)!
    var request = URLRequest(url: url)
    request.setValue("application/vnd.github.v3+json",
      forHTTPHeaderField: "Accept")

    let task = session.dataTask(with: request) { (data, response,
      error) in

    }
    task.resume()
}
```

You will note that after creating `URLRequest`, we set an HTTP header; this particular header ensures that we will always get back version 3 of the GitHub API.

We know from the GitHub API documentation (`https://developer.github.com/v3/`) that this response data is in JSON format. We need to parse the JSON data to turn it into something that we can use; enter `JSONSerialization`. `JSONSerialization` is part of the Foundation framework and provides class methods for turning Swift dictionaries and arrays into JSON data (known as **serialization**) and back again (known as **deserialization**).

2. Let's use `JSONSerialization` to turn our JSON response data into something more useful:

```swift
func fetchRepos(forUsername username: String) {

    let urlString = "https://api.github.com/users/\(username)/repos"
    let url = URL(string: urlString)!
    var request = URLRequest(url: url)
    request.setValue("application/vnd.github.v3+json",
        forHTTPHeaderField: "Accept")
    let task = session.dataTask(with: request) { (data, response,
        error) in

        // Once we have handled this response, the Playground
        // can finish executing.
        defer {
            PlaygroundPage.current.finishExecution()
        }

        // First unwrap the optional data
        guard let jsonData = data else {
            // If it is nil, there was probably a network error
            print(error ?? "Network Error")
            return
        }

        do {
            // Deserialisation can throw an error, so we have to `try`
            // catch errors
            let deserialised = try JSONSerialization.jsonObject(with:
                jsonData, options: [])
            print(deserialised)

        } catch {
            print(error)
        }
    }
    task.resume()
}
```

3. Now, let's fetch the public Packt repositories by executing our function and passing `PacktPublishing` in as the GitHub username:

```swift
fetchRepos(forUsername: "PacktPublishing")
```

Once executed, the print output should look like this:

```
(
    {
    "archive_url" = "https://api.github.com/repos/PacktPublishing/-.NET-Core-Microservices/{archive_format}{/ref}";
    archived = 0;
    "assignees_url" = "https://api.github.com/repos/PacktPublishing/-.NET-Core-Microservices/assignees{/user}";
    "blobs_url" = "https://api.github.com/repos/PacktPublishing/-.NET-Core-Microservices/git/blobs{/sha}";
    "branches_url" = "https://api.github.com/repos/PacktPublishing/-.NET-Core-Microservices/branches{/branch}";
    "clone_url" = "https://github.com/PacktPublishing/-.NET-Core-Microservices.git";
    "collaborators_url" = "https://api.github.com/repos/PacktPublishing/-.NET-Core-Microservices/collaborators{/collaborator}";
    "comments_url" = "https://api.github.com/repos/PacktPublishing/-.NET-Core-Microservices/comments{/number}";
    "commits_url" = "https://api.github.com/repos/PacktPublishing/-.NET-Core-Microservices/commits{/sha}";
    "compare_url" = "https://api.github.com/repos/PacktPublishing/-.NET-Core-Microservices/compare/{base}...{head}";
    "contents_url" = "https://api.github.com/repos/PacktPublishing/-.NET-Core-Microservices/contents/{+path}";
    "contributors_url" = "https://api.github.com/repos/PacktPublishing/-.NET-Core-Microservices/contributors";
    "created_at" = "2019-05-03T10:54:14Z";
    "default_branch" = master;
    "deployments_url" = "https://api.github.com/repos/PacktPublishing/-.NET-Core-Microservices/deployments";
    description = " .NET Core Microservices, published by [Packt]";
    disabled = 0;
    "downloads_url" = "https://api.github.com/repos/PacktPublishing/-.NET-Core-Microservices/downloads";
```

Figure 5.4 – Public GitHub repositories API response

`JSONSerializer` has turned our JSON data into familiar arrays and dictionaries that can be used to retrieve the information we need in the normal way. The JSON data is deserialized with the `Any` type, as the JSON can have a JSON object or an array at its root.

Since, from the preceding output, we know that the response has an array of JSON objects at its root, we need to turn the value from type `Any` to an array of dictionaries of the `[String: Any]` type. This is referred to as **casting** from one type to another, which we can do by using the `as` keyword and then specifying the new type. This keyword can be used in three different ways:

- `as` will perform a trivial cast. This is possible if the existing type is synonymous with the intended type, for instance, casting from a subclass to a superclass.
- `as?` will conditionally perform a cast, returning an optional value. If it is not possible to represent the value as the intended type, the value will be `nil`.
- `as!` will perform a forced cast. If it is not possible to represent the value as the intended type, you will get a crash.

So, let's cast the deserialized data to an array of dictionaries with string keys, with the `[[String: Any]]` type:

```
func fetchRepos(forUsername username: String) {
    //...
    let task = session.dataTask(with: request) { (data, response, error)
    in
        //...
        do {
            // Deserialisation can throw an error, so we have to `try` and
```

```
        // catch errors
      let deserialised = try JSONSerialization.jsonObject(with:
        jsonData, options: [])
      print(deserialised)
      // As `deserialised` has type `Any` we need to cast
      guard let repos = deserialised as? [[String: Any]] else {
        print("Unexpected Response")
        return
      }
      print(repos)
    } catch {
      print(error)
    }
  }
}
```

Now, we have an array of dictionaries for the repositories in the API response, which we need to provide as input for this function. A common pattern for providing results for asynchronous work is to provide a completion handler as a parameter. A completion handler is a closure that can be executed once the asynchronous work is completed.

Since the output we want to provide is the array of repository dictionaries, we will define this as an input for the closure if the request was successful, and an error if it wasn't:

```
func fetchRepos(forUsername username: String, completionHandler:
  @escaping ([[String: Any]]?, Error?) -> Void) {

  let urlString = "https://api.github.com/users/\(username)/repos"
  let url = URL(string: urlString)!
  var request = URLRequest(url: url)
  request.setValue("application/vnd.github.v3+json",
    forHTTPHeaderField: "Accept")
  let task = session.dataTask(with: request) { (data, response, error)
    in

    // Once we have handled this response, the Playground
    // can finish executing.
    defer {
      PlaygroundPage.current.finishExecution()
    }

    // First unwrap the optional data
    guard let jsonData = data else {
      // If it is nil, there was probably a network error
      completionHandler(nil, ResponseError.requestUnsuccessful)
      return
    }
```

```
do {
  // Deserialisation can throw an error, so we have to `try` and
  // catch errors
  let deserialised = try JSONSerialization.jsonObject(with:
    jsonData, options: [])
  // As `deserialised` has type `Any` we need to cast
  guard let repos = deserialised as? [[String: Any]] else {
    completionHandler(nil,
      ResponseError.unexpectedResponseStructure)
    return
  }

  completionHandler(repos, nil)

} catch {
  completionHandler(nil, error)
}
}
task.resume()
}
```

Now, whenever an error is generated, we execute `completionHandler`, passing in the error and `nil` for the results value. Also, when we have the repository results, we execute the completion handler, passing in the parsed JSON and `nil` for the error.

We passed in a few new errors in the preceding code, so let's define those errors:

```
enum ResponseError: Error {
  case requestUnsuccessful
  case unexpectedResponseStructure
}
```

This changes how we call this `fetchRepos` function:

```
fetchRepos(forUsername: "PacktPublishing") { (repos, error) in

  if let repos = repos {
    print(repos)
  } else if let error = error {
    print(error)
  }
}
```

Now that we have retrieved the details of the public repositories, we will submit an issue to the repository for this chapter. This issue can be any feedback you would like to give about this book; it can be a review, a suggestion for new content, or you can tell me about a Swift project you are currently working on.

This request to the GitHub API will be authenticated against your user account and therefore, we will need to include details of the personal access token that we created at the beginning of this recipe. There are a number of ways to authenticate requests to the GitHub API, but the simplest is basic authentication, which involves adding an authorization string to the request header.

Let's create a method to format the personal access token correctly for authentication:

```
func authHeaderValue(for token: String) -> String {
    let authorisationValue = Data("\(token):x-oauth-
    basic".utf8).base64EncodedString()
    return "Basic \(authorisationValue)"
}
```

Next, let's create our function to submit our issue. From the API documentation at `https://developer.github.com/v3/issues/#create-an-issue`, we can see that unless you have push access, you can only create an issue with the following components:

- `title` (required)
- `body` (optional)

So, our function will take this information as input, along with the repository name and username:

```
func createIssue(inRepo repo: String,
                 forUser user: String,
                 title: String,
                 body: String?) {

}
```

Creating an issue is achieved by sending a `POST` request, and information about the issue is provided as JSON data in the request body. To create our request, we can use `JSONSerialization`, but we will take our intended JSON structure and serialize it into `Data` this time:

```
func createIssue(inRepo repo: String,
                 forUser user: String,
                 title: String,
                 body: String?) {
    // Create the URL and Request
    let urlString = "https://api.github.com/repos/\(user)/\
    (repo)/issues"
    let url = URL(string: urlString)!
    var request = URLRequest(url: url)
    request.httpMethod = "POST"
```

```
        request.setValue("application/vnd.github.v3+json",
                        forHTTPHeaderField: "Accept")
        let authorisationValue = authHeaderValue(for: <#your personal
          access token>)
        request.setValue(authorisationValue, forHTTPHeaderField:
          "Authorization")
        // Put the issue information into the JSON structure required
        var json = ["title": title]
        if let body = body {
            json["body"] = body
        }
        // Serialise the json into Data. We can use try! as we know it is
         // valid JSON.
        // Just be aware that the this will fail if provided value can't be
         //  converted into valid JSON.
        let jsonData = try! JSONSerialization.data(withJSONObject: json,
          options: .prettyPrinted)
        request.httpBody = jsonData
        session.dataTask(with: request) { (data, response, error) in
            // TO FINISH
        }
    }
```

As with the previous API request, we need a way to provide the result of creating the issue, so let's provide a completion handler, try to deserialize the response, and provide it to the completion handler:

```
func createIssue(inRepo repo: String,
                 forUser user: String,
                 title: String,
                 body: String?,
                 completionHandler: @escaping ([String: Any]?, Error?)
                    -> Void) {
    //...
    session.dataTask(with: request) { (data, response, error) in
        guard let jsonData = data else {
            completionHandler(nil, ResponseError.requestUnsuccessful)
            return
        }
        do {
            // Deserialisation can throw an error, so we have to `try`
            // and catch errors
            let deserialised = try JSONSerialization.jsonObject(with:
              jsonData, options: [])
            // As `deserialised` has type `Any` we need to cast it
            guard let createdIssue = deserialised as? [String: Any]
              else {
                completionHandler(nil,
```

```
                    ResponseError.unexpectedResponseStructure)
                return
            }
            completionHandler(createdIssue, nil)
        } catch {
            completionHandler(nil, error)
        }
    }
}
```

The API response to a successfully created issue provides a JSON representation of that issue. Our function will return this representation if it was successful, or an error if it was not.

Now that we have a function to create issues in a repository, it's time to use it to create an issue:

```
createIssue(inRepo: "Swift-5-Cookbook-Second-Edition",
        forUser: "PacktPublishing",
        title: <#The title of your feedback#>,
        body: <#Extra detail#>) { (issue, error) in
            if let issue = issue {
                print(issue)
            } else if let error = error {
                print(error)
            }
}
```

I will check these created issues, so please provide genuine feedback on this book. How have you found the content? Too detailed? Not detailed enough? Anything I've missed or not fully explained? Any questions that you have? This is your opportunity to let me know.

There's more...

When we created our completion handlers, we gave them two inputs: the successful result (either the repository information or the created issue) or an error if there is a failure. Both these values are optional; one will be `nil`, and the other has a value. However, this convention is not enforced by the language, and a user of this function will have to consider the possibility that it may not be the case. What should the user of this function do if the `fetchRepos` function fires the completion handler with non-`nil` values for both the repository and the error? What if both are `nil`?

The user of this function, without viewing the function's internal code, can't be sure that this won't happen, which means they may need to write functionality and tests to account for this possibility, even though it may never happen.

It would be better if we could more accurately represent the intended behavior of our function, providing the user with a clear indication of the possible outcomes and leaving no room for ambiguity. We know that there are two possible outcomes from calling the function: it will either succeed and return the relevant value, or it will fail and return an error to indicate the reason for the failure.

Instead of optional values, we can use an enum to represent these possibilities, and the Foundation framework provides a generic enum for this purpose, called Result.

The Result enum has a success case, which has an associated type for a successful result, and a failure case with an associated type for the relevant error. Both associated types are defined as generic constraints, with the failure type needing to conform to the Error protocol.

We can now define the success and failure states and use associated values to hold the value that is relevant for each state, which is the repository information for the success state and the error for the failure state.

Now, let's amend our fetchRepos function to provide a Result enum in completionHandler:

```
func fetchRepos(forUsername username: String,
    completionHandler: @escaping (Result<[[String: Any]], Error?) -
      -> Void) {

    //...
    let task = session.dataTask(with: request) { (data, response,
      error) in

        //...

        // First unwrap the optional data
        guard let jsonData = data else {
            // If it is nil, there was probably a network error
            completionHandler(.failure(ResponseError.
              requestUnsuccessful))
            return
        }

        do {
            // Deserialisation can throw an error,
```

```
                    // so we have to `try` and catch errors
                    let deserialised = try JSONSerialization.jsonObject(with:
                      jsonData, options: [] )
                    // As `deserialised` has type `Any` we need to cast
                    guard let repos = deserialised as? [[String: Any]] else {
                        let error = ResponseError.unexpectedResponseStructure
                        completionHandler(.failure(error))
                        return
                    }
                    completionHandler(.success(repos))
                } catch {
                    completionHandler(.failure(error))
                }
            }
        task.resume()
    }
```

We need to update how we call the `fetchRepos` function:

```
fetchRepos(forUsername: "PacktPublishing", completionHandler:{ result
  in
    switch result {
        case .success(let repos):
            print(repos)

        case .failure(let error):
            print(error)
    }
})
```

We now use a `switch` statement instead of `if/else`, and we get the added benefit that the compiler will ensure that we have covered all possible outcomes.

Having made this improvement to the `fetchRepos` function, we can similarly improve the `createIssue` function:

```
func createIssue(inRepo repo: String,
                 forUser user: String,
                 title: String,
                 body: String?,
                 completionHandler: @escaping (Result<[[String:
                   Any]], Error?) -> Void) {
    //...
    let task = session.dataTask(with: request) { (data, response,
      error) in

        guard let jsonData = data else {
            completionHandler(.failure(ResponseError.
```

```
            requestUnsuccessful))
        return
    }

    do {
        // Deserialisation can throw an error,
        // so we have to `try` and catch errors
        let deserialised = try JSONSerialization.jsonObject(with:
          jsonData, options: [])

        // As `deserialised` has type `Any` we need to cast
        guard let createdIssue = deserialised as? [String: Any]
          else {
            let error = ResponseError.unexpectedResponseStructure
            completionHandler(.failure(error))
            return
        }

        completionHandler(.success(createdIssue))

    } catch {
        completionHandler(.failure(error))
    }
}
    task.resume()
}
```

Lastly, we need to update the contents of the completion handler that we provide to the createIssue function:

```
createIssue(inRepo: "Swift-5-Cookbook-Second-Edition",
        forUser: "PacktPublishing",
        title: <#The title of your feedback#>,
        body: <#Extra detail#>) { result in

    switch result {
        case .success(let issue):
            print(issue)

        case .failure(let error):
            print(error)
    }
}
```

Working with JSON data and extracting relevant information from it can be frustrating. Consider the JSON response for our `fetchRepos` function:

```
[
    {
        "id": 68144965,
        "name": "JSONNode",
        "full_name": "keefmoon/JSONNode",
        "owner": {
            "login": "keefmoon",
            "id": 271298,
            "avatar_url":
              "https://avatars.githubusercontent.com/u/271298?v=3",
            "gravatar_id": "",
            "url": "https://api.github.com/users/keefmoon",
            "html_url": "https://github.com/keefmoon",
            "followers_url":
              "https://api.github.com/users/keefmoon/followers",
            //... Some more URLs
            "received_events_url":
            "https://api.github.com/users/keefmoon/received_events",
            "type": "User",
            "site_admin": false
        },
        "private": false,
        //... more values
    }
    //... more repositories
]
```

If we want to get the username for the owner of the first repository, we need to deserialize the JSON and then conditionally unwrap multiple nested layers to get the username string:

```
let jsonData = //... returned from the network

guard
    let deserialised = try? JSONSerialization.jsonObject(with:
      jsonData, options: []),
    let repoArray = deserialised as? [[String: Any]],
    let firstRepo = repoArray.first,
    let ownerDictionary = firstRepo["owner"] as? [String: Any],
    let username = ownerDictionary["login"] as? String
    else {
        return
}
print(username)
```

That's a lot of optional unwrapping and casting just to get one value! Swift's strongly typed nature doesn't work well with JSON's loosely defined schema, which is why you have to do a lot of work to turn loosely typed information into strongly typed values.

To help with these problems, a number of open source frameworks are available, which make working with JSON in Swift easier. `SwiftyJSON` is a popular framework that can be found on GitHub at `https://github.com/SwiftyJSON/SwiftyJSON`.

I have also built a lightweight JSON helper called `JSONNode`, which can also be found on GitHub at `https://github.com/keefmoon/JSONnode`.

With `JSONNode`, you can perform the same task of retrieving the owner's username for the first repository with the following code:

```
let jsonData = //... returned from the network
guard
    let jsonNode = try? JSONNode(data: jsonData),
    let username = jsonNode[0]["owner"]["username"].string
    else {
        return
}

print(username)
```

Information within JSON, of any depth, can be retrieved in one line using subscripts.

Working with XML

XML stands for **eXtensible Markup Language** and is a popular way of representing data for storage and transfer across a network. XML is a very flexible format and is used to represent many types of data. The current specification of HTML, which powers most of the web, is an implementation of XML.

The version of XML that we will concern ourselves with in this recipe is **RSS**, which stands for **Really Simple Syndication**. RSS is used to define a collection of time-ordered pieces of digestible content; these RSS feeds can then be used to aggregate content from a number of different sources. RSS is typically used as a distribution mechanism for news articles and podcasts.

In this recipe, we will learn how to read and write XML data by fetching and parsing the BBC News RSS feed.

Getting ready

The functionality to deal with XML data is provided by the Foundation framework. However, while the classes that help with reading XML data are available on all of Apple's platforms, the classes that assist with writing XML data are only available on the macOS platform.

This is an unfortunate oversight and means that if you need to write XML data within an iOS app, you will likely need to look for a third-party helper or build your own. We will investigate third-party helpers at the end of this recipe.

To investigate both reading and writing XML using the Foundation framework, we need to create a new macOS-based playground instead of an iOS-based playground, which we have been using so far in this book.

Create a new Swift playground as usual, but choose a **Blank** template from the **macOS** tab:

Figure 5.5 – Choosing a template

The RSS feed that we will retrieve and parse is from the front page of the BBC News website, which is `http://feeds.bbci.co.uk/news/rss.xml`.

Our first step is to retrieve the data at this URL so that we can start making sense of it. Since we previously covered retrieving information over the network, I'll add the code without further comment; check out the *Fetching data with URLSession* recipe in this chapter for more information:

```
import Foundation
import PlaygroundSupport

PlaygroundPage.current.needsIndefiniteExecution = true

func fetchBBCNewsRSSFeed() {

    let session = URLSession.shared
    let url = URL(string: "http://feeds.bbci.co.uk/news/rss.xml")!
    let dataTask = session.dataTask(with: url) { (data, response,
      error) in

        guard let data = data, error == nil else {
            print(error ?? "Unexpected response")
            return
        }

        let dataAsString = String(data: data, encoding: .utf8)!
        print(dataAsString)
    }
    dataTask.resume()
}

fetchBBCNewsRSSFeed()
```

When you run the playground, you will get an output that looks like the following:

```
<?xml version="1.0" encoding="UTF-8"?>
<?xml-stylesheet title="XSL_formatting" type="text/xsl"
href="/shared/bsp/xsl/rss/nolsol.xsl"?>
<rss xmlns:dc="http://purl.org/dc/elements/1.1/"
xmlns:content="http://purl.org/rss/1.0/modules/content/"
xmlns:atom="http://www.w3.org/2005/Atom" version="2.0"
xmlns:media="http://search.yahoo.com/mrss/">
  <channel>
    <title><![CDATA[BBC News - Home]]></title>;
    <description><![CDATA[BBC News - Home]]></description>
    <link>https://www.bbc.co.uk/news/</link>
    <image>
 <url>https://news.bbcimg.co.uk/nol/shared/img/bbc_news_120x60.gif</url>
 <title>BBC News - Home</title>
 <link>https://www.bbc.co.uk/news/</link>
  </image>
```

```
    <generator>RSS for Node</generator>
    <lastBuildDate>Sat, 15 Aug 2020 00:41:41 GMT</lastBuildDate>
  <copyright><![CDATA[Copyright: (C) British Broadcasting
      Corporation, see http://news.bbc.co.uk/2/hi/help/rss/4498287.stm
        for terms and conditions of reuse.]]></copyright>
    <language><![CDATA[en-gb]]></language>
    <ttl>15</ttl>
    <item>
      <title><![CDATA[Coronavirus: Thousands return to UK to beat
        France quarantine]]></title>
      <description><![CDATA[Holidaymakers have just hours to return to
        the UK to avoid the 14-day self-isolation requirement.]]>
    </description>
      <link>https://www.bbc.co.uk/news/uk-53782019</link>
      <guid isPermaLink="true">https://www.bbc.co.uk/news/uk-
        53782019</guid>
      <pubDate>Fri, 14 Aug 2020 21:21:54 GMT</pubDate>
    </item>
    //... More items
  </channel>
</rss>
```

How to do it...

The overall structure should be familiar to anyone who has seen HTML. Apart from the first two lines, which define the version and formatting of the XML, the information is structured with opening and closing tags. Consider the following example:

```
<link>https://www.bbc.co.uk/news/uk-53782019</link>
```

The name of the opening tag defines the content of this element of XML; in this case, it is a link. Then follows the content of the element, and the end of the content is defined by a closing tag that has a / character before its name.

In addition to this simple example, an XML element can have attributes that describe extra information about the content of the element:

```
<guid isPermaLink="true">https://www.bbc.co.uk/news/uk-53782019</guid>
```

These are defined as key-value pairs within the opening tag.

The content of the XML element may be a string, as in the preceding examples, or it can be nested child XML elements:

```
<image>
    <url>http://news.bbcimg.co.uk/nol/shared/img/bbc_news_120x60.gif</url>
    <title>BBC News - Home</title>
    <link>http://www.bbc.co.uk/news/</link>
</image>
```

Lastly, the content of an XML element can be data. This data might be represented as a string, especially if the string is likely to be longer, and may include line breaks, special characters, and other components that may be confused for being part of the enclosing XML formatting:

```
<title><![CDATA[Coronavirus: Thousands return to UK to beat France
    quarantine]]></title>
```

Now that we have retrieved the XML, we want to parse it into something useful. The parser we will be using is provided by the Foundation framework and is available on iOS and macOS. It is called `XMLParser`. `XMLParser` is a **SAX** parser, which stands for **Simple API for XML**. The features of a SAX parser are as follows:

- Event-driven
- Low memory overhead
- Only retains relevant information
- One pass

The parser takes a delegate object that it will deliver event information to as it parses the document. It is the delegate object's responsibility to take and retain the relevant information from these delegate callbacks as the XML data is parsed, as the parser will not retain the parsed data.

We will step through a simple example to see how the parser reports events to the delegate. Here's the simple XML that we intend to parse:

```
<xml version="1.0" encoding="UTF-8"?>
<quotes>
    <quote attribution="Homer Simpson">
        Press any key to continue, where's the any key?
    <;/quote>
    <quote attribution="Unknown">
        Why do nerds confuse Halloween and Christmas? Because
            OCT31=DEC25
```

```
    </quote>
</quotes>
```

The parser will start parsing the XML, character by character, and as an event is triggered, the delegate will be informed:

1. The first event will be the start of the document, where the parser will call this:

   ```
   func parserDidStartDocument(_ parser: XMLParser)
   ```

   Here, we can do any setup or resetting of the state that is required.

2. Then, the parser will move through the document until it reaches this point:

   ```
   <?xml version="1.0" encoding="UTF-8"?>
   <quotes>
   ** Parser is here **
       <quote attribution="Homer Simpson">
           Press any key to continue, where's the any key?
       </quote>
       <quote attribution="Unknown">
           Why do nerds confuse Halloween and Christmas? Because
               OCT31=DEC25
       </quote>
   </quotes>
   ```

3. The parser has finished parsing the opening tag for the first element and so it fires the delegate callback:

   ```
   func parser(_ parser: XMLParser,
               didStartElement elementName: String,
               namespaceURI: String?,
               qualifiedName qName: String?,
               attributes attributeDict: [String : String] = [:]) {
       /*
       elementName = quotes
       namespaceURI = nil
       qName = nil
       attributeDict = [:]
       */

   }
   ```

4. The parser then continues until it reaches this point:

   ```
   <?xml version="1.0" encoding="UTF-8">
   <quotes>
       <quote attribution="Homer Simpson">
   ** Parser is here **
   ```

```
            Press any key to continue, where's the any key?
        </quote>
        <quote attribution="Unknown">
            Why do nerds confuse Halloween and Christmas? Because
                OCT31=DEC25
        </quote>
    </quotes>
```

5. Since the parser has seen another starting tag, it fires the same delegate callback with information about this new element:

```
func parser(_ parser: XMLParser,
            didStartElement elementName: String,
            namespaceURI: String?,
            qualifiedName qName: String?,
            attributes attributeDict: [String : String] = [:]) {
    /*
    elementName = quote
    namespaceURI = nil
    qName = nil
    attributeDict = ["attribution": "Homer Simpson"]
    */

}
```

This time, as the element has attribute information, it is provided by the delegate callback in the attributeDict dictionary.

6. The parser now moves through the content of the first quote element. At some point, it fires the delegate callback with the content it has collected up to that point:

```
<?xml version="1.0" encoding="UTF-8"?>
<quotes>
    <quote attribution="Homer Simpson">
        Press any key to continue, ** Parser is here **where's the
            any key?
    </quote>
    <quote attribution="Unknown>
        Why do nerds confuse Halloween and Christmas? Because
            OCT31=DEC25
    </quote>
</quotes>
```

It then provides this content collected so far to the delegate:

```
func parser(_ parser: XMLParser, foundCharacters string: String) {
    /*
    string = "Press any key to continue, "
    */
}
```

The reason the parser stops halfway through the content to fire the delegate callback is to make the most efficient use of memory. All the data that the parser processes must be kept in memory by the parser until it can be delivered to the delegate. Therefore, if the parser determines that memory usage is getting high, it will take the content it has collected so far and deliver it to the delegate. Once it has done this, it can free up the memory and start collecting further content afresh.

In this simple example, it is very unlikely that the parser will not provide all the content of the element in one delegate callback. It is, however, useful to see an example of this, as we have to account for the possibility, and it will affect how we implement the delegate later.

7. The parser will fire the same `foundCharacters` delegate callback until all of the content of an element has been delivered to the delegate:

    ```
    <?xml version="1.0" encoding="UTF-8"?>
    <quotes>
        <quote attribution="Homer Simpson">
            Press any key to continue, where's the any key?
                ** Parser is here **
        </quote>
        <quote attribution="Unknown">
            Why do nerds confuse Halloween and Christmas? Because
                OCT31=DEC25
        </quote>
    </quotes>
    ```

8. It then provides the new content since the last call to the delegate:

    ```
    func parser(_ parser: XMLParser, foundCharacters string: String) {
        /*
        string = "where's the any key?"
        */
    }
    ```

9. The parser now processes the closing tag for the first `quote` element:

```
<?xml version="1.0" encoding="UTF-8"?>
<quotes>
    <quote attribution="Homer Simpson">
        Press any key to continue, where's the any key?
    </quote>
** Parser is here **
    <quote attribution="Unknown">
        Why do nerds confuse Halloween and Christmas? Because
            OCT31=DEC25
    </quote>
</quotes>
```

10. Then, it fires the delegate callback, signaling the end of the element:

```
func parser(_ parser: XMLParser,
 didEndElement elementName: String,
 namespaceURI: String?,
 qualifiedName qName: String?) {
 /*
 elementName = "quote"
 namespaceURI = nil
 qName = nil
 */
 }
```

The parser will then continue to process the next `quote` element in the same way, firing the same sequence of `didStartElement`, followed by a number of `foundCharacters` callbacks, and finishing with a call to `didEndElement`.

11. Having finished processing the last `quote` element, the parser will process the closing tag of the `quotes` element:

```
<?xml version="1.0" encoding="UTF-8"?>
<quotes>
    <quote attribution="Homer Simpson">
        Press any key to continue, where's the any key?
    </quote>
    <quote attribution="Unknown">
        Why do nerds confuse Halloween and Christmas? Because
            OCT31=DEC25
    </quote>
</quotes>
** Parser is here **
```

It will fire another `didEndElement` callback for the `quotes` element:

```
func parser(_ parser: XMLParser,
            didEndElement elementName: String,
            namespaceURI: String?,
            qualifiedName qName: String?) {
    /*
    elementName = "quotes"
    namespaceURI = nil
    qName = nil
    */
}
```

12. Finally, the parser will fire a delegate callback to indicate that the parsing of the document is complete:

```
func parserDidEndDocument(_ parser: XMLParser) {

}
```

Now that you understand how the parser passes information to the delegate, we can return to our RSS example.

How it works...

You will remember that we retrieved XML data that looks like this:

```
<?xml version="1.0" encoding="UTF-8"?>
<?xml-stylesheet title="XSL_formatting" type="text/xsl"
href="/shared/bsp/xsl/rss/nolsol.xsl"?>
<rss xmlns:dc="http://purl.org/dc/elements/1.1/"
xmlns:content="http://purl.org/rss/1.0/modules/content/"
xmlns:atom="http://www.w3.org/2005/Atom" version="2.0"
xmlns:media="http://search.yahoo.com/mrss/">
    <channel>
        <title><![CDATA[BBC News - Home]]></title>
        <description><![CDATA[BBC News - Home]]></description>
        <link>https://www.bbc.co.uk/news/</link>
        <image>
            <url>https://news.bbcimg.co.uk/nol/shared/img/
                bbc_news_120x60.gif</url>
            <title>BBC News - Home</title>
            <link>https://www.bbc.co.uk/news/</link>
        </image>
        <generator>RSS for Node</generator>
        <lastBuildDate>Sat, 15 Aug 2020 00:41:41 GMT</lastBuildDate>
```

```
        <copyright><![CDATA[Copyright: (C) British Broadcasting
          Corporation, see http://news.bbc.co.uk/2/hi/help/rss/
            4498287.stm for terms and conditions of reuse.]]>
              </copyright>
        <language><![CDATA[en-gb]]></language>
        <ttl>15</ttl>
        <item>
            <title><![CDATA[Coronavirus: Thousands return to UK to beat
                France quarantine]]></title>
            <description><![CDATA[Holidaymakers have just hours to
                  return to the UK to avoid the 14-day self-isolation
                    requirement.]]></description>
            <link>https://www.bbc.co.uk/news/uk-53782019</link>
            <guid isPermaLink="true">https://www.bbc.co.uk/news/uk-
                53782019</guid>
            <pubDate>Fri, 14 Aug 2020 21:21:54 GMT</pubDate>
        </item>
        //... More items
    </channel>
</rss>
```

From this, we want to extract the news articles in a usable form, so let's define a `NewsArticle` model containing some useful information and place it near the top of the playground:

```
struct NewsArticle {
    let title: String
    let url: URL
}
```

Since the information we require will be spread over multiple delegate callbacks, our delegate will need to keep track of the information it has received, so it can be pieced together at the appropriate time.

Let's create a class object to be the delegate for the parser and have it conform to `XMLParserDelegate`:

```
class RSSNewsArticleBuilder: NSObject, XMLParserDelegate {

}
```

In the preceding XML, each news article is contained in an `item` element, so our delegate will need to keep track of when the parser is delivering content for the `item` element so that it can ignore content from other elements:

```
class RSSNewsArticleBuilder: NSObject, XMLParserDelegate {

    var inItem = false

    func parser(_ parser: XMLParser,
                didStartElement elementName: String,
                namespaceURI: String?,
                qualifiedName qName: String?,
                attributes attributeDict: [String : String] = [:]) {

        switch elementName {

        case "item":
            inItem = true

        default:
            break

        }
    }

    func parser(_ parser: XMLParser,
                didEndElement elementName: String,
                namespaceURI: String?,
                qualifiedName qName: String?) {

        switch elementName {

        case "item":
            inItem = false

        default:
            break
        }
    }
}
```

The two parts we want to extract from the `item` element to create our `NewsArticle` are the title and the URL. As we can see from the XML, the title is contained in a `CDATA` wrapper within a `title` element, and the URL is within a `link` element:

```
<item>
    <title><![CDATA[Coronavirus: Thousands return to UK to beat France
```

```
        quarantine]]></title>
    <description><![CDATA[Holidaymakers have just hours to return to the
        UK to avoid the 14-day self-isolation requirement.]]>
        </description>
    <link>https://www.bbc.co.uk/news/uk-53782019</link>
    <guid isPermaLink="true">https://www.bbc.co.uk/news/uk-
        53782019</guid>
    <pubDate>Fri, 14 Aug 2020 21:21:54 GMT</pubDate>
</item>
```

We will, therefore, also need to keep track of when the parser is in the `link` element, and while it is within the link element, append the received content to a `String` property. Similarly, we need to keep track of when the parser is in the `title` element, and when it is, append the received content to a `Data` property.

Let's add the extra properties we need to our `RSSNewsArticleBuilder` object:

```
class RSSNewsArticleBuilder: NSObject, XMLParserDelegate {
    var inItem = false
    var inTitle = false
    var inLink = false
    var titleData: Data?
    var linkString: String?

    //...
}
```

In the `didStartElement` method, we can check for these new element names we need to track. We must also remember to reset the link and title properties as we start the relevant element. This way, we don't continue to append content meant for the next item element onto content from the previous one:

```
func parser(_ parser: XMLParser,
            didStartElement elementName: String,
            namespaceURI: String?,
            qualifiedName qName: String?,
            attributes attributeDict: [String : String] = [:]) {
    switch elementName {
    case "item":
        inItem = true
    case "title":
        inTitle = true
        titleData = Data()
    case "link":
        inLink = true
        linkString = ""
    default:
```

```
        break
    }
}
```

Now that we know when we are in the right elements, we can implement two of the XMLParserDelegate methods to receive the relevant content and store it:

```
class RSSNewsArticleBuilder: NSObject, XMLParserDelegate {

    //...
    func parser(_ parser: XMLParser, foundCDATA CDATABlock: Data) {
        if inTitle {
            titleData?.append(CDATABlock)
        }
    }
    func parser(_ parser: XMLParser, foundCharacters string: String) {
        if inLink {
            linkString?.append(string)
        }
    }
}
```

In the didEndElement method, we need to update our new properties and we can print out the values we have retrieved from the XML:

```
class RSSNewsArticleBuilder: NSObject, XMLParserDelegate {
    //...
    func parser(_ parser: XMLParser,
                didEndElement elementName: String,
                namespaceURI: String?,
                qualifiedName qName: String?) {
        switch elementName {
        case "item":
            inItem = false
            guard
                let titleData = titleData,
                let titleString = String(data: titleData, encoding:
                    .utf8),
                let linkString = linkString,
                let link = URL(string: linkString)
                else { break }
            print(titleString)
            print(link)
        case "title":
            inTitle = false
        case "link":
            inLink = false
        default:
```

```
                    break
            }
        }
    //...
}
```

Now that we have extracted the title and URL of the news article, we can use this to create a `NewsArticle` model object. First, let's create an array to hold the `NewsArticle` objects we will be creating:

```
class RSSNewsArticleBuilder: NSObject, XMLParserDelegate {
    var inItem = false
    var inTitle = false
    var inLink = false
    var titleData: Data?
    var linkString: String?
    var articles = [NewsArticle]()
    //...
}
```

We can create the `NewsArticle` object at the end of the `item` element as this is when we will have all the relevant content:

```
class RSSNewsArticleBuilder: NSObject, XMLParserDelegate {
    //...
    func parser(_ parser: XMLParser,
                didEndElement elementName: String,
                namespaceURI: String?,
                qualifiedName qName: String?) {
        switch elementName {
        case "item":
            inItem = false
            guard
                let titleData = titleData,
                let titleString = String(data: titleData, encoding:
                    .utf8),
                let linkString = linkString,
                let link = URL(string: linkString)
                else { break }
            let article = NewsArticle(title: titleString, url: link)
            articles.append(article)
        case "title":
            inTitle = false
        case "link":
            inLink = false
        default:
            break
        }
```

```
        }
        //...
    }
```

Lastly, when the document starts, we should ensure that all the properties are reset:

```
class RSSNewsArticleBuilder: NSObject, XMLParserDelegate {
    //...
    func parserDidStartDocument(_ parser: XMLParser) {
        inItem = false
        inTitle = false
        inLink = false
        titleData = nil
        linkString = nil
        articles = [NewsArticle]()
    }
    //...
}
```

Now that we have completed the parser delegate, let's go back to our
`fetchBBCNewsRSSFeed` **function:**

```
func fetchBBCNewsRSSFeed() {
    let session = URLSession.shared
    let url = URL(string: "http://feeds.bbci.co.uk/news/rss.xml")!
    let dataTask = session.dataTask(with: url) { (data, response,
      error) in
        guard let data = data, error == nil else {
            print(error ?? "Unexpected response")
            return
        }
        let dataAsString = String(data: data, encoding: .utf8)!
        print(dataAsString)
    }
    dataTask.resume()
}
```

Once the XML data has been retrieved, we'll pass it to `XMLParser`, set up the delegate, and
tell the parser to parse the data:

```
func fetchBBCNewsRSSFeed() {
    let session = URLSession.shared
    let url = URL(string: "http://feeds.bbci.co.uk/news/rss.xml")!
    let dataTask = session.dataTask(with: url) { (data, response,
      error) in
        guard let data = data, error == nil else {
            print(error ?? "Unexpected response")
            return
```

```
        }
        let parser = XMLParser(data: data)
        let articleBuilder = RSSNewsArticleBuilder()
        parser.delegate = articleBuilder
        parser.parse()
        let articles = articleBuilder.articles
        print(articles)
    }
    dataTask.resume()
}
```

We want to provide the articles as an output from this function, so we can add a completion handler to provide an array of news articles or an error:

```
func fetchBBCNewsRSSFeed(completion: @escaping ([NewsArticle]?, Error?)
  -> Void) {
    let session = URLSession.shared
    let url = URL(string: "http://feeds.bbci.co.uk/news/rss.xml")!
    let dataTask = session.dataTask(with: url) { (data, response,
      error) in
        guard let data = data, error == nil else {
            completion(nil, error)
            return
        }
        let parser = XMLParser(data: data)
        let articleBuilder = RSSNewsArticleBuilder()
        parser.delegate = articleBuilder
        parser.parse()
        let articles = articleBuilder.articles
        completion(articles, nil)
    }
    dataTask.resume()
}
```

Finally, we can call this function, which will retrieve the RSS feed, parse it, and return an array of news articles:

```
fetchBBCNewsRSSFeed() { (articles, error) in
    if let articles = articles {
        print(articles)
    } else if let error = error {
        print(error)
    }
}
```

There's more...

Foundation also provides the ability to write XML data, although currently, this functionality is only available on macOS.

Having retrieved the RSS feed and created our news articles, let's write this information to an XML data structure and save it to disk. This XML will take the following form:

```
<articles>
    <article>
        <title>Donald Trump calls Fidel Castro 'brutal dictator'
            </title>
        <url>http://www.bbc.co.uk/news/world-latin-america-
            38118739</url>
    </article>
    <article>
        <title>Fidel Castro: Jeremy Corbyn praises 'huge figure'
            </title>
        <url>http://www.bbc.co.uk/news/uk-38117068</url>
    </article>
</articles>
```

At the root of the XML structure is an `articles` element, which contains multiple `article` elements, which in turn contain a `title` element and a `url` element.

To write the XML data, we will recreate the preceding structure using the `XMLDocument` and `XMLElement` objects. Once constructed, the `xmlData` property of the `XMLDocument` object provides the document as data.

Let's create a function to produce XML data from an array of `NewsArticle`:

```swift
func createXML(representing articles: [NewsArticle]) -> Data {
    let root = XMLElement(name: "articles")
    let document = XMLDocument(rootElement: root)
    for article in articles {
        let articleElement = XMLElement(name: "article")
        let titleElement = XMLElement(name: "title",
                                      stringValue: article.title)
        let urlElement = XMLElement(name: "url",
                          stringValue: article.url.absoluteString)
        articleElement.addChild(titleElement)
        articleElement.addChild(urlElement)
        root.addChild(articleElement)
    }
    print(document.xmlString)
    return document.xmlData
}
```

We create each XMLElement and add it as a child to the element that we want to nest it within.

If you are building this in a storyboard, ensure that you place this function after RSSNewsArticleBuilder, and before the code that calls fetchBBCNewsRSSFeed, as this function will need to be available to the completion handler soon.

Our call to fetchBBCNewsRSSFeed will provide an array of NewsArticle, so we can pass this to our new function to write this information to XML data:

```
fetchBBCNewsRSSFeed() { (articles, error) in
    if let articles = articles {
        let articleXMLData = createXML(representing: articles)
        print(articleXMLData.length)
    } else if let error = error {
        print(error)
    }
}
```

Now that we have the data, we can obtain a URL for the documents directory, append the name of the file we will create, and write it to disk:

```
fetchBBCNewsRSSFeed() { (articles, error) in
    if let articles = articles {
        let xmlData = createXML(representing: articles)
        let documentsURL = FileManager.default.urls(for:
            .documentDirectory, in: .userDomainMask).first!
        let writeURL = documentsURL.appendingPathComponent(
            "articles.xml")
        print("Writing data to: \(writeURL)")
        try! xmlData.write(to: writeURL)
    } else if let error = error {
        print(error)
    }
}
```

We have now retrieved an RSS feed, extracted useful information from it, written that information to a custom XML format, and saved that data to disk. Give yourself a pat on the back!

See also

Further information about XMLParser can be found in Apple's Foundation reference at http://swiftbook.link/docs/xmlparser.

Other XML parsers are available, which may have advantages over Apple's, including being able to write XML on iOS. They are as follows:

- RaptureXML: https://github.com/ZaBlanc/RaptureXML
- TBXML: https://github.com/71squared/TBXML

6

Building iOS Apps with Swift

In this chapter, we'll be building our very own iOS app using Swift and the Xcode IDE. Once we've built our app, we'll look at how we can incorporate unit tests and **user interface (UI)** tests. Finally, we'll take a look at backward compatibility in Swift and iOS development.

In this chapter, we will cover the following recipes:

- Building an iOS App using Cocoa Touch
- Unit and integration testing with XCTest
- User interface testing with XCUITest
- Backward compatibility

Let's get started!

Technical requirements

For this chapter, you'll need the latest version of Xcode from the Mac App Store.

All the code for this chapter can be found in this book's GitHub repository at `https://github.com/PacktPublishing/Swift-Cookbook-Second-Edition/tree/master/Chapter06`

Check out the following video to see the Code in Action: `https://bit.ly/3pMG44r`

Building an iOS App using Cocoa Touch

The focus of this book is ultimately on the Swift programming language itself, as opposed to the use of the language to produce apps for Apple platforms or to build server-side services. That being said, it can't be ignored that the vast majority of the Swift code being written is to build, or build upon, iOS and iPadOS apps.

In this recipe, we will take a brief look at how we can interact with Apple's Cocoa Touch frameworks using Swift and begin to build and create our very own iOS app.

Cocoa Touch is a name given to the collection of UI frameworks available as part of the iOS SDK. Its name derives from the Cocoa framework on macOS, which provides UI elements for macOS apps. While Cocoa on macOS is a framework in its own right, Cocoa Touch is a collection of frameworks that provide UI elements for iOS apps and handle the app's life cycle; the core of these frameworks is **UIKit**.

Getting ready

First, we'll need to create a new iOS app project:

1. From the Xcode menu, choose **File**, then **New**.
2. From the dialog box that opens, choose **App** from the **iOS** tab:

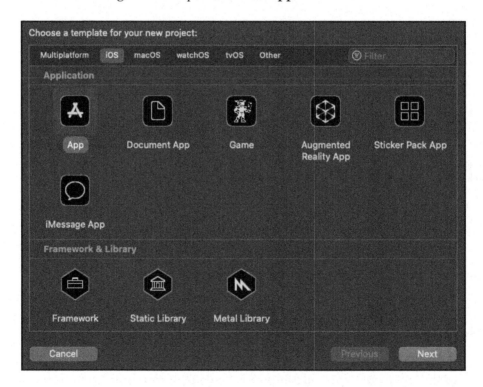

Figure 6.1 – Choosing a template

3. The next dialog box asks you to enter details about your app, pick a product name and organization name, and add an organization identifier in reverse DNS style.

Reverse DNS style means to take a website that you or your company owns and reverse the order of the domain name components. So, for example, `http://maps.google.com` becomes `com.google.maps`:

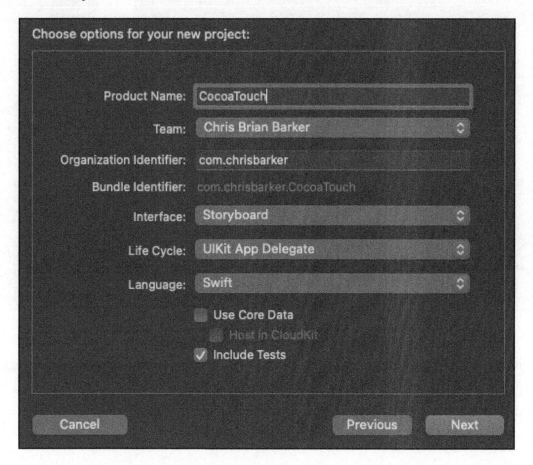

Pay attention to the preceding choices as not all of them may be selected by default. For this recipe, the ones that are important to us are **Interface** and **Include Tests**, both of which we'll cover later on this in the chapter when we look at unit testing with XCTest and user interface testing with XCUITest.

4. Once you've chosen a save location on your Mac, you will be presented with the following Xcode layout:

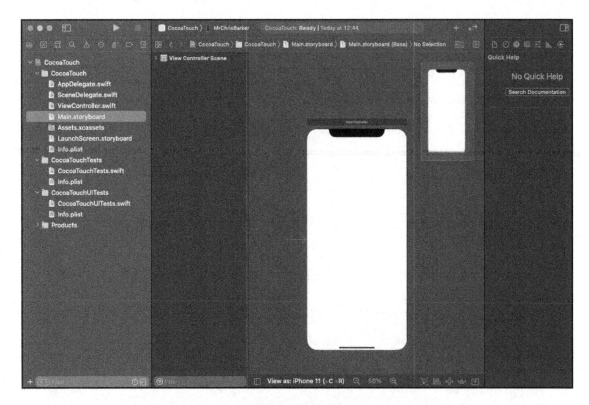

Figure 6.3 – New project template

Here, we have the start of our project – it's not much, but it's where all new iOS apps begin.

From this menu, press **Product** | **Run**. Xcode will now compile and run your app in a simulator.

How to do it...

Continuing from a previous recipe, we'll build our app based on data that is returned from the Public GitHub API:

1. In the File Explorer, click on **Main.storyboard**; this view is a representation of what the app will look like and is called **Interface Builder**. At the moment, there is only one blank screen visible, which matches what the app looked like when we ran it earlier. This screen represents a `View Controller` object; as the name suggests, this is an object that controls views.

2. We will display our list of repositories in a table. We actually want to create a view controller class that is a subclass of `UITableViewController`. So, from the menu, choose **File**, then **New**, and select a **Cocoa Touch Class** template:

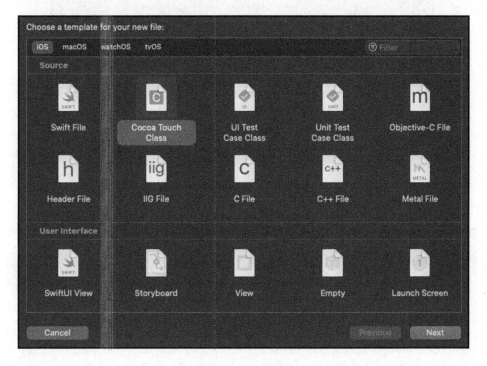

Figure 6.4 – New file template

3. We will be displaying repositories in this view controller, so let's call it `ReposTableViewController`. Specify that it's a subclass of `UITableViewController` and ensure that the language is **Swift**:

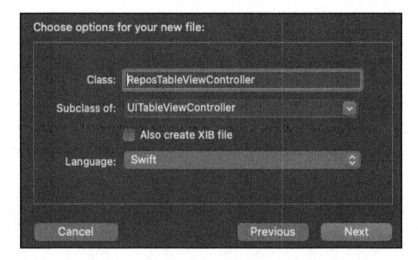

Figure 6.5 – New filename and subclass

Now that we have created our view controller class, let's switch back to `Main.storyboard` and delete the blank view controller that was created for us.

4. From the object library, find the **Table View Controller** option and drag it into the **Interface Builder** editor:

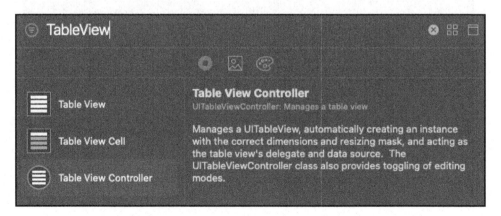

Figure 6.6 – Object library

5. Now that we have a table view controller, we want this controller to be part of our custom subclass. To do this, select the controller, go into the class inspector, enter `ReposTableViewController` as the **Class** type, and press *Enter*:

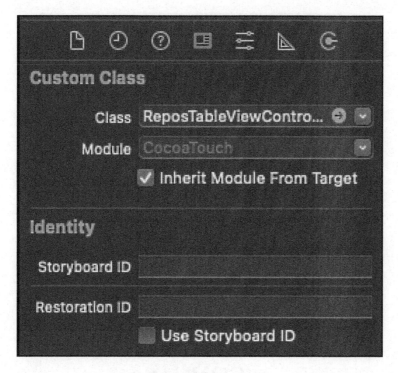

Figure 6.7: Custom class inspector

Although we have the view controller that will be displaying the repository names, when a user selects a repository, we want to present a new view controller that will show details about that particular repo. We will cover what type of view controller that is and how we present it shortly, but first, we need a mechanism for navigating between view controllers.

If you have ever used an iOS app, you will be familiar with the standard *push* and *pop* way of navigating between views. The following screenshot shows an app in the middle of that transition:

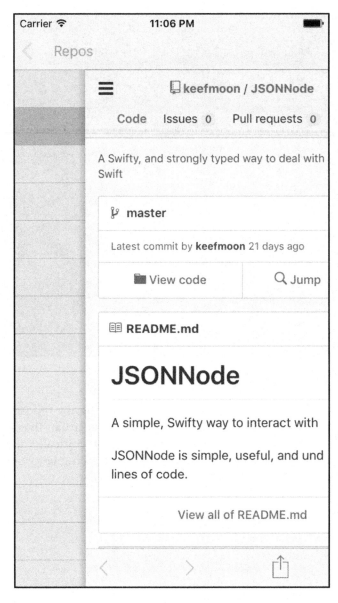

Figure 6.8 – Push and pop view controller

The management of these view controllers, as well as their presentation and dismissal transitions, are handled by a navigation controller, which is provided by Cocoa Touch in the form of `UINavigationController`. Let's take a look:

1. To place our view controller inside a navigation controller, select `ReposTableViewController` in **Interface Builder**. Then, from the Xcode menu, go to **Editor** and then **Embed In** and choose **Navigation Controller**.

    This will add a navigation controller to the storyboard and set the selected view controller as its root view controller (*if there is an existing view controller already inside the storyboard from the initial project we created, this can be highlighted and deleted*).

2. Next, we need to define which view controller is initially on the screen when the app starts. Select **Navigation Controller** on the left-hand side of the screen and within the property inspector, select **Is Initial View Controller**. You will see that an entry arrow will point toward the navigation controller on the left, indicating that it will be shown initially.

3. With this set up, we can start working on our `ReposTableViewController` by selecting it from the **File navigator** menu.

    When we created our view controller, the template gave us a bunch of code, with some of it commented out. The first method that the template provides is `viewDidLoad`. This is part of a set of methods that cover the life cycle of the root view that the view controller is managing. Full details about the view life cycle and its relevant method calls can be found at `http://swiftbook.link/docs/vc-lifecycle`.

    `viewDidLoad` is fired quite early on in the view controller's life cycle but before the view controller is visible to the user. Due to this, it is a good place to configure the view and retrieve any information that you want to present to the user.

4. Let's give the view controller a title:

```
class ReposTableViewController: UITableViewController {
    override func viewDidLoad() {
        super.viewDidLoad()
        self.title = "Repos"
    }
    //...
}
```

    Now, if you **Build and Run** the app, you'll see a navigation bar with the title we just added programmatically.

5. Next, we'll fetch and display a list of GitHub repositories. Implement the following snippet of code in order to fetch a list of repos for a specific user:

```
@discardableResult
  internal func fetchRepos(forUsername username: String,
      completionHandler: @escaping (FetchReposResult) -> Void)
      -> URLSessionDataTask? {
      let urlString = "https://api.github.com/users/\
        (username)/repos"
      guard let url = URL(string: urlString) else {
          return nil
      }
      var request = URLRequest(url: url)
      request.setValue("application/vnd.github.v3+json",
        forHTTPHeaderField: "Accept")
      let task = session.dataTask(with: request) { (data,
        response, error) in
          // First unwrap the optional data
          guard let data = data else {
              completionHandler(.failure(ResponseError.
                requestUnsuccessful))
              return
          }
          do {
              let decoder = JSONDecoder()
              let responseObject = try decoder.
                decode([Repo].self, from: data)
              completionHandler(.success(responseObject))
          } catch {
              completionHandler(.failure(error))
          }
      }
      task.resume()

      return task
  }
```

6. Let's add the following highlighted code to the top of the file, before the start of the class definition. We will also add a session property to the view controller, which is needed for the network request:

```
import UIKit

struct Repo: Codable {
    let name: String?
    let url: URL?
    enum CodingKeys: String, CodingKey {
        case name = "name"
```

```
            case url = "html_url"
        }
    }

    enum FetchReposResult {
        case success([Repo])
        case failure(Error)
    }

    enum ResponseError: Error {
        case requestUnsuccessful
        case unexpectedResponseStructure
    }

    class ReposTableViewController: UITableViewController {
        internal var session = URLSession.shared
        //...
    }
```

You may notice something a little different about the preceding functions since we're now making full use of Swift's **Codable** protocol. With Codable, we can map the JSON response from our API straight to our struct models, without the need to convert this into a dictionary and then iterate each key-value pair to a property.

7. Next, in our table view, each row of the table view will display the name of one of the repositories that we retrieve from the GitHub API. We need a place to store the repositories that we retrieve from the API:

```
    class ReposTableViewController: UITableViewController {
        internal var session = URLSession.shared
        internal var repos = [Repo]()
        //...
    }
```

The `repos` array has an initially empty array value, but we will use this property to hold the fetched results from the API.

We don't need to fetch the repository data right now. So, instead, we'll learn how to provide data to be used in the table view. Let's get started:

1. Let's create a couple of fake repositories so that we can temporarily populate our table view:

```
    class ReposTableViewController: UITableViewController {
        let session = URLSession.shared
        var repos = [Repo]()
```

```
      override func viewDidLoad() {
          super.viewDidLoad()
  let repo1 = Repo(name: "Test repo 1",
    url: URL(string: "http://example.com/repo1")!)
  let repo2 = Repo(name: "Test repo 2",
    url: URL(string: "http://example.com/repo2")!)
  repos.append(contentsOf: [repo1, repo2])
      }
      //...
  }
```

The information in a table view is populated from the table view's data source, which can be any object that conforms to the UITableViewDataSource protocol.

When the table view is displayed and the user interacts with it, the table view will ask the data source for the information it needs to populate the table view. For simple table view implementations, it is often the view controller that controls the table view that acts as the data source. In fact, when you create a subclass of UITableViewController, as we have, the view controller already conforms to UITableViewDataSource and is assigned as the table view's data source.

2. Some of the methods defined in UITableViewDataSource were created as part of the UITableViewController template; the three we will take a look at are as follows:

```
// MARK: - Table view data source
override func numberOfSections(in tableView: UITableView) -> Int {
    // #warning Incomplete implementation, return the number of
    // sections
    return 0
}

override func tableView(_ tableView: UITableView,
                        numberOfRowsInSection section: Int) -> Int
{
 // #warning Incomplete implementation, return the number of rows
    return 0
}

/*
override func tableView(_ tableView: UITableView,
    cellForRowAt indexPath: IndexPath) -> UITableViewCell {
      let cell = tableView.dequeueReusableCell(withIdentifier:
        "RepoCell", for: indexPath)
      // Configure the cell...
```

```
      return cell
   }
   */
```

Data in a table view can be divided into sections, and information is presented in rows within those sections; information is referenced through an `IndexPath` that consists of a section integer value and a row integer value.

3. The first thing that the data source methods ask us to provide is the number of sections that the table view will have. Our app will only be displaying a simple list of repositories, and as such, we only need one section, so we will return `1` from this method:

```
override func numberOfSections(in tableView: UITableView) -> Int {
    1
}
```

4. The next thing we have to provide is the number of rows the table view should have for a given section. If we had multiple sections, we could examine the provided section index and return the right number of rows, but since we only have one section, we can return the same number in all scenarios.

We are displaying all the repositories we have retrieved, so the number of rows is simply the number of repositories in the `repos` array:

```
override func tableView(_ tableView: UITableView,
   numberOfRowsInSection section: Int) -> Int {
    repos.count
}
```

Notice that in the preceding two functions, we no longer use the `return` keyword. This is because, starting with Swift 5.1, you can now use *implicit returns* in functions. As long as your function doesn't carry ambiguity about what should and should not be returned, the compiler can work this out for you. This allows for more streamlined syntax.

Now that we have told the table view how many pieces of information to display, we must be able to display that information. A table view displays information in a type of view called `UITableViewCell`, and this cell is what we have to provide next.

For each index path within the section and row bounds that we have provided, we will be asked to provide a cell that will be displayed by the table view. A table view can be very large in size as it may need to represent a large amount of data. However, there are only a handful of cells that can be displayed to the user at any one time. This is because only a portion of the table view can be visible at any one time:

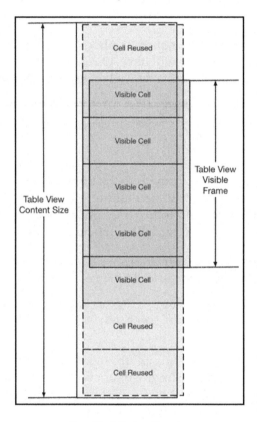

Figure 6.9 – Table view cell overview

In order to be efficient and prevent your app from slowing down as the user scrolls, the table view can reuse cells that have already been created but have since moved off-screen. Implementing cell reuse happens in two stages:

- Registering the cell's type with the table view with a reuse identifier.
- Dequeuing a cell for a given reuse identifier. This will return a cell that has moved off-screen or create a new cell if none are available for reuse.

How a cell is registered will depend on how it has been created. If the cell has been created and its subviews have also been laid out in the code, then the cell's class is registered with the table view through this method on `UITableView`:

```
func register(_ cellClass: AnyClass?,
              forCellReuseIdentifier identifier: String)
```

If the cell has been laid out in `.xib` (usually called a "nib" for historical reasons), which is a visual layout file for views that's similar to a storyboard, then the cell's nib is registered with the table view through this method on `UITableView`:

```
func register(_ nib: UINib?, forCellReuseIdentifier identifier: String)
```

Lastly, cells can be defined and laid out within the table view in a storyboard. One advantage of this approach is that there is no need to manually register the cell, as with the previous two approaches; registering with the table view is free. However, one disadvantage of this approach is that the cell layout is tied to the table view, so it can't be reused in other table views, unlike the previous two implementations.

Let's layout our cell in the Storyboard since we will only be using it with one table view:

1. Switch to our **Main.storyboard** file and select the table view in our `ReposTableViewController`.

2. In the attributes inspector, change the number of prototype cells to 1; this will add a cell to the table view in the main window. This cell will define the layout of all the cells that will be displayed in our table view. You should create a prototype cell for each type of cell layout you will need; we are only displaying one piece of information in our table view, so all our cells will be of the same type.

3. Select a cell in the storyboard. The attributes inspector will switch to showing the attributes for the cell. The cell style will be set to custom, and often, this will be what you want it to be. When you are displaying multiple pieces of information in a cell, you will usually want to create a subclass of `UITableViewCell`, set this to be the cell's class in the class inspector, and then lay out subviews in this custom cell type. However, for this example, we just want to show the name of the repository. Due to this, we can use a basic cell style that just has one text label, without a custom subclass, so choose **basic** from the style dropdown.

4. We need to set the reuse identifier that we will use to dequeue the cell later, so type an appropriate string, such as `RepoCell`, into the reuse identifier box of the attributes inspector:

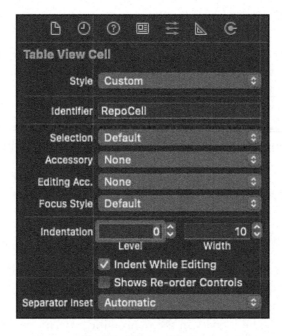

Figure 6.10 – Table view cell identifier

5. Now that we have a cell that is registered for reuse with the table view, we can go back to our view controller and complete our conformance with `UITableViewDataSource`.

6. Our `ReposTableViewController` contains some commented code that was created as part of the template:

```
/*
override func tableView(_ tableView: UITableView,
    cellForRowAt indexPath: IndexPath) -> UITableViewCell {
  let cell = tableView.dequeueReusableCell(withIdentifier:
    "RepoCell", for: indexPath)
  // Configure the cell...
  return cell
}
*/
```

7. At this point, you can remove the /* */ comment signifiers as we are ready to implement this method.

   This data source method will be called every time the table view needs to place a cell on-screen; this will happen the first time the table is displayed as it needs cells to fill the visible part of the table view. It will also be called when the user scrolls the table view in a way that will reveal a new cell so that it becomes visible.

8. Regarding the method's definition, we can see that we are provided with the table view in question and the index path of the cell that is needed, and we are expected to return a UITableViewCell. The code provided by the template actually does most of the work for us; we just need to provide the reuse identifier that we set in the storyboard and set the title label of the cell so that we have the name of the correct repository:

```
override func tableView(_ tableView: UITableView,
    cellForRowAt indexPath: IndexPath) -> UITableViewCell {
        let cell = tableView.dequeueReusableCell(withIdentifier:
          "RepoCell", for: indexPath)
        // Configure the cell...
        let repo = repos[indexPath.row]
        cell.textLabel?.text = repo.name
        return cell
}
```

The cell's textLabel property is optional because it only exists when the cell's style is not custom.

9. Since we've now provided everything the table view needs to display our repository information, let's click on **Build and Run** and take a look:

Figure 6.11 – Our app's first run

Great! Now that we have our two test repositories displayed in our table view, let's replace our test data with real repositories from the GitHub API.

We added our `fetchRepos` method earlier, so all we need to do is call this method, set the results to our `repos` property, and tell our table view that it needs to reload since the data has changed:

```
class ReposTableViewController: UITableViewController {
    internal var session = URLSession.shared
    internal var repos = [Repo]()
    override func viewDidLoad() {
        super.viewDidLoad()
        title = "Repos"
        fetchRepos(forUsername:"SwiftProgrammingCookbook"){ [weak self]
          result in
            switch result {
            case .success(let repos):
                self?.repos = repos
            case .failure(let error):
                self?.repos = []
                print("There was an error: \(error)")
```

```
        }
            self?.tableView.reloadData()
        }
    }
    //...
}
```

As we did in the previous recipes, we fetched the repositories from the GitHub API and received a result enum informing us of whether this was a success or a failure. If it was successful, we store the resulting repository array in our `repos` property. Once we have handled the response, we call the `reloadData` method on `UITableView`, which instructs the table view to requery its source for cells to display.

We also provided a weak reference to `self` in our closure's capture list to prevent a retain cycle. You can find out more about why this is important in the *Closures* recipe of `Chapter 1`, *Swift Building Blocks*.

At this point, there is an important consideration that needs to be addressed. The iOS platform is a multithreaded environment, which means that it can do more than one thing at once. This is critical to being able to maintain a responsive user interface, while also being able to process data and perform long-running tasks. The iOS system uses queues to manage this work and reserves the "main" queue for any work involving the user interface. Therefore, any time you need to interact with the user interface, it is important that this work is done from the main queue.

Our `fetchRepos` method presents a situation where this might not be true. Our `fetchRepos` method performs networking, and we provide closure to `URLSession` as part of creating a `URLSessionDataTask`, but there is no guarantee that this closure will be executed on the main thread. Therefore, when we receive a response from `fetchRepos`, we need to "dispatch" the work of handling that response to the main queue to ensure that our updates to the UI happen on the main queue. We can do this using the `Dispatch` framework, so we need to import that at the top of the file:

```
class ReposTableViewController: UITableViewController {
    let session = URLSession.shared
    var repos = [Repo]()
    override func viewDidLoad() {
        super.viewDidLoad()
        title = "Repos"
        fetchRepos(forUsername:"SwiftProgrammingCookbook"){ [weak self]
            result in
                DispatchQueue.main.async {
                    switch result {
                    case .success(let repos):
                        self?.repos = repos
```

```
                    case .failure(let error):
                        self?.repos = []
                        print("There was an error: \(error)")
                    }
                    self?.tableView.reloadData()
                }
            }
        }
    }
```

We will be discussing multithreading and the `Dispatch` framework in greater depth in `Chapter 9`, *Performance and Responsiveness in Swift*.

1. Click on **Build and Run**. After a few seconds, the table view will be filled with the names of various repositories from the GitHub API.

   Now that we have repositories being displayed to the user, the next piece of functionality we'll implement for our app is the ability to tap on a cell and have it display the repository's GitHub page in a WebView.

   Actions triggered by the table view, such as when a user taps on a cell, are provided to the table view's delegate, which can be anything that conforms to `UITableViewDelegate`. As was the case with the table view's data source, our `ReposTableViewController` already conforms to `UITableViewDelegate` because it is a subclass of `UITableViewController`.

2. If you take a look at the documentation for the `UITableViewDelegate` protocol, you will see a lot of optional methods; this documentation can be found at `https://developer.apple.com/reference/uikit/uitableviewdelegate`. The one that's relevant for our purposes is as follows:

   ```
   func tableView(_ tableView: UITableView, didSelectRowAt indexPath:
       IndexPath)
   ```

3. This will be called on the table view's delegate whenever a cell is selected by the user, so let's implement this in our view controller:

```
override func tableView(_ tableView: UITableView, didSelectRowAt
    indexPath: IndexPath) {
    let repo = repos[indexPath.row]
    let repoURL = repo.url
    // TODO: Present the repo's URL in a webview
}
```

4. For the functionality it provides, we will use `SFSafariViewController`, passing it the repository's URL. Then, we will pass that view controller to the `show` method, which will present the view controller in the most appropriate way:

```
override func tableView(_ tableView: UITableView,
                        didSelectRowAt indexPath: IndexPath) {
    let repo = repos[indexPath.row]
    guard let repoURL = repo.url else { return }

    let webViewController = SFSafariViewController(url: repoURL)
    show(webViewController, sender: nil)
}
```

5. Don't forget to `import SafariServices` at the top of the file.
6. Click on **Build and Run**, and once the repositories are loaded, tap on one of the cells. A new view controller will be pushed onto the screen, and the relevant repository web page will load.

Congratulations – you've just built your first app and it looks great!

How it works...

Currently, our app fetches repositories from a specific, hardcoded GitHub username. It would be great if, rather than hardcoding the username, the user of the app could enter the GitHub username that the repositories will be retrieved for. So, let's add this functionality:

1. First, we need a way for the user to enter their GitHub username; the most appropriate way to allow a user to enter a small amount of text is through the use of UITextField.

2. In the main storyboard, find **Text Field** in the object library, drag it over to the main window, and drop it on the navigation bar of our ReposTableViewController. Now, you need to increase the width of the Text Field. For now, just hard code this to around 300px by highlighting the respective Text Field and selecting the **Size Inspector** option:

Figure 6.12 – Adding a UITextField

Like a table view, UITextField communicates user events through a delegate, which needs to conform to UITextFieldDelegate.

3. Let's switch back to ReposTableViewController and add conformance to UITextFieldDelegate; it is a common practice to add protocol conformance to an extension, so add the following at the bottom of ReposTableViewController:

```
extension ReposTableViewController: UITextFieldDelegate {

}
```

4. With this conformance in place, we need to set our view controller to be the delegate of `UITextField`. Head back over to the main storyboard and select the text field, and then open the **Connections Inspector**. You will see that the text field has an outlet for its delegate property. Now, click, hold, and drag from the circle next to our delegate over to the symbol representing our **Repos Table View Controller**:

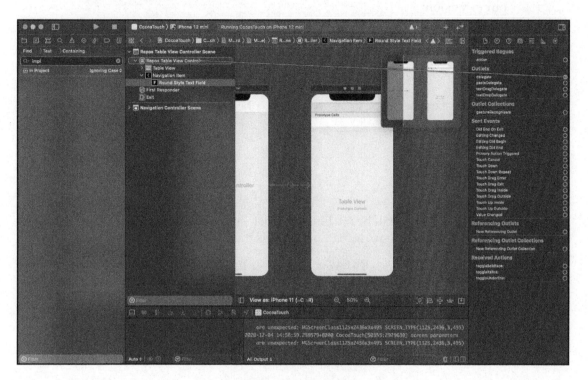

Figure 6.13 – UITextField with IBOutlet

The delegate outlet should now have a value:

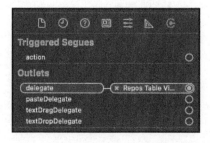

Figure 6.14 – UITextField delegate outlet

By taking a look at the documentation for UITextFieldDelegate, we can see that the textFieldShouldReturn method is called when the user presses the *Return* button on their keyboard after entering text, so this is the method we will implement.

5. Let's switch back to our ReposViewController and implement this method in our extension:

```
extension ReposTableViewController: UITextFieldDelegate {
    public func textFieldShouldReturn(_ textField: UITextField)
      -> Bool {
      // TODO: Fetch repositories from username entered into text
      // field
   // TODO: Dismiss keyboard

   // Returning true as we want the system to have the default
     // behaviour
   return true
       }
   }
```

6. Since repositories will be fetched here instead of when the view is loaded, let's move the code from viewDidLoad to this method:

```
extension ReposTableViewController: UITextFieldDelegate {
    public func textFieldShouldReturn(_ textField: UITextField)
      -> Bool {
        // If no username, clear the data
         guard let enteredUsername = textField.text else {
             repos.removeAll()
             tableView.reloadData()
             return true
       }
        // Fetch repositories from username entered into text field
        fetchRepos(forUsername: enteredUsername) { [weak self]
          result in
                switch result {
                case .success(let repos):
                    self?.repos = repos
                case .failure(let error):
                    self?.repos = []
                    print("There was an error: \(error)")
                }
                DispatchQueue.main.async {
                    self?.tableView.reloadData()
                }
          }
       }
```

```
        // TODO: Dismiss keyboard
        // Returning true as we want the system to have the default
          // behaviour
        return true
    }
}
```

Cocoa Touch implements the programming design pattern **MVC**, which stands for **Model View Controller**; it is a way of structuring your code to keep its elements reusable, with well-defined responsibilities. In the MVC pattern, all code related to displaying information falls broadly into three areas of responsibility:

- **Model** objects hold the data that will eventually be displayed on the screen; this might be data that was retrieved from the network or device, or that was generated when the app was running. These objects may be used in multiple places in the app, where different view representations of the same data may be required.

- **View** objects represent the UI elements that are displayed on the screen; these may just display information that they are provided, or capture input from the user. View objects can be used in multiple places where the same visual element is needed, even if it is showing different data.

- **Controller** objects act as bridges between the models and the views; they are responsible for obtaining the relevant model objects and for providing the data to be displayed to the right view objects at the right time. Controller objects are also responsible for handling user input from the views and updating the model objects as needed:

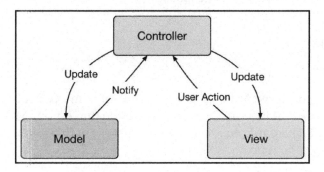

Figure 6.15 – MVC overview

With regards to displaying web content, our app provides us with a number of options for presenting web content:

- `WKWebView`, provided by the WebKit framework, is a view that uses the latest rendering and JavaScript engine for loading and displaying web content. While it is newer, it is less mature in some respects and has issues with caching content.
- `SFSafariViewController`, provided by the `SafariServices` framework, is a view controller that displays web content, and also provides many of the features that are available in Mobile Safari, including sharing and adding to reading lists and bookmarks. It also provides a convenient button for opening the current site in Mobile Safari.

There's more...

The last thing we need to do is dismiss the keyboard. Cocoa Touch refers to the object that is currently receiving user events as the first responder. Currently, this is the text field.

It's the act of the text field becoming the first responder that caused the keyboard to appear on-screen. Therefore, to dismiss the keyboard, the text field just needs to resign its place as first responder:

```
extension ReposTableViewController: UITextFieldDelegate {
    public func textFieldShouldReturn(_ textField: UITextField)
      -> Bool {
        //...
        // Dismiss keyboard
        textField.resignFirstResponder()
        // Returning true as we want the system to have the default
          // behaviour
        return true
    }
}
```

Now, click on **Build and Run**. At this point, you can enter any GitHub account name in the text field to retrieve a list of its public repositories. Note that if your Xcode simulator doesn't have the "soft keyboard" enabled, you can just press *Enter* on your physical keyboard to search for the repo.

See also

For more information regarding what was covered in this recipe, please refer to the following links:

- **Apple Documentation for GCD**: https://developer.apple.com/documentation/dispatch
- **Apple Documentation UIKit**: https://developer.apple.com/documentation/uikit

Unit and integration testing with XCTest

It goes without saying that testing plays a massive part of the software development life cycle. Primarily, a lot of the focus is on physical user testing – putting your piece of code in the hands of those using it day in day out. To a degree, this should be one of our main focuses, but what about testing what **we**, as software developers do? How do we test and check the integrity of our codebase?

This is where unit and integration testing comes in. In this recipe, we'll cook up a unit and integration test for our previously written Cocoa Touch app. This will be written entirely in Swift using the Xcode IDE.

Getting ready

Back in our existing CocoaTouch project, in the **File inspector**, look for a folder called `CocoaTouchTest`. Expand this and select the `CocoaTouchTests.swift` file.

Inside this file, you'll notice a class named `CocoaTouchTests`, which, in turn, inherits from the `XCTestCase` class. `XCTestCase` offers a suite of functions that we can use when writing out our unit tests.

So, what exactly is a unit test? Well, it's a test (or in our case, just a function) that checks that another function is doing what it's supposed to be doing. Writing tests or functions using XCTestCase allows us to not only use the previously mentioned suite of helpers but also allows Xcode to visualize and report on metrics such as test coverage.

With that, let's get stuck into cooking up our first unit test! In the `CocoaTouchTests.swift` file, you'll see some override functions that have already been generated by Xcode. Just ignore these for now; we'll work on them as/when we need to.

How to do it...

Let's start by creating the following function:

```
func testThatRepoIsNotNil() {
    XCTAssertNotNil(viewControllerUnderTest?.repos)
}
```

So, let's go through this one bit at a time. We'll start with the testThatRepoIsNotNil function. The common practice when naming a unit test is for the name to be as descriptive as possible. Depending on your coding standard, you can choose to either camel case these or snake case them (I much prefer camel case), but when writing tests with Xcode, you always have to prefix these with the word "test".

So, what are we testing? Here, we're checking that our repo array is not nil.

Looking back at our ReposTableViewController, you'll remember that we instantiated our "repo" model where the variable was declared, so this is a great test to start with. Let's say someone tries to change this to an optional, like this:

```
internal var repos: [Repo]?
```

If this happens, the code in our CocoaTouch App will compile, but the test will fail.

Let's take another look at our test. Note that the function we're calling to check our repo model is viewControllerUnderTest. This is how we access our RepoTableViewContoller. We can achieve this by adding the following class-level variable to our file:

```
var viewControllerUnderTest: ReposTableViewController?
```

Now, we need to instantiate this. Add the following override method from XCTestCase to your class:

```
override func setUp() {
    viewControllerUnderTest = ReposTableViewController()
}
```

When running your unit test for this particular class, setUp() will run prior to any of your test cases running, allowing you to prep anything you may need, such as instantiating a class. Once the tests are complete and you want to free anything up or close anything down, you can simply do this with the tearDown() function.

This was and is a very basic test, but the main purpose here was not necessarily to look at testing practice, but how we'd do that in Swift. However, before we go any further, let's take a look at the `Assert` options that are available to us.

Previously, we used `XCTAssertNotNil`, which worked perfectly for our scenario. However, the following options are also available:

```
XCTAssert
XCTAssertEqual
XCTAssertTrue
XCTAssertGreaterThan
XCTAssertGreaterThanOrEqual
XCTAssertLessThan
XCTAssertLessThanOrEqual
XCTAssertNil
```

These are just a handful of the common ones and they are pretty self-explanatory – an added bonus is that each one has an optional parameter of "message", which allows you to add a custom string. This allows you to be more specific about the assertion that took place (ideal for reporting in a CI/CD world).

Now that we understand the basics of how to write tests in Swift, we need to learn how to run them. There are two ways we can achieve this:

1. First, we can run all the tests in our class in one go. We can do this by simply clicking on the diamond to the left of the class's declaration:

Figure 6.16 – Class test case

2. If we want to run tests individually, then we can simply select the icon next to our individual test case, like this:

Figure 6.17 – Method test case

If everything goes to plan and our tests pass, we'll see the icon turn green:

Figure 6.18 – Method passed test case

However, if one or more of the tests in our class fail, we'll see the icon turn red:

Figure 6.19 – Method failed test case

Alternatively, the keyboard shortcut of *CMD + U* will also get Xcode to run any tests associated with the main project. Remember, only functions that start with the word `test` will be treated as a test case (excluding the class name), so feel free to add a private function in your test case should you need to.

Next, let's take a look at how we would test networking logic in Swift using mock data to help us out:

1. We'll start by creating the following test function:

```
func testThatFetchRepoParsesSuccessfulData() { }
```

2. Let's start by figuring out how we are going to call this. Once again, we'll take advantage of our `viewControllerUnderTest` variable:

```
func testThatFetchRepoParsesSuccessfulData() {
    viewControllerUnderTest?.fetchRepos(forUsername: "",
completionHandler: { (response) in
        print("\(response)")
    })
}
```

This works as expected, but unfortunately, it's not that simple – this will simply call the API just like our app would. If we were to add any XCAsserts inside our code, they wouldn't be executed as our test and function will have finished and been torn down before the API has a chance to respond.

3. To do this, we need to mock some objects in our `viewControllerUnderTest`, starting with **URLSession** and **URLSessionDataTask**. So, why do we need to mock these two? Let's start by taking a look at where we use them in our CocoaTouch app:

```
let task = session.dataTask(with: request) { (data, response,
error) in
```

Here, we are using **URLSession** and one of its functions, **URLSessionDataTask**, by mocking URLSession. We're creating our own local session here that we can then use to call our `MockURLSessionDataTask`. So, the real question here is, what is our `MockURLSessionDataTask` doing? We're using this to pass in some mock data – data that we should expect from the API – and then running this through our logic. This guarantees the integrity of our tests every time!

4. We could create the following input in our own files, but for now, we'll just append them to the bottom of our `CocoaTouchTests.swift` file. First, let's look at our `MockURLSession`:

```
class MockURLSession: URLSession {
    override func dataTask(with request: URLRequest,
completionHandler: @escaping (Data?, URLResponse?, Error?) -> Void)
-> URLSessionDataTask {
        return MockURLSessionDataTask(completionHandler:
completionHandler, request: request)
    }
}
```

The preceding function is pretty self-explanatory – we simply override the `dataTask()` function with the following `MockURLSessionDataTask`:

```
class MockURLSessionDataTask: URLSessionDataTask {
    var completionHandler: (Data?, URLResponse?, Error?) -> Void
    var request: URLRequest
    init(completionHandler: @escaping (Data?, URLResponse?, Error?)
-> Void, request: URLRequest) {
        self.completionHandler = completionHandler
        self.request = request
        super.init()
    }
    var calledResume = false
    override func resume() {
        calledResume = true
    }
}
```

At first glance, this looks a little complex, but all we are really doing here is adding our own `completionHandler`. This will allow it to be called synchronously from our test (stopping our test from running away with us).

Let's put this all together and head back over to our new test:

1. Let's start by setting our `MockURLSession` for our `viewControllerUnderTest`. This is nice and simple. Now, line by line, add the following:

```
func testThatFetchRepoParsesSuccessfulData() {
    viewControllerUnderTest?.session = MockURLSession()

    // ...
}
```

2. Let's start by adding in our main `responseObject`. This is what we are going to perform our XCAsserts against. Declare this as an optional variable:

```
var responseObject: FetchReposResult?
```

3. Now, we can call our function, much like we tried to earlier in this section. However, this time, we'll assign the result to a variable and cast this as a `MockURLSessionDataTask`:

```
let result = viewControllerUnderTest?.fetchRepos(forUsername: "",
completionHandler: { (response) in
        responseObject = response
    }) as? MockURLSessionDataTask
```

4. Remember that we can pass in anything we want for the `userName` variable as we're not going to be calling the API. Now, let's fire the completion handler we created and force through our `mockData`:

```
result?.completionHandler(mockData, nil, nil)
```

I've highlighted the `mockData` variable in the preceding code as we'll need to add this to the JSON response we want to test against. You can get this by simply visiting the GitHub URL and copying this into a new, **empty** file in the project. I did this for my username and created a file called `mock_Data.json`:

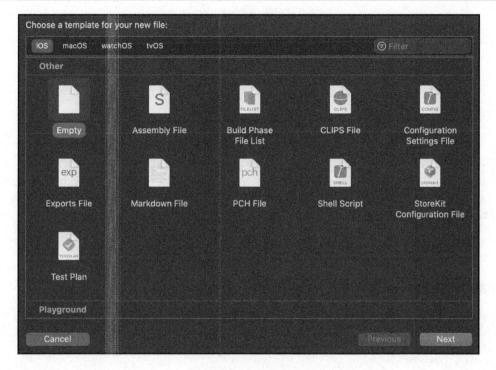

Figure 6.20 – Adding an empty file

Remember to select the CocoaTouch target when you're saving the file to disk; otherwise, the following steps won't work.

5. Now, create a computed property in our `Test` class that simply reads in the file and spits out the `Data()` object:

```
var mockData: Data {
    if let path = Bundle.main.path(forResource: "mock_Data",
ofType: "json"), let contents =
FileManager.default.contents(atPath: path){
        return contents
    }
    return Data()
}
```

6. At this point, we can successfully pass our mock data through our `fetchRepos` function without the need to call the API. All we need to do now is write some asserts:

```
switch responseObject {
    case .success(let repos):
```

```
            // Our test data had 3 repos, lets check that parsed okay
            XCTAssertEqual(repos.count, 9)
            // We know the first repo has a specific name... let's check
        that
            XCTAssertEqual(repos.first?.name, "aerogear-ios-oauth2")
            default:
            // Anything other than success - failure...
            XCTFail()
    }
```

What you test for here is really up to you – it's all based on the test cases you choose. Sometimes, thinking about what to test when you've already written a function can be a hard task. As a developer, it is easy for you to get "too close" to the project. This is where **test-driven development** (TDD) comes in, a methodology for writing tests prior to writing any code at all. Let's take a look at this and what we can achieve with it.

How it works...

Testing networking logic can be troublesome. I find that questions always arise, such as, what should you test? What exactly is being tested? However, if you can get your head around this, then you're well on your way to understanding the core fundamentals of unit testing.

Let's try and break this down. The logic we want to test is our `fetchRepos()` function. This is easy – we just call it with a repository username that we know and write some XCAsserts against the list of repos that come back.

While that will work for now, what happens when the user removes a repo? Your test will fail. This isn't good because your logic is not actually flawed – it's just the data that is wrong, much like if the API decided to return some malformed JSON due to an internal server error. This isn't your code's fault – it's the API's fault, and it's the API's job to make sure that it works.

All you want to do is check that if the server gives you a specific response, with a specific piece of data, your logic does what it says it should do. So, how can we guarantee the integrity of the data coming back from an API? We can't – that's why we mock the data ourselves and, in turn, don't actually call the service at all.

There's more...

TDD is a methodology that includes writing your unit test first, prior to actually writing your desired function. Some believe this is the only way to write code, while others preach about its usage when – and only when – necessary. For the record, I do the latter, but we're not here to get into the theory – we'll here to learn how to achieve this in Swift using XCTest.

Going back to our CocoaTouch app, let's say we'd like to write a function that validates UITextField for whitespaces. Perform the following steps to achieve this:

1. We'll start by writing out the stub function, which will look something like this:

   ```
   func isUserInputValid(withText text: String) -> Bool {
       return false
   }
   ```

   Normally, here, I would litter my function with comments about what I'd like to achieve, but for TDD, we're going to do this the other way around.

2. Back inside the `CocoaTouchTests.swift` file, add the following test:

   ```
   func testThatTextInputValidatesWithSingleWhitespace() {
   }
   ```

   Again, taking the name of our test as a literal description, we're going to check that our function correctly detects whitespaces in the middle of a `String()`.

3. So, let's write a test against the current function:

   ```
   func testThatTextInputValidatesWithSingleWhitespaces() {
       let result =
   viewControllerUnderTest?.isUserInputValid(withText: "multiple white
   spaces")
       XCTAssertFalse(result!)
   }
   ```

4. With that, we're happy we've asserted everything we set out to do in our test cases. Now, we can go ahead and run our test.

As expected, our test failed, which is obvious for two reasons. First, we didn't really write up our function, and second, we hardcoded the return type as **false**.

We actually hardcoded the return type as false on purpose – we did this as the TDD methodology is done in three stages:

1. **Fail test**: *Done, we did that.*
2. **Pass test**: *Can be as messy as you like.*
3. **Refactor code**: *We can do this with the utmost confidence.*

The idea is to write your unit test while covering all the scenarios and asserts that may be required for that test case and make it fail (like we did).

With the foundation set up, we can now confidently move over to our function and code away, safe in the knowledge that we'll be able to run our test to check if our function is broken or not:

```
func isUserInputValid(withText text: String) -> Bool {
    return !text.contains(" ")
}
```

This is nothing special, but for the purpose of this section, it doesn't need to be. TDD with Swift doesn't have to be daunting. After all, it's just a methodology that works perfectly well with XCTest.

See also

You can find out more information about **unit testing** at `https://developer.apple.com/documentation/xctest`.

User interface testing with XCUITest

User interface (UI) testing has been around for a while. In theory, it's done every day by any one person who is using, testing, or checking an app, but in terms of automation, it's had its fair share of critics.

However, with Swift and XCTest, this has never been easier, and the beauty regarding how we will implement this has an amazing hidden benefit.

Getting ready

Unlike unit testing, when we are testing against a function, piece of logic, or algorithm, user interface tests are exactly what they say on the tin. They are a way for us to test the UI and UX of the app – things that might not have necessarily been generated programmatically.

Head on over to the `CocoaTouchUITests.swift` file that was automatically generated when we created our project. Again, much like the unit tests, you'll notice some placeholder functions in there. We'll start by taking a look at one called `testExample()`.

How to do it...

With what we mentioned in the *Getting ready* section in mind, let's take a look at our app and see what we would like to test. The first thing that comes to my mind is the search bar:

Figure 6.21 – Search bar selected

Now that we've made this mandatory to populate in order for our app to work, we want to make sure this is here all the time, so let's write a UI test for this:

```
func testExample() throws {
    // UI tests must launch the application that they test.
    let app = XCUIApplication()
    app.launch()
}
```

As the comment correctly states, in order for the tests to be successful, the app needs to be launched, which is taken care of by the `launch()` function. However, once our app has been launched, how do we tell it to check for a UITextField and, more importantly, a specific one (in the future, we could have multiple on our screen)?

To do this, we must start with the basics:

1. I've edited the name of the function to make it more applicable to what we are testing here. As you can see from the following highlighted code, we've told our test to select the `textFields` element and tap it:

   ```
   func testThatUsernameSearchBarIsAvailable() throws {
       let app = XCUIApplication()
       app.launch()
       app.textFields.element.tap()
   }
   ```

2. Go ahead and run the test by clicking on the diamond to the left to watch your app come to life in the simulator. If you're quick enough, you'll see the cursor enter the text box just before the app closes.

Great work! The test passed, which means you've written your first UI test.

Regarding our previous test, we weren't specific about the element being identified. For now, this is okay, but building a much bigger and complex app may require that you test certain aspects of specific elements. Let's take a look at how we could achieve this:

1. One way would be to set an accessibility identifier for our UITextField – a specific identifier that's required for accessibility purposes that, in turn, will allow our UI test to identify the control we want to test.
2. Back over in our `RepoTableViewController.swift` file, create an `IBOutlet` for the `UITextField` object in question and add the following code, remembering to hook up the outlet to your ViewController:

   ```
   @IBOutlet weak var usernameTextField: UITextField! {
       didSet {
   ```

```
                    usernameTextField.accessibilityIdentifier =
                      "input.textfield.username"
            }
        }
```

3. With that in place, comment out or replace our generic `UTextField` tap test with the following:

```
app.textFields.element(matching: .textField, identifier:
  "input.textfield.username").tap()
```

4. Now, run your test and watch it pass. Great stuff!

   Notice that we are identifying a `textField` and then matching a control type from `textField`. This approach will work wonders when we're testing for nested components in specific views of your app. For example, you might want to search and match for a specific UIButton that you know is embedded within a specific UIScrollView:

```
app.scrollViews.element(matching: .button, identifier:
  "action.button.stopscrolling").tap()
```

5. With that done, let's take our test a little further. Notice the `.tap()` function we're calling at the end of our element identification. There's plenty more options to choose from, but we'll start by splitting the element into its own variable:

```
let textField = app.textFields.element(matching: .textField,
  identifier: "input.textfield.username")
```

6. Notice that's we've removed the `.tap()` function. Now, we can simply call this and any other available function via our `textField` variable:

```
textField.tap()
textField.typeText("MrChrisBarker")
```

7. Run this to see it in action for yourself. Now, what if we go a little further? Add the following line and run the code once more:

```
app.keyboards.buttons["return"].tap()
```

   Hopefully, at this point, you can see where we are going. One thing to bear in mind is that, since we are not mocking data here, we're making a live, asynchronous API call, which, depending on your connection speed or the API, could vary from test to test.

8. To check the results, we need our UI test to "wait" for a specific element to come into view. By design, we know that we are expecting a `UITableView` with populated cells, so let's write our test based on that:

```
let tableView = app.tables.staticTexts["XcodeValidateJson"]
XCTAssertTrue(tableView.waitForExistence(timeout: 5))
```

Line 1 of the preceding code should now be all but familiar to us – we're building an element based on cells within a UITableView (we're not being specific at the time) to look for a specific cell with a label of `XcodeValidateJson`.

Then, we're doing an XCAssert against this element. Allow for a timeout of 5 seconds for this to appear. If it appears beforehand, the test will pass; if not, it will fail.

There's more...

So far, we've seen how functions such as `.tap()` and `.typeText()` can be used when we're interacting with our app. However, these are not standard functions of a `UIButton` to `UITextField`. When we're identifying our controls, the return type we get back is that of an `XCUIElement()`.

There are more options available that we can use to enhance our UI tests, thus allowing for an intricate yet worthy automated test. Let's take a look at some of the additional options available to us:

```
tap()
doubleTap()
press()
twoFingerTap()
swipeUp()
swipeDown()
swipeLeft()
swipeRight()
pinch()
rotate()
```

Each comes with additional parameters that allow you to be specific and cover all the aspects of your user experience in the app (for example, `press()` has a duration parameter).

At the beginning of this section, I mentioned that UI tests come with a great additional benefit, and this is something we have seen already: accessibility. Accessibility is an important factor when building mobile apps, and Apple gives us the best possible tools to do this with Xcode and the Swift programming languages. However, from a theory perspective, if you take the time to build our accessibility into your app, you're indirectly making it much easier to build and shape the UI test around these identifiers – almost doing a good 50% of the work for you – while including an amazing feature.

Alternatively, writing a good UI test can lead to improved accessibility in your app, making it really easy to have one complement the other when building your app.

See also

You can find more information about **XCUITest** at `https://developer.apple.com/documentation/xctest/xcuielement`.

Backward compatibility

Backward compatibility is inevitable. Unless you build an app for the latest version of iOS and plan to support that – and only that – version of iOS, you're going to have to handle backward compatibility at some point. In this recipe, we'll take a look at what Apple offers in terms of building for APIs that have been built with older versions of Swift.

We'll also take a look at migration options from previous versions of Swift and if and how legacy projects can be updated to their latest versions.

How to do it...

We all want to use the latest shiny features in our app. Luckily, Apple makes this relatively easy for us to handle with the use of the **#available** check. So, how does this work? Well, primarily, it can work in three ways: at the function level, at the class level, and at the inline API level.

Let's start with the latter and have a look at how we would do this at the API level:

1. Here is an example of setting `maskedCorners` on a layer in `UIView()`:

```
UIView().layer.maskedCorners = [.layerMinXMaxYCorner,
 .layerMaxXMaxYCorner]
```

This is standard for APIs with iOS 11 and above, but what happens if your app supports iOS? In an ideal world, you only want to support two versions of iOS (including the current one), but that's not always possible. For example, in some retail apps, you may have an existing percentage of customers who you need to support. This also happens in the real world.

So, if your Xcode project has been set up to support iOS 10, you'll actually get a generated error, similar to the following:

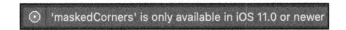

Figure 6.22 – Available API error

2. Click the red indicator to the left and you'll see the following options:

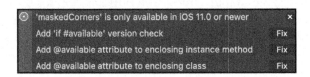

Figure 6.23 – Available API error options

As we mentioned previously we've got three options here: add a version check against the API itself, add a check against the method, or enclose the entire class.

3. Go ahead and click **Fix** for the first option. You'll see the following:

```
if #available(iOS 11.0, *) {
    UIView().layer.maskedCorners = [.layerMinXMaxYCorner,
        .layerMaxXMaxYCorner]
} else {
    // Fallback on earlier versions
}
```

Here, we're given the option to compile the API for a specific version of iOS, allowing us to make use of the API and use a fallback or contingency API, should we want to.

This is a great way to keep up to date with the latest changes that are being made to iOS and keep your code base fresh. However, this can come with some downsides. For example, if the API you've targeted is for a specific feature, you may find yourself struggling to find a suitable fallback (or worse, having to depend on a third-party library). You must also think about testing – you're potentially doubling your testing efforts when they may have only required a light regression test for earlier versions of iOS. Now, you'll have to make sure certain features are tested on multiple versions.

4. Next, let's take a look at the **enclosing instance method**, which allows us to wrap a whole function around a specific version check:

```
@available(iOS 11.0, *)
func availableCheck() {
    UIView().layer.maskedCorners = [.layerMinXMaxYCorner,
      .layerMaxXMaxYCorner]
}
```

As we can see, our function and its contents stay intact – we just decorate the function with the highlighted change.

5. This is all well and good, but let's try calling this function from somewhere else:

Figure 6.24 – Available method error options

That's right – we're met with the same problem that we came across earlier, but this does have some advantages. For example, if your function relies on a lot of code that has a higher API level – which would be a great way to maintain and manage your codebase – when the time comes to move up to higher SDK support, refactoring doesn't become a mammoth job.

6. The final "enclosing class" option follows a similar approach to the method approach, except this occurs at the class level. Your class is simply decorated like so:

```
@available(iOS 11.0, *)
class ReposTableViewController: UITableViewController { }
```

There's more...

Swift has come in many shapes and sizes since its release in 2013, with each new version offering a wider range of APIs and stability. The move to open source has had a massive part to play in that too, but moving from one version to another with each release has often been aided with the help of Xcode's migration tool.

But be warned: you can't simply take an app build in Swift 1.1 and migrate this to Swift 5.3 with Xcode 12 (as nice as that would be...).

Each release, from Swift 3.0 onward, allows you to migrate via the migration tool. For example, Xcode 9 would let you go from **Swift 2.2** to **Swift 3**, Xcode 10 would let you go from **Swift 3** to **Swift 4**, and so on.

This doesn't mean you have to support the latest version of Swift with the latest version of Xcode – the upgrade options are backward compatible too.

For example, our CocoaTouch project uses **Swift 5**, but options to use **Swift 4.2** and **Swift 4** are available via Xcode's **Build Settings**:

Figure 6.25 – Select Swift Language Version option

If you need to go back any further, you'll have to download a previous version of Xcode from the Apple Developer portal. More often than not, multiple versions of Xcode can play nicely together, although this was only really supported from Xcode 9 onward – you've been warned.

See also

You can find more information about **Swift Version History** at https://www.javatpoint.com/history-of-swift.

7
Swift Playgrounds

Throughout this book, we have been using Swift Playgrounds to work through code examples as we explore the Swift language. Playgrounds are great for this use case, as they allow you to explore code and framework APIs without needing the infrastructure of an iOS, macOS, or tvOS app to execute the code.

Their features go beyond how we have used them so far in this book, and in this chapter, we will explore some of those features, from using additional code and resources to creating fully interactive experiences.

In this chapter, we will cover the following recipes:

- Using Swift Playgrounds for UI
- Importing resources into playgrounds
- Importing code into playgrounds
- Multi-page playgrounds
- Using Swift Playgrounds on iPadOS

Technical requirements

All the code for this chapter can be found in this book's GitHub repository at `https://github.com/PacktPublishing/Swift-Cookbook-Second-Edition/tree/master/Chapter07`

Check out the following video to see the Code in Action: `https://bit.ly/37t4f0A`.

Using Swift Playgrounds for UI

We can use Playgrounds to experiment with UI and test custom views and interfaces. In this recipe, we will build a bar chart view that we can use to display numerical data in chart form and use a playground to test it.

Getting ready

First, we'll create an iOS-based playground to build our bar chart. In Chapter 1, *Swift Building Blocks*, we went through creating a new playground, so return there if you need a refresher.

We will create a custom view that will display information in bar chart form, and use that to test some features of playgrounds. You can either enter the following code into a new iOS-based playground or download the playground named `Simple_iOS.playground` from this book's GitHub repository:

1. Create a `Color` struct:

```
import UIKit

struct Color {
    let red: Float
    let green: Float
    let blue: Float
    let alpha: Float = 1.0
    var displayColor: UIColor {
        return UIColor(red: CGFloat(red),
                       green: CGFloat(green),
                       blue: CGFloat(blue),
                       alpha: CGFloat(alpha))
    }
}
```

2. Create a `Bar` struct and `BarView`:

```
struct Bar {
    var value: Float
    var color: Color
}

class BarView: UIView {
    init(frame: CGRect, color: UIColor) {
        super.init(frame: frame)
        backgroundColor = color
    }
    required init?(coder: NSCoder) {
        super.init(coder: coder)
        backgroundColor = .red
    }
}
```

3. Create the `BarChart` view:

```
class BarChart: UIView {
    private var barViews: [BarView] = []
    private var maxValue: Float = 0.0

    var interBarMargin: CGFloat = 5.0

    var bars: [Bar] = [] {
        didSet {
            self.barViews.forEach { $0.removeFromSuperview() }
            var barViews = [BarView]()
            let barCount = CGFloat(bars.count)
            // Calculate the max value before calculating size
            for bar in bars {
                maxValue = max(maxValue, bar.value)
            }
            var xOrigin: CGFloat = interBarMargin

            let margins = interBarMargin * (barCount+1)
            let width = (frame.width - margins) / barCount
            for bar in bars {

                let height = barHeight(forValue: bar.value)
                let rect = CGRect(x: xOrigin,
                                  y: bounds.height - height,
                                  width: width,
                                  height: height)
                let view = BarView(frame: rect,
                                   color: bar.color.displayColor)
```

```
                    barViews.append(view)
                    addSubview(view)
                    xOrigin = view.frame.maxX + interBarMargin
            }
            self.barViews = barViews
        }
    }
    private func barHeight(forValue value: Float) -> CGFloat {
        return (frame.size.height / CGFloat(maxValue)) *
          CGFloat(value)
    }
}
```

How to do it...

In the code that we defined in the **Getting ready** section, the BarChart view can be created with a frame and a background color, and then bars can be added in the form of a Bar struct containing a value and a color. The BarChart view uses these to create subviews of the correct relative size and scale to represent the values of the bars.

Let's write some code to make use of our BarChart view:

1. Enter the following into the playground at the bottom:

```
let barView = BarChart(frame: CGRect(x: 0, y: 0, width: 300,
height:
  300))
barView.backgroundColor = .white
let bar1 = Bar(value: 20, color: Color(red: 1, green: 0, blue: 0))
let bar2 = Bar(value: 40, color: Color(red: 0, green: 1, blue: 0))
let bar3 = Bar(value: 25, color: Color(red: 0, green: 0, blue: 1))
barView.bars = [bar1, bar2, bar3]
```

2. Press the blue play button at the bottom-left of the playground window to execute the code. As your code executes, you will see that the playground sidebar fills up with information.

3. In Chapter 1, *Swift Building Blocks*, we saw that playgrounds have a timeline that provides information about each line of execution. As you pass your cursor over the line, you see an eye-shaped icon that will display a preview of the result of that line of execution. Where the line involves a UI element such as view, the playground will render that view and display it in a preview box:

```
for bar in bars {

    let height = barHeight(forValue: bar.value)
    let rect = CGRect(x: xOrigin,
                      y: bounds.height - height,
                      width: width,
                      height: height)
    let view = BarView(frame: rect,
                       color: bar.color.displayColor)
    barViews.append(view)
    addSubview(view)

    xOrigin = view.frame.maxX + interBarMargin
}
self.barViews = barViews
```

Figure 7.1 – BarChart preview box

4. The same is true for the pinned inline preview that you can get by pressing the square button in the timeline:

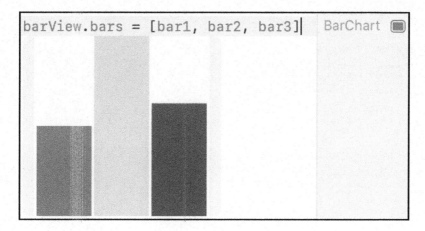

Figure 7.2 – BarChart inline preview

These features can be great for testing and tweaking view code.

If the purpose of the playground is to demo or experiment with a custom view component and you'd like a more prominent view output, you can use the playground's live view feature:

1. Import the `PlaygroundSupport` framework at the top of the playground:

   ```
   import PlaygroundSupport
   ```

   The `PlaygroundSupport` framework provides a number of features for accessing various features of the playground.

2. Add the following to set our `BarChart` view to be the playground's live view:

   ```
   PlaygroundPage.current.liveView = barView
   ```

3. If the playground's live view isn't visible, you can display it from the menu. Go to **Editor | Live View**:

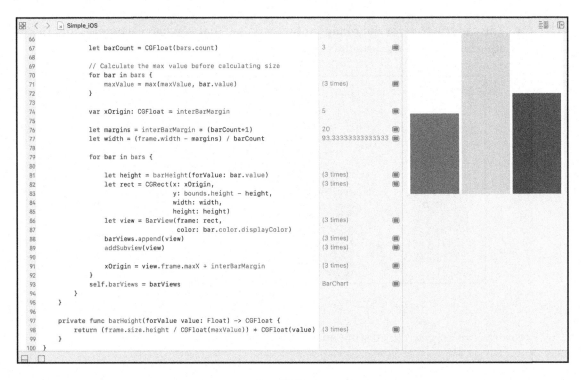

Figure 7.3 – Live view

This view will be updated as the code in the playground changes. Try changing the value of the bars and see the view change.

How it works...

A playground's live view can be anything that conforms to `PlaygroundLiveViewable`. On iOS, both `UIView` and `UIViewController` conform to `PlaygroundLiveViewable`, as do their equivalents on macOS: `NSView` and `NSViewController`.

In the preceding code, we construct a `BarChart`, which is a `UIView`, and assign it to the `liveView` property of the current `PlaygroundPage`.

These live views respond to touch events just as they would in a macOS app or in the iOS simulator. Therefore, you can use them to test interactive views and controls.

Unfortunately, playgrounds do not currently support interface builder layout files, which are the `.xibs` and `.storyboard` files. Therefore, to use Playgrounds with your custom views, you will have to lay out your views programmatically.

Be aware that iOS-based playgrounds support many, but not all, of the frameworks available in the iOS SDK, so this may limit what you can do in a playground.

There's more...

In the preceding example, and for most of this book, we focused on iOS-based playgrounds. However, macOS-based playgrounds are just as useful for the macOS platform and can also be used for UI testing and experimentation.

You will find a macOS-based playground called `Simple_macOS.playground` that also creates a simple bar chart view in this book's GitHub repository at `https://github.com/PacktPublishing/Swift-Cookbook-Second-Edition/tree/master/Chapter07/01_Using_Swift_Playgrounds_for_UI`

Alternatively, you can create a new macOS-based playground and enter the following code:

1. Create a `Color` struct:

```
import PlaygroundSupport
import Cocoa

struct Color {
    let red: CGFloat
```

```
        let green: CGFloat
        let blue: CGFloat
        let alpha: CGFloat = 1.0
        var displayColor: NSColor {
            return NSColor(calibratedRed: red,
                              green: green,
                              blue: blue,
                              alpha: alpha)
        }
    }
```

2. Create a `Bar` **struct and** `BarView`:

```
struct Bar {
    var value: Float
    var color: Color
}

class BarView: NSView {
    let color: NSColor
    init(frame: NSRect, color: NSColor) {
        self.color = color
        super.init(frame: frame)
    }
    required init?(coder: NSCoder) {
        self.color = .red
        super.init(coder: coder)
    }
    override func draw(_ dirtyRect: NSRect) {
        super.draw(dirtyRect)
        color.set()
        NSBezierPath.fill(dirtyRect)
    }
}
```

3. Create the `BarChart` **view:**

```
class BarChart: NSView {
    let color: NSColor
    init(frame: NSRect, color: NSColor) {
        self.color = color
        super.init(frame: frame)
    }
    required init?(coder: NSCoder) {
        self.color = .white
        super.init(coder: coder)
    }
    var bars: [Bar] = [] {
```

```
        didSet {
            self.barViews.forEach { $0.removeFromSuperview() }
            var barViews = [BarView]()
            let barCount = CGFloat(bars.count)
            // Calculate the max value before calculating size
            for bar in bars {
                maxValue = max(maxValue, bar.value)
            }
            var xOrigin: CGFloat = interBarMargin

            let margins = interBarMargin * (barCount+1)
            let width = (frame.width - margins) / barCount
            for bar in bars {

                let height = barHeight(forValue: bar.value)
                let rect = NSRect(x: xOrigin,
                                  y: 0,
                                  width: width,
                                  height: height)
                let view = BarView(frame: rect,
                                   color: bar.color.displayColor)
                barViews.append(view)
                addSubview(view)
                xOrigin = rect.maxX + interBarMargin
            }
            self.barViews = barViews
        }
    }
    var interBarMargin: CGFloat = 5.0
    private var barViews: [NSView] = []
    private var maxValue: Float = 0.0
    override func draw(_ dirtyRect: NSRect) {
        super.draw(dirtyRect)
        color.set()
        NSBezierPath.fill(dirtyRect)
    }
    private func barHeight(forValue value: Float) -> CGFloat {
        return (frame.size.height / CGFloat(maxValue)) *
          CGFloat(value)
    }
}
```

4. Use the `BarChart` to display information:

```
let frame = CGRect(x: 0, y: 0, width: 300, height: 300)
let barView = BarChart(frame: frame,
                       color: .white)
PlaygroundPage.current.liveView = barView
```

```
let bar1 = Bar(value: 20, color: Color(red: 1, green: 0, blue: 0))
let bar2 = Bar(value: 40, color: Color(red: 0, green: 1, blue: 0))
let bar3 = Bar(value: 25, color: Color(red: 0, green: 0, blue: 1))
barView.bars = [bar1, bar2, bar3]

PlaygroundPage.current.liveView = barView
```

This macOS version of our custom `barView` works exactly like the iOS version, and the live view for a macOS-based playground works exactly like its iOS-based counterparts.

Similar to iOS, macOS-based playgrounds support many, but not all, of the frameworks available in the macOS SDK, so this may limit what you can do in a playground.

Hopefully, you can see from this recipe that Swift Playgrounds can be really useful for viewing UI experimentation on both iOS and macOS.

See also

Apple's reference for the Playground Support framework can be found at `http://swiftbook.link/docs/playgroundsupport`.

Importing resources into playgrounds

While building apps, we will often need to include resources, such as images. How can we do the same with playgrounds so that our UI can incorporate these images? That is what we will investigate in this recipe.

We will improve our bar chart custom view from the previous recipe by adding a semi-transparent image to provide a texture for the bars.

Getting ready

For this recipe, we will start with the playground from the previous recipe. The playground is called `Simple_iOS.playground`, and you can get it from the GitHub repository for this book at `https://github.com/PacktPublishing/Swift-Cookbook-Second-Edition/tree/master/Chapter07/01_Using_Swift_Playgrounds_for_UI`

We will be using a semi-transparent texture image for this recipe. You can supply your own, or download a sample one from here: `https://github.com/PacktPublishing/Swift-Cookbook-Second-Edition/tree/master/Chapter07/02_Import_Resources_into_Playgrounds/EmbeddedResource.playground/Resources`

How to do it...

Let's take a look at the following steps to understand how to add our image to the playground:

1. We need to open up Xcode's project navigator, which is often not visible by default when a playground is opened. To reveal the project navigator, select **View | Navigators | Project** from the menu. Alternatively, you can select the **left pane reveal** button in the top-left corner of the Xcode window:

Figure 7.4 – Project navigator

The playground will be listed at the top of the project navigator, along with a disclosure triangle.

2. Select the triangle to reveal folders named `Sources` and `Resources`.

3. Drag the texture image from Finder into the `Resources` folder:

Figure 7.5 – Adding a file to the project

Now that we have embedded our texture image within our playground, we need to make use of it. We want each bar in the bar chart to have a settable color, but for the texture to sit on top of that color.

4. Update the `BarView` part of our code to use the texture image:

```
class BarView: UIView {
    init(frame: CGRect, color: UIColor) {
        super.init(frame: frame)
        backgroundColor = color
        setupTexture()
    }
    required init?(coder: NSCoder) {
        super.init(coder: coder)
        backgroundColor = UIColor.red
        setupTexture()
    }
    private func setupTexture() {
        guard let textureImage = UIImage(named: "texture") else {
            return }
        let textureColor = UIColor(patternImage: textureImage)
        let frame = CGRect(origin: .zero, size: bounds.size)
        let textureView = UIView(frame: frame)
        textureView.backgroundColor = textureColor
        addSubview(textureView)
    }
}
```

5. We can retrieve the image in the same way we would in a full app by referencing the filename of the image, without the file extension, in a `UIImage` initializer:

```
let textureImage = UIImage(named: "texture")
```

When the playground is executed, you will see that our bar chart looks a lot more interesting:

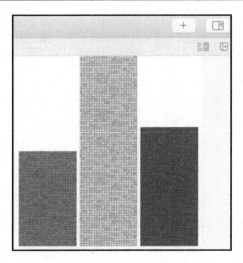

Figure 7.6 – Textured bar chart

How it works...

To understand where the image that we added is stored, it helps to know how playgrounds are structured.

A playground is actually a folder, but with a `.playground` file extension. We can see this by taking a playground file and showing the context menu, which can be done by right-clicking or holding *Ctrl* while clicking on the file. From this menu, select **Show Package Contents**:

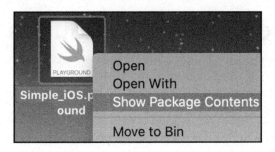

Figure 7.7 – Viewing Package Contents

This will open the playground as a folder, showing its contents. In there, you will find a number of files, including one called `Contents.swift`, which is the Swift file containing the code that is executed. There is also a folder called `Resources`, which contains the texture image we imported:

Figure 7.8 – Package Contents

By dragging the image into the file navigator, Xcode created this folder and placed the image in it. Alternatively, we could have created this folder manually and dropped it in the image. Playgrounds will look for a folder named `Resources`, and all the resources in it will be made available from the playground.

See also

The result of this recipe is available as `EmbeddedResources.playground` in the GitHub repository for this book, in the `chapter 7` folder.

Importing code into playgrounds

As we have seen throughout this chapter, and this book, playgrounds are a great canvas for exploring APIs, frameworks, and custom code. However, if you want to explore uses for your own code, it appears that you need to include all the code needed in the playground, and that can make it long and unwieldy.

It doesn't need to be that way. In this recipe, we will see how you can embed Swift code in your playground and make use of it from your playground code.

Getting ready

For this recipe, we will use the playground from the previous recipe, called `EmbeddedResources.playground`, which can be retrieved from this book's GitHub repository at `https://github.com/PacktPublishing/Swift-Cookbook-Second-Edition/tree/master/Chapter07/02_Import_Resources_into_Playgrounds`.

How to do it...

We will take the `BarChart` custom view and related code and move it to a separate file embedded within the playground, leaving us free to use the playground to experiment with our custom view:

1. If the playground's project navigator isn't visible, select **View | Navigators | Project** from the menu.
2. Select the **Sources** folder and then select **File | New | File** from the menu to create a new Swift file in your **Sources** folder:

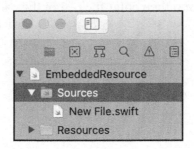

Figure 7.9 – Sources folder

3. If you already have Swift files that you want to embed in a playground, you can drag the files into the `Sources` folder, just like we did with our texture image in the previous recipe.
4. Rename the new file `Color.swift`, as we will use this to hold our `Color` struct that is currently in the main playground content.
5. Enter the following code into `Color.swift`:

```
import UIKit

public struct Color {
    let red: Float
    let green: Float
```

```
        let blue: Float
        let alpha: Float
        public init(red:Float, green:Float, blue:Float, alpha:Float =
1) {
            self.red = red
            self.green = green
            self.blue = blue
            self.alpha = alpha
        }
        var displayColor: UIColor {
            return UIColor(red: CGFloat(red),
                        green: CGFloat(green),
                        blue: CGFloat(blue),
                        alpha: CGFloat(alpha))
        }
    }
```

Note that we have added `public` access controls to the `Color` struct and its initializer; we will see more about that as we progress.

6. Create another new Swift file in the `Sources` folder as we did earlier, called `BarChart.swift`, and then enter the rest of the code needed to define the `BarChart` custom view, starting with the `Bar` struct:

```
import UIKit

public struct Bar {
    var value: Float
    var color: Color
    public init(value: Float, color: Color) {
        self.value = value
        self.color = color
    }
}
```

This is followed by `BarView`:

```
class BarView: UIView {
    init(frame: CGRect, color: UIColor) {
        super.init(frame: frame)
        backgroundColor = color
        setupTexture()
    }
    required init?(coder: NSCoder) {
        super.init(coder: coder)
        backgroundColor = UIColor.red
        setupTexture()
    }
}
```

```
    private func setupTexture() {
        guard let textureImage = UIImage(named: "texture") else {
          return }
        let textureColor = UIColor(patternImage: textureImage)
        let textureView = UIView(frame: bounds)
        textureView.backgroundColor = textureColor
        addSubview(textureView)
    }
}
```

And finally, we have `BarChart`:

```
public class BarChart: UIView {
    private var barViews: [BarView] = []
    private var maxValue: Float = 0.0

    var interBarMargin: CGFloat = 5.0
    public var bars: [Bar] = [] {
        didSet {
            self.barViews.forEach { $0.removeFromSuperview() }
            var barViews = [BarView]()
            let barCount = CGFloat(bars.count)
            // Calculate the max value before calculating size
            for bar in bars {
                maxValue = max(maxValue, bar.value)
            }
            var xOrigin: CGFloat = interBarMargin

            let margins = interBarMargin * (barCount+1)
            let width = (frame.width - margins) / barCount
            for bar in bars {

                let height = barHeight(forValue: bar.value)
                let rect = CGRect(x: xOrigin,
                                  y: bounds.height - height,
                                  width: width,
                                  height: height)
                let view = BarView(frame: rect,
                                   color: bar.color.displayColor)
                barViews.append(view)
                addSubview(view)
                xOrigin = view.frame.maxX + interBarMargin
            }
            self.barViews = barViews
        }
    }
    private func barHeight(forValue value: Float) -> CGFloat {
        return (frame.size.height / CGFloat(maxValue)) *
```

```
                    CGFloat(value)
          }
     }
```

7. With the `BarChart` implementation code contained in the `Sources` folder, the playground contents can be just for experimenting with the `BarChart` custom view. Remove the code we placed in the other files and you are left with the following:

```
import PlaygroundSupport
import UIKit

let barView = BarChart(frame: CGRect(x: 0, y: 0, width: 300,
height:
  300))
barView.backgroundColor = .white
let bar1 = Bar(value: 20, color: Color(red: 1, green: 0, blue: 0))
let bar2 = Bar(value: 40, color: Color(red: 0, green: 1, blue: 0))
let bar3 = Bar(value: 25, color: Color(red: 0, green: 0, blue: 1))
barView.bars = [bar1, bar2, bar3]
PlaygroundPage.current.liveView = barView
```

How it works...

In moving the `BarChart` implementation to embedded Swift files, we added `public` access control at points where we wanted it to be accessible from the playground content. This is because code within the `Sources` folder acts as a kind of lightweight module in terms of access control.

Anything with the default `internal` access control is only accessible to other code inside the `Sources` folder. To make it accessible to code in the main playground content, it needs to be declared as `public` or `open`. This is really useful, as it allows you to be in control of what you expose to the playground content; so, you can provide well-designed APIs that don't expose the underlying complexity.

 If you require a refresher on access controls or want to learn more, check out the recipe entitled *Controlling access with access control*, in `Chapter 2`, *Mastering the Building Blocks*.

See also

The result of this recipe can be found in `EmbeddedSources.playground` in this book's GitHub repository.

Further information about Swift access controls can be found in `Chapter 2`, *Mastering the Building Blocks*.

Multi-page playgrounds

We've discussed how playgrounds can be a great tool for exploring APIs and experimenting with UIs. However, playgrounds can also be used for documenting APIs, and providing rich, linkable content. Swift Playgrounds provides support for rich text formatting in comments and multiple pages of content, and we will explore those features in this recipe.

Getting ready

We will start with the playground we used in the last recipe, which displayed our custom `BarChart` view. You can get the playground, called `EmbeddedSources.playground`, from the GitHub repository for this book at `https://github.com/PacktPublishing/Swift-Cookbook-Second-Edition/tree/master/Chapter07`.

We will use our `BarChart` view to display the price in US dollars of three different cryptocurrencies over a 6-month period between January 2020 and June 2020. We can show each type of currency on a different playground page.

 If you want to know more about cryptocurrencies, you can watch this explanatory video:
`http://swiftbook.link/videos/cryptocurrencies`.

How to do it...

By default, playgrounds have just one Swift content file, but for our purpose, we want to have three pages in our playground, one for each of the three cryptocurrencies we will document: Bitcoin, Etherium, and Lightcoin. Let's get started:

1. If the project navigator isn't visible, you should make it visible using the menu by selecting **View** | **Navigators** | **Project**.

2. To create a new playground page, you can click on the plus button in the bottom left-hand corner of the project navigator, or select **File** | **New** | **Playground Page** from the menu:

Figure 7.10 – New Playground Page

When creating a new playground page, the existing contents of the playground become a playground page, and another blank page is created:

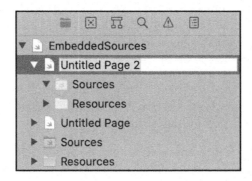

Figure 7.11 – Creating a new page in Playgrounds

3. Create three pages in total, as we will display data on three different cryptocurrencies, and rename them as follows:

   - Bitcoin
   - Etherium
   - Lightcoin

Each of these pages can use the `BarChart` code in the `Sources` folder that we added in the previous recipe, so we can create a `BarChart` view on each page to chart the value of each currency.

4. Enter the following code into the `Bitcoin` playground page:

```
import PlaygroundSupport
import UIKit

let frame = CGRect(x: 0, y: 0, width: 300, height: 300)
let barView = BarChart(frame: frame)
barView.backgroundColor = .white

let green =  Color(red: 0, green: 1, blue: 0)

let jan2020 = Bar(value: 9388.88, color: green)
let feb2020 = Bar(value: 8639.59, color: green)
let mar2020 = Bar(value: 6483.74, color: green)
let apr2020 = Bar(value: 8773.11, color: green)
let may2020 = Bar(value: 9437.05, color: green)
let jun2020 = Bar(value: 9164.54, color: green)

barView.bars = [jan2020,
                feb2020,
                mar2020,
                apr2020,
                may2020,
                jun2020]

PlaygroundPage.current.liveView = barView
```

5. Next, enter the following code into the `Etherium` playground page:

```
import PlaygroundSupport
import UIKit

let frame = CGRect(x: 0, y: 0, width: 300, height: 300)
let barView = BarChart(frame: frame)
barView.backgroundColor = .white

let blue = Color(red: 0, green: 0, blue: 1)

let jan2020 = Bar(value: 181.73, color: blue)
let feb2020 = Bar(value: 223.5, color: blue)
let mar2020 = Bar(value: 133.76, color: blue)
let apr2020 = Bar(value: 209.42, color: blue)
let may2020 = Bar(value: 245.76, color: blue)
let jun2020 = Bar(value: 225.71, color: blue)
```

```
barView.bars = [jan2020,
                feb2020,
                mar2020,
                apr2020,
                may2020,
                jun2020]

PlaygroundPage.current.liveView = barView
```

6. Lastly, enter the following code into the `Lightcoin` playground page:

```
import PlaygroundSupport
import UIKit

let frame = CGRect(x: 0, y: 0, width: 300, height: 300)
let barView = BarChart(frame: frame)
barView.backgroundColor = .white

let red = Color(red: 1, green: 0, blue: 0)

let jan2020 = Bar(value: 67.58, color: red)
let feb2020 = Bar(value: 58.09, color: red)
let mar2020 = Bar(value: 39.13, color: red)
let apr2020 = Bar(value: 46.19, color: red)
let may2020 = Bar(value: 44.23, color: red)
let jun2020 = Bar(value: 41.21, color: red)

barView.bars = [jan2020,
                feb2020,
                mar2020,
                apr2020,
                may2020,
                jun2020]

PlaygroundPage.current.liveView = barView
```

Each page displays the value history as a bar chart when run, and you can use the project navigator to switch between them.

How it works...

As we did in previous recipes, we can take a look inside the playground to see how each playground page is represented. Right-click on the playground, or hold *Ctrl* while clicking on it. From this menu, select **Show Package Contents**:

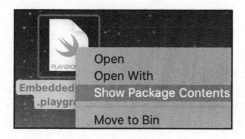

Figure 7.12 – Viewing Package Contents

You will see that the `Contents.swift` folder that we saw earlier has been replaced with a folder containing three `.xcplaygroundpage` files, one for each page in the playground:

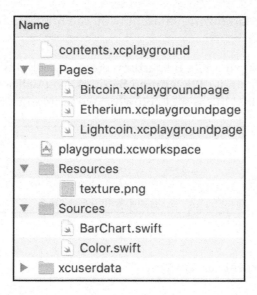

Figure 7.13 – Extracted content

Each of these `.playgroundpage` files is essentially a playground in itself. You can right-click on `.playgroundpage` and select **Show Package Contents**, and you will see the same playground structure that we saw previously. Much like the normal playground, a `.xcplaygroundpage` file can contain the `Sources` and `Resources` subfolders, and placing code and resources in these will make them visible to just that page.

There's more...

Since we can now add multiple pages of content and have the ability to embed code and resources, Swift Playgrounds appears very useful in terms of interactive code documentation. To assist in this use case, it would be great if we could have some control over the presentation of our comments; well we can, as playgrounds support comments in **Markdown**.

Markdown is a lightweight text formatting syntax, invented by *John Gruber*, and is widely used to write text that can then be rendered with rich text formatting. More details about Markdown can be found at `http://swiftbook.link/markdown/docs`.

We won't delve into the Markdown syntax, but you can find a useful *cheat sheet* at `http://swiftbook.link/markdown/cheatsheet`.

In our playground, open up the **File Inspector** window by selecting from the menu **View | Inspectors | File** and look under **Playground Settings**. You will see an option for **Render Documentation**. Ensure that this is set to off while we write some Markdown comments:

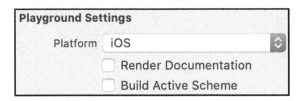

Figure 7.14 – Playground Settings

Let's now add some comments to our `Bitcoin` page:

```
/*:
 # Crypto Currencies
 ## Bitcoin
 */

import PlaygroundSupport
import UIKit
```

```
/*:
 ### Usage
 * Create Bar Chart
 * Create Bars and add to chart
 * Make Bar Chart the LiveView
 */
let barView = BarChart(frame: CGRect(x: 0, y: 0, width: 300, height:
   300))
barView.backgroundColor = .white
let green =  Color(red: 0, green: 1, blue: 0, alpha: 1.0)

/*:
 * Note:
 Bitcoin Price (in USD)
 - Jan 2017 -  $970.17
 - Feb 2017 -  $960.05
 - Mar 2017 - $1203.02
 - Apr 2017 - $1076.90
 - May 2017 - $1390.24
 - Jun 2017 - $2414.11

Taken from
[Statista](https://www.statista.com/statistics/326707/bitcoin-price-index)
 */
let jan2017 = Bar(value: 970.17, color: green)
let feb2017 = Bar(value: 960.05, color: green)
let mar2017 = Bar(value: 1203.02, color: green)
let apr2017 = Bar(value: 1076.90, color: green)
let may2017 = Bar(value: 1390.24, color: green)
let jun2017 = Bar(value: 2414.11, color: green)

barView.bars = [jan2017, feb2017, mar2017, apr2017, may2017, jun2017]
PlaygroundPage.current.liveView = barView
```

To indicate to the playground that your comments contain Markdown formatting, a colon, :, is added after the opening of the comment block. This works for multi-line comments, /*:, and single-line comments, //:.

With these comments in place, let's turn **Render Documentation** back on and see what the comments look like:

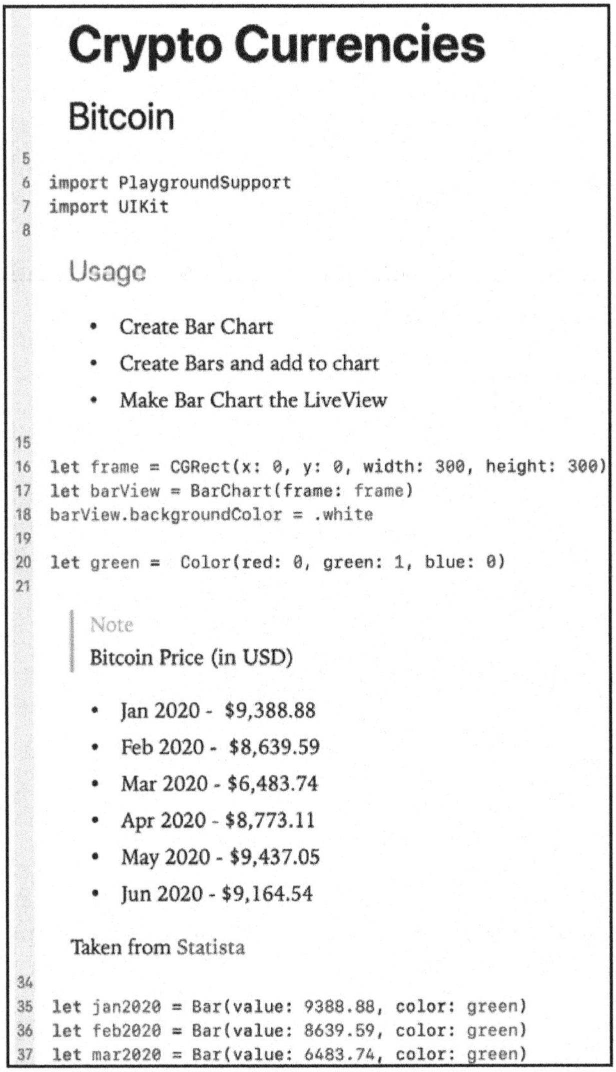

Crypto Currencies

Bitcoin

```
5
6   import PlaygroundSupport
7   import UIKit
8
```

Usage

- Create Bar Chart
- Create Bars and add to chart
- Make Bar Chart the LiveView

```
15
16  let frame = CGRect(x: 0, y: 0, width: 300, height: 300)
17  let barView = BarChart(frame: frame)
18  barView.backgroundColor = .white
19
20  let green =  Color(red: 0, green: 1, blue: 0)
21
```

> Note
>
> Bitcoin Price (in USD)
>
> - Jan 2020 - $9,388.88
> - Feb 2020 - $8,639.59
> - Mar 2020 - $6,483.74
> - Apr 2020 - $8,773.11
> - May 2020 - $9,437.05
> - Jun 2020 - $9,164.54

Taken from Statista

```
34
35  let jan2020 = Bar(value: 9388.88, color: green)
36  let feb2020 = Bar(value: 8639.59, color: green)
37  let mar2020 = Bar(value: 6483.74, color: green)
```

Figure 7.15 – Rendered document

In addition, playgrounds also support the creation of Markdown links between the playground pages; you can link to the next page with `@next` and to the previous page with `@previous`. So, in Markdown, the links will be as follows:

```
//: [Next page] (@next)
//: [Previous page] (@previous)
```

It is left as an exercise to the reader to add Markdown comments to the other two pages and provide links between the pages.

See also

The result of this recipe can be found as `MultiplePages.playground` in the GitHub repository for this book at `https://github.com/PacktPublishing/Swift-Cookbook-Second-Edition/tree/master/Chapter07/04_Multi-Page_Playgrounds/MultiplePages.playground`.

Further information pertaining to the Markdown syntax can be found at `http://swiftbook.link/markdown/docs`.

Using Swift Playgrounds on iPadOS

In 2016, Apple released an iPad-only app called Swift Playgrounds. Taken from the success of Playgrounds from Xcode, Swift Playgrounds for iPadOS went a step further and added an additional educational element to the app. In 2020, Apple also released a version for macOS, opening the doors for educational purposes and to those starting out who may feel a little intimidated by the Xcode IDE.

In this recipe, we'll take a look at how we can more easily replicate a recipe similar to that from `Chapter 6`, *Building iOS Apps with Swift*, straight on our iPad.

Getting ready

For this recipe, you'll need either an iPad running iOS 14.0 in order to download Swift Playgrounds from the App Store or alternatively, you can download the macOS version from the Mac App Store and follow along with this recipe too.

How to do it...

1. We'll start by launching the Swift Playgrounds app from your device. You should be presented with the following:

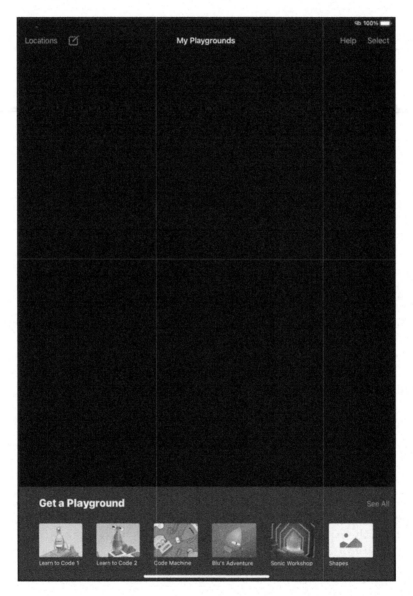

Figure 7.16 – Swift Playgrounds on iPadOS

2. Next, you can either scroll along with the **Get a Playground** carousel until you see **Blank** or tap on the new document icon on the top left next to **Locations**.

3. A new document will be created and added to your playgrounds. Tap on this to open it.

Welcome to the Playgrounds Editor. This is where we can go ahead and write code, with a sense of familiarity that you'll get from developing in Xcode:

Figure 7.17 – My Playground

We'll start by doing something simple, just to get familiar with the IDE (*yes, I'm calling it an IDE - it kind of is in a way...*):

1. Tap on the screen to raise the keyboard. If the keyboard doesn't raise, simply press the chevron on the right-hand side of the bottom toolbar. While you are down there, take a look at some of the available keyword suggestions – **let**, **var**, **if**, and so on.

2. Go ahead and tap on the **let** constant. You will notice that the following is autopopulated for you:

```
let name = value
```

3. With the name placeholder highlighted, simply start typing your variable name, create one called `isSwitchedOn`, and now press the *tab* key to move the highlighted placeholder over to the `value` here. Then, type the word `true`.

Just as you would expect in Swift, type inference kicks in and we've created a constant Bool called `isSwitchedOn` with the value of `true`.

4. Next, on a new line, tap on `if` and complete the following highlighted code snippet:

```
let isSwitchedOn = true
if isSwitchedOn {
    print("Switched On")
}
```

5. Once done, press the **Run My Code** button and you should observe that a red indicator appears on the icon to the left of this button. Tap on that to reveal the console window and check out your print statement.

Pretty cool hey! OK, so let's do something a bit more complex and fun. Create another project and call it `Quotes` (or whatever name you prefer):

1. First, we need to add a couple of imports if they are not already there:

```
import UIKit
import PlaygroundSupport

PlaygroundPage.current.needsIndefiniteExecution = true
```

This is followed by the third line, which sets the playground to run continuously. We'll go into more details as to why we need that in our *How it works...* section.

2. Next, we'll continue by creating a couple of structs, as follows:

```
struct RootResponse: Codable {
    let response: [Response]?
}

struct Response: Codable {
    let id: String?
    let quote: String
}
```

3. These match the response type from the API we are about to call. Next, let's create a function similar to the `fetchRepos()` function:

```
func fetchQuotes(completionHandler: @escaping ([Response]?) ->
Void)
  -> URLSessionDataTask? {
    var session = URLSession.shared
    let urlString = "https://api.bobross.dev/api/10"
    guard let url = URL(string: urlString) else {
        return nil
    }
    var request = URLRequest(url: url)
    let task = session.dataTask(with: request) { (data, response,
      error) in
        // First unwrap the optional data
        guard let data = data else {
            completionHandler(nil)
            return
        }
        do {
            let decoder = JSONDecoder()
            let responseObject = try
              decoder.decode(RootResponse.self, from: data)
            completionHandler(responseObject.response)
        } catch {
            completionHandler(nil)
        }
    }
    task.resume()
    return task
}
```

For simplicity, I've made some small tweaks here, as highlighted in the preceding code. We have just made an adjustment to the `return` type, returning our codable object that we created in the previous step.

We're also calling a different API, one that will return us with an array of quotes that we can iterate through.

4. Next, let's call our function:

```
fetchQuotes { (response) in
    guard let quotes = response as? [Response] else { return }
    for item in quotes {
        print(item.quote ?? "")
    }
}
```

Here, we're just iterating around the response, but you should see the following red badge appear next to our console icon:

Figure 7.18 – The Stop running button

5. Go ahead and tap on the icon and see the results logged to the console. If everything is going well, you should now see a list of 10 quotes.

With this all working, let's take a look at how we can arrange our code a little better, much like Playgrounds in Xcode. Our main Swift file is embedded within a single root file; however, we are given support for **modules** with the addition of shared code files:

1. To access these, press on the navigation icon in the top-left corner next to the close button. When pressed, it should look something like this:

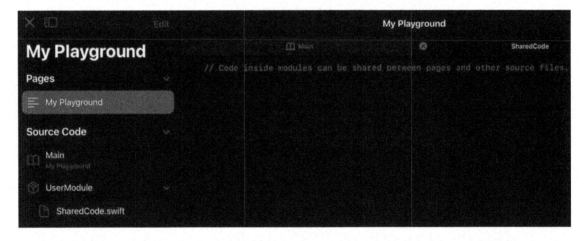

Figure 7.19 – Project navigation window

Don't worry too much about the file structure, we'll go through that in the *How it works...* section later; all you need to know for now is that all code that can be used (or *shared*) by the playground file is within a module called **UserModule** (which can be renamed should you wish).

2. Under here is a file called `SharedCode.swift`. Highlight this and cut and paste the codable structs from the main project into here. You can rename `SharedCode.swift` to `Models.swift` if you like.

3. Run the project again and you'll notice that you're given the following compiler error – **Property cannot be declared public because its type uses an internal type**. Basically, due to the way Swift Playgrounds interprets external files, you need to make the structs public:

```
public struct RootResponse: Codable {
    public let response: [Response]?
}

public struct Response: Codable {
    public let id: String?
    public let quote: String
}
```

Run this again and you'll see the logic working again in all its glory, but as nice as it is to see this in the output window, let's again take a look at how we can add this to our `liveView` canvas:

1. We start by programmatically creating a `TableViewController()`:

```
class TableViewController: UITableViewController { }
```

2. We'll override `viewWillLoad()` and add in our code here to call our `fetchQuotes()` function:

```
override func viewDidLoad() {
    super.viewDidLoad()
    // Fetch Quotes code to go here
}
```

3. Now we'll need to add a couple of class properties, so incorporate the following:

```
var quotes = [String]()
var session = URLSession.shared
```

`URLSession` will be used for our `fetchQuotes()` function just as we needed before. The quotes array will be where we store all our quotes from the API response.

4. Next, copy the `fetchQuotes()` function into the `TableViewController` class (currently this will sit outside).

5. Now, we can extend `viewDidLoad()` to call our function:

```
override func viewDidLoad() {
    super.viewDidLoad()
    fetchQuotes { (response) in
```

```
guard let quotes = response as? [Response] else { return }
for item in quotes {
    self.quotes.append(item.quote)
}
DispatchQueue.main.async {
    self.tableView.reloadData()
}
    }
}
```

Notice that in the preceding code, rather than printing the output to the console, we'll now add this to our quotes array. Once our array has been populated and we're no longer iterating around the response, we can call `reloadData()` on our table view, which we'll need to do inside `DispatchQueue.main.async` to force the reload on the main thread (as we're currently inside an asynchronous response callback from our API).

6. Once this is done, let's add in some `UITableView` delegates that are required in order for our Table view to display our data:

```
override func numberOfSections(in tableView: UITableView) -> Int {
    return 1
}
override func tableView(_ tableView: UITableView,
numberOfRowsInSection section: Int) -> Int {
    return quotes.count
}
```

We will now need to add `numberOfSections()` in any order, which will return 1 followed by `numberOfRowsInSection()`, which will return the number of quotes in our array.

7. Finally, we need to add in the `cellForRowAt()` delegate:

```
override func tableView(_ tableView: UITableView, cellForRowAt
indexPath: IndexPath) -> UITableViewCell {
    let quote = quotes[indexPath.row]
    var cell = UITableViewCell()
    if let _ = tableView.dequeueReusableCell(withIdentifier:
      "table.view.cell") {
        cell = UITableViewCell(style: .default, reuseIdentifier:
          "table.view.cell")
    }

    cell.textLabel?.text = quote
    return cell
}
```

Here, we simply create an instance of `UITableViewCell()`. If no reuse identifier is set, we'll add one to our cell (we've called ours `table.view.cell`, but you can call it anything you want). Then, using the current index of the cell being called, we obtain the text from our quotes array.

8. Finally, we need to assign `TableViewContoller` to our Live view:

```
PlaygroundPage.current.liveView = TableViewController()
```

9. Press **Run My Code** and you should see the following:

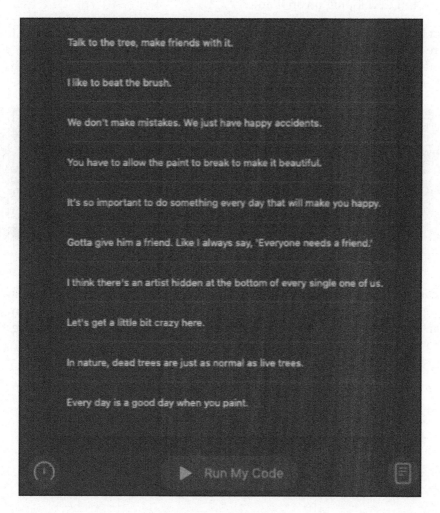

Figure 7.20 – Results live view

Whether your using Playground on the iPad or via the Mac App Store, it goes without saying that it's certainly a powerful alternative to Xcode.

How it works...

Swift Playgrounds has some powerful features, and especially if you're used to using Xcode, you'll immediately start to make a comparison (I know I did). But taking a step back and seeing how it all wonderfully knits together certainly opened my eyes to not only writing code but developing on an iPad.

Let's take a look at the code completion. Normally with Xcode, we'll expect this to show up when we're typing away, in a small dialog/table next to our text, but with Swift Playgrounds on iPadOS, we get this in the form of a horizontal scroll bar at the bottom of the screen:

Figure 7.21 – Syntax suggestions

Here, we can see an example of code completion on UITableView. Notice that immediately we're given multiple options that refer to just UITableViews. Go ahead and re-implement the delegate you did earlier, and you will then see another show up in the suggestions as you start to type numberOf – it just works.

Another thing to note is compiler errors, displayed in a similar way to how Xcode does it (although more in line with your code in the editor). The following red symbol with a description of your error will be presented when running your code. Tapping on the button will collapse the error, allowing you to inspect your code in a little more detail:

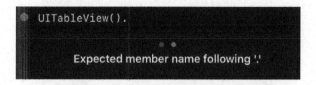

Figure 7.22 – Error inspection

Alternatively, if you have a number of errors, then you can simply click on the red icon to the left of the **+** icon in the menu bar to display a list of current errors:

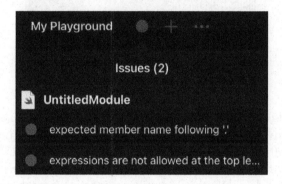

Figure 7.23 – Error indicator

With this in mind, the compiler may not always give you errors and you may be forced to "step through" your code in order to find out what exactly is going on in your logic. If we refer back to the *How to do it...* section, you'll remember that we needed to add the following line of code to make our function work:

```
PlaygroundPage.current.needsIndefiniteExecution = true
```

This was due to our playground finishing its execution before our API had returned the call. Let's comment this out for the moment and run our code and you will notice that it never displays our list of quotes, but we want to see what is happening.

To the left of the **Run My Code** button is a timer icon. Tap on this to see the following options:

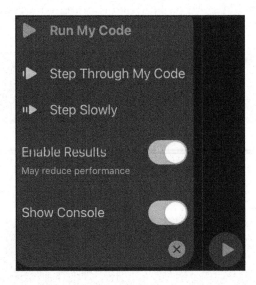

Figure 7.24 – Running my code options

Run My Code is highlighted by default, but two additional options exist – **Step Through My Code** and **Step Slowly**. What these do (essentially the same thing, although one does it more slowly than the other) is highlight each line of code as it is executed, or intended to be executed, allowing you to follow and check any potential logic issues. For those who are already familiar with Xcode's IDE, this is common practice for debugging.

Tap on one of these two options with the preceding code commented out and you'll see that our code never finishes (because the main, synchronous function finished before the completion handler fired). If you try this a few times, you'll notice that it does occasionally stop at different points inside the completion. Uncomment the line and watch it step through right to the end.

Another thing to note is the object menu to the top right. Pressing on the plus button provides a plethora of code snippets to choose from, while you can also import images into an asset like a catalog, allowing you to reference image literals just like you can in Xcode:

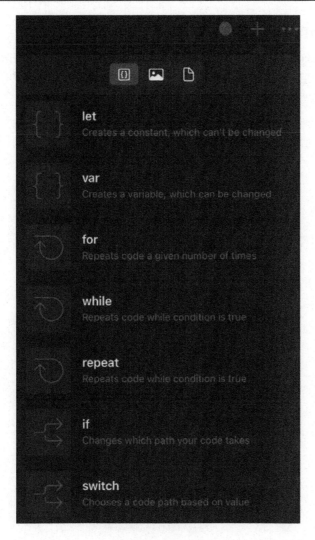

Figure 7.25 – Layout result

Finally, I'd like to touch on the file inspector again over on the left-hand side. If you open this up again, you'll see an Edit button, which, in turn, does what it says on the tin. It lets you edit, rename, and re-order Swift files for your project and module.

As mentioned earlier in this recipe, Swift Playgrounds is designed for both iPadOS and macOS, with both working in identical ways, and you should be able to follow this recipe perfectly on both (hint, I wrote half of this recipe on the iPad and the other on the Mac version just to test it out!).

There's more

One final section worth going over is the **Tools** section. Click on the three dots to the right of the + icon in the top-right corner. You should now be presented with the following:

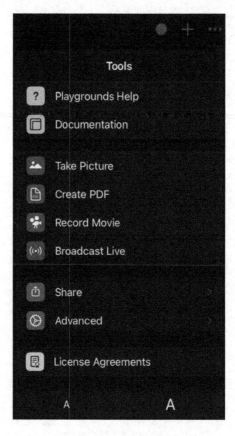

Figure 7.26 – Playground options

We will go through each of these individually or collectively:

- **Playgrounds Help / Documentation**

    As you would expect, **Help** is focused around the App/IDE and interface giving you an overview of what is available, while **Documentation** is Apple-specific API documentation.

- **Take Picture / Create PDF**

  These options share a screenshot or PDF of the canvas in its current state. Other standard iPadOS sharing options are also available.

- **Record Movie / Broadcast Live**

  Record Movie starts a "screen recorder"-like scenario with stop and record controls that appear at the top of your screen. Broadcasting alternatively hooks into third-party apps that can be found on the Apple App Store that support broadcasting.

- **Share / Advanced**

  Share initiates the default iPadOS share sheet for the option to share your current playbook.

  Advanced gives you two options, one to export your playbook, and the second to take a more in-depth look at your current playbook's hierarchy.

- **License agreements**

  This is nothing to write home about, just your usual software license agreement information.

See also

Apple's Swift Playgrounds page: `https://www.apple.com/swift/playgrounds/`

8
Server-Side Swift

From its very inception, Swift was intended to be a general-purpose programming language, applicable for multiple use cases and on multiple platforms, not just for building apps for Apple platforms. One of the obvious use cases, other than building apps, is creating server-side code. After all, interacting with a server is a vital component of almost any app. The vast majority of servers that power the internet run on Linux, which is arguably more suited to the task than any Apple platform. Therefore, being able to run Swift on Linux is vital to the goal of making Swift a viable server-side programming language option.

In this chapter, we will investigate installing the Swift toolchain on Linux, using a web server framework to build a REST API, and hosting our API via a hosting service.

In this chapter, we will cover the following recipes:

- Running Swift on Linux
- Building a REST API using Vapor and Fluent
- Database persistence with Fluent and Postgres
- Hosting your Vapor app on Heroku
- The Swift Package Manager
- Real-time communication using WebSockets
- Packaging and sharing models between server and app

Technical requirements

All the code for this chapter can be found in this book's GitHub repository: https://github.com/PacktPublishing/Swift-Cookbook-Second-Edition/tree/master/Chapter08

Check out the following video to see the Code in Action: https://bit.ly/3kgvhxe

Running Swift on Linux

The Linux operating system is a dominant force in the world of backend servers, so to be of any use for server-side development, Swift needs to be available on Linux. Fortunately, part of the open source release of Swift includes the Swift toolchain on Linux. Let's get it up and running with a "Hello World" program in Swift on Linux.

Getting started

This recipe will use Ubuntu 20.04, as this is a very popular and widely used Linux distribution, and 20.04 is the latest **Long-Term Support** (**LTS**) version. Additionally, pre-built binaries of the Swift toolchain are provided for this distribution by the Swift open source team. As a Mac user, I have tested this process on an instance of Ubuntu, running in the VirtualBox virtualization environment, but there should be no difference when running on bare metal.

How to do it...

Let's install the Swift toolchain and run our first Swift code on Linux:

1. We need to install some dependencies related to the compiler. If you are using Ubuntu with a **Graphical User Interface** (**GUI**), open up a Terminal window and run the following from the prompt to update the software repositories:

   ```
   sudo apt-get update
   ```

2. Run the next command to install a number of dependencies required for the Swift toolchain:

   ```
   sudo apt-get install \
               binutils \
               git \
               gnupg2 \
               libc6-dev \
               libcurl4 \
               libedit2 \
               libgcc-9-dev \
               libpython2.7 \
               libsqlite3-0 \
               libstdc++-9-dev \
               libxml2 \
               libz3-dev \
   ```

```
pkg-config \
tzdata \
zlib1g-dev
```

The Swift team released a prebuilt toolchain for Ubuntu, so we will need to download the latest released version and the associated `signature` file. Links for these releases can be found at `https://swift.org/download/#releases`.

3. Download the toolchain and PGP signature file for the relevant platform. For example, at the time of writing, the most recent release versions can be downloaded using `wget` with the following command:

```
wget
https://swift.org/builds/swift-5.3-release/ubuntu2004/swift-5.3-REL
EASE/swift-5.3-RELEASE-ubuntu20.04.tar.gz
wget
https://swift.org/builds/swift-5.3-release/ubuntu2004/swift-5.3-REL
EASE/swift-5.3-RELEASE-ubuntu20.04.tar.gz.sig
```

4. The signature file that we downloaded can be used to verify that the toolchain archive has not been tampered with or modified during the download. The verification will use public PGP keys provided by the Swift project in conjunction with the signature file. If you haven't done so before, you can use the following command to retrieve the PGP keys and import them into your keyring:

```
wget -q -O - https://swift.org/keys/all-keys.asc | gpg --import -
```

5. Next, we need to check for any key revocation certificates:

```
gpg --keyserver hkp://pool.sks-keyservers.net --refresh-keys Swift
```

6. With all that done, we can verify the integrity of our downloaded toolchain archive (replacing the signature filename below with the one downloaded):

```
gpg --verify swift-5.3-RELEASE-ubuntu20.04.tar.gz.sig
```

7. The response should contain the `gpg: Good signature from "Swift 5.x Release Signing Key <swift-infrastructure@swift.org>"` line; if it does, the archive has been successfully verified, and if not, the download may have been altered and should be retrieved from a trusted source on a trusted network.

Don't be alarmed if it says the key is not from a trusted `signature`. This is because the system can't find an unbroken chain of certificates from your computer to this key; it's okay to ignore this warning.

8. With our archive verified, let's unzip the archive and see what's inside (replacing the filename that follows with the toolchain downloaded):

```
tar -xzf swift-5.3-RELEASE-ubuntu20.04.tar.gz
```

Within the archive is a `usr` folder, and within that, a `bin` folder, which contains a number of binaries that are related to building Swift; key among them is the `swift` binary.

9. We want to interact with the Swift toolchain using just the command `swift`; to do this, we need to tell the system where to look for the Swift binaries. Open up `~/.profile` in your preferred text editor, and add the folder containing your Swift toolchain to the `$PATH` export command:

```
PATH="$HOME/bin:$HOME/.local/bin:<path to extracted swift
toolchain>/usr/bin:$PATH"
```

10. Save your `.profile` file.
11. Log out and log back in for the changes to take effect.
12. Now, when you type `swift` and press *Enter*, the Swift REPL will launch. It stands for the **read–eval–print loop (REPL)**; it's a way to interact with the Swift language in a very quick, easy way, much like a playground.

In the REPL, you can write Swift commands and press *Enter* to have them executed, with each command occurring within the same scope as the previous commands.

13. In the REPL, type the following Swift expression:

```
let greeting = "Hello world!"
```

14. Press *Enter*, and the REPL will display the outcome of your command, much like a playground does:

```
greeting: String = "Hello world!"
```

15. Now we can print our greeting:

```
print(greeting)
```

We get the expected response:

```
Hello world!
```

16. To leave the REPL and return to your normal command line, type the following and press *Enter*:

```
:quit
```

Congratulations! You just executed Swift code on Ubuntu Linux. The world of server-side Swift awaits.

There's more...

It's great to try out Swift code at the command line using the REPL, but what we really require is the ability to compile our code into an executable binary that we can run on demand. Let's take our "Hello world!" example and compile it into a binary:

1. Open your favorite text editor and save the following into a file called `HelloWorld.swift`:

```
print("Hello world!")
```

2. From the command line, in the folder that contains our Swift file, we can compile our binary using `swiftc`. We can specify the file or files to compile and use the -o flag to provide a name for the output binary:

```
swiftc HelloWorld.swift -o HelloWorld
```

3. Now, we can run the binary:

```
> ./HelloWorld
> Hello world!
```

Compiling one file is great, but to perform any useful work, we are likely to have multiple Swift files that define things like models, controllers, and other logic, so how can we compile them into a single, executable binary?

When we have multiple files, we need to be able to define one at the entry point of our application. When compiling a Swift binary with multiple files, one of them should be called `main.swift`. This file serves as the entry point so that when the binary is run, the code in the `main.swift` file is executed from start to end.

Let's make two Swift files, the first one named `Model.swift`:

```
// Model.swift

class Person {
    let name: String
    init(name: String) {
        self.name = name
    }
}
```

Next, we'll create the `main.swift` file:

```
// main.swift

let keith = Person(name: "Keith")
print("Hello \(keith.name)")
```

Now, let's compile these two files into a binary called `Greeter`:

```
swiftc Model.swift main.swift -o Greeter
```

This can then be executed:

```
> ./Greeter
> Hello Keith!
```

We have now written and compiled a binary from multiple files in Swift on Ubuntu.

Building a REST API using Vapor and Fluent

One of the main use cases for server-side Swift is building REST APIs. Interacting with network data is a key function of almost any app, and until now, that server-side component had to be built by someone else with the relevant server-side skills. Alternatively, it required an app developer to frequently switch between programming languages and development environments to build both the client-side and the server-side code of an app.

Swift on the server opens the possibility for a developer to work on everything involved in the app, and move seamlessly between the client side and server side.

Much has been done by the Swift team to encourage the use of Swift on the server, including creating a new networking framework for running servers. This new framework is called SwiftNIO and is available open-sourced on GitHub: `github.com/apple/swift-nio`.

This framework is quite low-level, and a number of higher-level frameworks exist to make creating a REST API easier using Swift.

In this recipe, we will use one of the more popular frameworks, Vapor, to build a REST API for an app that stores a user's tasks.

Getting started

Vapor is a Swift framework for building web services, that makes accomplishing common tasks very easy. At the time of writing, Vapor is at Version 4, which is required with Swift 5.2. More information about Vapor can be found on its website at `http://vapor.codes`.

For this recipe, we will assume that you are developing your Swift web service on a Mac, even if it may eventually be deployed to a Linux server.

When writing Swift code that will be deployed on Linux, it's very important to test your code by actually running it on Linux, especially if it's initially developed on macOS. There are significant differences between Swift's operation on macOS and Linux. These differences are often due to the different implementation of the Foundation framework on the different platforms.

Let's verify that we have the right version of Swift installed to run Vapor. Run the following command in Terminal to check your version of Swift:

```
swift --version
```

The output should indicate at least `version 5.2`; if this is not the case, you will need to update your version of Xcode.

We next need to install Vapor Toolbox, which is a set of command-line tools to simplify working with Vapor-based projects. The Vapor CLI is available through Homebrew, which is a package manager for macOS. You can find more details about Homebrew on its website at `https://brew.sh`.

At the time of writing, Homebrew has not been updated to support the recently released Apple Silicon Macs. If you are using one of these Macs, please check the Homebrew website for compatibility information.

If you don't already have Homebrew installed, run the following in Terminal:

```
/usr/bin/ruby -e "$(curl -fsSL
https://raw.githubusercontent.com/Homebrew/install/master/install)"
```

With Homebrew installed, we can add the `tap` for Vapor:

```
brew install vapor
```

Let's run Vapor to check whether it's installed correctly. You should see instructions on how to use Vapor:

```
vapor
```

We are now ready to use Vapor to build our REST API.

How to do it...

We will create a web service to store and manage tasks from an iOS app:

1. Create a new Vapor project called `TaskAPI` and then move to the new folder that is created:

    ```
    vapor new TaskAPI
    cd TaskAPI
    ```

    During this process, you will be asked *Would you like to use Fluent?* Answer yes to this. You will then be asked which database you would like to use. Select **Postgres** (this should be the recommended one).

    Additionally, you will be asked if you would like to install *Leaf*. Select **No** for now, as this goes slightly outside of the scope of this recipe.

    You can create your Vapor web service using any IDE, but we are familiar with using Xcode, so let's use that.

2. Vapor has support for creating an Xcode project containing our Vapor code, so let's launch Xcode for our Vapor project:

```
vapor xcode
```

Xcode will open and the project dependencies will be fetched automatically and appear under **Swift Package Dependencies** in the project navigator. Be patient – this can take a few minutes and you might not see any activity straight away.

Once all the dependencies have been fetched, the build and run button will become active.

3. Build and run the project to launch a local web server, which will handle requests to http://127.0.0.1:8080.

4. Open http://127.0.0.1:8080 in a browser and you will see this web page:

Figure 8.1 – Vapor project

It works! You now have your bare-bones Vapor project up and running. Now let's take a look at the Xcode project that Vapor has created for us.

In the Project Navigator, you will find a **Sources** group, and two subgroups: **Run** and **App**. The **Run** group contains main.swift, the file that will be executed when you run the app. The **App** group contains a number of files with some example code for setting up a REST API.

Open the main.swift file; it will contain the following template code:

```
import App
import Vapor

var env = try Environment.detect()
try LoggingSystem.bootstrap(from: &env)
let app = Application(env)
defer { app.shutdown() }
try configure(app)
try app.run()
```

You shouldn't really need to edit this file; it just performs the required setup and starts the web server that serves up our API. What we do need to do is to use this setup process to configure Vapor to provide the API we require.

Let's look at how the default Vapor template sets things up. In the **App** group, open the `configure.swift` file:

```
import Vapor

// configures your application
public func configure(_ app: Application) throws {
    // uncomment to serve files from /Public folder
    // app.middleware.use(FileMiddleware(publicDirectory:
      // app.directory.publicDirectory))

    if let databaseURL = Environment.get("DATABASE_URL"),
       var postgresConfig = PostgresConfiguration(url: databaseURL) {
       postgresConfig.tlsConfiguration =
         .forClient(certificateVerification: .none)
       app.databases.use(.postgres(configuration: postgresConfig),
         as: .psql)
    } else {
       app.databases.use(.postgres(
           hostname: Environment.get("DATABASE_HOST") ?? "localhost",
           port: Environment.get("DATABASE_PORT").flatMap(
             Int.init(_:)) ?? PostgresConfiguration.ianaPortNumber,
           username: Environment.get("DATABASE_USERNAME") ??
             "vapor_username",
           password: Environment.get("DATABASE_PASSWORD") ??
             "vapor_password",
           database: Environment.get("DATABASE_NAME") ??
             "vapor_database"
       ), as: .psql)
    }

app.migrations.add(CreateTodo())
    // register routes
    try routes(app)
}
```

In this file, we've imported the `Vapor` module, which contains all the code to set up and manage the Vapor web server. We've also got our code for our database, but we'll go further into that a little later on. If you look back at `main.swift`, you will see that it imports the `App` module; this is the module that will contain all of your code for setting up the web server and managing requests and responses.

Note in the preceding code, I've highlighted a required change for the latest version of Vapor which may now be included in the most recent template, if you are unsure, just copy the preceding code into your project from here or take a look at the source files.

Next, let's switch to `Routes.swift`, and we will see that this is where our routes are configured:

```
import Vapor

func routes(_ app: Application) throws {
    app.get { req in
        return "It works!"
    }

    app.get("hello") { req -> String in
        return "Hello, world!"
    }
}
```

A route defines a type of request that the web server may receive, and the response to send.

You will notice that the `"plaintext"` path is defined, which is the URL we visited to determine that everything was correctly configured:

```
app.get("hello") { req -> String in
    return "Hello, world!"
}
```

This route is for a `GET` request, with the path string parameter, `plaintext`; when our Vapor server was locally run, this related to the URL `http://0.0.0.0:8080`. The process of defining a route in Vapor involves providing a closure that takes a `Request` object and returns something that conforms to `ResponseRepresentable`; Vapor has already defined the string as conforming to `ResponseRepresentable`, so in the string, **Hello, world!** can be returned.

Build and run the **Run** scheme, if it's not already running, and visit `http://0.0.0.0:8080/hello` to see the JSON defined.

How it works...

The **TaskAPI** will accept new tasks as POST requests containing JSON representations of the tasks and will return all the existing tasks via `GET` requests.

First, let's define a task – in the **App** group of your Xcode project, create a new file called `Task.swift` in a new group called **Models**.

After creating this file, ensure that it is a member of the **App** target and not any others. The **Target Membership** panel for our new file should look like this:

Figure 8.2 – Target membership

Now, let's define our task as having two properties: `description` and `category`, plus an identifier:

```
class Task {
  let id: String
```

```
var description: String
var category: String

init(id: String, description: String, category: String) {
self.id = id
self.description = description
self.category = category
}
}
```

We can now create a `Task` in code, like this:

```
let task = Task(id: "1", description: "Remember the milk", category:
  "shopping")
```

However, we will always create our `Task` objects from the JSON received by the `POST` request, so being able to create our `Task` objects directly from JSON will be very helpful, and since we will be returning our `Task` objects as JSON, being able to convert them to JSON will also be helpful.

Vapor has a framework called Content for dealing with JSON data. Content is Vapor's version of Codable (which we learned about in `Chapter 6`, *Building iOS Apps with Swift*).

The Vapor project we created, in turn, creates example code of everything we're about to go through. If you get stuck at any time, simply refer to the template counterpart for guidance as to where you could be going wrong.

Let's add the `Content` conformance to our `Task` model object:

```
import Foundation
import Vapor

final class Task: Content {
    let id: String = UUID().uuidString
    var description: String
    var category: String
}
```

When we are creating a new task, we don't expect the JSON to include the identifier, so if it is missing, we can generate a `UUID` using the `Foundation` framework.

Now that we have our `Task` model object, which can be converted to and from JSON, let's create some routes for our API.

In `Routes.swift`, we need an array of `Task` objects to hold the tasks that get created; for the moment, we can just add that to the top of the file:

```
var tasks = [Task]()
```

Next, we'll add two routes to the `routes()` method:

```
app.post("task") { request -> String in
    let task = try request.content.decode(Task.self)
    tasks.append(task)
    return "Task Added"
}
app.get("task") { request in
    return tasks
}
```

In the first route, we look for a POST request to the `/task` path. If the request has JSON, then we can use it to attempt to create a `Task` object using the JSON; once created, we can store it in the `tasks` array.

The next route looks for a `get` request to that same path – `/task` – and returns a JSON representation of the tasks we stored in our array. This makes use of the fact that Vapor has an extension of `Sequence`, which `Array` conforms to, and if all items in the `Sequence` conform to `JSONRepresentable`, then the `Sequence` can be represented as JSON, too. With these routes defined, let's build and run the **Run** scheme and test them out.

We'll add a task, sending a POST request to `http://0.0.0.0:8080/task`; we can do this using the `curl` command:

```
curl -H "Content-Type: application/json" -X POST -d
'{"description":"Remember the Eggs","category":"Shopping"}'
http://0.0.0.0:8080/task
```

This should return a JSON representation of the task we just created, which looks like this, although the `id` will be different:

```
{
  "id": "CEC93BB9-2487-4207-97D8-E41196B44D24",
  "category": "Shopping",
  "description": "Remember the Eggs"
}
```

Next, let's test our route to show all the existing tasks:

```
curl http://0.0.0.0:8080/task
```

This should return the one `Task` we created in an array:

```
[
    {
        "id": "CEC93BB9-2487-4207-97D8-E41196B44D24",
        "category": "shopping",
        "description": "Remember the milk"
    }
]
```

We now have a simple API that stores our tasks.

Try adding a few more tasks and check whether they are returned from the `GET` request.

There's more...

The API we have created so far allows us to perform some operations on a task; namely, to create one and list all the current tasks. Implementing these actions, along with other operations such as modifying, deleting, and listing an individual task, is very common when building a REST API, so Vapor makes this really easy.

In Vapor, you can define a resource that will define how all these operations are performed, and Vapor handles the setting up of routes that follow standard practice for REST APIs.

Let's a new file called `TaskController.swift` – this will be our new `TaskControllerAPI` and will be responsible for housing our REST API response logic and will allow a degree of separation between our routing logic and our business logic:

```swift
import Foundation
import Vapor

var tasksByID = [String: Task]()

final class TaskControllerAPI {
    typealias Model = Task
    func getTasks(req: Request) -> [String: Task] {
        return tasksByID
    }
    func createTasks(request: Request) throws -> String {
        let task = try request.content.decode(Task.self)
        tasksByID[task.id] = task
        return "Task Added"
    }
}
```

We are storing the created tasks in a dictionary, with the key being the task ID; this allows us to easily retrieve them when the ID is passed as a URL parameter.

To create our resource, we provide functions that provide the response for each REST operation that we would like to support. These areas are listed here:

- `index`
- `store`
- `show`
- `replace`
- `modify`
- `destroy`
- `clear`
- `aboutItem`
- `aboutMultiple`

As you can see from the preceding code, we've just created a couple to get going. We can add the rest in later as and when we need them.

Now let's add in an extension that conforms to **RouteCollection**:

```
extension TaskControllerAPI: RouteCollection {
    func boot(routes: RoutesBuilder) throws {
        routes.get("task", use: getTasks)
        routes.post("create", use: createTasks)
    }

}
```

Here is where we take our routes that are specific to the core logic in `TaskControllerAPI` and define them as we need. With the routing code added here, we no longer need these in our `Routes.swift` file, so head on over there now and replace them with the following single line:

```
try app.register(collection: TaskControllerAPI())
```

Rerun the project and let's test whether everything still works as expected. Let's create a task:

```
curl -H "Content-Type: application/json" -X POST -d
'{"description":"Remember the milk","category":"shopping"}'
http://0.0.0.0:8080/create
```

Then, fetch all tasks to check our newly created task is returned (notice how we changed the URL to `create`):

```
curl http://0.0.0.0:8080/task
```

We've now created a simple REST API for storing and retrieving tasks.

In the next recipe, we will build on this to make it truly useful.

See also

More information about the Vapor framework can be found on its website at `https://vapor.codes`.

Here are some other popular Swift web frameworks:

- Kitura: `http://www.kitura.io`
- Perfect: `http://perfect.org`
- Zewo: `http://www.zewo.io`

Database persistence with Fluent and Postgres

In our previous project, our task editor would work a treat as long as the server kept running, but one quick re-start and everything we've saved would be lost forever – which is why persistence, particularly with databases, plays a massive part in software development.

In this section, we're going to continue to build on our TaskAPI project, adding persistence so that our data is always protected.

Getting ready

For this section, you'll need to install Docker on your Mac. Follow this link for information on Docker and containerization, along with a link to the installer: `https://www.docker.com/products/docker-desktop`.

How to do it...

First, we'll need to create our database. Luckily, Vapor can do that for us:

1. Start by creating a new file under the `Migration` folder called
   `CreateTasks.swift` and copy the following:

```
struct CreateTask: Migration {
    func prepare(on database: Database) -> EventLoopFuture<Void> {
        return database.schema("task")
            .id()
            .field("description", .string, .required)
            .field("category", .string, .required)
            .create()
    }

    func revert(on database: Database) -> EventLoopFuture<Void> {
        return database.schema("task").delete()
    }
}
```

Notice our struct conforms to `Migration` – don't worry, this is normal.
Migrations are used even for creating databases. In the preceding code, we're
doing the following:

- Creating a database with a schema called `task`
- Creating fields in our database called `"description"`, `"category"`, along with
  an **ID** column

And that is it, really – job done. However, we need to tell our server to run the
code and perform the migration (the `create` for us).

2. Go back over to `Configure.swift` and add in the following lines:

```
app.migrations.add(CreateTask())
try app.autoMigrate().wait()
```

When our server application starts, the database will be created. Don't worry –
Vapor only does this once, so if your database already exists, then it won't try and
create it again.

3. Next, we need to adjust our code to allow our models to persist to the database matching the properties in our model to the fields we just created. Head back over to the `Task.swift` file and make the following highlighted changes:

```
import Fluent

final class Task: Content, Model {
    static let schema = "task"
    @ID(key: .id)
    var id: UUID?
    @Field(key: "description")
    var description: String
    @Field(key: "category")
    var category: String
    init() { }

    init(id: UUID? = nil, description: String, category: String) {
        self.id = id
        self.description = description
        self.category = category
    }
}
```

We'll go through the structure of this later on in the *How it works...* section, but for now, you just need to make sure the changes are in.

4. Next, head back over to our `TaskController.swift` and make the following changes:

```
final class TaskControllerAPI {
    func index(req: Request) throws -> EventLoopFuture<[Task]> {
        return Task.query(on: req.db).all()
    }

    func create(req: Request) throws -> EventLoopFuture<Task> {
        let task = try req.content.decode(Task.self)
        return task.save(on: req.db).map { task }
    }

    func delete(req: Request) throws -> EventLoopFuture<HTTPStatus>
    {
        return Task.find(req.parameters.get("taskID"), on: req.db)
            .unwrap(or: Abort(.notFound))
            .flatMap { $0.delete(on: req.db) }
            .transform(to: .ok)
    }
}
```

```
extension TaskControllerAPI: RouteCollection {
    func boot(routes: RoutesBuilder) throws {
        let tasks = routes.grouped("tasks")
        tasks.get(use: index)
        tasks.post(use: create)
        tasks.group(":taskID") { task in
            tasks.delete(use: delete)
        }
    }
}
```

We're almost ready to go. Now we just need to get an instance of our database up and running. We'll achieve this by using a Docker container.

5. With Docker installed and running (if you are using Mac, you should have an icon that represents Docker on your toolbar), enter the following command in Terminal:

```
$ docker run --name postgres -e POSTGRES_DB=vapor_database \
    -e POSTGRES_USER=vapor_username \
    -e POSTGRES_PASSWORD=vapor_password \
    -p 5432:5432 -d postgres
```

Notice they perfectly match the details we've got in our `Configure.swift` file. Feel free to adjust them accordingly to suit your specific needs/conventions.

All being well, you should see the following in Terminal:

```
$ Unable to find image 'postgres:latest' locally
$ latest: Pulling from library/postgres
```

This means everything is going well. Once installed, we're ready to launch our new and improved REST API. Go ahead and run the project from Xcode. You should notice the database migration/creation in Xcode's console window.

6. Now launched, use our existing cURL command to add multiple items to our database:

```
curl -H "Content-Type: application/json" -X POST -d
'{"description":"Remember the eggs","category":"shopping"}'
http://0.0.0.0:8080/tasks
```

Now, restart the server (via Xcode) and call our `get` request. You should see a list of all the items we recently persisted. From this, you can now go on to update your API with `put` and `delete` commands, and many others that adhere to API standards. As this book concentrates on Swift as a programming language, we'll leave that up to you to have a play around with.

How it works...

With our API now up and running, let's dig a little deeper into how we made the persistence work. Let's start by taking a closer look at our `Task.swift` class model:

```
import Fluent

final class Task: Content, Model {
    static let schema = "task"
    @ID(key: .id)
    var id: UUID?
    @Field(key: "description")
    var description: String
    @Field(key: "category")
    var category: String
    init() { }

    init(id: UUID? = nil, description: String, category: String) {
        self.id = id
        self.description = description
        self.category = category
    }
}
```

As you can see, our class now conforms to Model – which is a protocol used by the Fluent framework. This allows us to add attributes to our properties so we can bind these to fields within our database, such as the `category` property:

```
@Field(key: "category")
var category: String
```

Without this, Fluent wouldn't know how to bind this causing a failure in persistence. Another added benefit is that our properties are not tied to the naming convention of the database; something that's not a problem when starting from scratch, but this is potentially helpful when working with legacy systems.

You'll also notice the `schema = "task"` constant we have in there, again another part of the inner workings of our binding that allows our Model to be bound only to a particular database schema.

Go back over to our `TaskControllerAPI()` class and you'll see that the changes we made reference a `.db` property. Let's take a look at these:

```
func create(req: Request) throws -> EventLoopFuture<Task> {
    let task = try req.content.decode(Task.self)
    return task.save(on: req.db).map { task }
}
```

In the preceding code, we decode our data using `content` to bind this to our Model (`Task()`). We are now able to perform a `.save` operation on our `task` object as this now conforms to **Model** from Fluent.

The save is being performed on the `req.db` and then in turn being **.map**(ed) – once the operation is complete and successful, we can see that the task is returned (which is why we see this in the output window when performing our cURL command).

If you break down the preceding, the syntax makes a little more sense:

```
func create(req: Request) throws -> EventLoopFuture<Task> {
    let task = try req.content.decode(Task.self)
    return task.save(on: req.db).map {
        task // Closure here is part of the return function, so will be
        // passed back up
    }
}
```

For those familiar with the previous way of implementing databases in Vapor, you'll certainly appreciate this new and much-improved way of setting up persistence.

See also

Vapor provides a number of other database providers that can be used instead of Postgres:

- **MySQL**: https://github.com/vapor/mysql-provider
- **SQLite**: https://github.com/vapor-community/sqlite-provider
- **Redis**: https://github.com/vapor/redis-provider
- **Mongo**: https://github.com/vapor-community/mongo-provider

Hosting your Vapor app on Heroku

In the previous recipes in this chapter, we created a REST API that stores and retrieves information from a Postgres database. We have our Vapor web server running on our local machine and can interact with it over HTTP requests; however, unless you plan on making your machine available to the public internet, this is of limited use, and we need to find somewhere to host our data and REST interface.

At the time of writing, Swift's support on hosting services is the exception rather than the norm; however, support is growing. Heroku is a popular hosting service that provides dynamic scaling of resources and a really simple deployment mechanism. It also has support for Swift and Postgres, so in this recipe, we will deploy our REST API to Heroku.

Getting started

Heroku provides simple and scalable infrastructure for your server-side projects. Once deployed, instances of your app are called Dymos, and additional Dymos can be started to cope with increased load.

Deployment to Heroku happens through a remote Git repository. When you are ready to deploy your app, simply push the code to Heroku.

First, visit `http://www.heroku.com` and sign up for a free account. Next, we will install the Heroku CLI (**Command-Line Interface**), as this is helpful for interacting with Heroku. Since we installed Homebrew in the previous recipes, we can use it to get the Heroku CLI:

```
brew install heroku
```

Next, we need to log into the Heroku CLI with the account that we just created. Run the `login` command and follow the instructions:

```
heroku login
```

We now have our Heroku CLI set up and ready to use.

How to do it...

Since the deployment mechanism for Heroku is Git, we need to create a local Git repo.

In Terminal, navigate to the folder containing our `TaskAPI` app that we built in the previous recipes, and create a local Git repo:

```
git init
```

Now we need to stage all the files:

```
git add .
```

Then, commit all the code:

```
git commit -m "Initial commit"
```

Next, we will set up this Vapor project to use Heroku and follow the instructions:

```
vapor heroku init
```

You will be asked if you would like a custom name for your app. If you choose not to have a custom app name, then a random app name will be assigned in the form of two words and a number; for example, `afternoon-bastion-18185`. Therefore, the app's URL will be `https://afternoon-bastion-18185.herokuapp.com`.

You will also be asked if you want to provide a custom build pack and a custom executable name. You can answer no to both of these.

We need to associate our local Git repository with the Heroku app we just created. Run the following command, replacing the final parameter with the name of the app that Heroku just created for you:

```
heroku git:remote -a afternoon-bastion-18185
```

To get our database-backed API up and running on our local machine, we ran a `Postgresql` service and configured Vapor's connection to it using a configuration JSON file in `Config/secret`. However, this configuration is specific to our local machine, and so we need to start a `PostgreSQL` database service on Heroku and configure Vapor to connect to it.

Luckily, the Heroku CLI makes this really easy; just run the following:

```
heroku addons:create heroku-postgresql:hobby-dev
```

In this command, `hobby-dev` is the pricing plan to use for the database, which is free for up to 10,000 database rows.

This will cause the database to be made available to your Heroku Dymo whenever your app is deployed. By running `heroku config`, we can see that an environment variable called `DATABASE_URL` is created, containing the connection URL for the database.

Now, we need to ensure that Vapor knows how to connect to the database when it's running on Heroku. To do this, we will add a configuration to `Procfile`, which is used by Heroku to set up the environment.

In the root of the project, create a file named `Procfile`; open this file and add the following:

```
web: Run serve --env production" --hostname 0.0.0.0 --port \$PORT
```

This will allow Vapor to use the PostgreSQL database set up on Heroku.

Now, let's commit the change:

```
git add .
git commit -m "Added Procfile with databse URL"
```

We are now ready to push our code to Heroku, which will then be deployed:

```
git push heroku master
```

 At the time of writing this book - there was/is an open pull request to fix an issue with a missing file `LinuxTests.swift` if Heroku gives you an error performing the above push, simply create a blank file called `LinuxTests.swift` and re-commit & push again.

It may take a while, but eventually, Heroku will report that the code has been deployed and will provide the URL for the deployed app, which will look similar to this:

```
https://afternoon-bastion-18185.herokuapp.com
```

You have a deployed version of our `TaskAPI` running on Heroku. You can rerun all the cURL tests from the last recipe, but with the preceding hostname in the place of `http://0.0.0.0:8080`.

See also

What we have built in this chapter is just the tip of the iceberg of what Vapor is capable of. Vapor has built-in support for authentication, templating, and much more, so check out `http://vapor.codes` for the full documentation.

The team behind Vapor has launched its own hosting service, Vapor Cloud. This really simplifies the process of getting your Vapor app online. At the time of writing, this service is in open beta; you can find out more and sign up at `https://vapor.cloud`.

The Swift Package Manager

Dependency package management has been around for a while now in software development – the ability to add a dependent framework or snippet to your code base without the need for any major integration has often been seen as a benefit to many.

Managers such as NuGet and NPM are widely used and maintained by the community. Specifically for iOS development, CocoaPods and Carthage have been the big players; that was until the introduction of the **Swift Package Manager** or **SPM** for short.

Although it's been around much longer than you might think, it was recently announced at WWDC 2019 that Xcode 11 would have full integration support for the Swift Package Manager.

In this recipe, we are going to learn how to add a dependency to our project using the Swift Package Manager.

Getting started

For this project, we'll continue using our recent Xcode project where we implemented Fluent and Postgres – you can follow along in the sample recipe from GitHub or alternatively make a copy on disk of your current project and work from that.

How to do it...

1. First, open Xcode and from the file tree, locate the following filename:

   `Package.swift`

2. Here, you should see the start of the following code:

```
import PackageDescription

let package = Package(
    name: "TaskAPI",
    platforms: [
```

```
        .macOS(.v10_15)
    ],
    dependencies: [
        // A server-side Swift web framework.
        .package(url: "https://github.com/vapor/vapor.git", from:
          "4.0.0"),
        .package(url: "https://github.com/vapor/fluent.git", from:
          "4.0.0"),
        .package(url: "https://github.com/vapor/fluent-postgres-
          driver.git", from: "2.0.0"),
    ],

    // ...


)
```

In the preceding code, I've highlighted our main area of interest. Here, we currently have a list of existing dependencies – in our case, the Vapor framework and two Fluent dependencies.

3. So let's go ahead and add another one in:

```
.package(url: "https://github.com/vapor/vapor.git", from: "4.0.0"),
.package(url: "https://github.com/vapor/fluent.git", from:
"4.0.0"),
.package(url:
"https://github.com/vapor/fluent-postgres-driver.git",
  from: "2.0.0"),
.package(url: "https://github.com/Kitura/BlueSocket.git", from:
  "1.0.0"),
```

4. Give Xcode a moment or so and it should start to download the new dependency. Failing that, you can push this along a little by using the following command in Terminal:

```
$ vapor build
```

If there are any errors with your package file, you'll see them here. Once completed, you'll see your new dependency alongside the existing ones in the File Explorer to the left of Xcode.

Xcode also allows you to add package dependencies via the GUI, from Xcode. Select **File** | **Swift Packages** to see a list of options. Unfortunately, these are only currently supported for .xcproject files (which Vapor does not use).

How it works...

So now we've added in our framework, how does SPM work its magic? We'll start by taking a look at the dependency section of our `Packages.swift` file again:

```
.package(url: "https://github.com/vapor/vapor.git", from: "4.0.0"),
.package(url: "https://github.com/vapor/fluent.git", from: "4.0.0"),
.package(url: "https://github.com/vapor/fluent-postgres-driver.git",
  from: "2.0.0"),
.package(url: "https://github.com/Kitura/BlueSocket.git", from:
  "1.0.0"),
```

I've highlighted two main areas here from our recent addition – the first is the URL. Much like other dependency packages such as Cocoapods and Carthage, SPM pulls its code from a (or your) Git repository.

Without going into too many details about how a package is actually made, versioning for dependencies is done using tags. In the preceding code, we're looking for any version of the package that starts from 1.0.0 (so the latest could be version 10.2.2, for all we know), but we've made a decision that at the very least, version 1.0.0 is good enough for us.

But maybe we want to be more specific. Let's see how we'd do that:

```
.package(url: "https://github.com/Kitura/BlueSocket.git", .exact("1.2.3")),
```

Here, we're specifying that we only want to use version 1.2.3. The format of the version numbers that we are checking against is what is called semantic versioning.

This allows us to add additional conditions to our packages such as `upToNextMajor` and `upToNextMinor` from a specific set version. Here is an example:

```
.package(url: "https://github.com/Kitura/BlueSocket.git",
  .upToNextMajor("1.2.3")),
.package(url: "https://github.com/Kitura/BlueSocket.git",
  .upToNextMinor("1.2.3")),
```

`upToNextMajor` will include any version up to version 2.0.0.

`upToNextMinor` will include any version up to version 1.3.0 (so 1.2.x basically).

More often than not, you won't really need to worry about this, but with a framework dependent on other frameworks, sometimes this can really come in handy to keep everything nice and tidy in your project.

There's more...

Finally, let's take a look at the remaining code in our `Packages.swift` file – let's start at the top:

```
// swift-tools-version:5.2
```

Although this appears to be commented out, it actually plays a big part in our packages file. Here, we're setting the version of Swift that our dependencies must comply with. So if a dependency being downloaded is built with an older version of Swift and is currently unsupported, SPM will let us know about it.

On the flip side too, if our dependency is newer than our version of Swift, this will be handled.

Next, let's take a look at the targets section. At first glance, you might feel a little overwhelmed as to what is going on in here, but it is actually straightforward, and for those familiar with other dependency management tools, this will be familiar ground:

```
targets: [
    .target(
        name: "App",
        dependencies: [
            .product(name: "Fluent", package: "fluent"),
            .product(name: "FluentPostgresDriver", package: "fluent-
                postgres-driver"),
            .product(name: "Vapor", package: "vapor")
        ],
        swiftSettings: [
            // Enable better optimizations when building in Release
                // configuration. Despite the use of
            // the `.unsafeFlags` construct required by SwiftPM, this
                // flag is recommended for Release
            // builds. See <https://github.com/swift-
                // server/guides#building-for-production> for details.
            .unsafeFlags(["-cross-module-optimization"],
                .when(configuration: .release))
        ]
    )

    // ..

]
```

In the preceding code, I've highlighted some key areas. The first is the list of targets. All we are doing here is identifying one of our targets (in our case our **App** target) and adding a list of specific dependencies for that target.

These names are the actual package names once installed – not the Git URL. These are defined outside the targets array on a more global scale for our project. Here, we are simply cherry-picking what should be used for what specific target.

The same goes for `swiftSettings` too, a place where we can set Swift-specific optimizations for the build when in either release or debug mode (but generally we do this for release builds).

See also

For more information, refer to the following links:

- Semantic versioning: `https://semver.org`
- Building for production: `https://github.com/swift-server/guides#building-for-production`
- CocoaPods: `https://cocoapods.org`
- Carthage: `https://github.com/Carthage/Carthage`

Real-time communication using WebSockets

Communicating via WebSockets has been around for a long time and plays an integral part in server-to-server, server-to-client, and client-to-server communications. WebSockets allow open and constant communication between both parties, thus allowing data to be sent and received without the need for "polling" for changes.

A commonplace where you might see WebSockets being used would be a chat window – a constant line of communication between each device (usually via a server). Think of it as the "telephone line" of the internet (which is actually not too far from the truth).

In this section, we are going to take our previously built Vapor project and communicate in real time with a companion iOS app.

Getting started

For this section, you'll need the completed project from our previous section. Feel free to continue to work on the sample project found in the Git repository.

In addition, you'll need the **TaskAPIApp** project.

How to do it...

First of all, let's head over to our `Routes.swift` file and add in the following:

```
app.webSocket("talk-back") { req, ws in
}
```

Look familiar? Here, we are ultimately creating an "endpoint" for our WebSocket called "talk-back". When successfully connected, all data will be received via the ws parameter in the function. But how can we intercept this? Well, there are a couple of ways actually. Let's take a look:

```
app.webSocket("talk-back") { req, ws in
    ws.onText { ws, text in
        print(text)
    }
    ws.onBinary { (ws, buffer) in
        print(buffer)
    }

}
```

Our client, when connected to our server via WebSockets, can send a number of specific commands, such as sending plain text or sending binary text. For this recipe, we'll just be using `onText`.

Add the following code and run your server:

```
app.webSocket("talk-back") { req, ws in
    ws.onText { ws, text in
        if text.lowercased() == "hello" {
            ws.send("Is it me your are looking for...?")
        }
    }

}
```

So, essentially, what we are doing here is listening for a message from our client (any message), but if the message meets our specific condition, we're going to send a response straight back.

Now, from the GitHub repository, fire up the **TaskAPIApp** project in Xcode. Here, you'll notice we're using a third-party dependency called Starscream to enable our app as a WebSocket client – we could have gone through and built our own but that was a little out of scope and unnecessary for this recipe.

One thing to note: we used SPM in order to obtain the Starscream dependency – take a look in the Xcode project and compare it to our Vapor project to see how it matches up!

Okay, with the iOS app loaded, check out the `ViewController.swift` file and make sure the localhost URL is correct as per your current setup (it should be the same if you are following along):

```
guard let url = URL(string: "http://127.0.0.1:8080/talk-back") else {
    return }
```

If you take a closer look in the `ViewController.swift` file, you'll see the following hooked up to an `IBAction`:

```
@IBAction func onSendRequest(_ sender: Any) {
    socket.write(string: "Hello")
}
```

We've got the option to send a String via our WebSocket connection – boom!

Launch the project (still making sure your Vapor server is running locally) and click the button. What do you see? All being well, you should see the words **Is it me you are looking for...?** appear in the `UILabel` – nice!

How it works...

WebSockets in Vapor act in a similar way to routes. Just as we said about our talk-back endpoint we created that the only difference was that the connection was open, the difference here is there have been no additional calls made – our server didn't need to rebuild and re-connect a new URL request, so there's no additional authorization or authentication. Our client (much like our server) was just listening for a response.

All WebSocket calls are asynchronous – and don't reply in the usual request/response pattern that we see with HTTP. However, it is up to you, the client or the server, to manage this connection, checking to make sure it is still not alive, and being ready to handle the requests at any time.

There's more...

We touched earlier on the `onText` and `onBinary` functions available to us when receiving a message from our client, but by default, WebSockets constantly ping each other to make sure they are still active (or alive). We can monitor these requests by intercepting them with the following functions:

```
ws.onPong { (ws) in }
ws.onPing { (ws) in }
```

Alternately, we can use our Vapor project to connect to a WebSocket too:

```
WebSocket.connect(to: "ws://talk-back.websocket.org", on: eventLoop) {
    ws in
        print(ws)
}
```

Sending messages whilst connected as a client is performed in the same way as we sent a message earlier, either through plain text or binary:

```
ws.send("Is it me your are looking for...?") // Plain "String" Text
ws.send([1, 2, 3]) // Binary as UIInt
```

While sending messages is done asynchronously, sometimes we would like to know if our message has been sent successfully – we can do this with the use of the `eventLoop` promise:

```
let promise = eventLoop.makePromise(of: Void.self)
ws.send("Hello", promise: promise)
promise.futureResult.whenComplete { result in
    // Succeeded or failed to send.
}
```

And finally, we have these options to close and handle our open WebSocket connections:

```
ws.close()
ws.close(promise: nil)
ws.onClose.whenComplete { result in
    // Succeeded or failed to close.
}
```

WebSockets really are a way of opening up your server in terms of real-time connectivity to your client. There are usually many things that it can be used for, such as dashboard reporting and chat messaging.

See also

WebSockets: `https://docs.vapor.codes/4.0/websockets/`

Packaging and sharing models between server and app

Server-side Swift is credited for the fact that web application developers can harness the power of the Swift programming language first hand. This, along with the power of the open source community behind it – even in what is still classed as its infancy - means that server-side Swift is already a worthy production-quality option.

But what about other advantages, specifically for iOS developers who now build their apps using Swift? Other than knowledge of syntax and specific APIs, what else can they benefit from?

As we saw earlier in this chapter, with the integration of the Swift Package Manager into Xcode, we can now build out some of our code into a module that we can reuse in both our server-side Swift apps and our iOS apps.

Getting started

For this section, we'll continue to work on our Vapor project and will continue to work on a Mac using Xcode.

How to do it...

For a moment, let's take a step away from our Vapor app. We'll start by creating a new Swift package module. In Xcode, click on **File** | **New** | **Swift Package** – call it `TaskModule` and click **Save**. You should now be presented with a brand-new project.

If you take a look at File Explorer, you'll see some familiar files, such as `Packages.swift`. Our main concern is the files that live inside the **Sources** folder – here is where your files and classes will live and will grow as part of the module you want to use:

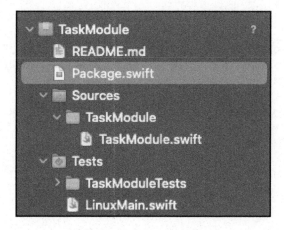

Figure 8.3 – Sources folder

Let's start by creating a new file called `TaskViewModel.swift` – this file will be a view model to the model we created in our Vapor project.

 A view model is basically a model that only houses data based on what is required to render a particular view, for example, a response model from a server might have 20 properties all containing information such as date timestamps, created by, and so on, but our rendered view may only be interested in a handful of that information or may want to manipulate or compute some of the data into one single property.

Add the following code:

```
import Foundation

enum Category: String {
    case shopping = "shopping"
    case work = "work"
}

public final class TaskViewModel {
    var category: Category?
    var title: String?
    var imageUrl: URL?
    public convenience init(title: String, category: String) {
        self.init()
```

```
        self.category = Category(rawValue: category)
        self.title = title
        self.imageUrl = URL(string: "https://www.test.com/\(category)")
    }


}
```

In the preceding code, we are building a very basic view model, an enum class to bind our category to a 1-1 match on our title property, and a computed property for an image URL.

As it stands, that code can be used in either our server-side Swift project or an iOS app – but how do we get it to do both? Well, easy! As we've created this as a Swift package, we can just import it as a Swift package. Close this project from Xcode (important) and head on over to `Packages.swift` in your Vapor app.

Add the following highlighted changes. Note that the local path must be the one on your machine – this needs to point to the directory where your `Packages.swift` file lives:

```
dependencies: [
        // A server-side Swift web framework.
    .package(url: "https://github.com/vapor/vapor.git", from: "4.0.0"),
    .package(url: "https://github.com/vapor/fluent.git", from:
      "4.0.0"),
    .package(url: "https://github.com/vapor/fluent-postgres-
      driver.git", from: "2.0.0"),
    .package(path: "/path/to/your/TaskModule")
],
targets: [
    .target(
        name: "App",
        dependencies: [
            .product(name: "Fluent", package: "fluent"),
            .product(name: "FluentPostgresDriver", package: "fluent-
              postgres-driver"),
            .product(name: "Vapor", package: "vapor"),
            .product(name: "TaskModule", package: "TaskModule"),
],
```

Here, we're doing just as we did previously – adding in our package and then referencing a module name to the package for our specific target.

Give Xcode a moment to pick up this change and, as if by magic, you'll see our recently created module inside our dependency tree. Let's go ahead and try and use it.

For now, let's add this into our `TaskControllerAPI()` file as it is in here that we find bind our original **Task** model from our response.

We'll start by importing our Module:

```
import TaskModule
```

All being well, this should resolve nicely. Now let's try and access our view model:

```
let viewTask = TaskViewModel(title: "", category: "")
```

And it really is as simple as that. Let's take a look at this from the other side now and see how we can use this same module in our iOS app:

1. First, we need to make sure that our `TaskModule` folder is initialized as a Git repo and there is an initial commit performed – I'll explain why shortly, but for now, just simply perform the following commands in Terminal to initialize a repository for the project:

   ```
   $ git init
   $ git add .
   $ git commit -m "Initial commit"
   ```

Now open our existing project, `TaskAPIApp`, in Xcode and select **File** | **Swift Package** | **Add Package Dependency**.

You'll be presented with a GUI asking for the URL for a Git repository. As ours is currently local, we need to give it in the following format:

```
file:///Users/chris/Source/TaskModule
```

Xcode requires an active Git repository in order to pull a dependency – so we've just created one locally, as opposed to remotely. Xcode is happy and will allow us to continue:

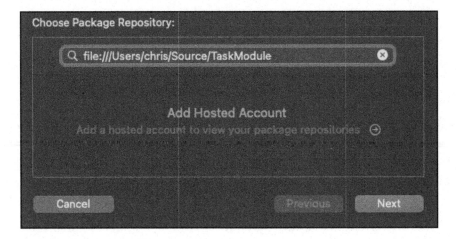

Figure 8.4 – Choose a package repository

The next screen should now look like this:

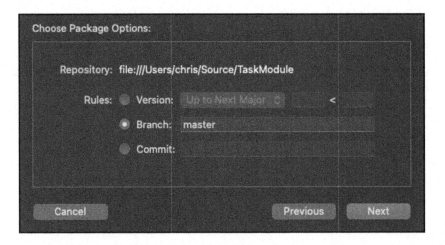

Figure 8.5 – Choose the package option

Specify a **Branch** and enter `master` and click **Next**. All being well, Xcode should be ready to import your dependency – click **Finish**.

Go back over to your Xcode project and you'll now see `TaskModule` successfully imported into your project. Let's make sure this is all working as expected. Head on over to your `ViewControler.swift` file and let's try and use our view model.

We'll start by importing our `TaskModule`:

```
import TaskModule
```

And now we should be able to access our view model perfectly from anywhere within our iOS code base:

```
let _ = TaskViewModel(title: "", category: "")
```

Wonderful – we've now successfully created and reused our view model in both our iOS and server-side Swift project.

How it works...

The beauty of being able to use our code in both server-side Swift and iOS projects doesn't have to stop at things like view models; specific computed logic can sit in here too, but you just have to be aware of a couple of things: remember your server-side Swift project is 99% likely to be running on a Linux server, so frameworks such as UIKit won't be available for use; however, this works both ways too.

Our `Codable` equivalent `Content` on Vapor which won't be available in our iOS project (as it simply just isn't needed there), so think carefully about how you want to split and share your logic. Take time to understand your requirements and separation of concerns when developing your application.

That aside, there are ways to target specific operating systems that our apps could be running on. Let's have a look at how we would achieve this:

```
#if os(Linux)
import LinuxModule
#else
import GlobalModule
#endif
```

If you need to be a bit more specific, you can identify operating systems with the following:

```
#if os(macOS)
#if os(iOS)
#if os(watchOS)
#if os(tvOS)
```

Again, if you're running your server-side Swift project on macOS, you'll be fine – but you're not really future-proofing your code as you may find at some point in the future, it's going to be more cost-effective and versatile to run your app on a Linux box.

Looking a little deeper into how the Swift Package Manager works is not as complex as you might think – although, I may add, it has exceptional convenience and power.

For those familiar with workspaces in Xcode, this follows a not too dissimilar pattern – essentially, your module is a link to the project we created earlier. The version of the code that is pulled into your project is defined by the `version number`, `branch`, or even `commit` we specify.

There's more...

Creating a package to use internally is one thing, but distributing it to others – either within your organization or the community – is another.

This is where hosting your package in a remote Git repository comes in handy. This not only allows you to version-control the changes in your package independently, but you can choose to administer these with a private repository, allowing for controlled internal use.

9
Performance and Responsiveness in Swift

We have covered a lot of ground in the previous chapters, and we have a lot of Swift tools in our tool belt. Now it's time to delve into more advanced topics, looking at how certain Swift types are implemented, how they can be used, and what their performance characteristics are. We will also look at how we can perform asynchronous tasks using **Grand Central Dispatch** (**GCD**) through the Dispatch framework and the higher-level operations in the Foundation framework that are also built on GCD.

Understanding the multithreaded environment available on all Apple platforms, as well as the performance profile of the Swift constructs you use, is vital to building a fast and responsive app.

In this chapter, we will cover the following recipes:

- Value and reference semantics
- Using Dispatch queues for concurrency
- Concurrent queues and dispatch groups
- Implementing the operation class

Technical requirements

All the code for this chapter can be found in this book's GitHub repository at `https://github.com/PacktPublishing/Swift-Cookbook-Second-Edition/tree/master/Chapter09`

Check out the following video to see the Code in Action: `https://bit.ly/3bn2l2O`

Value and reference semantics

We saw back in `Chapter 1`, *Swift Building Blocks*, that certain Swift types behave differently from others, specifically regarding ownership and the mutation of properties. We even defined this difference, saying that classes are *reference* types, while structs and enums are *value* types. In this recipe, we will examine why these types behave differently and the performance implications this entails.

Let's create the model for an app that allows a user to schedule events that they do every day and reminds them when these events should occur.

Getting ready

We need to decide how we will model our daily event. The key to this decision is whether we want our event to have reference semantics or value semantics. We discussed the differences between the two in `Chapter 1`, *Swift Building Blocks*, but let's re-examine the differences.

Value types are simple data structures that you can think of as just bundles of data. Swift makes these types more useful by allowing them to have methods, but any change or *mutation* of the underlying data results in a whole new bundle of data. In contrast, *reference* types are more complex data structures that have an identity outside of their component properties. Therefore, a change in the component properties will be available via any references to the object.

A value type's simple composition has the advantage of being very cheap on resources to create and maintain. However, this simplicity comes at the expense of dynamic dispatch, which enables sub-classing.

How to do it...

Given this distinction, what behavior do we want for our daily event? If we change the name of our event, should we expect anything that has a reference to it to also see that change? That sounds like the behavior we want, so our daily event should be a reference type:

```
class DailyEvent {
    var name: String
    init(name: String) {
        self.name = name
    }
}
```

Let's check that this gives us the behavior we expect:

```
var event1 = DailyEvent(name: "have bath")
var event2 = event1
print("Event 1 - \(event1.name)") // have bath
print("Event 2 - \(event2.name)") // have bath
event1.name = "have shower"
print("Event 1 - \(event1.name)") // have shower
print("Event 2 - \(event2.name)") // have shower
```

We want to be reminded of our event every day at a certain time, but for our purpose, Date in Foundation is a bit of an overkill, since it contains both date and time information, and we only need to maintain time information. Let's create something to represent the time, irrespective of the date. What behavior is most appropriate for our time model? Should it have reference semantics or type semantics?

Let's try both and see which seems to most accurately model the situation we are after:

1. We'll create time as a class, with reference semantics:

```
class ClockTime {
    var hours: Int
    var minutes: Int
    init(hours: Int, minutes: Int) {
        self.hours = hours
        self.minutes = minutes
    }
}
```

2. Now, let's see how this will behave when its properties are changed:

```
let defaultEventTime = ClockTime(hours: 6, minutes: 30)
var event1Time = defaultEventTime // 6:30
```

```
var event2Time = defaultEventTime // 6:30
// Event 2 has been moved to 9:30
event2Time.hours = 9
print("Event 1 - \(event1Time.hours):\(event1Time.minutes)")
   // Event 1 - 9:30
print("Event 2 - \(event2Time.hours):\(event2Time.minutes)")
   // Event 2 - 9:30
```

When we change the properties of an instance of ClockTime, it has the unintended consequence of changing all references to that same instance of ClockTime. Since reference semantics aren't a perfect fit for ClockTime, let's change it to a value type and see whether that is more appropriate.

3. We now have two options for value types in Swift; we can model ClockTime as a struct or an enum. Enums are great for modeling concepts that have a small number of finite values. While there are a finite number of minutes in a day, it's not a small number, and we might want to do math calculations on the hours and minutes in ClockTime, so a struct is more appropriate:

```
struct ClockTime {
    var hours: Int
    var minutes: Int
}
```

4. Let's see how this changes the behavior when we change the properties of a ClockTime instance:

```
let defaultEventTime = ClockTime(hours: 6, minutes: 30)
var event1Time = defaultEventTime // 6:30
var event2Time = defaultEventTime // 6:30
// Event 2 has been moved to 9:30
event2Time.hours = 9
print("Event 1 - \(event1Time.hours):\(event1Time.minutes)") //
Event 1 - 6:30
print("Event 2 - \(event2Time.hours):\(event2Time.minutes)") //
Event 2 - 9:30
```

With ClockTime as a value type, changing a property of a ClockTime instance results in a new instance, so the change doesn't have the unintended consequences that we saw when it was a reference type.

Lastly, let's consider some of the dynamic features that we will give up by making `ClockTime` a value type. Will we ever want to subclass `ClockTime`? This doesn't seem likely, and it is right to characterize `ClockTime` as a simple bundle of data. So, in this scenario, modeling `ClockTime` as a value type is the right decision.

5. To complete the model, we will add a `ClockTime` property to the `DailyEvent` class:

```
class DailyEvent {
    var name: String
    var time: ClockTime
    init(name: String, time: ClockTime) {
        self.name = name
        self.time = time
    }
}
```

How it works...

We've already covered how value types differ from reference types. Now, let's examine why they behave differently.

When storing new instances of a type in memory, Swift has two different data structures that it can use for storage: the **Stack** and the **Heap**. These structures are common to many programming languages. Value types are stored on the **Stack**, and reference types are stored on the **Heap**. Understanding how data is stored in these structures, even at the superficial level that we will cover, will help us to understand why value types and reference types have differing behaviors.

The stack can be thought of as sequential blocks of data. An instance of a type may be represented by multiple blocks of data, and an instance can be referenced using the memory position of its first piece of data. A **Stack Pointer**, which is a reference to the memory position at the end of the stack, is maintained. New instances are always added to the end of the stack, and then the stack pointer's position is updated to the new end of the stack.

Let's go through adding a value type instance using a simplified diagram of the stack. Before anything is added, the stack pointer is at the top of the stack:

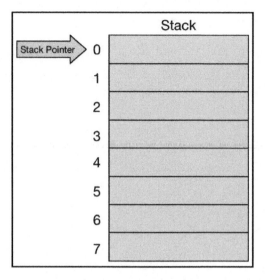

Figure 9.1 – Representation of the stack and stack pointer

A `ClockTime` struct for 07:00 is added to the stack. This takes up three blocks, and the stack pointer moves to the next empty block on the stack:

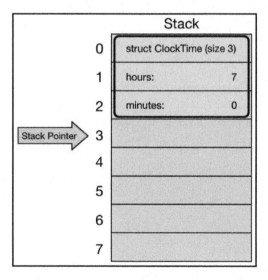

Figure 9.2 – Stack pointer after adding a ClockTime struct for 7:00

Another `ClockTime` struct for 09:30 is added to the stack. This has a size of four blocks, and the stack pointer moves to the next empty block on the stack:

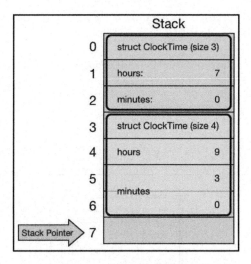

Figure 9.3 – Stack pointer after adding a ClockTime struct for 9:30

Once data is placed on the stack, it is immutable. To see why this is an important restriction, let's try and change our first `ClockTime` instance on the stack. The simplicity and efficiency of the stack is predicated on the fact that it is a continuous block of memory. If we try and change any data already on the stack, it may take up more space, which will cause data in the subsequent blocks to be overwritten:

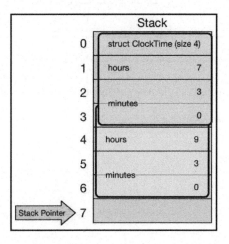

Figure 9.4 – Changing the first ClockTime instance on the stack

Therefore, any change to a struct results in a new, changed version of the struct appended at the end of the stack.

Let's mutate a ClockTime instance and see how that looks in our simplified stack representation by taking it step by step:

1. We have a ClockTime struct for 9:00 assigned to the variable named event1Time:

```
var event1Time = ClockTime(hours: 9, minutes: 0)
```

See the following diagram for a visual representation of how this may look:

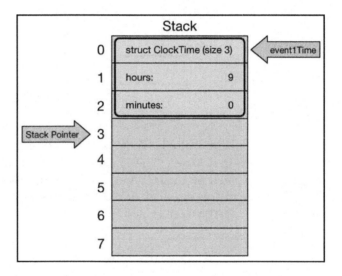

Figure 9.5 – Assigning the event1Time variable to a ClockTime struct for 09:00

2. The value of event1Time is also assigned to a new variable, called event2Time:

```
var event2Time = event1Time
```

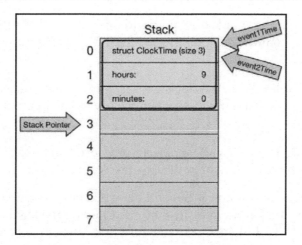

Figure 9.6 – Assigning the value of event1Time to event2Time

3. When we mutate `event2Time`, changing the minute value to `30`, a new `ClockTime` instance with the changed minute value is placed at the end of the stack:

```
event2Time.minutes = 30
```

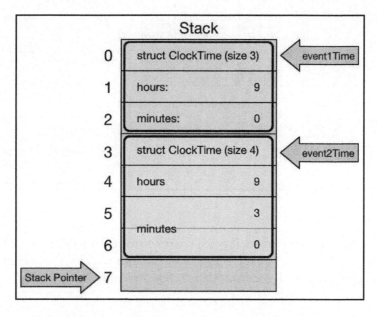

Figure 9.7 – The new ClockTime instance placed at the end of the stack

The event2Time variable now points to this new stack position, while
event1Time continues to point to the stack position of the original ClockTime
struct for 09:00.

As the preceding examples show, the stack is a very simple and efficient data structure, and
its properties explain the behavior we see when we use value types such as struct and
enums.

In contrast, reference types, such as class objects, are stored on the heap, which enables
more dynamic and complex behavior at the expense of efficiency.

An accurate look at heap allocations is beyond the scope of this book, but let's take a very
simplified look at how a reference type instance is stored on the **Heap**. The heap is not a
continuous chain of blocks, but an area of memory that can be free or already allocated:

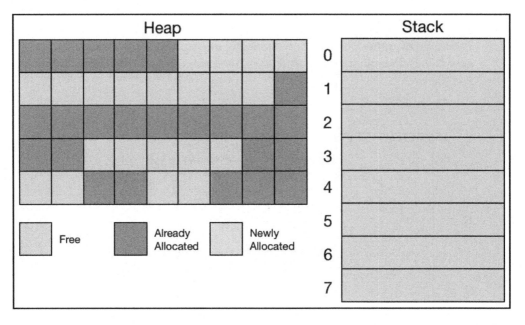

Figure 9.8 – Representation of the heap

When a class is allocated to the heap, it must search through the heap to find a set of free
blocks appropriate for its size. The reference type instance may include references to other
reference types or value types by storing their stack positions:

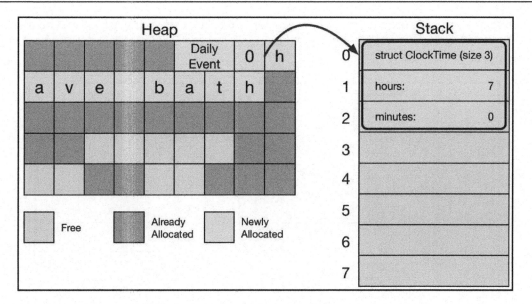

Figure 9.9 – Allocation of a class in the heap

Multiple variables can hold references to the same instance:

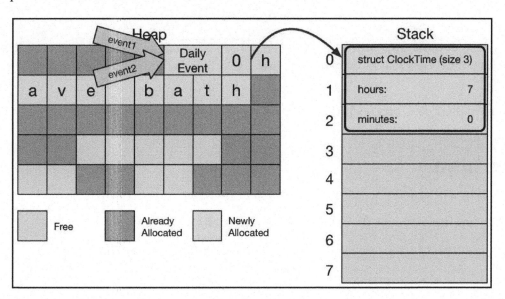

Figure 9.10 – Multiple variables holding references to the same instances

When reference types are modified, they aren't copied. Instead, extra space must be found to accommodate the extra information. All references to the instance have the changed information:

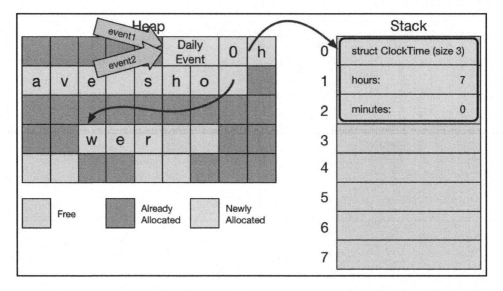

Figure 9.11 – Modifying reference types

This recipe describes the difference between reference semantics and value semantics, and hopefully illustrates that these behaviors arise from the way in which they are stored in memory.

Both have their uses, and it's important to choose the right type when building your model.

See also

Swift blog: Value and reference types: `http://swiftbook.link/blog/type-semantics`

Apple Developer Videos (developer account needed):

- WWDC 2016 - Protocol and Value-Oriented Programming in UIKit Apps: `https://developer.apple.com/videos/play/wwdc2016/419`

Using Dispatch queues for concurrency

We live in a multicore computing world. Multicore processors are found in everything, from our laptops and mobile phones to our watches. With these multiple cores comes the ability to work in parallel. These concurrent streams of work are known as *threads*, and programming in a multithreaded way enables your code to make the best use of the processor's cores. Deciding how and when to create new threads and manage the available resources are complex tasks, so Apple has built a framework to do the hard work for us. It is called *Grand Central Dispatch*.

Grand Central Dispatch (GCD) handles the thread maintenance and monitors the available resources while providing a simple, queue-based interface for getting concurrent work done. With the open-sourcing of Swift, Apple also open-sourced GCD in the form of `libdispatch`, since Swift does not yet have built-in concurrency features.

In this recipe, we will explore some of the features of `libdispatch`, also known as the Dispatch framework, and see how we can use concurrency to build apps that are efficient and responsive.

Getting ready

We will see how we can improve the responsiveness of an app using GCD, so first, we need to start with an app that requires some improvement. Go to `https://github.com/ PacktPublishing/Swift-Cookbook-Second-Edition/tree/master/Chapter09/ PhotobookCreator_DispatchGroups`. Here, you will find the repository of an app that takes a collection of photos and turns them into a PDF photo book. You can download the app source files directly from GitHub or by using `git`:

```
git clone https://github.com/PacktPublishing/Swift-Cookbook-Second-
Edition/tree/master/Chapter09/PhotobookCreator_DispatchGroups/
PhotobookCreator.git
```

If you build and run the app, you will see a collection of sample images, with the ability to add more:

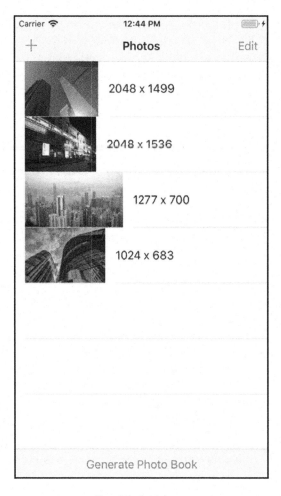

Figure 9.12 – Sample images

When you tap on **Generate Photo Book**, the app will take the photos you have chosen, resize them to the same size, and save them as a multi-page PDF that can then be exported or shared. Depending on how many photos are included and the performance of the device, this process can take a little time to complete. During this time, the whole interface is unresponsive; for example, you can't scroll through the pictures.

How to do it...

Let's examine why the app is unresponsive during photo book generation and how we can fix this:

1. Open up the `PhotoBookCreator` project and navigate to `PhotoCollectionViewController.swift`. In this file, you will find the following method:

```
func generatePhotoBook(with photos: [UIImage]) {
    let resizer = PhotoResizer()
    let builder = PhotoBookBuilder()
    // Scale down (can take a while)
    var photosForBook = resizer.scaleToSmallest(of: photos)
    // Crop (can take a while)
    photosForBook = resizer.cropToSmallest(of: photosForBook)
    // Generate PDF (can take a while)
    let photobookURL = builder.buildPhotobook(with:
        photosForBook)
    let previewController = UIDocumentInteractionController(url:
        photobookURL)
    previewController.delegate = self
    previewController.presentPreview(animated: true)
}
```

In this method, we call three functions that can take quite a long time to complete. We take the output of one function and feed it into the next function, and the result is a URL for our photo book, which we then launch with some UI to preview and export.

This work to resize and crop the photos, and then generate the photo book, is taking place in the same queue where UI touch events are processed, the main queue, which is why our UI is unresponsive.

2. To free up the main queue for UI events, we can create our own private queue, which we can use to execute our long-running functions:

```
import Dispatch

class PhotoCollectionViewController: UIViewController {
    //...
    let processingQueue = DispatchQueue(label: "Photo processing
        queue")
    func generatePhotoBook(with photos: [UIImage]) {
        processingQueue.async { [weak self] in
```

```
        let resizer = PhotoResizer()
        let builder = PhotoBookBuilder()

        // Get smallest common size
        let size = resizer.smallestCommonSize(for: photos)

        // Scale down (can take a while)
        var photosForBook = resizer.scaleWithAspectFill(photos,
          to: size)
        // Crop (can take a while)
        photosForBook = resizer.centerCrop(photosForBook, to:
          size)
        // Generate PDF (can take a while)
        let pbURL = builder.buildPhotobook(with: photosForBook)
        // Show preview with export options
        let previewController =
          UIDocumentInteractionController(url: pbURL)
        previewController.delegate = self
        previewController.presentPreview(animated: true)
      }
    }
  }
```

By calling the `async` method on our `DispatchQueue` and providing a block of
code, we are scheduling that block to be executed. GCD will execute that block
when resources are available. Now, our long-running code isn't blocking the main
queue, so our UI will remain responsive; however, if you were to run the app
with just this change, you would get some very odd behavior when the app tried
to show the preview view controller.

We just discussed the fact that UI touch events are delivered to the main queue,
which is why we wanted to avoid blocking it; however, `UIKit` expects *all* UI
events to happen on the main queue. Since we are currently creating and
presenting the preview view controller from our private queue, we are defying
this `UIKit` expectation, which can produce a number of bugs, including UI
elements that never appear, or appear long after they were presented.

3. To solve this problem, we need to ensure that when we are ready to present our
   UI, we do that operation on the main queue:

   ```
   func generatePhotoBook(with photos: [UIImage], using builder:
     PhotoBookBuilder) {
       processingQueue.async { [weak self] in

           let resizer = PhotoResizer()
           let builder = PhotoBookBuilder()
   ```

```
// Get smallest common size
let size = resizer.smallestCommonSize(for: photos)

// Scale down (can take a while)
var photosForBook = resizer.scaleWithAspectFill(photos, to:
  size)
// Crop (can take a while)
photosForBook = resizer.centerCrop(photosForBook, to: size)
// Generate PDF (can take a while)
let pbURL = builder.buildPhotobook(with: photosForBook)
DispatchQueue.main.async {
  // Show preview with export options
  let previewController = UIDocumentInteractionController
    (url: pbURL)
  previewController.delegate = self
  previewController.presentPreview(animated: true)
}
    }
  }
```

Now, if you run the app, you will find that you can generate a photo book while still being able to interact with the UI; for instance, being able to scroll the table view.

How it works...

GCD uses queues to manage blocks of work in a multithreaded environment. Queues operate on a **first in first out (FIFO)** policy. When GCD determines that resources are available, it will take the next block from the queue and execute it. Once the block has finished executing, it will be removed from the queue:

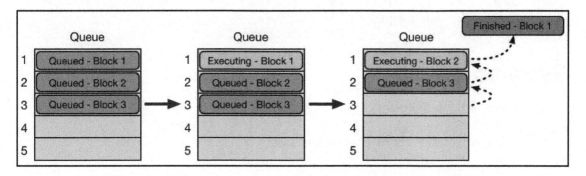

Figure 9.13 – FIFO policy

There are two types of `DispatchQueue`: *serial* and *concurrent*. With the simplest form of a queue, a serial queue, GCD will only execute one block at a time from the top of the queue. When each block finishes executing, it is removed from the queue, and each block moves up one position.

The main queue, which processes all UI events, is an example of a serial queue, and this explains why performing a long-running operation on the main queue will cause your UI to become unresponsive. While your long-running operation is executing, nothing else on the main queue will be executed until the long-running operation has finished.

With the second type of queue, a concurrent queue, GCD will execute as many blocks on different threads as resources allow. The next block to execute will be the block closest to the top of the stack that isn't already executing, and blocks are removed from the stack when finished:

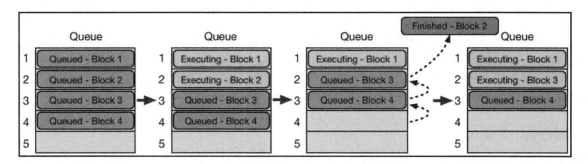

Figure 9.14 – Execution when the second type of queue is added

Concurrent queues can be really useful when you have numerous operations that are independent of each other. We will look into concurrent queues further in the *Concurrent queues and dispatch groups* recipe.

See also

- The GitHub repository for `libdispatch`:
  `https://github.com/apple/swift-corelibs-libdispatch`
- Documentation for dispatch queues: `http://swiftbook.link/docs/dispatchqueue`

Concurrent queues and dispatch groups

In the previous recipe, we looked into using a private serial queue to keep our app responsive by moving long-running operations off the main queue. In this recipe, we will break our operations down into smaller, independent blocks and place them on a concurrent queue.

Getting ready

We are going to build on the app we improved in the last recipe, which is an app that will produce a PDF photo book from a collection of photos. You can get the code for this app at `https://github.com/PacktPublishing/Swift-Cookbook-Second-Edition/tree/master/Chapter09` and choose the `PhotobookCreator_DispatchGroups` folder.

Open the project in XCode and navigate to the `PhotoCollectionViewController.swift` file.

How to do it...

We saw in the last recipe how dispatch queues operate on a FIFO policy. GCD will execute a block from the top of the queue and remove it from the queue when it has finished executing. The number of blocks that GCD will allow to execute at the same time will depend on the type of queue being used. *Serial* queues will only have one block of code being executed at any time; other blocks in the queues will have to wait until the block at the top of the queue has finished executing. However, for a *concurrent* queue, GCD will concurrently execute as many blocks as there are resources available. We can make more efficient use of a concurrent queue by breaking down the work into smaller, independent blocks, allowing them to be executed concurrently.

Take a look at the current implementation of the `generatePhotoBook` method. The only thing that has changed since the last recipe is that we now present the preview UI within a completion that is passed to the `generatePhotoBook` method. This simplifies the method and prevents us from needing to weakly capture `self` within the `async` block:

```
func generatePhotoBook(with photos: [UIImage], completion: @escaping
  (URL) -> Void) {
    processingQueue.async {
        let resizer = PhotoResizer()
        let builder = PhotoBookBuilder()
        // Get smallest common size
        let size = resizer.smallestCommonSize(for: photos)
        // Scale down (can take a while)
        var photosForBook = resizer.scaleWithAspectFill(photos,
          to: size)
        // Crop (can take a while)
        photosForBook = resizer.centerCrop(photosForBook, to: size)
        // Generate PDF (can take a while)
        let photobookURL = builder.buildPhotobook(with: photosForBook)
        DispatchQueue.main.async {
            // Fire completion handler which will show the preview UI
            completion(photobookURL)
        }
    }
}
```

The work we are doing is in one block of code that we place on a queue. Let's see whether we can break this down into smaller, independent pieces of work that can be executed concurrently. We can't perform the scale and crop operations concurrently, as they will be operating on the same `UIImage` objects, and we will not get the intended result if the image is cropped before it's scaled.

However, we can apply the scale and crop operation to each photo separately and perform that operation concurrently on the other photos. Once each photo has been scaled and cropped, we can use the processed images to generate the photo book:

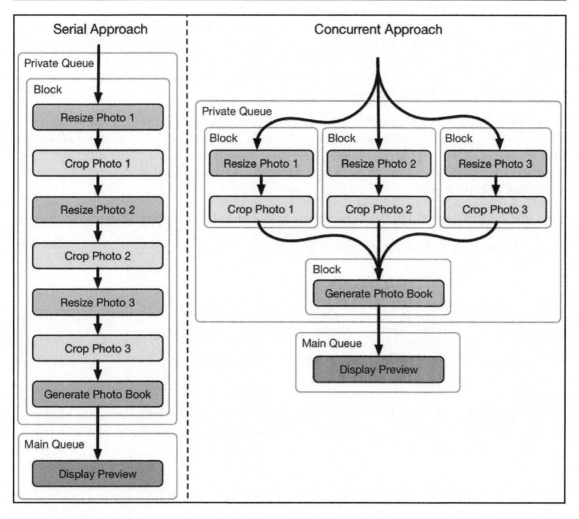

Figure 9.15 – Serial approach and concurrent approach

Splitting the work up in this way may not make the overall operation faster, as there is an overhead to each block of work. The efficiency improvement of dividing the work into concurrent blocks will depend on the operation involved, and how many concurrent operations can run.

We now have blocks of work that can run concurrently, but we have given ourselves a new problem; how do we coordinate all these concurrent pieces of work so that we know they are all completed and we can start generating the photo book? Here, GCD can help us. We can use a `DispatchGroup` to coordinate our operations on each of the images and be notified when they are all completed.

A dispatch group is like a turnstile at a stadium. Every time someone enters the stadium, they pass through the turnstile, and one extra person is counted as being in the stadium, and at the end of the day, as people leave the stadium and pass through the turnstile, the number of people in the stadium decreases. Once there is no one left in the stadium, the lights can be turned off.

Let's use a dispatch group to coordinate the work of our photo book creator:

1. First, we will create a dispatch group:

   ```
   let group = DispatchGroup()
   ```

2. Every time we start a blockwork to resize a photo, we will enter the group:

   ```
   group.enter()
   ```

3. Once the work is finished, we will leave the group:

   ```
   group.leave()
   ```

4. Finally, we will ask the group to notify us when the last resize operation has finished and left the group. Then, we can take the processed files and generate the photo book:

   ```
   group.notify(queue: processingQueue) {
       //.. generate photo book
       //.. execute completion handler
   }
   ```

5. Let's take a look at our `generatePhotoBook` method, now using a concurrent queue and dispatch groups:

   ```
   let processingQueue = DispatchQueue(label: "Photo processing
       queue", attributes: .concurrent)

   func generatePhotoBook(with photos: [UIImage], completion:
   @escaping
       (URL) -> Void) {
       let resizer = PhotoResizer()
       let builder = PhotoBookBuilder()
   ```

```
        // Get smallest common size
        let size = resizer.smallestCommonSize(for: photos)
        let processedPhotos = NSMutableArray(array: photos)
        let group = DispatchGroup()
        for (index, photo) in photos.enumerated() {
            group.enter()
            processingQueue.async {
                // Scale down (can take a while)
                var photosForBook = resizer.scaleWithAspectFill(
                  [photo], to: size)
                // Crop (can take a while)
                photosForBook = resizer.centerCrop([photo], to: size)
                // Replace original photo with processed photo
                processedPhotos[index] = photosForBook[0]
                group.leave()
            }
        }
        group.notify(queue: processingQueue) {
            guard let photos = processedPhotos as? [UIImage] else {
              return }
            // Generate PDF (can take a while)
            let photobookURL = builder.buildPhotobook(with: photos)
            DispatchQueue.main.async {
                completion(photobookURL)
            }
        }
    }
```

How it works...

Dispatch queues are serial by default, so to create a concurrent queue instead, we pass the .concurrent attribute when it is created:

```
let processingQueue = DispatchQueue(label: "Photo processing queue",
                                    attributes: .concurrent)
```

Before we loop through all the photos, we set up anything that isn't specific to each photo:

```
let resizer = PhotoResizer()
let builder = PhotoBookBuilder()
// Get smallest common size
let size = resizer.smallestCommonSize(for: photos)
let processedPhotos = NSMutableArray(array: photos)
let group = DispatchGroup()
```

This includes creating the `DispatchGroup`, which we will use to coordinate the work. Since our photo resizing will now be happening concurrently, we need a place to collect the photos once they have been processed. We can use a Swift array for this; however, a Swift array is a value type, so we can't use it from within multiple blocks, as each block will be taking a copy of the array, not the original array itself.

To solve this with a Swift array, we would need to make the `processedPhotos` array property on the view controller, which would mean we would have to weakly capture self in the blocks that we would need to unwrap. A simpler way to solve this problem is to use a collection that has reference semantics; the `Foundation` framework provides that in the form of `NSArray` and `NSMutableArray`. As we saw earlier in this chapter, it's important to understand the semantics of the construct being used and pick the right tool for the right job:

```
for (index, photo) in photos.enumerated() {
    group.enter()
    processingQueue.async {
        // Scale down (can take a while)
        var photosForBook = resizer.scaleWithAspectFill([photo],
          to: size)
        // Crop (can take a while)
        photosForBook = resizer.centerCrop([photo], to: size)
        // Replace original photo with processed photo
        processedPhotos[index] = photosForBook[0]
        group.leave()
    }
}
```

For each photo, we enter the group and place the resize work on the concurrent queue. We can use the same scale and crop methods that we used previously, just passing an array containing one photo. Once the work is completed, we'll replace the original photo with the processed photo in the array and leave the group.

Once every block has left the group, this `notify` block will execute. We retrieve the processed photos and use them to generate the photo book. Finally, we ensure that the completion handler is executed on the main queue:

```
group.notify(queue: processingQueue) {
    guard let photos = processedPhotos as? [UIImage] else { return }
    // Generate PDF (can take a while)
    let photobookURL = builder.buildPhotobook(with: photos)
    DispatchQueue.main.async {
        completion(photobookURL)
    }
}
```

If you build and run the app, you can still generate a photo book and the UI is still responsive, and now GCD can make the best use of the available resources to generate our photo book.

See also

- Documentation relating to dispatch queues: `http://swiftbook.link/docs/dispatchqueue`
- Documentation relating to dispatch groups: `http://swiftbook.link/docs/dispatchgroup`

Implementing the operation class

In this chapter so far, we have taken our long-running operations and scheduled them as blocks of code, called **closures**, on dispatch queues. This has made it really easy to move long-running code off of the main queue, but if we intend to reuse this long-running code, pass it around, track its state, and generally deal with it in an object-orientated way, a closure is not ideal.

To solve this, the `Foundation` framework provides an object, `Operation`, that allows us to wrap up our block of work within an encapsulated object.

In this recipe, we will take the photo book app we used throughout this chapter and convert our long-running blocks to an `Operation` instance.

Getting ready

We are going to build on the app we improved in the last recipe, which is an app that will produce a PDF photo book from a collection of photos. You can get the code for this app at `https://github.com/PacktPublishing/Swift-Cookbook-Second-Edition/tree/master/Chapter09` and choose the `PhotobookCreator_StartOperations` folder.

Open the folder and navigate to the `PhotoCollectionViewController.swift` file.

How to do it...

Let's recap how we broke the work down into independent parts:

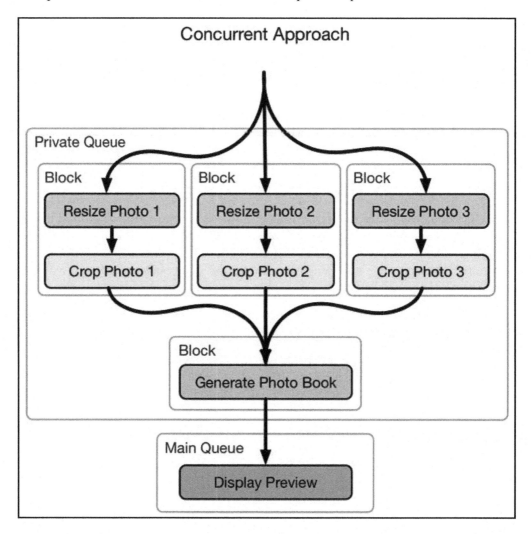

Figure 9.16 – Concurrent Approach blocks

We can turn each of these blocks of work into separate operations:

1. Let's create an operation to scale and crop each photo.

2. We define an operation by sub-classing the `Operation` class, so in the project, create a new Swift file and call it `PhotoResizeOperation.swift`.

3. In the simplest `Operation` implementation, we only need to override one method, `main()`, so let's copy and paste the relevant code from our `generatePhotobook` method. This `main()` method will be executed when the operation starts:

```
import UIKit

class PhotoResizeOperation: Operation {
    override func main() {
        // Scale down (can take a while)
        var photosForBook = resizer.scaleWithAspectFill([photo],
            to: size)
        // Crop (can take a while)
        photosForBook = resizer.centerCrop([photo], to: size)
        // Replace original photo with processed photo
        processedPhotos[index] = photosForBook[0]
    }
}
```

4. Copying and pasting the code is not enough, as there are a number of dependencies that were previously being captured by the block. Now we have to explicitly provide these dependencies to the operation:

```
class PhotoResizeOperation: Operation {
    let resizer: PhotoResizer
    let size: CGSize
    let photos: NSMutableArray
    let photoIndex: Int
    init(resizer: PhotoResizer, size: CGSize,
        photos: NSMutableArray, photoIndex: Int) {

        self.resizer = resizer
        self.size = size
        self.photos = photos
        self.photoIndex = photoIndex
    }
    override func main() {
        // Retrieve the photo to be resized.
        guard let photo = photos[photoIndex] as? UIImage else {
            return }
```

```
            // Scale down (can take a while)
            var photosForBook = resizer.scaleWithAspectFill([photo],
               to: size)
            // Crop (can take a while)
            photosForBook = resizer.centerCrop(photosForBook, to: size)
            photos[photoIndex] = photosForBook[0]
        }
    }
```

5. We have converted our resize block to an operation. We now need to do the same for the block that generates the photo book:

```
import UIKit

class GeneratePhotoBookOperation: Operation {
    let builder: PhotoBookBuilder
    let photos: NSMutableArray
    var photobookURL: URL?
    init(builder: PhotoBookBuilder, photos: NSMutableArray) {
        self.builder = builder
        self.photos = photos
    }
    override func main() {
        guard let photos = photos as? [UIImage] else { return }
        // Generate PDF (can take a while)
        photobookURL = builder.buildPhotobook(with: photos)
    }
}
```

We pass the dependencies into the operation, just like in PhotoResizeOperation. The output of this operation is a URL for the resulting photo book. We expose that as a property on the operation so that it can be retrieved outside the operation.

6. With our blocks of work converted to operations, let's switch over to PhotoCollectionViewController.swift and update our generatePhotoBook method to use this new operation:

```
let processingQueue = OperationQueue()

func generatePhotoBook(with photos: [UIImage], completion:
@escaping
  (URL) -> Void) {
    let resizer = PhotoResizer()
    let builder = PhotoBookBuilder()
    // Get smallest common size
    let size = resizer.smallestCommonSize(for: photos)
```

```
        let processedPhotos = NSMutableArray(array: photos)
        let generateBookOp = GeneratePhotoBookOperation(builder:
          builder, photos: processedPhotos)
        for index in 0..<processedPhotos.count {
            let resizeOp = PhotoResizeOperation(resizer: resizer,
                                                size: size,
                                                photos: processedPhotos,
                                                photoIndex: index)
            generateBookOp.addDependency(resizeOp)
            processingQueue.addOperation(resizeOp)
        }
        generateBookOp.completionBlock = { [weak generateBookOp] in
            guard let pbURL = generateBookOp?.photobookURL else {
                return
            }
            OperationQueue.main.addOperation {
                completion(pbURL)
            }
        }
        processingQueue.addOperation(generateBookOp)
    }
```

Let's walk through the changes step by step:

1. Where we were previously using a `DispatchQueue` to manage the execution of our blocks, operations are now managed with an `OperationQueue`:

   ```
   let processingQueue = OperationQueue()
   ```

2. The method signature in the following code and the dependencies we need to generate upfront remain the same:

   ```
   func generatePhotoBook(with photos: [UIImage], completion:
   @escaping (URL) -> Void) {
       let resizer = PhotoResizer()
       let builder = PhotoBookBuilder()
       // Get smallest common size
       let size = resizer.smallestCommonSize(for: photos)
       let processedPhotos = NSMutableArray(array: photos)
   ```

3. Next, we create the operation to generate the photo book, passing in the dependencies:

   ```
   let generateBookOp = GeneratePhotoBookOperation(builder: builder,
       photos: processedPhotos)
   ```

4. Although the operation will be executed last, we create it first so that we can make it dependent on the resize operations we are about to create. An operation does not execute immediately upon creation. It will only execute when the `start()` method of `Operation` is called, which can be called manually, or, if an `Operation` is placed on an `OperationQueue`, it will be called by the queue as appropriate:

```
for index in 0..<processedPhotos.count {
    let resizeOp = PhotoResizeOperation(resizer: resizer,
                                        size: size,
                                        photos: processedPhotos,
                                        photoIndex: index)
    generateBookOp.addDependency(resizeOp)
    processingQueue.addOperation(resizeOp)
}
```

Now, as you can see from the preceding code, we loop through the number of photos that we intend to process and create a resize operation for each, passing in the dependencies.

With our move to use `Operation`, one thing we have lost is the use of `DispatchGroup`, which we used to ensure that we only generated the photo book once all the photo resize blocks had completed. We can, however, achieve the same goals using operation dependencies. An operation can be declared as dependent on a set of other operations, so it will not begin executing until the operations it depends on have finished. To ensure that the `generateBookOp` operation, which we just created, only executes when all the `PhotoResizeOperation` operations are complete, we add each of them as a dependency of `generateBookOp`.

With this done, we can place each `PhotoResizeOperation` on the `OperationQueue`:

```
generateBookOp.completionBlock = { [weak generateBookOp] in
    guard let pbURL = generateBookOp?.photobookURL else {
        return
    }
    OperationQueue.main.addOperation {
        completion(pbURL)
    }
}
```

`Operation` has a `completionBlock` property; any block set here will be executed once the operation has completed. We can use this to fire our completion handler on the main queue. Since we need to provide the completion handler with the URL to the photo book created by `generateBookOp`, we can retrieve this from within the block, as we know that the operation will be finished and the URL will be there. However, we need to be careful. We are providing a closure to `generateBookOp`, which will be retained, and we are using, and therefore capturing and retaining, the `generateBookOp` operation in the same block. This will lead to a retain cycle, and `generateBookOp` will never get released from memory. To avoid this retain cycle, we specify that we want to weakly capture `generateBookOp` in the block we provide, using the `[weak generateBookOp]` capture list. This won't increment the retain count, preventing the retain cycle from happening.

Much like `DispatchQueue`, `OperationQueue` has an available property that provides a reference to the main queue, upon which the UI events are processed. Also, `OperationQueue` has a convenience method that will take a block of code, wrap it in an `Operation`, and add it to the queue. We use this to ensure that the completion handler is executed on the main queue:

```
processingQueue.addOperation(generateBookOp)
```

As the final step, we put the `generateBookOp` operation on the processing queue. It's important that we do this as the last step because, once placed on the queue, the operation may be executed immediately, but we don't want it executed immediately. We only want `generateBookOp` executed once all the resize operations are complete, and if we placed the operation on the queue before setting up the dependencies, this could happen.

Now that we have transitioned our app over to using `Operation`, let's build and then run and verify that everything works just as it did before.

Users of our photo book app currently do not have the ability to cancel the generation of a photo book once the process has started, so let's add that functionality:

1. We will examine our two operations and look for opportunities to check the `isCancelled` property and exit early. Switch to `PhotoResizeOperation.swift` and add `isCancelled` checks to the `main()` method:

```
override func main() {
    // Check if operation has been cancelled
    guard isCancelled == false else { return }
    guard let photo = photos[photoIndex] as? UIImage else { return
}
    // Scale down (can take a while)
```

```
    var photosForBook = resizer.scaleWithAspectFill(
      [photo], to: size)
    // Check if operation has been cancelled
    guard isCancelled == false else { return }
    // Crop (can take a while)
    photosForBook = resizer.centerCrop(photosForBook, to: size)
    photos[photoIndex] = photosForBook[0]
}
```

Before each piece of long-running work, we check the isCancelled property, and if it is true, we return early, which will finish the operation.

2. We can do the same in GeneratePhotoBookOperation.swift:

```
override func main() {
    // Check if operation has been cancelled
    guard isCancelled == false else { return }
    guard let photos = photos as? [UIImage] else { return }
    // Generate PDF (can take a while)
    photobookURL = builder.buildPhotobook(with: photos)
}
```

3. Next, we will need to add some UI that allows the user to cancel the photo book generation once it is in progress. This is an exercise for the reader, or you can switch to the end-operations branch to see how I have implemented it.

4. Once the user chooses to cancel generating a photo book, we can call the following command:

```
processingQueue.cancelAllOperations()
```

This will fire the cancel() method on all the operations in the queue.

We now have an app with a cancelable, long-running operation.

How it works...

How does OperationQueue know when to start an operation and when to remove it from the queue? It knows by monitoring the operation's state. The Operation class goes through a number of state transformations during its life cycle. The following diagram describes how these state transformations occur:

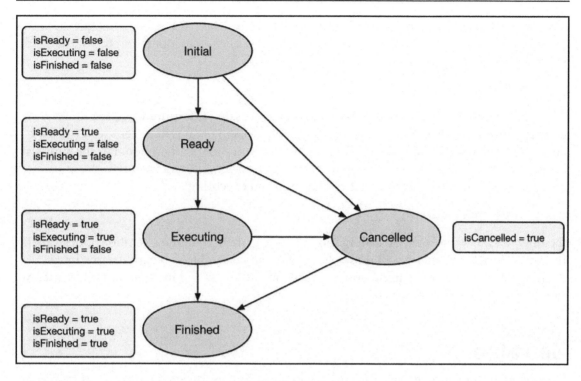

Figure 9.17 – Operation life cycle

Information about the operation's state is exposed through a number of Boolean properties on Operation, and the operation queue uses the properties to know when to perform certain actions on the operations. Let's look at these properties one by one:

```
var isReady: Bool
```

An operation will return true for isReady when all its dependencies are finished. If it doesn't have any dependencies, it will always return true. The queue will only start executing an operation if isReady is true:

```
var isExecuting: Bool
```

Once start is called on an operation, either manually or by a queue, isExecuting will return true, and when the operation has finished executing, isExecuting will revert to returning false.

Since operations remain on the queue until they have finished, the queue uses the `isExecuting` property to ensure that it doesn't call `start` on an operation that has already started:

```
var isFinished: Bool
```

Once the operation has finished doing whatever processing is required, `isFinished` should return `true`. When `isFinished` starts to return `true`, it will be removed from the queue, and the queue will no longer maintain a reference to the operation. For the simplest implementation of `Operation`, as we implemented earlier, `isFinished` returns `true` automatically when the `main()` method has finished executing:

```
var isCancelled: Bool
```

Operations can be canceled by calling the `cancel()` method on the operation. Once called, the `isCancelled` property will return true. This can be used to exit early from a long-running operation, but it is up to you to check the `isCancelled` method and interrupt any long-running code if it returns `true`.

See also

Documentation relating to the `Operation` class: `http://swiftbook.link/docs/operation`

10
SwiftUI and Combine Framework

At the Apple **Worldwide Developer Conference (WWDC)** in 2019, Apple took a lot of us by surprise with the announcement of SwiftUI, a brand new **user interface (UI)** framework written from the ground up, entirely in Swift.

Making use of the declarative programming paradigm, SwiftUI not only offers a powerful way to programmatically create and design your UI but a functional and logical approach too.

Alongside many other announcements at WWDC 19, Apple also announced its very own entry into the reactive programming stream with a new framework called **Combine**. Combine replaces the traditional delegate pattern most of us will be accustomed to in iOS and macOS development.

With SwiftUI's change to the dynamics of how UI patterns are written programmatically, Combine is a welcome addition alongside the SwiftUI framework. In this chapter, we'll take a tour of the inner workings of SwiftUI and how to build our very own app—alongside this, we'll integrate the power of Combine to give us a truly unique and reactive workflow.

In this chapter, we will cover the following recipes:

- Declarative syntax
- Function builders, property wrappers, and opaque return types
- Building simple views in SwiftUI
- Combine and data flow in SwiftUI

Technical requirements

You can find the code files for this chapter on GitHub at `https://github.com/ PacktPublishing/Swift-Cookbook-Second-Edition/tree/master/Chapter10`

Check out the following video to see the Code in Action: `https://bit.ly/3qE2mpv`

Declarative syntax

With the introduction of SwiftUI comes a new coding paradigm called declarative syntax. Well, I say "new"—it's actually been around for a while; it's just something we've never really used in iOS or macOS development. In this section, we'll take a look at what exactly declarative syntax is and how it compares to the style of syntax we might be used to seeing already.

Getting ready

For this section, you'll need the latest version of Xcode available from the Mac App Store.

How to do it...

1. Open Xcode and select **File | New | Playground**, then select **Blank** in order to open a new Playground canvas to work from.
2. Once open, add in the following syntax:

   ```
   import PlaygroundSupport
   import SwiftUI
   ```

   The first `import` statement we've seen before and should be familiar with already. The next is our one for SwiftUI—pretty self-explanatory as to why we need this.

3. Now, let's create a view in SwiftUI by adding in the following highlighted code:

   ```
   import PlaygroundSupport
   import SwiftUI

   struct MyView: View {
       var body: some View {
           VStack {
   ```

```
                    Text("Swift Cookbook")
                }
            }
        }
```

All SwiftUI views are built in a struct that conforms to the `View` type—this then houses another struct, which looks a bit like a computed property called `body`, which in turn conforms to `some View`. Inside this property—or "function builder", as it's known (which we'll touch on later in this chapter)—we have certain elements that start to make up our UI.

There is a `VStack` or **vertical stack**, which will wrap all enclosing views "vertically" within itself. A VStack is, again, a `View`.

Inside here, we have a `Text()` view where we set our text to be displayed.

4. If we add the following to our Playground, we'll be able to see our SwiftUI in action:

```
PlaygroundPage.current.setLiveView(MyView())
```

However, where does the declarative syntax come into all this? Well, it already has done; you've written it, right there in your struct. Let's dig a little deeper into how declarative syntax works.

How it works...

In SwiftUI everything is made from Views, from the main container that is presented to the app's window, to text, a button, or even a toggle.

Thinking back to how UIKit works, this theory isn't too dissimilar—most objects are a subclass of `UIView()`.

The only fundamental difference is that with SwiftUI, the layout and construction of all this is much more visible; this is the declarative syntax coming into play. The best way to think about declarative syntax is in a functional and logical way.

I want to vertically align items on my view:

```
VStack {}
```

I then want to add a `Text` box:

```
Text("Swift Cookbook")
```

Then, let's add a button:

```
Button(action: {
    print("Set Action Here...")
}, label: {
    Text("I'm going to perform an action")
})
```

Even the construction of the button is declarative itself: *set an action*; *set a label*. Everything is just... functional.

Another way to think of this would be similar to how we would work through a food recipe:

1. Chop onions.
2. Fry onions.
3. Add seasoning.
4. And so on...

With our more traditional style of programming (or **imperative** programming, as it's known), you might perform things a little differently and a little less logically:

1. Get seasoning
2. Get onion
3. Peel onion
4. Chop onion
5. Heat pan
6. And so on...

While with declarative syntax all the preceding steps still need to exist to make it work, the framework that it is written on does a lot of the work for you—we just simply "tell it" what to do.

There's more...

Declarative syntax has been around for a while now; you may have used it before without even realizing it. Let's take a look at the following **Structured Query Language** (SQL) syntax:

```
SELECT column1, column2, ...
FROM table_name
WHERE condition;
```

Notice anything familiar? That's right: declarative syntax right there... give me `column1` and `column2` from a ***particular table*** where this `condition` is met.

Most recently, the declarative syntax has been making its way into even more UI frameworks such as Google's Flutter and, most recently, into Android's new Jetpack Compose, both of which use a declarative syntax style to allow developers and designers to build a UI.

We've mentioned a few times already that declarative syntax gives us a much more functional and logical approach to programming. They are paradigms that sit beneath the declarative paradigm as a whole. SQL, for example, sits within **DSL (Domain-Specific Language)**, along with HTML and other markup languages.

See also

- Android Jetpack Compose: `https://developer.android.com/jetpack/compose`
- Google's Flutter: `https://flutter.dev/`

Function builders, property wrappers, and opaque return types

SwiftUI certainly brings a lot to the table, especially as it's been built from the ground up using Swift at its core. This itself has a plethora of benefits, which include making use of some of the features we are about to cover in this section.

Getting ready

For this section, you'll need the latest version of Xcode available from the Mac App Store.

How to do it...

1. Continuing with our existing Playground project, let's take another look at how things "stack up". We'll start by taking another look at our VStack:

```
VStack {
    Text("Swift Cookbook")
```

```
Button(action: {
    print("Set Action Here...")
}, label: {
    Text("I'm going to perform an action")
})
}
```

Here is a block of code, which in SwiftUI terms is a View to be displayed. The view is a vertical stack—think `UITableView`, but at the same time don't think `UITableView`, as it's bad practice to try to compare SwiftUI to UIKit.

All the code sitting within our VStack will be displayed vertically and then presented back to the main View, but where is the logic that adds our `Text()` and `Button()` views to the VStack? There's no `item` or `row` for index (see, it's bad to compare this to `UITableView`); there's no `.add()` or `.append()` function that you would see when building an array. Everything just sits inside what are called **function builders**.

2. Let's add another in for good measure:

```
VStack {
    Text("Swift Cookbook")
    Button(action: {
        print("Set Action Here...")
    }, label: {
        Text("I'm going to perform an action")
    })
    HStack {
        Text("By Keith & Chris")
        Image(systemName: "book")
    }
}
```

In the preceding code, we've added an `HStack`, which (yep, you guessed it) gives us a horizontal stack of Views—another function builder like before, this time housing a `Text()` and an `Image()` view.

Notice how we've added our `HStack` function builder inside our existing VStack? This is like we said before: our Stacks are just Views, so our top-level VStack just treats it like that and our `HStack` does all the work of arranging its `Text()` and `Image()` views.

But what is being returned here? When building Views in functions programmatically, you might expect to see the `return` keyword, with the return type specific to the object type being returned.

3. However, with Swift 5.1, we can harness the power of **opaque return types**. Let's look back at the body of our SwiftUI view:

```
struct MyView: View {
    var body: some View {
    }
}
```

Notice the `some View` return type. This is an opaque return type and allows SwiftUI to return any type that conforms to the View protocol, such as `Text`, `Button`, `Image`, and so on. Without this, SwiftUI would not be as versatile in terms of allowing us to build up a view, and our view builder would simply not exist.

But the beauty of **opaque return types** is that they are not SwiftUI-specific; they are just a natural evolution of the Swift language, again demonstrating how much SwiftUI has been built from the core Swift programming language.

Another thing we see here is the omission of the `return` keyword. Again, a new feature introduced in Swift 5.1: our SwiftUI code can now interpret a final return type to be passed back up the View hierarchy. But what about our `HStack` or `VStack`? Well, as these are **function builders**, they are not being returned back as such; it is more that they are being added to the Stack, which then, in turn, is passed back up.

However, there is always the possibility that you may need an `HStack` sitting alongside a `VStack`, like so:

```
VStack { }
HStack {
    Text("I'm sitting underneath a HStack")
}
```

At this point, the compiler will need a little help. Unfortunately, we can't just add in a `return` keyword as we want both to be returned, so we could add these into another Stack—but as we don't really need one that would be unnecessary, so we simply wrap these in a `Group()` view instead:

```
Group {
    VStack { }
    HStack {
        Text("I'm sitting underneath a HStack")
    }
}
```

A `Group` view itself is another view that can then be passed back up as `some View` to our body—nice!

4. We're certainly getting all the ingredients together in order to make a start with SwiftUI, but before we get stuck in, let's take a look at another feature introduced in SwiftUI, again from our ever-evolving Swift programming language.

Property wrappers in SwiftUI are one of the features that really help make it shine, and are used for a wide variety of things. The main purpose that each one holds is to reduce the amount of maintenance required for your specific view. Let's take a look at some of the more common ones you might use:

```
@State
```

`@State` allows SwiftUI to modify specific properties of specific views without the need to call a specific function to do so. For example, make the following highlighted changes to your code:

```
struct MyView: View {
    @State var count: Int = 0
    var body: some View {
        Group {
            VStack {
                Text("Swift Cookbook")
                Button(action: {
                    count += 1
                }, label: {
                    if actionPerformed > 0 {
                        Text("Performed \(count) times")
                    } else {
                        Text("I'm going to perform an action")
                    }
                })
                HStack {
                    Text("By Keith & Chris")
                    Image(systemName: "book")
                }
            }
            HStack {
                Text("I'm sitting underneath a HStack")
            }
        }
    }
}
```

We've added a variable called `count` and have given this the `@State` property wrapper, and we now update our button click to increase the integer by 1. Next, we add some logic based on the value of `count`.

By changing the value of `count` we have now bound our property that is being used within SwiftUI to the value and any changes that are made, thus invalidating the SwiftUI layout and rebuilding our view using the new value.

Go ahead—run this in the Playground and try it out for yourself.

`@Binding` is another well-used property wrapper specifically used in conjunction with passing values to state properties that may live in another view. Let's take a look at how we might do this, starting by separating out some code and creating another SwiftUI view. We can do this just underneath our current `MyView`:

```
struct ResultView: View {
    @Binding var count: Int
    var body: some View {
        Text("Performed \(count) times")
    }
}
```

Here, we're simply just creating a SwiftUI view that returns a `Text` view, but this is a great way to see how easy it is to separate out specific view logic that you might want to work on separately (or make reusable).

Notice here we were also using our `count` variable, although this time with the `@Binding` wrapper. This is because we won't be controlling the value of `count` from within this view; this will be done externally back in `MyView`:

```
struct MyView: View {
    @State var count: Int = 0
    var body: some View {
        Group {
            VStack {
                Text("Swift Cookbook")
                ResultView(count: $count)
                Button(action: {
                    count += 1
                }, label: {
                    Text("Perform Action")
                })
                HStack {
                    Text("By Keith & Chris")
                    Image(systemName: "book")
                }
```

```
        }
        HStack {
            Text("I'm sitting underneath a HStack")
        }
    }
  }
}
```

In the preceding highlighted code, notice we still have our `@State` variable, and our `Button` action is still updating this value on each press. We've also added in our new `ResultView`, passing in our `@State` variable and "binding" this to our variable in `ResultView`, thus forcing a change to that view every time `count` is updated. Go ahead and try it for yourself.

There's more...

We've covered some of the property wrappers that you are more than likely to be exposed to with SwiftUI from the outset, but there are plenty more where they came from, some of which we'll cover later on in this chapter, specifically when it comes to working with the Combine framework. However, here is a run-through of some of the others and what they have to offer:

@EnvironmentObject

Think of this as a global object—sometimes you might want to keep track of certain things throughout your app that you might not necessarily need or feel the need to pass through to every view. However, it's important to know that `EnvironmentObject` isn't a single source of truth; it's data—it's merely referencing it from the source, and should the source change, `EnvironmentObject` will trigger a state change (which is what we want).

An example of how we could use this is to create a class we want to observe, conforming to `ObservableObject`:

```
class BookStatus: ObservableObject {
    @Published var released = true
    @Published var title = ""
    @Published var authors = [""]
}
```

Then, reference it from anywhere in our SwiftUI project, like this:

```
@EnvironmentObject var bookStatus: BookStatus
```

Another great and certainly convenient property wrapper is `@AppStorage`, used as a way to access data stored within `UserDefaults`. As of iOS 14, we can incorporate this straight into our SwiftUI views, without the need for additional logic or functions. Let's take a look at how we would do this:

```
@AppStorage("book.title") var title: String = "Book Title"
```

Notice here that we have a default value should there be no data already persisted. If we want to write to this, we simply assign the property a value:

```
title = "Swift Cookbook"
```

Go ahead and try this in your Playground. If you get stuck, have a look at the GitHub resource to see how I did it.

Due to the architecture of SwiftUI, there is—and will be—an ever-growing list of available property wrappers. We'll cover some more later on in this chapter, but here are some others to be aware of:

- `@GestureState`—Tracks the current gesture that is being performed
- `@FetchRequest`—Performs a fetch for Core Data entities

See also

- States: `https://developer.apple.com/documentation/swiftui/state`
- Bindings: `https://developer.apple.com/documentation/swiftui/binding`

Building simple views in SwiftUI

We've covered some of the fundamentals of how SwiftUI is built up from the Swift programming language, but it's time now to get into how we build an actual app in SwiftUI.

In this section, we'll take everything we've learned so far and apply it in order for us to build a list app similar to the one we created previously.

Getting ready

For this section, you'll need the latest version of Xcode from the Mac App Store.

How to do it...

1. Let's get going. First, we'll create a brand new project—in Xcode, click on **File |
New | Project**. Then, select **Single View App** and make sure you've selected
SwiftUI for the **Interface** style, just like I've done here:

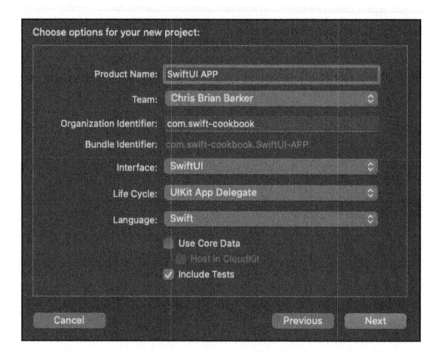

Figure 10.1 – Creating a new project

2. Click **Next** and select a location on your disk. Once that is done, the familiar site
of Xcode should appear; however, you may notice something new. On the right-
hand side, you'll see the **Live Window** screen. Go ahead and click **Resume**—you
should see the following:

Figure 10.2 – Xcode and Live Window screen

Here, we've got a generated preview of our boilerplate SwiftUI code. Notice our `ContentView()` struct, just as we expect with its **body**. Now, look at the struct below it:

```
struct ContentView_Previews: PreviewProvider {
    static var previews: some View {
        ContentView()
    }
}
```

This is our `PreviewProvider` struct, allowing us to test out our SwiftUI views at design time, without the need to keep rerunning the simulator and rebuilding our application—neat!

Now, for our initial list, we're going to need some mock data:

1. Create the following struct (this can be in a new file if you want):

```
struct Task: Identifiable {
    var description: String
    var category: String
    var id = UUID()
}
```

Comparing this to our `Task` model in Chapter 8, *Server-Side Swift*, it's pretty much identical in terms of properties and the data we want it to hold. The only difference we've had to make is for our model to conform to `Identifiable` and be given a unique ID—this is required by SwiftUI for anything that we are going to iterate around.

2. Next, let's create a little helper function for some mock data:

```
struct MockHelper {
    static func getTasks() -> [Task] {
        var tasks = [Task]()
        tasks.append(Task(description: "Get Eggs", category:
          "Shopping"))
        tasks.append(Task(description: "Get Milk", category:
          "Shopping"))
        tasks.append(Task(description: "Go for a run", category:
          "Health"))
        return tasks
    }
}
```

This mock data will come in handy in SwiftUI in more than one way, but we'll get to that shortly. Let's hook this up to our app.

3. Back over to our `ContentView`, replace the `Hello World` text view with the following:

```
List(MockHelper.getTasks()) { task in
    Text(task.description)
}
```

Notice something about our `List()` view? That's right: another function builder accepts an argument of an array of items, where the items conform to `Identifiable`. A variable is given back to us in the closure, representing each one of these items so that we can then use them inside our list builder as we see fit.

4. Here, we are just adding the description to a text view for now. If not already showing in the live preview, click **Resume** (sometimes this is needed in Xcode), and you should now see the following:

Figure 10.3 – Preview screen

Now, run this in the simulator, and you should see the exact same thing—great job!

Time for a little refactoring now, so make the following highlighted changes to the
`ContentView`:

```
var tasks = [Task]()
var body: some View {
    List(tasks) { task in
        Text(task.description)
    }
}
```

Here, we're removing our call to our mock data helper as, for production code, we
shouldn't be calling this in here. With this change, let's head on over to `PreviewProvider`
and make the following highlighted changes there:

```
struct ContentView_Previews: PreviewProvider {
    static var previews: some View {
        ContentView(tasks: MockHelper.getTasks())
    }
}
```

As our `ContentView` struct now has a non-optional `tasks` variable, it requires us to pass
some data in; here, we'll pass in our `MockHelper` function.

If not already showing, go ahead and resume the live preview. All being well, everything
should be working as expected. However, let's see what happens when we try to run this in
the simulator—that's right: no data.

If you take a closer look at the change we just made, you'll see why we're now only
injecting our mock data into our `ContentView` via the Preview Provider so that when our
actual app runs, our `tasks` array is empty.

But this is right; as we'll be hooking our app up to the **REpresentational State Transfer
application programming interface (REST API)** we created in `Chapter 8`, *Server-Side Swift*,
by injecting the mock data via the Preview Provider, we can continue to build our UI long
before we build in any networking functionality, so let's continue.

Remember from the previous section how we refactored out our `Result` view? We're going
to do the same again here for each row in our `List` view.

Create a new SwiftUI file and call it `ListRowView`, then update the boilerplate code to look like the following:

```
var description: String = ""
var category: String = ""
var body: some View {
    VStack {
        Text(description)
        Text(category)
    }
}
```

From here, head back over to `ContentView.swift` and make the following highlighted changes:

```
var body: some View {
    List(tasks) { task in
        ListRowView(description: task.description,
                    category: task.category)
    }
}
```

Just like before, we're replacing our text view with the view we just created. Click **Resume** to view the live preview and see for yourself.

Now we know that's working, we want to work on the style of our `ListRowView` a little, so let's head back on over there now and start by updating the Preview Provider so that we can work from there:

```
struct ListRowView_Previews: PreviewProvider {
    static var previews: some View {
        ListRowView(description: "Description Field",
                    category: "Category Field")
    }
}
```

As you can see from the preceding highlighted code, we've added some mock data for use in our **Live Preview**. If this is not already showing, click **Resume** and you should see the following:

Figure 10.4 – Live Preview screen with some mock data

It works but doesn't look much like a `List` row, but that's fine—we just need to tell the Preview Provider what we intend to use it for:

```
List {
    ListRowView(description: "Description Field",
                category: "Category Field")
}
```

It really is that simple. We just wrap it around a `List` view and SwiftUI does the rest, and we can now get to work on decorating our row.

Back in the body of our `ListRowView`, make the following highlighted changes:

```
var body: some View {
    VStack(alignment: .leading) {
        Text(description)
            .font(.title)
            .padding(EdgeInsets(top: 0,
                                leading: 0,
                                bottom: 2,
                                trailing: 0))
            .foregroundColor(.blue)
        Text(category)
            .font(.title3)
            .foregroundColor(.blue)
    }
}
```

Here, we've added modifiers to our views. Modifiers allow us to decorate and style our views just like we would with properties in UIKit, and each modifier is tied specifically to its type of view.

SwiftUI has gone a little further with some of the modifiers available, giving us a wide variety of options. Let's take the `.font` modifier, for example:

```
.font(.largeTitle) // A font with the large title text style.
.font(.title) // A font with the title text style.
.font(.title2) // Create a font for second level hierarchical headings.
.font(.title3) // Create a font for third level hierarchical headings.
.font(.headline) // A font with the headline text style.
.font(.subheadline) // A font with the subheadline text style.
.font(.footnote) // A font with the footnote text style.
.font(.caption) // A font with the caption text style.
.font(.caption2) // Create a font with the alternate caption text
                 // style.
```

The preceding fonts are all available to use straight out of the box; however, if you still want to specify your own font, you can do so by using the following:

```
public static func system(_ style: Font.TextStyle, design: Font.Design
   = .default) -> Font
```

Let's finish off the base of our app by adding in an image based on the category type:

```
HStack {
    VStack(alignment: .leading) {
        Text(description)
            .font(.title)
            .padding(EdgeInsets(top: 0,
                                leading: 0,
                                bottom: 2,
                                trailing: 0))
            .foregroundColor(.blue)
        Text(category)
            .font(.title3)
            .foregroundColor(.blue)
    }
    Spacer()
    Image(systemName: "book")
        .foregroundColor(.blue)
        .padding()
}
```

Notice in the preceding code how we've now introduced an HStack and wrapped this around our current VStack, which allows us to now add views outside of our original VStack and align them horizontally, just like we've done with the Image view.

The use of the Spacer() view in SwiftUI has pushed out our two horizontal views (our VStack on the left and Image on the right) so that they act as leading and trailing views to the parent view (the body, in this case).

How it works...

The base of our app is now ready to hook up to an external data source, but first, let's go over how modifiers work and how we can create our very own. Either add the following code to your ListRowView.swift file or create a new file (it's up to you):

```
struct CategoryText: ViewModifier {
    func body(content: Content) -> some View {
        content
            .font(.title3)
```

```
                  .foregroundColor(.blue)
        }
    }
```

Here, we've created a struct called `CategoryText` that conforms to the `ViewModifier` protocol. In here, there is a function called `Body` for which we are setting the modifiers of `.font` and `.foregroundColor`. These modifiers are available on anything that inherits from `View`.

Feel free to have a play around with some of the modifiers available. You could add the following and really give the `Category` label a little punch:

```
struct CategoryText: ViewModifier {
    func body(content: Content) -> some View {
        content
            .font(.footnote)
            .foregroundColor(.blue)
            .padding(4)
            .overlay(
                RoundedRectangle(cornerRadius: 8)
                    .stroke(Color.blue, lineWidth: 2)
            )
            .shadow(color: .grey, radius: 2, x: -1, y: -1)
    }
}
```

Let's now add this to our `Text` view:

```
Text(category)
    .modifier(CategoryText())
```

We're using the `.modifier` (modifier) in order to call our custom struct; this is good from a readability point of view as it allows you to quickly identify anything that could potentially be custom as opposed to anything that is a system API. However, if you are like me and want it to look just right, simply create an extension of `View`:

```
extension View {
    func styleCategory() -> some View {
        self.modifier(CategoryText())
    }
}
```

Then, use it like this:

```
Text(category)
    .styleCategory()
```

You might have noticed we glossed over assigning a specific image to a category. This was with good reason, as I wanted to expand further on the use of SF Symbols within SwiftUI.

Also available for use with UIKit, SF Symbols works exceptionally well in SwiftUI, especially when used with modifiers like the ones we've just been playing with.

SF Symbols are exactly what they say they are—symbols (not images), they are fonts and can be treated just like fonts too:

```
Image(systemName: "book")
    .font(.system(size: 32, weight: .regular))
    .foregroundColor(.blue)
    .padding()
```

No need for stretching images or **2x** or **3x** images' assets. SF Symbols will handle this just like having your own vector right in the app, with the added benefit that it's all included in the Swift API without extra assets bulking up your app.

As the name of the symbol is just written in plain text, let's write a little function that works out what we need to display:

```
struct Helper {
    static func getCategoryIcon(category: String) -> String {
        switch category.lowercased() {
        case "shopping":
            return "bag"
        case "health":
            return "heart"
        default:
            return "info.circle"
        }
    }
}
```

In an ideal world, our categories would be enums with `String` values that we could cast to, but for this demo, a basic string match will suffice. Now, replace the static text in the `Image` constructor to call this new static function:

```
Image(systemName: Helper.getCategoryIcon(category: category))
```

The only drawback is the following: is the image you want to use included in the library?

With iOS 14, Apple introduced a much wider range of SF Symbols. There's even a Mac app you can download that catalogs all these for you in a nice **graphical UI (GUI)**.

There's more...

We've touched on the Preview Provider a couple of times so far, but this handy little feature of SwiftUI does have a couple more tricks up its sleeve.

By default, the device it will preview on will be that of the one currently selected in Xcode, but if you want to change this, simply add in the following:

```
struct ListRowView_Previews: PreviewProvider {
    static var previews: some View {
        List {
            ListRowView(description: "Description Field",
                        category: "Category Field")
        }
        .previewDevice(PreviewDevice(rawValue: "iPhone 12 Pro Max"))
        .previewDisplayName("iPhone 12 Pro Max")
    }
}
```

`.previewDevice`—This specifies the device you want to use—the raw value string matched that of an internal enum for that specific device (*basically the string name as you would see in the simulator list*).

`.previewDisplayName`—This is a custom name given for that device, as shown in the **Live Preview** window.

The display name can come in handy for other reasons too, specifically if we have more than one preview running:

```
struct ListRowView_Previews_MockData2: PreviewProvider {
    static var previews: some View {
        List {
            ListRowView(description: "Very Long Description Field, Very
                Long Description Field", category: "Very Long Category
                Field, Very Long Category Field")
        }
        .previewDevice(PreviewDevice(rawValue: "iPhone 12 Pro"))
        .previewDisplayName("iPhone 12 Pro - Data #2")
    }
}
```

As highlighted, we've created an additional preview to run in our **Live Preview** window, which in turn passes in different data and tests on a different device.

With this, we could create mock data for every condition or style we wanted and have them previewing on all manner of device types, allowing us to test right there without the need to launch each version on a simulator.

SwiftUI is no doubt powerful and, especially with the latest release of iOS 14 at WWDC 2020, things have improved vastly, but we must not forget that at less than 2 years old it's still well within its infancy, and there will be more than one occasion when you'll need to revert back to UIKit for some form of component.

Luckily for us, Apple has us ready to go with `UIViewRepresentable`, a protocol that we can use to harness UIKit components and return them as SwiftUI views.

A good example would be `UITextView()`, currently not available in SwiftUI or any direct equivalent (*although with iOS 14, TextEditor for SwiftUI now does a lot of what we want, but is still not a direct replacement as such*).

Create a new Swift file and call it `TextView`, then start by pasting the following methods in one by one:

```
struct TextView: UIViewRepresentable {

    @Binding var text: String

    func makeUIView(context: Context) -> UITextView {
        let textView = UITextView()
        return textView
    }
}
```

Our `UIViewRepresentable` protocol requires us to conform to certain functions such as `makeUIView()`, which is, in turn, responsible for instantiating the UIKit component we want to wrap.

Next, add the following:

```
struct TextView: UIViewRepresentable {

    // ...

    func updateUIView(_ uiView: UITextView, context: Context) {
        uiView.text = text
    }

    func makeCoordinator() -> Coordinator {
        Coordinator($text)
    }
```

```
    // ...
}
```

With `updateUIView()`, we set the instance of our `UITextView` with whatever we want. Here, we are setting the `text` value from our variable.

Next, we'll add the `makeCoordinator()` function, which returns an instance of `Coordinator`, padding in our `@Binding` text field. The best way to think about the `Coordinator` is as a way of handling the delegate methods we might use for our UIKit component. Add in the following, and this should make more sense:

```
struct TextView: UIViewRepresentable {

    // ...

    class Coordinator: NSObject, UITextViewDelegate {
        var text: Binding<String>
        init(_ text: Binding<String>) {
            self.text = text
        }
        func textViewDidChange(_ textView: UITextView) {
            self.text.wrappedValue = textView.text
        }
    }
}
```

See how our `Coordinator` conforms to `UITextViewDelegate`, and we have `textViewDidChange()` in there. As our text variable being passed in is a `Binding` string, changes made will reflect in the delegate method being called, just as they would in UIKit:

```
@State var textViewString = ""
TextView(text: $textViewString)
```

In order to call this, we would simply add this as we would any other SwiftUI view.

See also

SF Symbols Mac app: `https://developer.apple.com/design/human-interface-guidelines/sf-symbols/overview/`

`UIViewRepresentable`: `https://developer.apple.com/documentation/swiftui/uiviewrepresentable`

Combine and data flow in SwiftUI

For many years, the reactive programming stream has played a big part in development architecture in terms of iOS and macOS. You may have heard of RxSwift and RxCocoa, a massive community committed to the reactive stream that allows for asynchronous events to be processed.

If you are not familiar with the terminology of Rx or reactive programming, you may have seen the use of **Publishers**, **Subscribers**, and **Operators** in your code base. If you have, then you've most likely been subject to reactive programming at some point.

In this section, we are going to take a look at Apple's offering for reactive programming, called **Combine**. Introduced alongside SwiftUI at WWDC 2019, Combine is the perfect accompaniment for the new layout and structure of SwiftUI (although not bound solely to SwiftUI). We'll take a look at how we can create a seamless flow of data from our REST API, right up to our UI layer.

Getting ready

For this section, you'll need the latest version of Xcode from the Mac App Store and the project from the previous section.

How to do it...

First, we'll start by updating our `Task` model to a class, by making the following highlighted changes:

```
class Task: Identifiable {
    var id = UUID()
    let response: TaskResponse
    init(taskResponse: TaskResponse) {
        self.response = taskResponse
    }
    var category: String {
        return response.category ?? ""
    }
    var description: String {
        return response.description ?? ""
    }
}
```

Here, we've converted our model to a class (more on that later), and have added a custom initializer and a couple of computed properties too.

We've also added a variable of type `TaskResponse`, so let's go ahead and create that now in a new file:

```
struct TaskResponse: Codable {
    let category: String?
    let description: String?
}
```

Here, we have a basic codable response from the REST API we created earlier.

Now, for a bit of boilerplate networking code; create a new file called `NetworkManager.swift` and add the following code into it:

```
class NetworkManager {
    static func loadData(url: URL, completion: @escaping
      ([TaskResponse]?) -> ()) {
        URLSession.shared.dataTask(with: url) { data, response, error
          in
            guard let data = data, error == nil else {
                completion(nil)
                return
            }
            if let response = try? JSONDecoder().decode(
              [TaskResponse].self, from: data) {
                DispatchQueue.main.async {
                    completion(response)
                }
            }
        }.resume()
    }
}
```

Here, we have a basic implementation of `URLSession`, which is being passed a **Uniform Resource Locator (URL)**, parsing the **JavaScript Object Notation (JSON)** response into a `Codable` object (our `TaskResponse` model). The function we've created has a completion handler that returns an array of our `TaskResponse` model, should the response and decoding be successful.

Next, create a file called `TaskViewModel` and add in the following code:

```
class TaskViewModel: ObservableObject {
    init() {
        getTasks()
    }
```

```
    @Published var tasks = [Task]()
    private func getTasks() {
        guard let url = URL(string: "http://0.0.0.0:8080/tasks") else {
            return
        }
        NetworkManager.loadData(url: url) { taskResponse in
            if let taskResponse = taskResponse {
                self.tasks = taskResponse.map(Task.init)
            }
        }
    }
}
```

In the preceding code, I've highlighted some areas of interest. First is how we've conformed our class to `ObservableObject`—this is required as our `tasks` variable has the `@Published` wrapper and will be looking for changes as and when they occur.

Next is the local URL we're passing into our `NetworkingManager`—this is our local instance of the REST API we created earlier.

Now, head on back over to our `ContentView.swift` file and make the following highlighted changes:

```
struct ContentView: View {
    @ObservedObject var model = TaskViewModel()
    var body: some View {
        List(model.tasks) { task in
            ListRowView(description: task.description,
                        category: task.category)
        }
    }
}
```

We've now renamed our `tasks` variable to `model`, and this in turn has now created a new instance of `TaskViewModel()`.

As we've updated a few things here, the structure of how we inject our mock data will need adjusting too, so make the following highlighted changes to our `MockHelper` function:

```
var task = [Task]()
task.append(Task(taskResponse: TaskResponse(category: "Get Eggs",
    description: "Shopping")))
task.append(Task(taskResponse: TaskResponse(category: "Get Milk",
    description: "Shopping")))
task.append(Task(taskResponse: TaskResponse(category: "Go for a run",
    description: "Health")))
```

```
let taskViewModel = TaskViewModel()
taskViewModel.tasks = task

return taskViewModel
```

As our `ContentView` now accepts an array of `TaskResponse`, we've just made the adjustment accordingly.

Now for the magic—from our previous project, launch our local instance of our Task API and add a couple of things into the database:

```
curl -H "Content-Type: application/json" -X POST -d
'{"description":"Remember the Eggs","category":"Shopping"}'
http://0.0.0.0:8080/tasks

curl -H "Content-Type: application/json" -X POST -d
'{"description":"Bread","category":"Shopping"}' http://0.0.0.0:8080/tasks

curl -H "Content-Type: application/json" -X POST -d '{"description":"Ring
Mandy","category":"Home"}' http://0.0.0.0:8080/tasks
```

With this done, it's time to see the magic happen. Launch the app, and if all's going well, you should see something like this:

Figure 10.5 – Launching the app

Here is a simple yet exceptionally effective demonstration of how Combine can and should be used within SwiftUI. Let's take a look now at how all this actually works.

How it works...

Let's start at the `ContentView` and work our way back:

```
@ObservedObject var model = TaskViewModel()
```

Two things to note here—our model is that of an `@ObservedObject`, meaning any changes made to this model will result in an update being fired and thus forcing a refresh of our UI (just like we saw with `@State` earlier).

Next, we're instantiating our `TaskViewModel()` when the `ContentView` is rendered. Let's dive into our `TaskViewModel` and see why:

```
class TaskViewModel: ObservableObject {
    init() {
        getTasks()
    }
    @Published var tasks = [Task]()
    // ...
}
```

We already touched earlier on our class conforming to `ObservableObject`. This is what allows us to use `@ObservedObject` when declaring this back over in our `ContentView` (we're creating a **data flow** connection, so to speak).

Notice here that we've also added a call to our `getTasks()` function so that when we initialize the class (back over in `ContentView`), we'll kick off a networking request to get a list of tasks.

If we now have a quick look inside our `getTasks()` function, you'll see that once we get a successful response, we assign this to our `@Published tasks` variable:

```
NetworkManager.loadData(url: url) { articles in
    if let articles = articles {
        self.tasks = articles.map(Task.init)
    }
}
```

And as soon as the variable is updated, our `Observable` object class lets anything listening know about a change (our `@ObservedObject` in our `ContentView`, for example).

If you think back to how the `UITableView` works, if there are any updates or changes to the data source, we then have to call `UITableView.reloadData()` manually, and within our UI layer.

With this approach, everything has been handled the way it should be and is in the right place, passing data changes from the source of truth up to the UI layer.

See also

- Swift Combine: `https://developer.apple.com/documentation/combine`

Using CoreML and Vision in Swift

11

The Swift programming language has come a long way since its first introduction, and in comparison to many other programming languages, it's still well within its infancy.

However, with this in mind, with every release of Swift and its place in the open source community, we've seen it grow from strength to strength over such a short period of time. We already covered server-side Swift back in Chapter 8, *Server-Side Swift*, another evolution that was again fueled by the open source community.

Another fast-moving train is that of machine learning, once again driven by the power of the community, and recognized giants in the industry, such as TensorFlow, now support the Swift programming language.

In this chapter, we're going to look at Apple's offering for machine learning – CoreML – and how we can build an app using Swift to read and process machine learning models, giving us intelligent image recognition.

We'll also take a look at Apple's Vision Framework and how it works alongside CoreML to allow us to process video being streamed to our devices in real time, recognizing objects on the fly.

In this chapter, we will cover the following recipes:

- Building an image capture app
- Using CoreML models to detect objects in images
- Building a video capture app
- Using CoreML and the Vision Framework to detect objects in real time

Technical requirements

You can find the code files present in this chapter on GitHub at `https://github.com/PacktPublishing/Swift-Cookbook-Second-Edition/tree/master/Chapter11`

Check out the following video to see the Code in Action: `https://bit.ly/2NmP961`

Building an image capture app

In this first recipe, we're going to create an app that captures either an image from your camera roll or an image taken from your camera. This will set up our iOS app ready for us to incorporate CoreML to detect objects in our photos.

Getting ready

For this recipe, you'll need the latest version of Xcode available from the Mac App Store.

How to do it...

With Xcode open, let's get started:

1. Create a new project in Xcode. Go to **File** | **New** | **Project** | **iOS App**.
2. In `Main.storyboard`, add the following:
    1. Add `UISegmentedControl` with two options (**Photo / Camera Roll** and **Live Camera**).
    2. Next, add a `UILabel` view just underneath.
    3. Add a `UIImageView` view beneath that.
    4. Finally, add a `UIButton` component.
3. Space these accordingly using AutoLayout constraints with `UIImageView` being the prominent object:

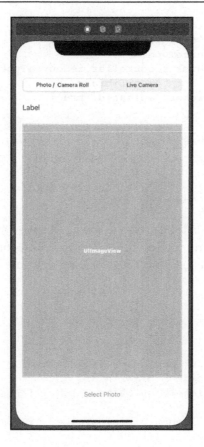

Figure 11.1 – Camera/photo app

4. Once we have this in place, let's hook these up to our `ViewController.swift` file:

```
@IBOutlet weak var imageView: UIImageView!
@IBOutlet weak var labelView: UILabel!
@IBAction func onSelectPhoto(_ sender: Any)
```

Take note that in the preceding, we have two IBOutlet and one IBAction (we don't need an outlet for UIButton, we just care about its action).

5. Next, populate IBAction with the following code:

```
@IBAction func onSelectPhoto(_ sender: Any) {
    let picker = UIImagePickerController()
```

```
          picker.delegate = self
          picker.allowsEditing = false
          picker.sourceType =
            UIImagePickerController.isSourceTypeAvailable(.camera) ?
              .camera : .photoLibrary
          present(picker, animated: true)
      }
```

6. Now, let's create an extension of `UIViewController`. You can do this at the bottom of the `ViewController` class if you like:

```
extension ViewController: UIImagePickerControllerDelegate,
    UINavigationControllerDelegate
```

7. Our extension needs to conform to the `UIImagePickerControllerDelegate` and `UINavigationControllerDelegate` protocols. We can now go ahead and populate our extension with the following delegate method:

```
func imagePickerControllerDidCancel(_ picker:
    UIImagePickerController) {
    dismiss(animated: true, completion: nil)
}

func imagePickerController(_ picker: UIImagePickerController,
    didFinishPickingMediaWithInfo info:
      [UIImagePickerController.InfoKey : Any]) {

    guard let image = info[UIImagePickerController.InfoKey
      .originalImage] as? UIImage else {
        return
    }
    imageView.image = image
    labelView.text = "This is my image!"
    dismiss(animated: true, completion: nil)
}
```

8. Before we go any further, we'll need to add a couple of lines to our `info.plist`:

```
NSCameraUsageDescription
NSPhotoLibraryUsageDescription
```

9. Add these in with the following string description: `Chapter 11 wants to detect cook Stuff`. This is an iOS security feature that will prompt the user when any app/code tries to access the camera, photo library, or location services. Failure to add this in could result in an app crash.

For our app, we can add whatever we want, but for a production app, make sure the text you enter is useful and informative to the user. Apple will check this when reviewing your app and has been known to potentially block a release until this is resolved.

Go ahead and run your code, and then launch the app. One of the following things should happen:

- If you are running the app from the simulator, our `UIButton` press should present the photo picker (along with the default images supplied by the iOS simulator).
- If you are running from a device, then you should be presented with the camera view, allowing you to capture a photo.

Either way, whether a photo was selected or a picture was taken, the resulting image should show in `UIImageView`!

How it works...

Let's step through what we've just done. We'll begin at `IBAction` and have a look at the `UIPickerView` view we've created:

```
let picker = UIImagePickerController() // 1
picker.delegate = self // 2
picker.allowsEditing = false // 3
picker.sourceType = UIImagePickerController.isSourceTypeAvailable
  (.camera) ? .camera : .photoLibrary // 4
present(picker, animated: true) // 5
```

Let's go through this one line at a time:

1. We instantiate an instance of `UIImagePickerController` – an available API that will allow us to choose an image based on a specific source.
2. We set the delegate as `self`, so we can harness any results or actions caused by `UIImagePickerController`.
3. We set `allowEditing` to `false`, which is used to hide controls when the camera is our source.
4. In this instance, we set the source type based on whether the camera is available or not (so it works well with the simulator).
5. Finally, we present our view controller.

Now, let's take a look at our delegate methods:

```
func imagePickerControllerDidCancel(_ picker: UIImagePickerController)
func imagePickerController(_ picker: UIImagePickerController,
   didFinishPickingMediaWithInfo info: [UIImagePickerController.InfoKey
     : Any])
```

The first is pretty self-explanatory; `imagePickerControllerDidCancel` handles any instances where `UIImagePickerController` is canceled by the users. In our case, we just dismiss the instance returned – job done!

`didFinishPickingMediaWithInfo` is where interesting things happen. Notice how we are given a dictionary of **info** in our response. Here, we have various segments of information. The one we are looking for is under the `UIImagePickerController.InfoKey.originalImage` key. This gives us a `UIImage` of what we've just selected, allowing us to assign this straight back to `UIImageView`.

Now that we've got an app that allows us to take or choose a photo, we can apply it to some real work with the power of CoreML and object detection.

There's more...

A quick note to mention: you'll also have noticed that we were required to conform our extension to `UINavigationControllerDelegate`. This is required by iOS to allow `UIImageContoller` to be handled and presented correctly from its "presenting" stack (`ViewController` in our instance).

See also

For more information on `UIImagePickerController`, refer to `https://developer.apple.com/documentation/uikit/uiimagepickercontroller`.

Using CoreML models to detect objects in images

In this recipe, we'll take the app we just built and incorporate the CoreML framework in order to detect objects in our images.

We'll also take a look at the generated CoreML models available for us to use and download directly from Apple's Developer portal.

Getting ready

For this recipe, you'll need the latest version of Xcode available from the Mac App Store.

Next, head on over to the Apple Developer portal at the following address: `https://developer.apple.com/machine-learning/models/`.

Here, you will find out a little bit more about the models available for us to download and use in our Xcode project.

You'll notice there are options for image models and text models. For this recipe, we're going to be using image models, specifically one called **Resnet50**, which uses a residual neural network that attempts to identify and classify what it perceives to be the dominant object in an image.

 For more information on the different types of machine learning models, see the links in the *See also* section at the end of this recipe.

From here, download the **Resnet50.mlmodel** (32-bit) model. If you are having trouble downloading the file, you can just take a copy from the sample project in our GitHub repository.

Once downloaded, add this to your Xcode project by simply dragging it into the file explorer tree in our previous app.

How to do it...

Let's make a start where we left off in our previous project:

1. With everything in place, head back into `ViewController.swift` and add the following global variable and addition to our `viewDidLoad()` function:

```
var model: Resnet50!

override func viewDidLoad() {
    super.viewDidLoad()
    model = Resnet50()
}
```

2. Now, head on over to the sample project and obtain a file called `ImageHelpers.swift`; add this to our project. Once this has been added, we'll head on back over to our `didFinishPickingMediaWithInfo` delegate and expand on this a little further.

3. Add in the following highlighted changes:

```
guard let image = info[UIImagePickerController.InfoKey.
  originalImage] as? UIImage else {
    return
}

let (newImage, pixelBuffer) =
  ImageHelper.processImageData(capturedImage: image)

imageView.image = newImage

var imagePredictionText = "no idea... lol"

    guard let prediction = try? model.prediction(
      image: pixelBuffer!) else {
        labelView.text = imagePredictionText
        dismiss(animated: true, completion: nil)
        return
    }
    imagePredictionText = prediction.classLabel
labelView.text = "I think this is a \(imagePredictionText)"

dismiss(animated: true, completion: nil)
```

With everything in place, run the app and select a photo. As long as you didn't point it at a blank wall, you should be seeing some interesting feedback.

With all that in place, let's break down the changes we just made to understand what just happened a little more.

How it works...

The first thing is to take a look at the following line we added in:

```
let (newImage, pixelBuffer) =
  ImageHelper.processImageData(capturedImage: image)
```

Here, we added in a call to a helper method we took from our sample project. This helper contains the following two functions:

```
static func processImageData(capturedImage: UIImage) -> (UIImage?,
  CVPixelBuffer?)
static func exifOrientationFromDeviceOrientation() ->
  CGImagePropertyOrientation
```

These functions and what they do are a little out of the scope of this book, and this chapter in particular. However, at a very high level, the first function, `processImageData()`, takes an instance of `UIImage` and transforms this to `CVPixelBuffer` format.

This essentially returns the `UIImage` object back to its raw format that it was captured in (`UIImage` is merely a UIKit wrapper for our true raw image).

During this process, we need to flip the orientation too as with all captured images. This is almost certainly in landscape mode (and more often than not, you've taken a picture or selected a photo in portrait mode).

Another reason for performing this is that our ResNet50 model is trained to observe images at only 224 x 224. So, we need to readjust the captured image to this size.

 If you need more information on the model you have in your project, simply select the file in the file explorer and view the details in the main window. From here, the **Predictions** tab will give you all the details you need about the input file required.

So, with our helper function implemented, we receive a new `UIImage` object (modified to our new spec) and the image in `CVPixelBuffer` format, all ready to pass over to CoreML for processing.

Now, let's take a look at the following code:

```
guard let prediction = try? model.prediction(image: pixelBuffer!) else {
    labelView.text = imagePredictionText
    dismiss(animated: true, completion: nil)
    return
}

imagePredictionText = prediction.classLabel
```

In the preceding code, I've highlighted some areas of interest. First is our `prediction()` function call on our `model` object. Here, we pass in our image in the `CVPixelBuffer` format we got back from our helper method earlier. From this, wrapped in a `try` statement, CoreML will now attempt to detect an object in the photo. If successful, we'll exit our `guard` statement gracefully and be able to access the properties available in our `prediction` variable.

If you take a look at the properties available in our ResNet50 model, you'll see the various options we have:

```
.classLabel
.classLabelProbs
```

The class label we've already seen, but the class label probability will return us a dictionary of the most likely category for our image with a value based around a confidence score.

Each model will have its own set of properties based on its desired intention and how it's been built.

There's more...

At the beginning of this section, we obtained a model that allowed us to detect objects in our images. Touching on this subject a little more, models are a set of data that has been trained to identify a pattern or characteristics of a certain description.

For example, we want a model that detects cats; so, we train our model by feeding it images of around 10,000 various pictures of cats. Our model training will identify features and shapes common to each other and categorize them accordingly.

When we then feed our model an image of a cat, we hope that it is able to pick up those categorized features within our image and successfully identify the cat.

The more images you train with, the greater the performance; however, that still depends on the integrity of the images too. Training with the same image of a cat (just in a different pose) 1,000 times might give you the same results as if you take 10,000 images of the same cat (again in a different pose).

The same goes the other way too; if you train with 500,000 images of a panther and then 500,000 images of a kitten, it's just not going to work.

Away from CoreML, you are now able to train a model using Swift with TensorFlow. TensorFlow is a Google product that is leading the way in terms of machine learning and with an ever-growing community of developers behind it coupled with Swift's own open source community. Advancement in this particular technology is certainly looking bright.

See also

For more information, please refer to the following links:

- Apple CoreML documentation: `https://developer.apple.com/documentation/coreml`
- TensorFlow Swift: `https://www.tensorflow.org/swift/tutorials/model_training_walkthrough`

Building a video capture app

So, what we have seen so far of CoreML is pretty neat, to say the least. But taking a look back over this chapter so far, we have probably spent more time building our app to harness the power of CoreML than actually implementing it.

In this section, we're going to take our app a little further by streaming a live camera feed that in turn will allow us to intercept each frame and detect objects in real time.

Getting ready

For this section, you'll need the latest version of Xcode available from the Mac App Store.

Please note that for this section, you'll need to be connected to a real device for this to work. Currently, the iOS simulator does not have a way to emulate the front or back camera.

How to do it...

Let's begin:

1. Head over to our `ViewContoller.swift` file and make the following amendments:

```
import AVFoundation

private var previewLayer: AVCaptureVideoPreviewLayer! = nil
var captureSession = AVCaptureSession()

var bufferSize: CGSize = .zero
var rootLayer: CALayer! = nil

private let videoDataOutput = AVCaptureVideoDataOutput()
private let videoDataOutputQueue = DispatchQueue(label:
    "video.data.output.queue", qos: .userInitiated, attributes: [],
    autoreleaseFrequency: .workItem)
```

2. Now, create a function called `setupCaptureSession()` and we'll start by adding in the following:

```
func setupCaptureSession() {
    var deviceInput: AVCaptureDeviceInput!
    guard let videoDevice =
            AVCaptureDevice.DiscoverySession(deviceTypes:
                [.builtInWideAngleCamera], mediaType: .video,
                    position: .back).devices.first else {
        return
    }

    do {
        deviceInput = try AVCaptureDeviceInput(device: videoDevice)
    } catch {
        print(error.localizedDescription)
        return
    }

    // More to go here

}
```

In the preceding code, we are checking our device for an available camera, specifically `.builtInWideAngleCamera` at the back. If no device can be found, our guard will fail.

3. Next, we initialize `AVCaptureDeviceInput` with our new `videoDevice` object.

4. Now, continuing in our function, add the following code:

```
captureSession.beginConfiguration()
captureSession.sessionPreset = .medium

guard captureSession.canAddInput(deviceInput) else {
    captureSession.commitConfiguration()
    return
}
captureSession.addInput(deviceInput)

if captureSession.canAddOutput(videoDataOutput) {
    captureSession.addOutput(videoDataOutput)
    videoDataOutput.setSampleBufferDelegate(self, queue:
      videoDataOutputQueue)
} else {
    captureSession.commitConfiguration()
    return
}

do {
    try videoDevice.lockForConfiguration()
    let dimensions = CMVideoFormatDescriptionGetDimensions(
      (videoDevice.activeFormat.formatDescription))
    bufferSize.width = CGFloat(dimensions.width)
    bufferSize.height = CGFloat(dimensions.height)
    videoDevice.unlockForConfiguration()
} catch {
    print(error)
}
```

Essentially, here we are attaching our device to a capture session, allowing us to stream what the device input (camera) is processing programmatically straight into our code. Now we just to point this at our view so that we can see the output.

5. Add the following additional code to our function:

```
captureSession.commitConfiguration()

previewLayer = AVCaptureVideoPreviewLayer(session: captureSession)
previewLayer.videoGravity = AVLayerVideoGravity.resizeAspectFill
rootLayer = imageView.layer
previewLayer.frame = rootLayer.bounds
rootLayer.addSublayer(previewLayer)
```

With the code we've just added, we are essentially creating a visible layer from our current capture session. In order for us to process this on our screen, we need to assign this to a `rootLayer` (our `CALayer` variable we added earlier). While this seems a little overkill and we could just add this to the layer of our `UIImageView`, we're prepping for something we need to do in our next recipe.

6. Finally, with our camera and device all set up, it's time to set the camera rolling:

```
captureSession.startRunning()
```

Go ahead and run the app. Note again that this will only work on a real device and not a simulator. All going well, you should have a live stream from your camera.

How it works...

The best way to explain this would be to think of the capture session as a wrapper or a configuration between the device's hardware and software. The camera hardware has a lot of options, so we configure our capture session to pick out what we want for our particular instance.

Let's look back at this line of code:

```
AVCaptureDevice.DiscoverySession(deviceTypes:
    [.builtInWideAngleCamera], mediaType: .video, position: .back)
```

Here, you could control the enum bases on a UI toggle, allowing the user to specify which camera to use. You could even use the following:

```
captureSession.stopRunning()
```

Re-configure the session and then `startRunning()` again. Essentially (albeit at a much more complex level), this is what happens when you switch from the front to the back camera when taking a photo.

With the session captured, we can now stream the output directly to any view we like just like we did here:

```
previewLayer = AVCaptureVideoPreviewLayer(session: captureSession)
```

But the fun comes when we want to manipulate the image that is being streamed, by capturing them one frame at a time. We do this by implementing the `AVCaptureVideoDataOutputSampleBufferDelegate` protocol, which allows us to override the following delegate methods:

```
func captureOutput(_ output: AVCaptureOutput, didOutput sampleBuffer:
    CMSampleBuffer, from connection: AVCaptureConnection) { }
```

Notice something familiar here... we're being given `sampleBuffer`, just like we got in `UIImagePickerDelegate`. The difference here is that this will be called with every frame, not just when one is selected.

There's more...

Playing around with capture sessions and `AVCaptureOutputs` is an expensive operation. Always make sure you stop your session from running when it's not needed, and make sure your delegates are not unnecessarily processing data when they don't need to be.

Another thing to note is that the initialization of a capture device can in some instances be slow, so make sure you have the appropriate UI to handle the potential blocking it may cause.

Final note: if you are struggling with memory leaks and high CPU times, take a look at a suite of tools called Instruments. Bundles of Xcode Instruments can offer a wide range of performance tracing tools that can really help you to get the most out of your Swift code.

See also

For more information, refer to the following links:

- Instruments overview: `https://help.apple.com/instruments/mac/current/#/dev7b09c84f5`
- AVFoundation: `https://developer.apple.com/documentation/avfoundation`

Using CoreML and the Vision Framework to detect objects in real time

We've seen what CoreML can do in terms of object detection, but taking everything we've done so far into account, we can certainly go a step further. Apple's Vision Framework offers a unique set of detection tools from landmark detection and face detection in images to tracking recognition.

With the latter, tracking recognition, the Vision Framework allows us to take models built with CoreML and use them in conjunction with CoreML's object detection to identify and track the object in question.

In this section, we'll take everything we've learned so far, from how AVFoundation works to implementing CoreML, and build a real-time object detection app using a device camera.

Getting ready

For this section, you'll need the latest version of Xcode available from the Mac App Store.

Next, head on over to the Apple Developer portal at the following address: `https://developer.apple.com/machine-learning/models/`.

Here, you will find out a little bit more about the models available for us to download and use in our Xcode project. You'll notice there are options for image models or text models. For this recipe, we're going to be using image models, specifically one called **YOLOv3**, which uses a residual neural network that attempts to identify and classify what it perceives to be the dominant object in the image.

 For more information on the different types of machine learning models, see the links in the *See also* section at the end of this recipe.

From here, download the **YOLOv3.mlmodel** (32-bit) model. If you are having trouble downloading the file, you can just take a copy from the sample project in our GitHub repository.

Once downloaded, add this to your Xcode project by simply dragging it into the file explorer tree in our previous app.

How to do it...

We'll start by creating a new `UIViewController` for all our vision work, in Xcode:

1. Go to **File** | **New** | **File**.
2. Choose **Cocoa Touch Class**.
3. Name this `VisionViewController`.
4. Make this a subclass of `UIViewController`.

With that done, we can now head on over to our new `VisionViewController` and add in the following highlighted code. We'll start by importing the Vision Framework:

```
import Vision
```

Now, we'll subclass our existing `ViewController` so that we can get the best of both worlds (without the need for copious amounts of code duplication):

```
class VisionViewController: ViewController
```

With that done, we can now override some of our functions in `ViewContoller.swift`. We'll start with `setupCaptureSession()`:

```
override func setupCaptureSession() {
    super.setupCaptureSession()
    setupDetectionLayer()
    updateDetectionLayerGeometry()
    startVision()
}
```

 When overriding from another class, always remember to call the base function first. In the case of the preceding code, this can be done by calling `super.setupCaptureSession()` as highlighted.

You'll notice some functions in the **ViewControler.swift** file that we've not yet created. Let's go through these now one by one:

1. First, we'll add a detection layer to our `rootLayer` that we created earlier. This `CALayer` will be used as the drawing plane for our detected object area:

```
func setupDetectionLayer() {
    detectionlayer = CALayer()
    detectionlayer.name = "detection.overlay"
    detectionlayer.bounds = CGRect(x: 0.0,
                                   y: 0.0,
```

```
                                            width: bufferSize.width,
                                            height: bufferSize.height)
        detectionlayer.position = CGPoint(x: rootLayer.bounds.midX, y:
            rootLayer.bounds.midY)
        rootLayer.addSublayer(detectionlayer)
    }
```

As you can see from the code, we create its bounds based on the height and width taken from our `bufferSize` property (which is being shared back over in our `ViewController` class).

2. Next, we need to add some geometry to `detectionLayer()`. This will re-adjust and scale the detection layer based on the device's current geometry:

```
func updateDetectionLayerGeometry() {
    let bounds = rootLayer.bounds
    var scale: CGFloat
    let xScale: CGFloat = bounds.size.width / bufferSize.height
    let yScale: CGFloat = bounds.size.height / bufferSize.width
    scale = fmax(xScale, yScale)
    if scale.isInfinite {
        scale = 1.0
    }
    CATransaction.begin()
    CATransaction.setValue(kCFBooleanTrue, forKey:
      kCATransactionDisableActions)
  detectionlayer.setAffineTransform(CGAffineTransform(rotationAngle:
    CGFloat(.pi / 2.0)).scaledBy(x: scale, y: -scale))
  detectionlayer.position = CGPoint(x: bounds.midX, y:
    bounds.midY)
    CATransaction.commit()
}
```

3. Finally, let's hook up our `startVision()` function:

```
func startVision(){
    guard let localModel = Bundle.main.url(forResource: "YOLOv3",
      withExtension: "mlmodelc") else {
        return
    }
    do {
        let visionModel = try VNCoreMLModel(for: MLModel(
          contentsOf: localModel))
        let objectRecognition = VNCoreMLRequest(model: visionModel,
          completionHandler: { (request, error) in
            DispatchQueue.main.async(execute: {
                if let results = request.results {
                    self.visionResults(results)
```

```
                }
            })
        })
        self.requests = [objectRecognition]
    } catch let error {
        print(error.localizedDescription)
    }
}
```

4. With this comes a new function, `visionResults()`. Go ahead and create this function in `VisionViewController` too.

> We could have simply used an extension in our original `ViewController` to house all these new functions, but we'd run the risk of overloading our view controller to the point where it could become too unmaintainable. Also, our logic and extension for `UIImagePicker` was in here, so the separation is nice.

5. With this, let's build out `visionResults()` function. We'll do this a section at a time so it all makes sense:

```
func visionResults(_ results: [Any]) {
    CATransaction.begin()
    CATransaction.setValue(kCFBooleanTrue, forKey:
      kCATransactionDisableActions)
    detectionlayer?.sublayers = nil
    // Other code to follow
}
```

We start with some basic housekeeping; performing `CATransaction` locks in memory any changes we're going to make to `CALayer`, before we finally commit them for use. In this code, we'll be modifying `detectionLayer`.

6. Next, we'll iterate around our `results` parameter to pull out anything that is of class type `VNRecognizedObjectObservation`:

```
for observation in results where observation is
  VNRecognizedObjectObservation {
    guard let objectObservation = observation as?
      VNRecognizedObjectObservation else {
        continue
    }
    let labelObservation = objectObservation.labels.first
    let objectBounds = VNImageRectForNormalizedRect(
      objectObservation.boundingBox, Int(bufferSize.width),
      Int(bufferSize.height))
```

```
        let shapeLayer = createRoundedRectLayer(with: objectBounds)
        let textLayer = createTextSubLayer(with: objectBounds,
          identifier: labelObservation?.identifier ?? "",
            confidence: labelObservation?.confidence ?? 0.0)
        shapeLayer.addSublayer(textLayer)
        detectionlayer.addSublayer(shapeLayer)

    updateDetectionLayerGeometry()
    CATransaction.commit()
    }
```

From this, we'll continue to use Vision to obtain the `Rect` and position of the identified object(s) using `VNImageRectForNormalizedRect`. We can also grab some text information about the objects detected and use that too.

7. Finally, we'll gracefully close off any changes to `detectionLayer` and update the geometry to match the detected objects. You'll notice there are two new functions we've just introduced:

    createRoundedRectLayer()
    createTextSubLayer()

These again are helper functions, one to draw the rectangle of the detected object and the other to write the text. These functions are generic boilerplate sample code that can be obtained from Apple's documentation. Feel free to have a play around with these to suit your needs. One thing I will mention: you'll notice how we do all this again using layers rather than adding `UIView` and `UILabel`. This again is because UIKit is a wrapper around a lot of core functionality. But adding a UIKit component on top of another component is unnecessary and with what is already an intense program, this could be performed much more efficiently by updating and manipulating the layers directly on a UIKit object.

These objects can be found in the sample project on GitHub; just copy them into your project (either in `VisionViewController` or your own helper file).

With our AV Foundation camera streaming in place and Vison and CoreML ready to do their magic, there is one final override we need to add to our `VisionViewController`:

```
override func captureOutput(_ output: AVCaptureOutput, didOutput
  sampleBuffer: CMSampleBuffer, from connection: AVCaptureConnection) {
    guard let pixelBuffer = CMSampleBufferGetImageBuffer(sampleBuffer)
      else {
        return
    }
    let exifOrientation =
      ImageHelper.exifOrientationFromDeviceOrientation()
    let imageRequestHandler = VNImageRequestHandler(cvPixelBuffer:
```

```
        pixelBuffer, orientation: exifOrientation, options: [:])
    do {
        try imageRequestHandler.perform(self.requests)
    } catch {
        print(error)
    }
}
```

Using the delegate for AV Foundation, we grab each frame again, converting this to `CVPixelBuffer` in order to create `VNImageRequestHander`. This now kicks off the requests in our `startVision()` function, stitching everything together nicely.

We're almost done; let's finish off with some bits and pieces to tie all this together now:

1. Head on over to `ViewController.swift` and add the following `IBAction` and logic from `UISegmentedControl` that we created earlier:

   ```
   @IBAction func onInputTypeSelected(_ sender: UISegmentedControl) {
       switch sender.selectedSegmentIndex {
       case 0:
           captureSession.stopRunning()
       case 1:
           startLivePreview()
       default:
           print("Default case")
       }
   }
   ```

2. Now, create a function called `startLivePreview()`:

   ```
   func startLivePreview() {
       captureSession.startRunning()
   }
   ```

3. Remove `captureSession.startRunning()` from `setupCaptureSession()`.

4. Finally, in our `Main.storyboard` view controller, change the class from `ViewController` to `VisionViewController`.

5. Now, go ahead and run the app. All going well, you should be live-detecting images with an overlay that looks like this:

Figure 11.2 – Vision detection

As you can see, both Vision and CoreML have successfully detected my cell phone and its location in the image (all in real time).

How it works...

A high-level overview goes something like this:

1. Capture a real-time camera feed (using AV Foundation).
2. Use a trained CoreML model to detect whether the image contains an object (that it recognizes).
3. Use Vision to detect the position of the object in the picture.

We covered the camera streaming elements in the previous recipe, but let's take a deeper look at how *steps 2* and *3* work.

Let's actually start with *step 3*. We saw in the last section how we use `VNImageRequestHander` to pass back `CVPixelBuffer` of each image frame. This now fires off calls in our `setupVision()` function, so let's take a closer look in there.

First, we grab our model from the apps bundle so that we can pass this over to Vision:

```
guard let localModel = Bundle.main.url(forResource: "YOLOv3",
   withExtension: "mlmodelc") else {
      return
}
```

Next, we head back to *step 2*, where we create an instance of `VNCoreMLModel()`, passing in our `localModel`. With this `visionModel`, we can now create our `VNCoreMLRequest` call, along with its completion handler, which will fire from requests that come in via our AV Foundation delegate.

This one simple request does the work of both the Vision Framework and CoreML – first detecting whether an object is found, then supplying us with the details on where that object is located inside the image.

This is where the bulk of our work is done. If you look again at our `visionResults()` function and all the helper functions within, these are merely just ways of parsing data that has come back, and in turn, decorating our view.

In our "results" from the `VNCoreMLRequest()` response, we take an instance of `VNRecognizedObjectObservation`, which in turn gives us two properties, a label (of what CoreML thinks it has found) along with a confidence score.

See also

For more information on `CALayer`, refer to `https://developer.apple.com/documentation/quartzcore/calayer`.

Subscribe to our online digital library for full access to over 7,000 books and videos, as well as industry leading tools to help you plan your personal development and advance your career. For more information, please visit our website.

Why subscribe?

- Spend less time learning and more time coding with practical eBooks and Videos from over 4,000 industry professionals

- Improve your learning with Skill Plans built especially for you

- Get a free eBook or video every month

- Fully searchable for easy access to vital information

- Copy and paste, print, and bookmark content

Did you know that Packt offers eBook versions of every book published, with PDF and ePub files available? You can upgrade to the eBook version at www.packt.com and as a print book customer, you are entitled to a discount on the eBook copy. Get in touch with us at customercare@packtpub.com for more details.

At www.packt.com, you can also read a collection of free technical articles, sign up for a range of free newsletters, and receive exclusive discounts and offers on Packt books and eBooks.

Other Books You May Enjoy

If you enjoyed this book, you may be interested in these other books by Packt:

iOS 14 Programming for Beginners - Fifth Edition
Ahmad Sahar

ISBN: 978-1-80020-974-9

- Get to grips with the fundamentals of Xcode 12 and Swift 5.3, the building blocks of iOS development
- Understand how to prototype an app using storyboards
- Discover the Model-View-Controller design pattern and how to implement the desired functionality within an app
- Implement the latest iOS features, such as widgets and App Clips
- Convert an existing iPad app into an Apple Silicon Mac app
- Design, deploy, and test your iOS applications with design patterns and best practices

Mastering Swift 5.3 - Sixth Edition

Jon Hoffman

ISBN: 978-1-80056-215-8

- Understand core Swift components, such as operators, collections, control flows, and functions
- Identify how and when to use classes, structures, and enumerations
- Use protocol-oriented design with extensions to write easy-to-manage code
- Leverage design patterns with Swift to solve commonly occurring design problems
- Apply copy-on-write for your custom value types to improve performance
- Add concurrency to your applications using Grand Central Dispatch and operation queues
- Implement generics to write flexible and reusable code

Packt is searching for authors like you

If you're interested in becoming an author for Packt, please visit `authors.packtpub.com` and apply today. We have worked with thousands of developers and tech professionals, just like you, to help them share their insight with the global tech community. You can make a general application, apply for a specific hot topic that we are recruiting an author for, or submit your own idea.

Leave a review - let other readers know what you think

Please share your thoughts on this book with others by leaving a review on the site that you bought it from. If you purchased the book from Amazon, please leave us an honest review on this book's Amazon page. This is vital so that other potential readers can see and use your unbiased opinion to make purchasing decisions, we can understand what our customers think about our products, and our authors can see your feedback on the title that they have worked with Packt to create. It will only take a few minutes of your time, but is valuable to other potential customers, our authors, and Packt. Thank you!

Index

36824309R00275